THE philistine

RAMON BENNETT

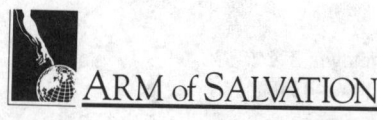

ARM of SALVATION
Jerusalem

Unless noted otherwise, Scripture quotations are from THE NEW KING JAMES VERSION of the Bible. Copyright © 1979, 1980, 1982, Thomas Nelson, Inc., Publishers. Used by permission.

Scriptures marked NIV are taken from the HOLY BIBLE, NEW INTERNATIONAL VERSION. Copyright © 1973, 1978, 1984, International Bible Society. Used by permission of Zondervan Bible Publishers.

Scriptures marked NASB are taken from the NEW AMERICAN STANDARD BIBLE. Copyright © 1960, 1962, 1963, 1968, 1971, 1972, 1973, 1975, 1977, 1988, The Lockman Foundation. Used by permission.

All bold emphasis within quotations is the author's own. Italics within quotations are as given in the source.

Copyright © 1995 Ramon Bennett
All Rights Reserved

Written permission must be secured from the publisher to use or reproduce, by any means, any part of this book, except for brief quotations in reviews or articles.

Cover design by Ramon Bennett:
Shows an actual PLO photograph of one of Yasser Arafat's *Fatah* terrorists about to enter Israel from Lebanese territory. The black and white checkered head-cloth is the distinctive *keffiyeh* worn by *Fatah* gunmen. The name *Fatah* is the reversed letters of the Arabic word *Hataf*, meaning, "sudden death."

Published and Distributed in Israel by:
    Arm of Salvation
    P.O. Box 32381, Jerusalem 91322.
    Tel: (02) 247-667 Fax: (02) 250-532

New Zealand Distributor:
    Christian Products
    P.O. Box 23 786, Papatoetoe.
    Tel: (09) 277-6909

United Kingdom Distributor:
    Faith Builders
    P.O. Box 40, Knutsford, Cheshire, WA16 9EW.
    Tel: (01565) 654-414   Fax: (01565) 652-706

United States Distributor:
    Shekinah Books
    4118 Rustle Cove, Georgetown, TX 78628.
    Telephone and Fax: (512) 869-4848

Printed in Israel

"O my soul, my soul! I am pained in my very heart! My heart makes a noise in me; I cannot hold my peace, because you have heard, O my soul, the sound of the trumpet, the alarm of war."

Jeremiah 4:19

To the nation of Israel—the world's scapegoat.

Contents

Acknowledgements ix
Author's Preface xi

1 The Middle East 15
2 The Arab Mind 21
3 Islam and the Koran 39
4 The Great Satan 59
5 Arafat and the PLO 69
6 Palestinian Refugees 105
7 Palestine 125
8 The United Nations 165
9 The News Media 181
10 The Israeli Connection 199
11 Peace: The Road that Leads to War 231
12 Judgment of Nations 267

For Your Information 297
Chapter Notes 301
Select Bibliography 345

ACKNOWLEDGEMENTS

Readers of this book will recognize the debt I owe to all the wonderful people who uphold me daily with their love and prayers. I am also indebted to my editor, whose help and suggestions were invaluable, and whose encouragement was stimulating. Grateful thanks are extended to those who sent newspaper and magazine clippings, especially Ann in New Zealand. Most of all, I want to thank my dear wife, companion and friend, Zipporah, for loving and believing in me.

Author's Preface

This has been a difficult book to write. Much of what I had to read while I researched facts over a period of 18 months was utterly depressing. Out of respect for the reader, I have deliberately left out many details but, even so, some things are sure to shock the average Western mind. The ever-changing political scene also made writing difficult. Some predictions I had made concerning men's intentions, or situations that would arise from political ineptitudes, came to pass during the writing of the book. I have rewritten those passages and attempted to guard against making further short term predictions in order not to date the book too rapidly.

It has been difficult, too, because a virtual mountain of gleaned material had to be condensed into the relatively small number of pages in this book (600 page books are not popular). As I write this brief preface, there are still several reference books on my desk from which, because of the space restriction, I took not one single quotation. And of the massive number of magazine and newspaper clippings that I had initially prepared for inclusion, hundreds have not been referred to for the same reason. Be aware that for every quotation given for reinforcement of my presentation there are many more that could have easily been given. I have attempted to present a well documented, readable book that sufficiently strips away the deception that masks the Israeli-PLO Peace Accord and presents the truth—the real intention.

The early chapters, especially 2, 3 and 5, are the pivotal chapters—providing understanding for the rest of the book as well as the keys for understanding the events of the Middle East. I would like to qualify what I have written about the Arab mind by saying that this is, of itself, an abstraction, as there can only be individual minds or psyches. It is, therefore, a generalization of the great mass, but not necessarily true of each individual. My sincere apologies go to the small percentage who are not part of the great mass.

Author's Preface

Today, we have in existence the most powerful nations in history, but the weakest men are in charge of them—men who are either stuck in a veritable bog of ignorance or who flounder in a sea of naiveté. Along with this weak leadership, we have a powerful, anti-Semitic, unprincipled news media, and the common people have been sucked into a carefully and craftily contrived morass of deception concerning the storm that is brewing in the Middle East.

It is important, even essential, for the reader to understand that God, *"the Holy One of Israel,"* is in complete control of events. It is He who *"deprives of intelligence the chiefs of the earth's people, and makes them wander in a pathless waste"* (Job 12:24 NASB). And it is He who *"brings the counsel of the nations to nothing; He makes the plans of the peoples of no effect"* (Psalms 33:10). Today's events are those recorded in His Word thousands of years ago, written down by His Spirit according to His foreknowledge. Nothing is out of control; everything is right on schedule. And the One who foretells the future in such detail and can reveal the mysteries of history, is the One who controls history and the future. God is sovereign. The world's leaders, including the President of the United States and the Prime Minister of Israel, together with Yasser Arafat and his terrorist minions, are all under His indirect control. Human beings do indeed make decisions that shape history, but such decision-making is not necessarily the last word. God sets events in motion, and He also terminates them. And our understanding would profit by knowing that God's kingdom comes by catastrophe, not by development.

The men in the headlines sincerely believe that it is they who control destiny. They are willing to sacrifice other's lives and indulge in deceit to achieve personal ambitions or gain political honor and prestige. This book is an attempt to set the record straight about the current Middle East "peace process." In the limited space available, I have endeavored to present the thoughts and intentions of the hearts of men in the headlines—some of whom say, like Neville Chamberlain after his September 1938

Author's Preface

meeting with Adolf Hitler in Munich, "There will be peace in our time." Chamberlain's "Peace in our time" led to World War II. In the seven years following his naive statement, 47 million lives were lost. This book, therefore, should be taken as a very serious warning to Israel and the West.

Ramon Bennett
Jerusalem
May 14, 1995

> ! Did you read the Author's Preface on page xi? It might help you to better understand this book.

1
The Middle East

As a small boy I remember hearing my father say again and again, "Keep your eyes on the Middle East—that's where World War III will come from." I was too young even to be aware of the Middle East's existence, but after surviving World War II's German V1 and V2 rocket attacks on England, the 1940 Battle of Britain, and the "Blitz"—the systematic German blanket-bombing of the city of London that began with 57 consecutive nights of bombing by armadas of up to a thousand warplanes—I was painfully aware of some of the more gruesome aspects of warfare.

My two older brothers and I spent many hours sandwiched between mattresses under our heavy, old oak dining table where our parents bundled us each time the sirens wailed their warning cries. My earliest recollections of life are of watching firestorms of incendiary bombs descending from the skies and setting the city on fire; of windows blown in and roofs blown off (our house lost its windows and roof seven times in one 24 hour period!);[1] of explosions with bricks, mortar and roof-tiles flying high into the air before cascading down like an avalanche; of seemingly mountainous heaps of rubble; of headless bodies and dead neighbors.

From time to time, after our family had immigrated to New Zealand in 1953, my father would repeat the same statement to anyone willing to lend him their ear but I, at least, remained completely disinterested and never once asked him to elaborate. I became a Christian in June 1965, but living in a remote country that is literally one of the "corners of the world," neither Israel nor the Middle East presented any attractions for my parochial mind. But, when the results of the Arab-Israeli June 1967, Six Day War became known, the focus of my attention made a quantum shift from real estate brokering to studying Biblical prophecy.

Before the outbreak of that June war, watching the situation on television and reading of the massive lineup of troops and military hardware facing Israel, like countless millions of other onlookers I felt that Israel had less than a fifty-fifty chance of survival. But God was obviously on the side of the Israelis, and He stunned the world with the outcome. I was impressed—so impressed that I began to devour the Bible, reading it from cover to cover, over and over again, never missing a single word. I continued for a number of years to read the Bible on an average of five hours each day, and whenever the opportunity presented itself, I would read for the entire day—that God-given hunger has remained with me for 28 years.

I saw in the Scriptures an enormous discrepancy between the traditional teaching of the Church—that she was the new Israel—and what was clearly presented in the Holy Spirit-inspired Scriptures. In the Bible, Israel is Israel. Israel is not used as a synonym for the Church. Modern Israel is the fulfillment of Biblical prophecy concerning ancient Israel, and the result of the Six Day War was simply another manifestation of God's intervention on behalf of His ancient people.

Even though I saw a distinct correlation between Bible prophecy and the founding of the State of Israel in 1948, which resulted in the subsequent ingathering of the dispersed Jewish nation, I did not become an "Israel fanatic," neither did I rush over to Israel to observe firsthand what God was doing. In 1979 I accepted an invitation to help a Christian ministry in Israel, but I had no inclination that my sojourn would become permanent.

I arrived on May 14, 1980—the 32nd anniversary of the founding of the Jewish state—with one suitcase and a heavy piece of hand-luggage containing nine translations of the Bible and a Biblical Encyclopedia. Only my faith in the God of Abraham, Isaac and Jacob and a deep love for His Word has sustained me throughout the long, difficult, frustrating years of living in the Middle East. We Westerners so readily complain of "red tape" or "bureaucracy" in our mother countries, but one needs to live in the Middle East to practically understand those terms. Believe

The Middle East

me, the novelty of camel dung on the sidewalk wears off after a short period of time, and the crude reality of paying some of the highest taxes in the world as well as dealing with government and municipal clerks with Middle Eastern mentalities, is somewhat akin to Chinese water torture.

At this juncture I would like to make it abundantly clear that I do not equate Israel with God—that is, I do not believe that it can do nothing wrong. Israel, like every nation on planet earth, makes blunders and initiates wrong actions. But despite its warts and wrinkles, Israel is a unique nation for a number of reasons.

First, Israel is unique because she is God's inspiration. It is, He says, *"the dearly beloved of My soul"* (Jeremiah 12:7). Israel was birthed by God and is protected by Him; whoever touches it, *"touches the apple of His eye"* (Zechariah 2:8).

Second, Israel is unique because practically every nation in the world looks upon it as the only obstacle to world peace. The State of Israel has replaced the wandering Jew as the world's scapegoat. She has become the irresistible target upon which the nations' politicians, diplomats, journalists and television personalities vent their baseless biases and ignorances with almost total freedom.

And, thirdly, it is unique because it is the only democracy in the entire inflammable region known as the Middle East. With the exception of Israel, one party systems rule in the Middle East, and these systems are usually dominated by military men unfit to rule by the very fact that they have no experience in economics or any other field necessary for successful government.

Army officers are touted to be "intellectuals," but the Arabic use of "intellectual" is such that it simply means they can read and write[2]. Having usually come into power by masterminding a military coup, the leaders make no concessions to the survival of any that criticize or oppose their party's rule. They treat every word not spoken in total agreement of current policy as a threat, or even the beginnings of another coup. The unfortunate person will be arrested and after torture extracts a "confession" from his lips, he is summarily executed. "Assassination and terror are seen as legitimate political methods; elimination of possible rivals is accepted practice. Whichever party rules has a list of victims—

an administrative list—for murder is systematized. No man can stay on top without murder."[3] Heads of ruling parties—especially despots like Saddam Hussein of Iraq, Mu'ammar Qaddhafi of Libya, Hafez Assad of Syria, etc.—place a high value upon their own skin but absolutely none upon that of others, whether they be Moslems or infidels (non-Moslems).

This story is told of Saddam Hussein: At a Baghdad cabinet meeting, his uncle was foolish enough to disagree with a suggestion Saddam had made. Saddam rose from the table and requested that his uncle come with him to an adjoining room. On entering the room Saddam produced a knife and calmly slit his uncle's throat. After trampling on the body, he re-entered the cabinet room and continued directing the country's affairs. For this and other similar actions, the Iraqis named him "The Butcher of Baghdad." In an interview with a Western newspaper, Saddam was asked to comment on his "Butcher of Baghdad" nickname. "Weakness doesn't assure achieving the objectives required by a leader,"[4] he replied. Due to the 1991 Gulf War situation most of the world learned about Saddam's use of poison gas to annihilate Iraqi Kurdish villages. In defending his use of poison gas, he stated in a recent press conference: "I reject any criticism of my use of gas against civilian populations. No one has come to me and said they are personally bothered by these gases. Frankly, I'm sick of having these self-righteous anti-gas types **infringe on my personal freedom.**"[5]

The average Western mind simply does not understand the violence and cunning that makes up the Middle Eastern mentality. Saddam considers it to be an infringement of his personal freedom to be criticized for gassing thousands of his Iraqi countrymen. And among the dictators in the Middle East, this type of behavior is the norm rather than the exception. President Hafez Assad of Syria is also on record for having killed some 20,000 fellow Syrians because they did not like his policies. The Syrian army surrounded the city of Hama, sealed the houses, pumped in cyanide gas, and later buried the city under a mound of dirt. A lone survivor miraculously escaped and told the tale.[6] The Egyptian army also used mustard gas in its dispute with Yemen back in the 1960's.[7] And during the eight year war between Iran and Iraq, which took a greater toll of lives than did World War I, the opposing sides used some 1,000 tons of poison gas against each other.[8] It is essential that the West comes to understand that life simply has no value in the eyes of those who "govern" the oil-rich desert regions.

Since the independent Arab states were created in the first half of this century, virtually all of them have been engaged in one or more wars against their Arab neighbors, besides the wars against non-Arab neighbors. The list of assassinations, attempted assassinations and executions of Arab rulers, army officers, cabinet ministers, opposition leaders, diplomats, minor officials, etc. reads like the New York telephone directory. War, violence and bloodshed is the Middle East's perpetual-motion machine that requires no outside assistance. The Middle East is the world's deadliest neighborhood—it "has spent more on weapons, fought more wars and suffered more casualties than any other part of the Third World."[9]

Considering the history of the Middle East and its propensity for war, one could rationally assume that the leaders of the world's nations would be careful to limit the amount and type of weaponry that enters the region. The United States, for example, is always talking about "strategic arms balances" and "limitation of arms," but she is very quick to jostle for position at the head of the queue at arms bazaars, and since the collapse of the Soviet Union, has become the region's largest supplier.[10] Arms sales into the Middle East between 1973 and 1993 were valued at the staggering figure of almost one trillion United States Dollars, and almost 92% of these weapons are in the hands of unstable Middle East Islamic regimes.[11] The United States and other nations might talk about "strategic balances," but they really mean "bank" balances, not arms balances—the weapons industry is the world's most lucrative business, and wars are necessary to keep the industry rolling and populations employed.

Since the breakup of the Soviet Union, nuclear missiles are known to find their way into the hands of the Middle East states, particularly those of Iran. And it is a debatable point as to which is Iran's largest export commodity—oil or terrorism. But, this could almost be said of any one of a dozen states in the Middle

East. In fact, it has been recorded by one of the most knowledgeable individuals on international terrorism, that "international terrorism is the quintessential Middle Eastern export."[12] Given the oft-declared and absolute hatred of both Israel and the West (especially the United States) by most of the Islamic nations of the Middle East, as well as their undeniable instability, it is only a matter of time before these weapons spark a conflict of cosmic proportions.

My father was a declared agnostic until 1979, at which time he, too, became a Christian. The closest he ever came to being in the Middle East was when our family passed through the Suez canal en route to New Zealand. After studying Biblical prophecy for nearly 28 years and living in the Middle East for 15 of them, coupled with carefully studying and monitoring the political, religious, and ethnic situations of the region, I now realize how perceptive my father really was. World War III will indeed be ignited from within the volatile Middle East, and all the signs of dawn are clearly visible in the skies to those who watch for the day.

2
The Arab Mind

A volatile region is volatile by reason of the cast of mind peculiar to the people dwelling there and that of those who govern it. Peoples and their leaders are prisoners of their cultural values. Arab culture, customs and mind-sets took root thousands of years ago and were the common denominators that ensured survival for this ancient people. Descended from Abraham, the Bedouin Arab desert dwellers possess, to the mind of the modern city or village dwelling Arab, the epitome of everything desirable in manners and customs. Some wealthy Arabs, whose families have lived in cities for generations, send their sons to noble Bedouin villages to experience their traditional customs much the same as the British gentry send their sons to Eton or Cambridge. Arab culture and custom remain the factors that govern the action and thought patterns of the Arab people. This culture is imbibed with the mother's milk, and its pattern is burned into the very cells that make up the modern Arab mind. It is, more often than not, a prison from which there is no possible escape.

The Arab world has some customs of which it can be justifiably proud. Arab hospitality, for example, is legendary and has changed little from the Biblical patterns of their ancestors. Just as Abram, in Genesis 18:2-8, killed the fatted calf for three passing strangers, so will today's Arab feed a stranger the finest of everything he has, and as much as that person can humanly hold. And just as Lot, in Genesis 19:1-3, insisted that the two travelers stay in his house for the night, so, also, will the modern Arab pressure a stranger to remain under his roof and partake of his hospitality. The customs of hospitality and generosity have changed little in 4,000 years, nor have the customs of raiding (thieving, rustling), saving face or savagery.

For the ancient Bedouin, raiding neighboring tribes and villages was a favorite pastime as well as an economic necessity. It was practically the only way they could improve their situation or standard of living. Raiding your enemy, your neighbor and even your own brother was considered to be "one of the few manly occupations."[1] Today's farmers, living in the regions of Israel where Bedouin Arabs abound, complain of losing tractors, implements, equipment, livestock, fertilizers, fencing, etc. to their neighbors. And when, because of a rash of murders of Israeli citizens, the Israeli government closed off the administered territories and refused entry to some 100,000 Arab workers from the West Bank and Gaza in 1993, Israeli police reported a 30 percent drop in car and house thefts. These workers constituted a small percentage of the 5.5 million people in the land, yet they were responsible for nearly one-third of the nation's car thefts and house burglaries! Some 650,000 Arabs hold Israeli citizenship and live in Israel proper; the reader can thus imagine what percentage of car thefts and burglaries that number is probably responsible for!

"Face"

The terms, "saving face," and "loss of face," are Western terms that describe prominent characteristics endemic to the Eastern world. The Arab either "whitens" the face (saves face), or "blackens" the face (loses face). "Face is the outward appearance of honor, the 'front' of honor which a man will strive to preserve even if, in actuality, he has committed a dishonorable act."[2] In the Arab world "honor" and "face" are so closely related that the words are almost interchangeable. This "face," or "honor," is such an integral part of the Arab mind that a person is considered perfectly justified in resorting to deceit and falseness in order to "whiten," or save, their own, someone else's or the entire Arab world's face. The Arab mind is in perpetual motion—working against "blackening" the face (losing face), and thus sculptures its words accordingly. When it comes to "whitening" or saving somebody else's face or the face of the Arab world, lying is even considered to be "a duty."[3]

Arab lying, like Arab hospitality, generosity and raiding, is an echo from the past, as made clear by an early Islamic theologian: "We must lie when truth leads to unpleasant results"[4] "It is sometimes a duty to lie."[5] "If a lie is the only way to reach a good result, it is allowable.[6] And a medieval Syrian poet also wrote: "I lift my voice to utter lies absurd, for when I speak the truth, my hushed tones scarce are heard."[7] Lying, therefore, has been a normal, integral, prevalent and perfectly acceptable facet of Arab culture since time immemorial. And until the West, its leaders and its politicians understand the full implications of this reflex action of the Arab mind when dealing with members of the Arab world, they can never hope to arrive at the results they aim for. So often one reads statements made by prominent politicians to the effect that it is not what is said by Arab leaders in Arabic that counts, but what they say publicly in English. Such statements are not only naive, but also completely absurd. When push comes to shove, it is only what is said in Arabic that contains the truth. Former United States Ambassador, Malcom Toon, understood this when he said: "If you want to know what leaders of non-democratic regimes really believe, don't listen to their declarations to Western statesmen and journalists, but to what they say among themselves."[8]

One aspect of "whitening" another's face is to tell a person, usually with all sincerity intended, what he really wants to hear. Thus, when the conversation is terminated, that person comes away with a positive but completely inaccurate view of the events discussed. As John Laffin, the English Arabist and author of a book entitled *The Arab Mind*, succinctly put it: "The Arab means what he says at the moment he is saying it. He is neither a vicious nor, usually, a calculating liar but a natural one."[9]

The most incredible thing about the Arab mind's ability to lie and its unlimited creativity in conjuring up the preposterous, is that it sincerely believes the lies it creates. In Madrid in October 1991, Hanan Ashrawi, the spokeswoman for the PLO negotiating team and the darling of the news media, sidestepped a legitimate question from a Christian journalist and said: "I am a Palestinian Christian and I know what Christianity is. I am a descendant of the first Christians in the world, and Jesus Christ was born in my country, in my land. Bethlehem is a Palestinian town."[10] Like most of her other statements, political or otherwise, this one was a series of colossal lies also. Ashrawi is an Arab, and Arabs did not come into the land until Islam conquered the Christians in 637 A.D. All the first Christians were Jews, as was Jesus himself. Bethlehem was in Judea, *"in the land of Israel"* (Matthew

2:21,22). Most of those who heard or read her outrageous statement believed it as much as she did, and this only helps to delegitimatize Israel's presence in the land.

Jordan entered the Arab's coalition against Israel in the humiliating and devastating 1967 war, because the commander of Egypt's forces sent a coded communiqué to King Hussein claiming that Egypt had destroyed 75 percent of Israel's attacking warplanes, destroyed Israel's bases in a counterattack, and that its ground forces had penetrated Israel itself.[11] The world now knows that Israel almost entirely destroyed Egypt's airforce along with those of three other nations in less than three hours from the commencement of hostilities. But on the strength of repeated Egyptian claims of massive victories, Jordan entered the war and not only added the loss of its airforce to that of the other four, but also lost more territory than all of the other aggressors combined. King Hussein of Jordan said: "These [Egyptian] reports—fantastic to say the least—had much to do with our confusion and false interpretation of the situation."[12] John Laffin comments: "To claim to have inflicted heavy military losses on an enemy makes this a fact, even if no military action whatever took place."[13] And an Egyptian Arab notes that, "When we Arabs praise some imaginary deed, we are carried away by the same feeling of satisfaction that we would feel if we had really carried it out."[14]

"This is a difficult concept for a Westerner to grasp, but until he does so, many Arab actions and statements make little sense."[15] The Arab mind struggles with reality and, therefore, usually operates more in the realm of fantasy. It lives in the glories of its people's past and not in actualities—it fabricates events to explain current or past failures.

Violence

One needs only to read the Bible to gain some understanding of the savage and cruel nature of the people who inhabit the Middle East. With the exception of around 40 percent of today's Israelis, the inhabitants of the Middle East have had their roots firmly fixed there for thousands of years—they are the descendants of men who have fought each other for thousands of years, and who still threaten war in the same sun-scorched desert sands.

Approximately 60 percent of Israeli Jews were either born in Arab lands or were born to those who came from Arab lands. Hundreds of thousands of Jews lived among the Arabs during their almost 2,000 years of exile from the Promised Land.

While the contemporary Israeli is in no way barbarous like the inhabitants of the modern Arab nations (particularly Iraq and Syria), there is a definite tendency among many of the Jews of Eastern origin to exhibit rather violent behavior with very little provocation. This has been most evident in recent days when Israeli policemen from this background disburse those demonstrating against the government's agreements with the PLO. Wife beating is also prevalent among Israelis of Eastern origin. Some 200,000 women—five percent of Israel's Jewish population—are victims of domestic violence.[16] And the "shame" culture is very much in evidence. Many Israelis will readily tell a lie rather than lose face. All these behavior patterns are the result of exposure to centuries of Arab culture. But Israelis in general are both shocked and outraged by violent or brutal acts, and brutality is neither condoned nor acceptable in Israeli society.

The Arab propensity for barbarity, however, is as old as the Arab people themselves. The LORD said of Ishmael, Abraham's son by Hagar: *"He will be a wild donkey of a man; his hand will be against everyone and everyone's hand against him, and he will live in hostility toward all his brothers"* (Genesis 16:12 NIV). The truth of those words are contained in an widespread, oft-quoted Arab proverb today: "I against my brothers; I and my brothers against my cousins; I and my cousins against the world."[17] And an Arab writing of his people said, "all our people are armed, all fight, and all kill for the least thing. We are very jealous of our rights...If in this village two houses should suddenly engage in a fight, the entire population would split into two parties and join in the fight. War could break out in the village. When it subsides, and only then, would the people ask what the cause of the fighting was. They fight first, and then inquire as to the cause of the fight. This is our way of life."[18]

Another feature of the Bedouin ethos is the law of blood revenge. A much quoted Arab proverb is, "Blood demands blood."

Relatives must avenge the blood of the slain by killing either the actual murderer or one of his relatives. Even when a murderer is apprehended, convicted in a court of law, and executed, it does not fulfill the requirements of blood revenge. One of the relatives of the executed man must die by the hand of one of the victims relatives. And, of course, the murdered relative's blood must be avenged by his relatives. Thus it continues *ad infinitum*. An Arab man once remarked that "both the Japanese and the Arabs are ready to kill to regain their lost honor; but the Japanese will kill himself, while the Arab will kill somebody else."[19]

Terrorism

Almost every native English speaker is conversant with the words, assassin, assassinate and assassination. But few would know that these words originate in the Middle East. Assassins was the name given to a medieval "murderous group of Syrian Moslems."[20] The Assassins belonged to a sect of Islam known as Isma'ili, and in a calculated war of terror, they murdered sovereigns, princes, generals, governors and even the divines of Islam. Their murders were designed to frighten, to weaken and ultimately to overthrow the Sunni sect of Islam.

The Assassins terrorized the Middle East from the 11th to the 13th century and derived their name from the Arabic word, *Hashshashin*, meaning "smokers of hashish." They whipped themselves into a religious frenzy by the smoking of hashish before committing their murders and were the "forerunners of today's terrorists."[21] The Assassins seized or bought fortresses for use as bases for their campaign of terror. They gained a great deal of influence and were given a building (traditionally a palace) in Damascus itself for use as their headquarters.[22] Another name by which the ancient Assassins were known was *Fedayeen*. This word is in common use in Arabic today and is generally applied to all Arab terrorists.

Little has changed in the Middle East. Numbers of well financed, murderous terrorist groups have bases and headquarters today throughout the entire region. Names like Abu Nidal, reputedly the world's most wanted man, Ahmed Jibril (believed to be the mastermind behind the bombing of the 1989 Pan Am

Flight 103 over Lockerbie, Scotland, that killed all 269 people on board and another 11 on the ground), considered to be the world's most dangerous terrorist,[23] George Habash, Yasser Arafat, Nayef Hawatmeh and a host of others whose names are synonymous with murder and terror, operate from within the Middle East. Their victims include both Arabs and non-Arabs, and the numbers killed, maimed or injured annually is in the tens of thousands. Terrorism is so much a part of Arab culture that most Arab countries "levy a two percent *fedayeen tax*' on all entertainment tickets."[24]

"Terrorist warfare has allowed Arab regimes to attack Western targets while denying any responsibility for these attacks. Sovereign Arab states such as Syria, Iraq and Libya have provided arms, embassies, intelligence services and money to various terror organizations operating against the West and other objects of their animosity, thereby transforming terrorism that had been a local peculiarity of Middle Eastern politics into an International malignancy. For international terrorism is the quintessential Middle Eastern export, and its techniques everywhere are those of the Arab regimes and organizations that invented it. The hijacking and bombing of aircraft, the bombing of embassies, the murder of diplomats, and the taking of hostages by Arab terrorists have since been adopted by non-Arab terrorists the world over."[25]

Arabs are unpredictable—"a gentle, peaceful man, on the spur of the moment may commit brutal murder."[26] A man's best friend of yesterday might well be his murderer tomorrow—once aroused, his wrath has no limits. How true is the Arab proverb: "At each meal a quarrel, with each bite a worry."[27]

Arab spokesmen tell Westerners, "If it were not for the Israelis, all would be peace and harmony in the Middle East."[28] The Middle East was a bloody and insecure region long before Israel raised her head in 1948. And most of the coups, conflicts and killings in the Arab states and Iran in the last 40 years have not been connected to Israel at all. The current Secretary General of the United Nations, Boutros Boutros-Ghali, wrote in 1982: "In the last three decades alone, more than 30 conflicts between Arab states have erupted."[29] Some of these "conflicts" were, in fact, full-scale wars. In addition to these conflicts, John Laffin writes:

"Between 1948 and 1973 the Arab world suffered thirty successful revolutions and at least fifty unsuccessful ones."[30] Laffin adds that in the same period, "22 heads of state and prime ministers were murdered."[31] Laffin gives the main reason for conflicts as "the desire for power,"[32] and says that some of the wars were "hideously brutal."[33]

Savagery

It was mentioned earlier that Arabs in general endeavor to emulate Bedouin customs, holding them in high esteem and believing them to be virtually sacrosanct. Next to Mohammed himself, an Arab philosopher of the 14th century, Ibn Khaldun, has had the most influence on the Arab world. He wrote: "Bedouin are a savage nation, fully accustomed to savagery and the things that cause it. Savagery has become their character and their nature. They enjoy it...They care only for the property they might take away from people through looting...civilization always collapsed in places the Bedouin took over and conquered."[34] Centuries have passed since Khaldun wrote those words, but the Bedouin qualities, including savagery, survives throughout the modern Arab world. "Western soldiers who fought the Arabs were always trained to keep their last bullet for themselves—an insurance against the torture they inevitably faced."[35] During the Arab's war with France between 1954–1962 French soldiers caught by Arabs in Morocco, Algeria, Tunisia or Syria were "buried to their necks in sand to die in the blazing sun and were sometimes smeared with honey or jam to attract the ants. Bestial indignities were inflicted on captives before they were killed. When the Arabs captured a group of Frenchmen they would sometimes cut off their hands, shuffle them and leave them in odd pairs stuck in the sand in attitudes of prayer. To the disgust of the French, women were usually more barbarous than their men."[36]

Arabists believe that each particular Arab group has its own particular type of barbarism, but my own research shows a uniform bestiality common to all parts of the Arab world. A military coup brought an end to Iraqi royalty when King Feisal II and all but one of the other members of the Royal Family were murdered.

The Arab Mind

The body of the heir apparent, Prince Abd al-Ilah, was given into the hands of the Iraqi populace. "With ropes the regent's body was attached by the neck and the armpits to the back of a lorry which dragged it through the streets to shouts of 'Allah is great!' Men armed with knives and choppers dismembered the body, and the young men ran off waving the limbs with joyful shouts. When the procession reached the ministry of defense the body was no more than a mutilated trunk but it was hoisted to a balcony where a young man with a knife climbed a lamp-post and repeatedly stabbed the corpse in the back. He then began cutting off the flesh, working from the buttocks upwards. From the street a long white stick was brought which was inserted into the corpse and forcibly pushed inside. What was left of the regent's body that evening was soaked with petrol and set on fire, the remains being thrown into the Tigris."[37]

Of eight captured Israelis that were returned to Israel from Syria, only "one was in mental condition to give a coherent account of their sufferings and to restart a normal life. Another of the eight committed suicide in his parent's home in Tel Aviv a few months after his release. The remaining six are likely to spend their lives in mental institutions."[38] Numbers of Israeli soldiers, who were overrun on the Golan Heights in the first hours of the 1973 *Yom Kippur* War, were found tied hand and foot with bullet holes in the backs of the heads. Their genitals had been cut off and stuffed in their mouths.

During the current *intifada* (Palestinian uprising), the local Arabs have killed nearly twice as many of their own people as have the Israeli army. Many of these Arabs have been butchered in the most cruel fashion for no reason at all. Simply for working in an Israeli administered hospital in Gaza, a nine-months pregnant Arab nurse was dragged out of the operation room in the middle of an operation and hacked to death in the corridor.[39] Arab violence is "handed on from father to eldest son to youngest son to the family donkey or dogs."[40] The whole Arab tradition is "one of violence. They know no better."[41] "Arab violence is non-selective; the identity of the victims is immaterial. For the Arab, violence in itself is consolatory."[42] "Violence," a Libyan cabinet minister told Laffin, "is the Moslem's most positive form of prayer."[43] "Violence has become a commodity. It was always exportable within the Arab world, but in modern times it reaches further afield and has the more open sanction of governments and political leaders."[44]

Books dealing with the issues of the Arab world are full of brutal accounts of Arab savagery. Newspapers, magazines and periodicals chronicle them also. There is arguably no other people quite so determinedly violent and pitiless as the people of the Arab world, where violence is "a chronic mental condition."[45] What is it that feeds this barbarism and actually fuels the fires of cruelty? To find the answer to the question, it is necessary to study Islam (addressed in the next chapter), works by eminent authorities on the Arab mind, Arab literature and statements made by Arab leaders and politicians. Almost all Arab cruelty is generated by one or more of the following—honor (face), hatred and sex.

Hatred

Hatred of anything non-Arab or Islamic is axiomatic in the Arab world. And to the Arab mind, either Israel or the West (or both) is responsible for the stagnant conditions prevailing within the Arab world—for disease, for illiteracy, for the lack of Arabic literature, for maliciously falsifying and distorting their glorious Arab history, etc. Just as the failing student will blame the exams instead of himself, so will the Arab world lay the blame for its failures upon others. "Most Westerners have simply no inkling of how deep and fierce is [that] hate."[46]

Arab children are first indoctrinated with hate in the home, and for those fortunate enough to receive an education, the school system and text books ensure its students will graduate in the subject. Hatred, especially toward Israel and the Jews, is nurtured and developed in the minds of Arab children and occupies a great deal of space in Arabic text books. A former Syrian Minister of Education, wrote: **"The hatred which we indoctrinate into the minds of our children from their birth is sacred."**[47] Throughout the Arab world school children are constantly faced with the following type of exercises: "Israel was born to die. Prove it."[48] "We shall expel all the Jews from the Arab countries."[49] "The Arabs do not cease to act for the extermination of Israel."[50] "Israel shall not live if the Arabs stand fast in their hatred."[51] And on the back of a standard exercise book there is map of Israel. "The Arab armies are shown encircling it, and a missile is aimed at Tel Aviv."[52]

A Jew, born and educated in Syria, but who later escaped to Israel recalls: "I remember that the Moslem boys threw stones at me, and I remember, too, the education I received in school. The Jewish school, but the majority is Moslem. I remember it is written that the Jews are evil, I don't know why. And their God is a God who wants to drink the blood of all the other peoples. This was in the Arabic book at the education system. I was taught this in the Jewish school, because I am a student and want to pass through these schools to graduate."[53] And an Arab boasted on Israeli television that his eight-year-old son is fed no breakfast before he throws his quota of rocks on Israeli vehicles.[54]

But no education of Arab children would be complete without the actual witnessing of brutality and violence. Arab nations execute most of their victims in public squares. In Baghdad's Liberation Square, for example, when Jews were hanged, hundreds of thousands of Iraqis converged on the square "to view the bodies dangling on the gallows; large parties of school children [were] taken to view the scene."[55]

Several hundred Israelis have been brutally murdered by Arab terrorists, many of those murdered were women and children. The weak and innocent have always been prime targets for Arab terrorists. Typical attacks took place in April 1994: A 23 year-old mother was stabbed seven times as she nursed her two-week old baby[56]—miraculously both the mother and baby survived. A bus taking on high school pupils in Afula was the target for a car bomb in which eight died and another 51 were injured, some critically—severed limbs were strewn over a wide area. The car was detonated right next to the bus. Investigation revealed that "the car, which had been stolen, contained several gas canisters to increase the force of the explosion, and a large quantity of nails to maximize the number of wounded. Many of the victims were teenagers from two nearby junior high schools where classes had just let out. 'Two boys were burning like torches. They came running toward me, and I took one and doused the flames with a rag, and then I ripped off his clothes,' said Albert Amos, 43, a driving teacher. 'He was burned all over. When I touched him, pieces of his skin came off in my hand. The other boy was put into an ambulance. He was shouting: 'What happened to me? What did I do?'"[57]

The great majority of the victims of the 1974 massacres in Kiryat Shmonah and Ma'alot were children, and those murders were "publicly applauded throughout the Arab world,"[58] just as today's terrorist actions are. The Kiryat Shmonah massacre left 18 dead, including five women and eight children.[59] The attack on the Ma'alot school left 20 dead and wounded another 70, nearly all children.[60] "In Arab thought," says Laffin, "a victim is responsible for his own suffering. Against all this it is pointless to appeal to conscience and ask, 'How can you wage war on children?' Given a lifetime's indoctrination, a man can wage war on anyone."[61]

A word needs to be added here concerning the February 1994 massacre of 29 Moslems in a Hebron mosque by Baruch Goldstein, a Jewish doctor from Kiryat Arba. The mosque was in the Cave of the Patriarchs (cave of Machpelah, Genesis 25:8-10), where Abraham, Isaac, Jacob, Sarah, Rebekah and Leah are all buried. The area inside the Cave of the Patriarchs is partitioned, enabling Jews to pray there also.

Goldstein was an immigrant from America and was described by all who knew him as "a quiet, kind, gentle man." Goldstein attended to a number of Kiryat Arba's victims of Arab terror. And his friend, Mordechai Lapid, a father of 14 and a former Russian "Prisoner of Zion," together with one of Lapid's sons, died in the doctor's arms from a terrorist attack a few weeks before he committed the Hebron massacre. The evening prior to the massacre, Goldstein left the Cave without completing his prayers because "a large group of Arabs **inside** the Cave of Patriarchs were chanting 'Slaughter the Jews'...'Death to the Jews,' and no one responsible among the Arab community found anything wrong with such pronouncements and conduct."[62] The next day Goldstein came to the Cave dressed in his IDF uniform and carrying his IDF-issue automatic rifle. He gained access to the Cave by convincing the guards that he was on duty, and while the Moslems were kneeling in prayer, he opened fire.

There was universal shock and outrage in Israel. The Prime Minister, Yitzak Rabin, spoke of his absolute disgust at the massacre as did all of Israel's leaders. The President of Israel, Ezer Weizeman, spoke of the shame the massacre had brought upon the Jewish people and visited Hebron to bring Israel's condolences to the families of the victims. Nearly 80 percent of all Israelis loudly condemned the massacre,[63] and the Israeli government paid NIS 40 million (U.S.$13.3 million) in compensation to the families of the dead and injured. The Hebron massacre was a rare, isolated incident, and both the reactions of the public and the actions of the government were those of shock, repulsion, sorrow and shame. This is in stark contrast to Arab reactions to news of the murders of Israelis.

Sex

Unlike the western world, sexual restraints upon Arab women are strictly enforced. Throughout almost the whole of the Arab world, death follows a girl's loss of virginity except to her new husband. And adultery brings death for married women. But a married man is not expected to refrain from extramarital sexual activity, he is guilty of sexual offense "only if the woman with whom he has sexual relations commits thereby an act of sexual dishonor."[64] It is the female's duty to protect both her honor and her life.

Men are usually circumcised without anesthesia at age 13, primarily as a means to increase virility but also as a test of their "manliness, bravery, and courage."[65] Female circumcision is also very widespread among the Arab peoples, but in the case of clitoridectomy, it is performed to prevent the girl from desiring premarital sex. And in the case of infibulation (either affixing a device to the vulva, or operating so that only an opening the size of a matchstick is left for the passing of urine and the menses), to make it altogether impossible, until her genitals are either cut or forced open.[66] During the traditional wedding night, "the husband is sometimes obliged to cut open hardened scar tissue with a knife."[67]

The traditional unavailability of willing girls with which to satisfy a young Arab's high sexual urge accounts for the extremely high rate of homosexuality among Arab males. The active homosexual act is considered to be an "assertion of one's aggressive masculine superiority,"[68] with the result that male homosexuality continues after marriage, with sheiks and the "well-to-do men lending their sons to each other."[69]

Professor Raphael Patai, the eminent Israeli Arabist, who also wrote a book entitled *The Arab Mind*, says the "rules that restrict contact between men and women, have the effect of making sex a prime mental preoccupation in the Arab world."[70] And an Arab wrote of his own people: "**Sex is our eternal headache, the incubus that devours us day and night.** If you ask me about the size of the sexual problem I will tell you that it is exactly the same size as our cranium, so that there is not a single convolution in the Arab brain which is not tumescent with sex."[71]

A favorite topic of discussion among Arabs is the immorality of Western women, and John Laffin says: "Because of the frustrations and repressions which follow the rigidly held sexual mores and prohibitions of his own society, the Arab is dangerous to women of other nationalities...When Arabs go abroad their projected sexual adventures loom more important than any work or study."[72] Dr. Sania Hamady, herself an Arab and one of the leading authorities on Arab psychology, observes that "whenever an Arab man finds himself alone with a woman, he makes sexual approaches to her."[73]

Sex is an all-consuming passion. It occupies an Arab's thoughts night and day and often expresses itself in violence and brutality brought about by sheer sexual frustration. Sigmund Freud,[74] and other psychoanalysts and psychologists, find a clear link between aggression and sexuality. The intensity of aggression is always related to the intensity of the sex drive. The continuous upheavals and violence in the Arab world is a way of "taking the mind off the consuming pre-occupation with sex."[75] This "pre-occupation" is "expressed by going to near certain death in a coup against the establishment, in a factional fight, or in an act of terrorism. Death in such an event would bring its own reward—the martyr would find himself among many beautiful, and more importantly, willing girls in paradise."[76]

Substituting Words for Actions

The Arab is notorious for substituting words for actions. It is believed by most Western Arabists and even by many Arabs themselves, that Arabs never carry out their threats or intentions. Students of the Arab world rightly conclude that there is a penchant to substitute words for actions, but this is not an ironclad rule, and it is extremely dangerous to regard it as such. Certainly, there are topics on which the Arabs have waxed eloquent for over 50 years without any action having taken place, but given a sufficiently powerful motivation, they will always attempt to carry out their threats. Israeli defeats of Arab armies in 1948, 1956, 1967, 1969, 1973, and again in 1982 provides such motivation. The Arab world has been repeatedly shamed—honor must be restored, and Arabs will patiently plan revenge for years, even decades, if need be.

Concerning the belief that words are always substituted for actions, take as an example the October 1973 *Yom Kippur* War. The Egyptian Deputy Foreign Minister, Salah Gohar, was asked by *Time* magazine about all the sabre-rattling declarations against Israel. Gohar replied: "When Arabs argue, they start on opposite sides of the sidewalks and shout at one another, 'I will carve you in pieces!' and 'You'll never see another sunset!' Then, after ten of 15 minutes, they walk away and nobody gets hurt."[77] *Time* believed him. The world believed him. The Israeli government believed him. Even Yitzhak Rabin, Chief of General Staff during the 1967 Six Day War and currently Israel's Prime Minister and Minister of Defense, believed him. Three months prior to the outbreak of war Rabin wrote: "There is no need to call up our forces even when the enemy makes threats and deploys its forces along the cease fire-line."[78]

But the Arabs had a sufficiently powerful motivation. On October 6, 1973, they attacked Israel on its most holy day of the year and almost succeeded in destroying it. An avalanche of over 1.2 million men[79] and a formidable array of equipment came against an unprepared Israel. It took three days to mobilize its small army that reached only 300,000 men with all the reserves mobilized.[80] Believing that Arabs always substitute words for actions almost cost Israel its life.

Another case in point is Saddam Hussein's December 1990 statement that if the United States and her coalition partners launched a "first strike" against Iraq for her invasion of Kuwait in August of the same year, "Israel will suffer the second (blow) in Tel Aviv."[81] The coalition forces, of whom Israel was not a part, delivered their "first strike" at Iraqi targets in the Gulf War on January 16, 1991. That day saw the first of the 39 Iraqi missile strikes on the civilian population centers of Israel which destroyed or damaged some 5,000 Israeli homes. Believing that Arabs now want to make peace and not war with Israel is equally as naive and dangerous as believing that they always substitute words for actions.

The motivation to destroy Israel has increased, not decreased. Only the tactics have changed. Arab honor must be restored, and only the annihilation of Israel can restore it. The establishment of the State of Israel and the defeat of the Arab armies is described by the leaders of the Arab world as "the disaster" or "the great defeat;"[82] "the day of the greatest shame in the modern history of the Arabs;"[83] and, "a smear on the entire Arab Nation. No one can forget the shame brought by the battle of 1948."[84] According to the Arabs that "smear," that "shame," can only be removed from the Arab nation's face by "Israel's total and absolute annihilation."[85] Five further wars against Israel since 1948, each more devastating that the last, should be ample proof that the greatest of motivations to restore Arab honor courses through the veins of the entire Arab world. It should be carefully noted that the Arab's preoccupation with revenge against Israel is all that restrains them from unleashing all their violence upon the West.

Arab?

At this point the question should be asked, "Who is an Arab?" It is generally believed that the Arab world has its roots in the union of Abraham and Hagar, the Egyptian maid of Sarah, Abraham's wife. This is only true to a point. There are numbers of nations described today as "Arab" that are not really Arab at all. The word "Arab" means "Bedouin" or "nomad," and the name was given to those who inhabited the Arabian peninsular and the Syrian Desert.

Abraham himself came from Chaldea, known today as Iraq.

Iran is not Arab and neither is its language Arabic. Iran is ancient Persia; Islam is her only common denominator with the Arab nations. The founding father of Egypt, Mizraim (*Mizraim* is Hebrew for Egypt—the leader of the so called "Arab" nations), was a grandson of Noah as were the fathers of Libya, Canaan and Ethiopia (Genesis 10:6). Obviously, if Ishmael, the son of Abraham, had an Egyptian mother, he is not responsible for fathering the nation. From Mizraim came the Philistines (Genesis 10:14). Lot, Abraham's nephew (Genesis 12:5), was also an Iraqi. He fathered Ammon and Moab in an incestuous drunken spree (Genesis 19:36-38), and these men were the fathers of modern-day Jordan. The father of the nation of Yemen (Hebrew: *Teman*) was the grandson of Jacob's brother Esau (Genesis 36:11,34). From the genealogies we can see that many of those living in the Middle East are indeed blood relations, but it is as equally incorrect to say that Abraham is responsible for the nations of the Middle East, as it is to say that all the nations of the Middle East are Arab.

In the Arab world the answer to the question, "Who is an Arab" is usually this: "One whose mother tongue is Arabic."[86] Scholars, both Arab and Western, give rather more defined answers to the question, but their thoughts seem to converge upon Arabs as being those who speak Arabic, are brought up in Arab culture, and live in an Arabian country. Neither of these answers are satisfactory, however, because the Christian Copts of Egypt satisfy all of the above requirements but fervently deny being Arab. Hundreds of thousands of Jews born and raised in Arab lands, and who also satisfy all the given requirements, neither consider themselves to be Arabs, nor would the Arabs dream of considering them as such. Therefore, from what has been written here, we can arrive at the correct answer to the contemporary question of "Who is an Arab?"

Iran is radically Islamic, the only Middle Eastern country not considered to be Arab and the only Middle Eastern country to have held to its ancestral language after embracing Islam. The Egyptian Copts never converted to Islam, and neither did the Jews. Thus, leaving history aside, today's Arabs are those whose mother tongue is Arabic, and who hold to the teachings of Islam.

3
Islam and the Koran

The words, "Arab," and "Islam," are as synonymous as "snow" and "ice." Arabs were responsible for the introduction of Islam, and Islam is responsible for keeping the Arab world in the dark ages. Arabs are cruel, and Islam is a cruel religion. They suit each other. The adherents of Islam are exhorted to kill for the sake of Allah, and where the Islamic holy law (*Sharia*) is in effect, there can be no resisting of Islam nor turning to another religion or faith. To do so invites severe punishment—by sword, hanging, stoning or crucifixion.

Violent, savage behavior is traditionally found among primitive tribal people who hold fast to a belief in one or more demon spirits. Islam is a primitive, tribal religion. Islam mandates that the only food to be eaten today is what Mohammed was accustomed to eating in Arabia 1,300 years ago, and the only clothing to be worn in any nation (East or West) is that which was worn by illiterate desert dwellers in 7th century Arabia.

For those who are not enamored with Islam, the Koran (the Moslem holy book) commands their punishment to be: "execution, or crucifixion, or the cutting off of hands and feet from the opposite sides."[1] In October 1993, in Saudi-Arabia, where the laws do not allow the practice of any religion other than Islam, a father and son were beheaded together for "having come to faith in Christ. Had it not been for the international outcry, the Saudi authorities would have executed two other Christians on Christmas day."[2]

A friend, who cannot be identified here, was recently in Riyadh, Saudi-Arabia, on a Friday, at what is called "Chop-Chop Square." Here executions take place following prayers. He wrote: "The square was filled with thousands of Moslems. We heard the Moslem priest preach from the mosque through the loudspeaker. The Friday prayer ended with all turning towards Mecca and bowing down on the ground. Immediately they stood up from their prayer, two policemen led a blindfolded man into the center of the crowd to a circle where policemen were standing. He had to bow down on his knees on the square with his head bowed forward. Two huge black men went forward. One carried a sword and gave it to the largest of the two. He lifted the sword and with one stroke the head was cut from the body of a Pakistani man. This is the way Moslems end their Friday prayer gathering in Riyadh. The executions for the day are announced on the TV-news in the evening." My friend also wrote: "The religious police arrest people in the streets in downtown Riyadh if they are not in the mosque at prayer time." The *matowa,* the powerful religious police, "enforce the closure of all businesses during prayer time and coerce people into the mosques. People late for a prayer session are beaten with sticks."[3]

Even acts of compassion can be classified as an affront to Allah and are dealt with accordingly. During the fast of Ramadan, for example, when no food or water is allowed between sunrise and sunset for an entire month, extreme hardship is undergone by those laboring in the searing desert heat, and many workers collapse. In 1986, during Ramadan in Saudi Arabia, a man fell unconscious, and another worker poured some water into his mouth in an effort to revive him. The compassionate man forfeited his life, and the distressed man had his right hand amputated.

The Koran teaches that women are inferior to men and even admonishes husbands to "scourge" their wives.[4] According to a recent poll, 80 percent of Arab women believe that routine wife-beating is "normal and beneficial for family stability and discipline."[5] And at least one sect believes that women have no souls and, therefore, will not be resurrected.[6]

The discrimination against females is hard for Westerners to imagine. In Bangladesh, in December 1994, a young woman was raped in a field where she was gathering vegetables. Instead of her violator being brought to justice, the 20-year-old herself was sentenced "to 80 lashes with a supple green bamboo cane for having unlawful sex."[7] The woman, who passed out under the gaze of 200 onlookers after 35 lashes, failed to "produce three male witnesses to support her allegation that she was raped."[8]

In some Islamic countries a woman who turns from Islam to embrace Christianity will be publicly hung. And if she has young children, those under the age of five years will be hung along with their mother. Petty crimes, committed by both men and women, are punished by the severing of hands or feet, or both. The "cutting off of hands, feet, ears, tongues, and heads; and the gouging out of eyes—all of these things are part of Islamic law today."[9]

Under Islamic law the death penalty for adultery is administered by stoning, but the method of administration varies. In the Iranian city of Qom, "women are buried in the ground up to their armpits, while men are buried to their waist as the stoning begins."[10]

Most Jews resist conversion to Islam, and many pay with their lives. Feysulla Mechubad, age 77, a leader in the small, Iranian Jewish community, paid the penalty for being Jewish on February 25, 1994. He "had his eyes gouged out before his death. He had also been connected to torture instruments and severely flogged on his back, limbs and face before being executed."[11]

Like the Arabs themselves, the religion of Islam is savage and rules by fear and terror. And Iran's own brand of fanatical Islam has executed 95,000 political prisoners—dissidents and apostates—since the 1979 revolution.[12] Welcome to the world of Islam—the "supreme" religion that Iran and the Arabs plan to bring by force upon the entire inhabited world.

Ignorance and Naiveté

In this last decade of the 20th century, as we move rapidly toward the last days of the End Times, two things stand out beyond all others: that the Western nations possess a cosmic ignorance of the reason for the Arab-Israeli conflict, and that the Church is abysmally naive in her thinking toward Islam.

The great majority of Westerners think that disputed ownership of land is the cause of the Arab-Israeli conflict. Scarcely a day passes without the news media propagating and enforcing this line of thought into the minds of the world's masses. And the widely-held heretical belief that Jews, Christians and Moslems all serve the same God and that there must be "understanding and interfaith-dialogue," will benefit the Church as much as the hunter benefited from his compromise with the grizzly bear. The hunter needed a fur coat, and the grizzly bear needed a meal, so the nice hunter compromised; the grizzly bear got his meal and the hunter was inside the grizzly bear's fur coat.

I have expressed for a number of years my belief that Islam is the Western world's most potentially dangerous enemy. Long before the collapse of the Soviet Union and its communist ideology, I had said that Communism did not nearly equal Islam's threat to the West. I have repeatedly warned of what lies ahead unless definite steps are taken to curb the increasing momentum of fundamental Islam, but my warnings have thus far fallen upon deaf ears.

If leaders and law makers are to sufficiently comprehend the danger that Islam presents to both Israel and the West, in order to motivate them to action, they first need to know something about it. **Islam is the antithesis of Biblical Christianity.** Christianity advocates love and compassion toward God and one's neighbor; Islam promotes hatred and cruelty—diabolical cruelty. Execution, crucifixion, the severing of hands, feet and tongues, the gouging out of eyes are all part of Islam's "submission to the will of Allah."

The Koran

Mohammed, the founder of Islam, wrote the Koran, the Moslem holy book. It is a mixture of desert folklore and customs, revelations of Mohammed, and elements of teaching from both Judaism and Christianity. The Koran is believed by Moslems to be the direct, precise, divine revelation of Allah to his prophet by the medium of angels and that the book is perfect and without error. Moslems also believe that Arabic is the language of Allah and that the Arabic of the Koran is, "the perfect, exact representation of Allah's words."[13]

These claims, like most other Arab claims, are patently false. The Arabic of the Koran has numerous grammatical errors, such as in "Suras 2:177,192; 3:59; 4:162; 5:69; 7:160; 13:28; 20:66; 63:10, etc."[14] The Koran contains: "sentences which are incomplete and not fully intelligible,"[15] and more than 100 "aberrations from the normal rules and structure of Arabic."[16] And the Koran is certainly not "pure Arabic," as it also contains over 100 "Egyptian, Hebrew, Greek, Syriac, Akkadian, Ethiopian and Persian words and phrases."[17] Many Moslems claim that the original manuscript of the Koran is still in existence and that all copies of the Koran come from this one single manuscript. Another

Islam and the Koran

manifestly absurd claim. Not only have parts of the Koran been lost or deliberately removed, but "entire verses and chapters have been added to it."[18]

Much of the information contained in the Koran bears little resemblance to historical fact. Mary, the mother of Jesus, lived 600 years before Mohammed. The Arabic form of her name is Maryam. Miriam, the sister of Moses and Aaron, whose Arabic name is also Maryam, lived 1,300 years before Mary, the mother of Jesus. But early in the Koran, the two women are portrayed as one and the same person! It says the wife of Moses' father, Imram (Amram), gave birth to Maryam, who in turn, gave birth to Jesus![19] And even in the second half of the Koran Maryam the mother of Jesus is still addressed as "sister of Aaron."[20] Moslem commentators and translators fail miserably in their weak attempts to explain these errors.

Similarly, Haman, the villain of the Book of Esther, is made a contemporary of the Pharaoh of the Israelite Exodus and is said to have helped build the tower of Babel![21] The Koran also claims that Abraham was thrown into a fire by Nimrod.[22] The mere fact that Nimrod died centuries before Abraham was born appears to be of no account! The Koran contains many such errors.

Mohammed

As a young child Mohammed was nursed by a Bedouin woman by the name of Halima. In his third and fourth years, "The child had had numerous fits, which made Halima think he was demon possessed."[23] Early Moslem tradition records that when Mohammed was about to receive a revelation from Allah: "...he would often fall down on the ground, his body would begin to jerk, his eyes would roll backward, and he would perspire profusely. They would often cover him with a blanket during such episodes."[24] It was while Mohammed was in this "trancelike" state that he received his "divine" revelations. "After the trance, he would rise and proclaim what had been handed down to him."[25] Most Western and many Arab biographers of Mohammed believe he suffered from epilepsy.

Mohammed was adept at receiving "divine" revelations that would allow him to live his own lifestyle. The Koran forbids the taking of more than four wives,[26] but Mohammed had "an appetite for women"[27] and married 15 wives,[28] including a ten year-old girl.[29] He even married the ex-wife of his adopted son who was divorced from her husband specifically for that purpose.[30] The marriage caused such a scandal that Mohammed received "divine" revelation to the effect that he was married by Allah's direct command.[31] The same sura (a division or chapter of the Koran) he received from Allah to justify marrying his adopted son's wife, also allowed him to take more than the prescribed four wives to which all other Moslems were, and are, restricted.[32] Mohammed also made provision for Moslems to have an unlimited number of concubines (sexual partners), in addition to the four wives prescribed by law.[33]

The Satanic Verses

In February 1989, Salman Rushdie, a Moslem living in the United Kingdom, wrote a novel entitled *Satanic Verses* which caused a worldwide storm among Moslems. Instead of receiving a literary award, the late Ayatollah Khomeini of Iran placed a price of $3 million on his head, and this reward is to be paid to whoever kills him. Rushdie went into hiding and still remains completely hidden six years later. In February 1995, Iran reiterated both the death sentence and the reward, and said: "Moslems will not forget Rushdie's insults against Islamic sanctities."[34] Publishers became fearful of handling Rushdie's book, especially since his Italian publisher was murdered by a Moslem in 1992. The book was based upon the "Satanic verses" which Mohammed is alleged to have received from Satan, and which are reputed to have been part of the earlier versions of the Koran.

A question we should ask is this: "Did those verses ever exist?" The answer, according to the experts, is a loud and unequivocal, Yes! The verses concerned Mohammed's appeasement of the pagans in Mecca. He received "divine" revelation that it was "perfectly proper to pray to and worship the three daughters of Allah: Al-lat, Al-Uzza and Manat."[35]

The verses caused another storm within Islam because it showed rejection of monotheism in favor of polytheism. But Mohammed later returned to monotheism and subsequently

Islam and the Koran

received revelation of Allah's ability to "abrogate," that is, cancel a past revelation and replace it with a "similar" or "better revelation."[36] The "Satanic verses" were not included in the text of the Koran after Mohammed's death—they were "abrogated."[37] The evidence for the existence of the Koran's "Satanic verses" is overwhelming: "The literature on the 'Satanic verses' is so vast that an entire volume could be written just on this one issue. Every general and Islamic reference work, Moslem or Western, deals with it as well as all the biographies of Mohammed."[38]

Hajj

Every Moslem is expected to make at least one pilgrimage to Mecca during his lifetime. This pilgrimage is known as *hajj,* and "*hajj* is an essential part in gaining salvation."[39] An attractive inducement is offered to Moslems as an encouragement to make the journey: "Since a pilgrimage to Mecca automatically wins pardon for sins already committed and any that may be committed in the future, this, in effect, confers immunity on the pilgrim."[40]

While Mohammed was trying to encourage the Jews to accept him as a prophet, Moslems prayed five times each day facing Jerusalem and also kept the Jewish Sabbath and other Jewish laws. When it became increasingly obvious that the Jews were not at all interested in becoming his disciples, the incensed prophet changed the direction of prayer by turning his back to Jerusalem and faced Mecca instead. He also dropped the Jewish laws, and adopted the pagan Friday sabbath in place of the Jewish Sabbath.[41] The pagans of pre-Islamic Arabia had already established set times of prayer facing Mecca, and had also insisted that everyone should make at least one pilgrimage to Mecca to worship at the Ka'abah,[42] where their idols were kept.

Concerning the Moslem pilgrimage to Mecca, Moslem scholar and statesman Ali Dashti writes: "The historical evidence is crystal clear that Mohammed adopted the pagan religious rite of a pilgrimage to Mecca to worship at the Ka'abah in order to appease the Meccan merchants who made a tremendous amount of money out of these pilgrimages. Thus for financial and cultural reasons Islam adopted the pagan pilgrimage to Mecca."[43]

Allah, god of Islam

Most Christians and Jews think that Allah is merely the Arabic name for God—the Creator God, the God of Abraham, Isaac and Jacob—*the Holy One of Israel.* This belief is the result of ignorance and is very dangerous, because it simply is not true. Moslems even delight in ridiculing the God of the Jews, who is also the God of Biblical Christians. They say, for example: "If you knew the attributes which they attributed to their God, those which they wanted and those which they have adorned him with, then you would certainly be astounded. Jehovah, Lord of Hosts, Lord of Israel, commands them to smear their houses with sheep's blood in order to save their sons and let the Egyptians perish. He is a God who feels remorse for creating Adam and for setting Saul on the throne. He is bloodthirsty, fickle-minded, harsh and greedy. He is pleased with imposture and deceit. He is loquacious and passionately fond of long speeches."[44]

If Islam's Allah is not the God of the Jews and Christians, then exactly who is he? To answer this we must take a journey to the Ka'abah, to the roots of Islam.

The roots of Islam are buried in Arabia—in Mecca—in a square, stone building called the Ka'abah which, according to the Koran, was built by Abraham. In the Ka'abah, there were 360 *jinn* (genies—idols, angels and demons), one of whom was called Allah.[45]

"The word 'Allah' comes from the compound Arabic word *al-ilah. Al* is the definite article 'the,' and *ilah* is an Arabic word for 'god.'"[46]

"Allah is a purely Arabic term used in reference to an Arabian deity."[47]

"'Allah' is a proper name, applicable only to their [Arabs] peculiar God."[48]

"The origin of this [Allah] goes back to pre-Moslem times. Allah is not a common name meaning 'God' (or a 'god').[49]

"'Allah' is a pre-Islamic name...corresponding to the Babylonian Bel."[50]

"Allah was known to the pre-Islamic Arabs; he was one of the Meccan deities."[51]

"Allah-worship, as well as the worship of Baal, were both astral religions in that they involved the worship of the sun, the moon, and the stars."[52]

"In Arabia, the sun god was viewed as a female goddess and the moon as the male god...The name Allah was used as the *personal* name of the moon god."[53]

"Allah, the moon god, was married to the sun goddess. Together they produced three goddesses who were called 'the daughters of Allah.' These three goddesses were called Al-lat, Al-Uzza, and Manat [of the 'Satanic verses']."[54]

"The Allah of the Koran is not the God of the Bible."[55]

Convinced? Can you now guess what the ancient symbol of Allah, the moon god was? Correct. The crescent moon. "His symbol was the crescent moon which now graces every mosque throughout the Moslem world."[56]

After the Jews had consistently refused to follow Mohammed, he changed the direction of prayer from Jerusalem to Mecca and joined the pagans of Arabia who prayed toward the Ka'abah in Mecca, because that was where their gods were. And "Since the idol of their moon god, Allah, was at Mecca, they [Moslems] prayed toward Mecca."[57] It was the Jewish refusal to accept Mohammed as their prophet that instigated the raw Islamic hatred against them. And from the time of the change in the direction of prayer toward the Ka'abah, Mohammed began to use his sword against the "Jewish infidels."

Allah subsequently commanded Mohammed to destroy all the other idols in the Ka'abah, and thus Allah, the moon god, became Allah, and Islam—"absolute submission,"[58] was born. Islam is the only post-Christian religion and the world's second largest religion. It is also the world's fastest growing religion. Governed by a demon spirit, Islam is "more oppressive than communism."[59]

Islam and Israel

It has been stated previously that the words "Arab" and "Islam" are synonymous. It is a grave mistake, indeed, to think that religion has the same meaning for Moslems as it has for those in the Western world. Westerners are generally lukewarm at best in their attitude to religion. Only for the zealous few does religion regulate their lives. Not so for the Arab and Iranian. Religion, for the traditional majority in every Arab country and Iran, remains the central normative of life. Islam permeates the Middle Eastern Moslem's life. It is the hub from which all else radiates. Every activity, every thought, feeling or custom is regulated by the laws of Islam, which are unquestioningly believed by minds that give unpledged allegiance. In this the Moslems are in "sharp contrast with those who profess other religions."[60]

The Middle East is the homeland of Islam. It is where Islam was born. It is—to the Arab mind—Allah's land. And in 1948, the Jews (whom Mohammed, the prophet of Allah, belittles in the Koran and urges his followers to kill) dispossessed Allah from a portion of his land. Not only did these "vile" Jews dispossess Allah and establish a sovereign Jewish state on his land, but they established it in the very heart of the Islamic homeland.

The Koran, implicitly believed by Moslems to be the final and true revelation of God, vilifies Jews as an insidious people worthy only of contempt, punishment and death. The *Hadith* (Moslem tradition) continues the hatred: "The one sent by Allah [Mohammed] has already said the great hour will not come until the Moslems make war upon the Jews and kill so many of them that when a Jew would hide behind a tree or a stone these objects will speak and say: 'O Moslem, servant of God, there is a Jew behind me. Come and kill him.'"[61] Other Moslem writings are also carried along with the momentum: "Allah's messenger—may peace be upon him—has commanded: Fight against the Jews and kill them. Pursue them until even a stone would say: Come here Moslem, there is a Jew hiding himself under me. Kill him. Kill

Islam and the Koran

him quickly."[62]

The Jewish victory in 1948, therefore, created the ultimate challenge to the Islamic world—it struck at the very heart of Islamic theology and belief and undermined it. The size of the State of Israel is immaterial; the Arabs hold 5.4 million sq. mi.[63] (14 million sq. km.) of territory, and Israel only 7,847 sq. mi.[64] (12,628 sq. km.) without "occupied territories." But this tiny speck on a world map is an affront to Islam.

For this reason, 1948 became "the day of the greatest shame in the modern history of the Arabs."[65] The "face" of the Arab nation was "blackened" with shame, as was the face of its god. The continuous call for Israel's annihilation comes not from the Arab world *per se,* but from Islam and for the honor of Allah. Perhaps some of the statements made by Arab leaders will now make more sense to the reader. Note the Islamic inferences:

> "Our war against the Jews is an old struggle that began with Mohammed...**It is our duty to fight the Jews for the sake of Allah and religion**, and it is our duty to end the war that Mohammed began."[66]

> "I promise to crush Israel and **return it to the humiliation and wretchedness established in the Koran.**"[67]

> "Surely **the judgment of Allah is reserved for them** [Jews] until Palestine is transferred from *Dar al-Harb* [House of War] to *Dar al-Islam* [House of Islam]."[68]

> "Israel will exist and continue to exist **until Islam eliminates it, just as it eliminated what preceded it**" (referring to the defeat of the Crusaders).[69]

> "We shall only **accept war**—*jihad*—**the holy war**. We have resolved to drench the lands of Palestine and Arabia with **the blood of the infidels or to accept martyrdom for the glory of Allah.**"[70]

> "The Jews in Palestine must be exterminated. There can be

no option for those of us who revere the name of Allah. There will only be *jihad*."[71]

"The Zionist conquest of Palestine is **an affront to all Moslems**. There can be no compromise until every Jew is dead and gone."[72]

"**Allah has bestowed upon us the rare privilege of finishing what Hitler only began. Let the** *jihad* **begin. Murder the Jews. Murder them all.**"[73]

"**The enemies of God have committed aggression on Moslem lands** and desecrated our sanctuaries. It has become **the duty of every Moslem to make the sacrifice to liberate Moslem territories.**"[74]

"**Fighting the Jews and Israel is a religious obligation and a divine duty.**"[75]

"Every problem in our region can be traced to this single dilemma: **the occupation of** *Dar al-Islam* **[House of Islam] by Jewish infidels**."[76]

The conflict between Arabs and Israelis began in the 7th century when the Jews refused to follow Mohammed and his new religion that has been described today as "heathenism in monotheistic form."[77] Today's conflict is the result of the "despicable" Jews having defeated the Islamic "warriors of *jihad.*"[78] No true Moslem can rest until Israel as a nation is obliterated. Allah, the god of Islam, has been dispossessed of a portion of his land, and his honor has been sullied, as has that of his "warriors"—Israel must be annihilated to restore that honor.

Current events give the appearance that the Arab nations are finally making peace with their common enemy, and the world is ecstatic. But the Koran forbids the existence of the Jewish state, and there can be no peace in the Middle East while it exists. All of the above statements from Islamic leaders were made prior to the signing of the September 1993 agreements between Israel

Islam and the Koran

and the PLO in Oslo. The Oslo agreements will bring no change in Islamic attitudes to Israel, and the following statement made four months after the signing proves this:

> "You don't understand...**Islam can never negotiate or recognize Israel.**"[79]

Nothing has changed! And nothing can change because Mohammed, whom all Moslems revere, said, as he was dying: "Never do two religions exist in Arabia."[80] The Arab's purpose for the "Peace Accord" is not to make lasting peace, but to create a tactical Islamic "truce" in order to destroy Israel at an appropriate time within 10 to 20 years from September 1993. Israel has proven time and time again that it cannot be defeated by direct military confrontation. Even when taken by complete surprise and outnumbered four-to-one in men, planes and tanks, Israel inflicted an incisive defeat in just 10 days. Israel's current borders reflect the outcome of its battles against Arab aggression. These borders must be reduced by "negotiations" around the "peace" table, reduced down to where the nation is indefensible, and where a launching pad can be obtained for Islam's next, and perhaps final, war against Israel.

Jihad and World Domination

Moslems believe that their Islamic nations form a single Islamic state, and that this "state" is destined to become an "Islamic world republic"[81] encompassing every country of the world. The Islamic state is divided into two houses: *Dar al-Islam* (House of Islam), and *Dar al-Harb* (House of War). Those nations under Islamic control belong to the "House of Islam." All others are in the abode of the "House of War."

Nations in the "House of War" are subject to *jihad,* or holy war, until they submit to Islam and become part of the "House of Islam." There can be "no peace and no treaty."[82] *Jihad* means "to remove obstructions impeding the propagation of Islam in non-Moslem countries."[83] *Jihad* is "an Islamic word which other nations use in the meaning of 'War.'"[84] "To struggle in the cause of Allah with pen, speech or sword—that is *jihad.*"[85]

The sword brings results faster than either the pen or speech. Therefore, practically everywhere that Moslems are found in large numbers, violence is found also. All the countries in the following list are either currently in the news, or have recently made the news, for having outbreaks of violence involving Moslems: Afghanistan, Algeria, Armenia, Azerbaijan, Bangladesh, Egypt, Ethiopia, Fiji, France, India, Iraq, Israel, Jordan, Kenya, Lebanon, Libya, Morocco, Niger, Pakistan, the Philippines, Russia, Saudi Arabia, Somalia, Sudan, Tunisia, Turkey, Yemen and Yugoslavia.

Unrest is everywhere within and without the Moslem world. If an area is not under Islam, *jihad* is waged to bring it under Islam. If it is already under Islam, the fanatical Moslem brotherhoods fight to bring a stricter code of Islam. The Islamic religion is often referred to as "the sword of Islam" due to its mania to wage war and shed blood. The late Ayatollah Khomeini, the fanatical leader of Iran who ousted the Shah and brought a resurgence of fundamental Islam to the Middle East, even preached that "the purest joy in Islam is to kill and be killed for Allah."[86]

Such preaching merely echoes that of Mohammed, the founder of Islam, who taught his followers that: "A day and night of fighting on the frontier is better than a month of fasting and prayer."[87] And his followers fought. They fought for Allah, and they died for paradise. An eyewitness account at that time says: "It is almost as if they are driven by the very demons of hell itself...they relish the ardor of battle and welcome the horrors of death."[88] Mohammed's teachings urged his followers on, and still initiates statements like the one previously cited from the Moslem cabinet minister, that "Violence is the Moslem's most positive form of prayer."

To kill and be killed for Islam ensures, for the "warriors of *jihad*," entry into Allah's paradise, which holds the promise of "the services of *houris*, those eternally young, beautiful and virginal black-eyed maidens."[89] Considering the "warrior's" obsession with sex we can understand why they are eager to die and enter paradise. John Laffin comments: "I have asked many Arabs what happens to the virgins once they have lost their virginity in the gardens of paradise, which they must assuredly do very quickly.

Are they thrown out of paradise and fresh virgins brought in? Nobody has been able to give me an answer."[90]

In the 7th century Mohammed said, "Swords are the keys to paradise." For today's 20th century Moslem "warrior," bombs are the keys. Moslem leaders in Gaza encourage young Arabs to detonate explosives worn on their bodies and become "suicide bombers" for Allah. In their hatred of Jews, these Moslem clerics promise their young, lusty recruits "pleasure in the Garden of Eden at the side of 70 virgins."[91] A 15-year-old boy, Mousa Ziada, taken into custody in April 1995, on the night he was to die, told how the clerics promised "to attach a key to his 8kg (nearly 18lb) of explosives, with which he could enter the Garden of Eden."[92] By blowing himself and a number of Jews to pieces, the boy would have become a "hero" and a "holy one," and earned a place next to Allah in paradise. Ziada said he "so much wanted to die and have the 70 beautiful women that Allah would put at his disposal."[93]

The world today is divided between the House of Islam and the rest of us. And Iranian Ayatollah Fazl-Allah Mahalati writes: "But he who takes up a gun, a dagger, a kitchen knife or even a pebble with which to harm and kill the enemies of the Faith has his place assured in Heaven...An Islamic state is a state of war until the whole world sees and accepts the light of the True Faith."[94]

In the book, *War and Peace in the Law of Islam,* Professor Majid Khadduri, one of the foremost experts on Islamic law, writes that the Islamic state seeks to "establish Islam as the dominant reigning ideology over the entire world."[95] And that the Islamic state refuses "to recognize the coexistence of non-Moslem communities, except perhaps as subordinate entities."[96] By "subordinate entities" Khadduri means that minority groups might be allowed to remain in the Islamic state as *dhimmi*—low-class unbelievers submitting to Moslem rule and paying a poll tax to the Islamic state.[97]

The Arab kings and Moslem Imams (holy rulers) believe it to be the divine destiny of Islam to hold "mastery over the earth."[98] Only a fool would dismiss this lightly. Islam today holds sway over 20 percent of the earth's total population—one person in every five, of every nation on the earth. And Islam is spreading, urged on by fiery rhetoric:

> "The governments of the world should know that Islam cannot be defeated. Islam will be victorious in all the countries of the world, and Islam and the teachings of the Koran will prevail all over the world."[99]

> "Weapons in our hands are used to realize divine and Islamic aspirations. The more people who die for our cause, the stronger our *jihad* shall become."[100]

> "We shall export our revolution to the whole world. Until the cry *'Allahu Akbar'* resounds over the whole world, there will be struggle. There will be *jihad*."[101]

Whenever a Moslem plunges a knife or axe into an innocent Jewish victim he screams *"Allahu Akbar"* (Allah is greater), and this war cry accompanies Moslem gunfire, handgrenade and petrol bomb attacks also. It was used by Mohammed as an expression of delight,[102] but later became the Moslem battle-cry which "sanctifies the killings and converts what would otherwise be murder into a righteous deed."[103]

Jews and Christians

Let the reader make no mistake; both Jews and Christians are targeted for total annihilation, unless they are willing to submit to Islam. And let the Christian reader also take note that Islam might well be the instrument that God will use to purge and purify His Church of spots and wrinkles in preparation for His glorious, soon coming. Christians must heed what Moslems in the Middle East chant in their demonstrations: "First we will fight the Saturday people; then we will fight the Sunday people."[104] And during wars they sing in the streets: "We shall fight on Saturday and then on Sunday."[105] In an article entitled *The Hidden Sword of Islam*, an American writer clarifies the two previous quotations: "Perhaps the simple formula articulated by the Moslems themselves is the best way to view their intentions. In their holy war against the

Islam and the Koran

infidels of the Judeo-Christian faiths, they declare that they will first reckon with 'Saturday' (that is, conquer the Jews). Then 'Sunday' will succumb to the conquering hordes of the prophet and his god, Allah. Islam will thus triumph over the 'Christian' world."[106]

When Islam conquers, it establishes memorials to its conquest. Islam's most holy sites (apart from the two in Mecca and Medina) are former Jewish or Christian holy sites. Thus the Omar mosque (Dome of the Rock) stands over the site of the Jewish temple to denote Islam's superiority over Judaism. And, just a stone's throw away, stands the monument to Islam's superiority over Christianity, the Aqsa mosque—built over the site of Solomon's porches where the Christian Church began (John 10:23; Acts 3:11, 5:12). Many hundreds of churches throughout the world (around 500 in Britain) have now been turned into mosques. Islam is marching; the Church is retreating.

And Moslems will brook no criticism of their religion, be it of the Koran, Mohammed or Allah. Just as the death penalty was passed upon Salman Rushdie for writing about the Satanic verses, so it was passed upon another writer, Taslima Nasrin, of Bangladesh, in June 1994. Nasrin had the temerity to suggest that the Koran "should be thoroughly revised."[107] The Bangladesh government ordered her arrest and the police are still hunting her. The local Islamic leader, Mufti Nazrul Islam, announced a reward of 100,000 taka (U.S.$2,500) to anyone who would kill Nasrin because she has "committed an unforgivable offense against Islam and must be condemned to death."[108] "Tens of thousands of fundamentalists have since demonstrated in Dhaka and elsewhere in the country, calling for her death."[109] I am acutely aware that I have placed my life in grave danger by the writing of this book, but I feel compelled to make known the very real threat that faces us, our children, our grandchildren, and the whole Western world.

Moslems feel at total liberty to criticize the Bible and denigrate both God and Jesus. As we saw earlier, they will print their reviling of God even in school text books and think nothing of it. And in any discussion concerning religion, nearly every Moslem will say something similar to this Arab man: "Look! Your Jewish and Christian writers of their Bibles made mistakes. The prophet made no mistakes because he took down God's exact words."[110] To point out that the Koran contains numerous glaring inaccuracies is to invite the full vent of his wrath. The one who would dare to criticize the Koran, Mohammed or Allah usually leaves home and takes up residence in a cemetery. When Islam holds the reigns of power, Christians can expect no mercy. And by siding with the Islamic-Arab states against Israel, "Western nations are helping to dig the grave in which Islam plans to bury Christian civilization once it has finished with the Jews."[111]

Currently there is a call for the execution of the entire Iranian community of converts to Christianity that is estimated to be around 10,000 in number.[112] On January 4, 1994, the Iranian president, Hashemi Rafsanjani, predicted an increase in *jihad* against Christians and indicated that this year might see the last Christmas celebrated in Tehran.[113] And observers report: "All the evidence points to the fact that a massive Middle East holocaust against Christians has begun."[114]

The traditional Islamic *Sharia* law was introduced into Sudan in 1983. Sudan's government led by Omar al Bashir has "targeted Christians and animists for assimilation or annihilation."[115] It was reported in *The New York Times* that the government had "driven 400,000 black Christians into the desert without food or drink to die of starvation, thirst and exposure – unless they converted to Islam."[116] Another source reports that "Christians are being crucified throughout southern Sudan."[117]

A Sudanese Christian, now living in the United States, wrote: "In 1989, radical Iranian-style fundamentalists seized power. Armed by the Arab world and also by Iran, they waged genocide against us. Our women were raped by the tens of thousands, our young men kidnapped and compelled to fight against loved ones. Entire regions were burned to the ground, their people burned alive or taken into slavery. Over 2 million of my people have been butchered or starved to death by those who once pledged peace."[118] The almost unbelievable death toll given above is not exaggerated; reliable sources, such as the United States Committee for Refugees, reveal that at least "1.8 million have died since

May 1983."[119]

Moslem attacks against Christians are currently taking place throughout the entire Middle East. In Egypt "Moslem terrorists opened fire with automatic weapons on a crowd of Coptic Christian worshippers in southern Egypt, killing five—two of them priests—and wounding four others. This massacre, which took place at an ancient Coptic monastery at the start of the Lent holiday period, was the latest in a long series of Moslem attacks on Christians in Egypt."[120]

The murders of a French monk and a French nun in early May 1994, and four Catholic priests—three French and one Belgian—in December 1994, helped bring the murder toll of foreigners in Algeria to more than 70 since September 1993.[121] Moslem fundamentalists issued a statement that the murders were "within the framework of a policy to liquidate Jews, Christians and unbelievers."[122] Since January 1992, an estimated 30,000 people have died violent deaths in Algeria at the hands of Islamic fundamentalists.[123]

Lebanon was the only "Christian" nation in the Middle East, and its Christian population constituted the majority of those living in the land. Today they barely attain to 25 percent of the population due to incessant Moslem pressure and ugly brutality.

As recently as February 1994, a bomb hidden under the altar of a Beirut church exploded during a communion service, killing three priests and nine congregants (including a four year-old girl), and wounding 54 others.[124] Three other unexploded bombs were found in the church and defused.

Israel has traditionally been blamed for the high rate of emigration of local Arab Christians, but recently the myth was exploded publicly by an Arab-Catholic parish priest in Bethlehem when he wrote that, "the emigration of Arab Christians from the country is the result of pressure from Moslems...The Moslems... are seeking to 'Islamize' the land; and to this end considerable sums have been contributed by the Moslem states...In my own parish, a Christian family wishing to sell their property told prospective buyers they would rather sell to Christians. Soon after, their home was set on fire. In the Moslem world there cannot be...a pluralistic or democratic society."[125] A furor erupted on publication of his article and the priest was "compelled to deny that he authored the article."[126]

Arab Christians in Bethlehem are witnessing a steadily increasing number of Islamic attacks against their community. The Moslems have literally taken over many Christian homes, and replaced the crosses with pictures of the Al Aqsa mosque and verses from the Koran.[127]

Only Israel's 27-year-long restraining hand in the occupied territories has prevented a Christian blood bath thus far. Now Gaza and Jericho have been handed over to the control of the PLO. The graffiti on the walls of Gaza repeat the above warnings to its Christians stating that when the Islamic fundamentalists "are through with the Saturday people, they will start on the Sunday people."[128] And PLO flags displayed in the traditionally Christian Arab towns of Bethlehem and Beit Sahour in December 1993, carried the same printed message: "On Saturday we will kill the Jews; on Sunday we will kill the Christians."[129]

Today, between 17 to 20 million Christians live in the lands of the Middle East, but experts are predicting: "In 30 years there will be no Christians left in the Middle East."[130]

The Imams and Ayatollahs in Iran are calling for World War III. The 21st century is the century of Islam. Iran and the Arab world, therefore, should logically deal with Israel either by the year 2,000 or shortly thereafter. In March 1994, 140 members of the Iranian parliament signed a document calling for the destruction of Israel.[131] Also in March 1994, militant Moslem fundamentalist leaders in Britain, referring to the "century of Islam," told students at the Islamic University of London that "the messianic age—the acceptance of Islam by all the Earth's inhabitants—would not arrive unless there was a mass slaughter of Jews. 'We've been talking about killing Zionists. Let's not mention Zionists. The Jews are our enemy and, please God, we should finish them."[132]

Islam is a "satanic religion,"[133] and the spirit of the god of Islam is rampaging throughout the earth. It is on a collision course with the most awesome power in the universe—the *Mighty One of Jacob*.

4
The Great Satan

In Islam the Western world faces a potentially highly dangerous destroyer of its democracies without believing that such a thing could be even possible. Islamic leaders make their intentions clear but Western leaders refuse to listen. World domination is Islam's stated and actual aim, and tolerance and compromise are anathema to it. Others writers pen their warnings also:

> "Islamic radicalism has surfaced as the number one threat to world peace. Its goal? The tyrannization and subjugation of the entire planet under Allah. Its method? An all-out race for nuclear and other arms, while its champions prepare the seed-beds of revolt in nation after nation through persecution and terror; demanding conversion, an end to opposition, or death. Its route? Like a circling snake through the nations—three or four deep—around Israel, then tightening to crush the Jewish state. After thus proving Allah's omnipotence and winning millions more souls, its venomous gaze will turn outwards."[1]

Preoccupied with an all consuming passion for wealth and material goods, the Western nations are arming those who desire, seek and pray for their destruction. The West has already poured the greater part of one trillion dollars of highly sophisticated arms into the hands of the Islamic nations of the Middle East during the past two decades. Western leaders, therefore, should not be surprised when sometime in the very near future they are threatened by the exact same weapons they sold to make themselves rich. Moslems even anticipate the day when their Western "enemies" will no longer sell them arms: "There [must] be built up inside the World of Islam armaments plants, so that Moslems might be in no need of importing from enemy countries which would certainly make a ban on such exports for fear of their possible use against them."[2]

It is a harsh fact of life that Moslem groups are responsible for the major proportion of international terrorist actions. The United States State Department's Office of Counter-Terrorism officially placed the blame on fanatical Moslems for the great majority of international terrorist attacks as far back as 1985 when some 800 incidents claimed 2,223 lives.[3] That year was considered a "bloody year,"[4] holding a 60 percent increase in attacks over the average of other years. But the rate of annual increase continues to climb alarmingly, and there were "5,404 attacks in 1992, up 11% from 1991, and the number of people killed rose above 10,000 for the first time."[5]

The Middle East's oil war against the West began with "terrifying hikes in oil prices since 1973"[6] that wrought havoc among the nations' economies, crippling many and sending others into a dizzying downward spiral from which they had not fully recovered over a decade later. The oil blackmail brought untold billions of dollars into the coffers of the Moslem regimes. This, in turn, allowed them to purchase vast amounts of weapons from those who desperately needed their petro-dollars, and with which they established Moslem centers in "every major city in the world and every sizable city (over 500,000 population) in the United States."[7]

The drop in the demand for oil that began in the latter half of 1980 brought a radical drop in the price of oil effectively disarming Moslem oil as a weapon for blackmail. But with the advent of missing Russian nuclear warheads turning up in Iran,[8] and Pakistan already producing (and other Moslem nations close to producing) atomic weapons, the West will be vulnerable to another form of Islamic blackmail such as has only been conceived by writers of science fiction.

Iran, with the recent discovery of a new oil field, is now the second largest oil producing country in the world, and despite the fall in oil prices, it has an enormous annual income from which it finances much of the world's terrorism. Ayatollah Ahmad Jannati, a close ally of the fanatical Ayatollah Khomeini, stated in November 1992, that "Iran is activating agents around the world for 'the Third World War'—between Islam and the West."[9]

America: the Great Satan

Moslems see the West as a "single whole,"[10] and Western civilization as a whole "is personified as a ghoul—a particularly obnoxious subvariety of demon."[11] Only on Israel is more virulent Arab and Iranian hatred vented than on the United States, and that is wholly due to Israel's continued existence in the Islamic Middle East. America has not usurped Moslem land, but it has usurped Moslem culture, ethics and morality. This is almost as unforgivable as Israel's existence, and the passionate hatred of America smolders within the breasts of Arab and Iranian Moslems.

Islam is not a religion as Westerners know religion; it is a whole civilization built upon the Koran and its *Sharia* law. Islamic law legislates, in the strictest and most brutal terms, a moral code of conduct that will execute or maim its every transgressor. The United States has no moral law, although some might say it has. God has been thrown out onto the trash heap. Only lip service is paid to America's Christian roots by government officials; even less by educators, and corruption is rife throughout the judicial system.[12] The moral has been exchanged for the immoral.

The United States pornographic industry is the biggest in the world, earning billions of dollars annually—more than the incomes of its giant commercial movie and recording industries combined.[13] And it is not just males that drool over this filth; almost half of all American women surveyed admitted to using pornographic material prior to having sexual intercourse.[14] And this "made with pride in the U.S.A." trash is peddled throughout the world, polluting almost the entire earth.

American television overflows with vulgarity, profanity, nudity, violence and murder. Its actors are in continual motion—killing, cursing or running from bed to bed, copulating with an unlimited supply of willing, nay, eager women. Whether this lineup of lusty, breathless females are married or unmarried matters not a wit to the program producers. This, too, pollutes the minds of the spiritually bankrupt, television addicted masses and portrays for them the norm of life in the United States. And few, indeed, are the movies that adults or youngsters can comfortably view without their minds being contaminated by sewerage packaged as "family entertainment."

The American population is mollified—deceived by *Satan—the deceiver of the whole world* (Revelation 12:9 Phillips). This great nation was founded and built upon the Bible, but has since gone a whoring after other gods. And its whoredom manifests itself largely in sex for profit—pornography, promiscuity and scantily clad women—all of which are an affront to the pivotal religious aspect of Moslem life. Even the poorest Moslem able to own, rent or view a television is exposed to the proselytizing of a Western culture that he finds so repulsive—complete with nudity, drugs, sexual freedom and normative legal equality between the sexes. The corruption of the sexual mores of the young, especially the girls, is beyond all of Islam's impermissibility. Radical Islamic leaders call America the "Great Satan," and hold it responsible for most of the evil on the earth.

America, believing the answer to the ills of the Middle East to be simply a matter of Westernization, increases its aggressive marketing thrust into the Moslem states through the media, adding fuel to the already smoking fires of bitter hatred, and boosts Islamic fundamentalism instead of decreasing it. All that stands between fanatical Islam and the unleashing of the full fury of its hatred upon the West (especially upon the United States) is Israel.

American Moslems Flex Their Muscles

In January 1993, two Moslem Arab-Americans were arrested by Israeli security police on suspicion of distributing funds to members of Moslem terror groups in Israel. The United States State Department in Washington "complained to Israel about the delay between the arrest of the two and their being visited by a U.S. official."[15] The State Department "dismissed charges"[16] that Americans were involved in organized terror or the funding of terror groups. But one of the men, Mohammed Saleh, subsequently proved to be the world commander of Hamas's military arm[17] responsible for the mutilation and death of hundreds of Israelis and Palestinians. Saleh had come to distribute a further $650,000[18] which had been raised by American Moslems for use in the Islamic struggle against Israel. Israel warned United States agencies that Moslem fundamentalist organizations were active in the United States, but "the warnings were contemptuously ignored."[19]

On Friday, February 26, 1993, at a little past noon, a massive explosion rocked the Twin Towers of New York's World Trade Center, blasting a 100 foot (30.5 meter) crater three floors deep. Six people died and more than 1,000 were injured.[20] The property damage alone was estimated in hundreds of millions of dollars. The terrorist bombers were Moslem Arab-Americans.[21]

In June of the same year, eight Moslems (six of whom were permanent United States residents), were arrested in New York only days away from their planned day of mayhem when they were to unleash terror, bombings and assassinations throughout New York city. The arrest came as they mixed the same deadly mixture of explosives used in the World Trade Center bombing. Their targets included: "the United Nations building, the Federal Building in lower Manhattan which houses the FBI headquarters in New York, and the Lincoln and Holland tunnels."[22] The Moslems intended to blow up all these locations in a single day.

Several members of both terrorist groups—that which bombed the World Trade Center and that which planned to cripple New York City—had fought with the Islamic fundamentalist guerillas against the Soviets in Afghanistan.[23] And the spiritual leader of both groups is the radical Egyptian Islamic cleric, Sheik Omar Abdel Rahman, who after the arrest of his followers, "sat smiling at a press conference"[24] in New Jersey. A chilling warning came from the arrested leader of the second terrorist group, Siddig Ibrahim Siddig Ali, who was quoted as saying: "We [Moslems] can get you [America] anytime!"[25]

When I originally penned these pages in the middle of 1994, American officials were uptight with Israel due to its insistence that the principle source of funds for Islamic terrorism in Israel now came from Moslems within the United States. Scattered pieces of evidence began to be collected together on American Islamic groups training for armed conflict and terrorism against the United States. Passing on this information to the State Department only seemed to increase its animosity toward Israel. But, when a PBS documentary, *Jihad in America*, was aired in the United States and Israel in October 1994, State Department and FBI officials began eating platefuls of crow for breakfast.

Steven Emerson, an American investigative reporter, gained access to numerous mosques, Islamic conferences and training camps across America, and secretly recorded speeches and events on film. In one chilling scene, militant Islamic leader Fayis Azram tells a 1990 conference in Atlanta: "Blood must flow. There must be widows, there must be orphans. Hands and limbs must be cut, and the limbs and blood must be spread everywhere." Emerson uncovered and documented nine fanatical Islamic training camps in the United States in the past five years. He recorded a whole string of spine-tingling video clips showing radical Islamic fundamentalists, organizers and terrorists urging followers in the United States to wage *jihad* against Jews, Christians and America.[26]

After the tragic car bombing of the downtown federal office building in Oklahoma City in April 1995, it was at first believed that Islamic fundamentalists were responsible. A short program was quickly put together on the Islamic community in Oklahoma and aired on television. I, personally, sat through only a few minutes of the program before switching off the television. I had just witnessed a blond American lady being interviewed as a professing Moslem. As she sat before the cameras dressed in fashionable Western clothing and nicely made up with cosmetics, she endeavored to convey to the viewers that Islamic *jihad* was not a violent part of Islam. The obviously sincere lady showed herself to be appallingly ignorant of the religion she professed to follow. The religion that she adheres to is a form of an alternative lifestyle, not Islam. If she were to live under Moslem *Sharia* law she would be summarily executed for showing her blond hair, for wearing cosmetics and her Western dress. All that she portrayed on television is anathema to Islam. As for *jihad* not being a violent part of the Islamic religion, it is worth noting that there are 123 verses in the Koran about fighting and killing for Allah. As a fundamentalist Moslem spokesman succinctly put it: "Ours is not a passive religion."[27]

Western Islamic Population Increase

America is home to over eight million Moslems,[28] and there are nearly 2,000 mosques scattered throughout the length and

The Great Satan

breadth of the land. During the 1991 Gulf War against Iraq, a survey was taken of Arab-American Moslems living in the United States, and the results were startling for those that conducted the survey. They reported that a staggering 82 percent said they would not fight nor would they allow their sons or daughters to fight for the United States in the war![29] And over half of Arab-American Moslems said they would never support a United States war against any Arab nation.[30] If surveys were to be taken in other Western countries where Moslems have found acceptance, much the same findings would be recorded. Moslem allegiance is to Islam, never to a country—not even a Moslem country. He will take advantage of all that his host country's culture offers but will, at the same time, despise it and work toward its ultimate downfall.

Of the 25 fastest growing nations in the world, 11 have Moslem majorities, and their birthrates are more than triple that of the West.[31] Islam now rules 40 countries, and much of the worldwide turmoil involving Moslems (mentioned in the last chapter) is part of a militant enterprise directed at non-Moslem governments by Moslem minorities demanding secession. Moslems in Azerbaijan and Tajikistan gained independence from the Soviet Union; those in Kashmir gained their independence from India; in Kosovo from Yugoslavia; in Xin Jian from China; and so on.[32] Chechnya has apparently failed in its current, determined bid to secede from Russia. Whenever a significant majority of Moslems is established in any part of a non-Moslem country, a demand for secession is eventually made, accompanied by customary violent and bloody conflict. Given Islam's aggressive march forward in the West, it is only a matter of time before demands are made of Europe or of the United States.

In France Moslems number six million, of which 600,000 are eligible to vote. Ironically, this was the figure by which the current French president was elected. It is conceivable, therefore, that "Islam could wield pivotal influence in future French elections."[33] Moslems are also the second largest religious groups in Sweden, Germany, Britain and the Benelux states. In Britain, "more people attend services in mosques than in Christian churches,"[34] and during the Anglican Lambeth Conference, the Koran has been read at the Eucharist service. At the International Islamic Conference in 1976, it was said, "If we can win London for Islam, it won't be hard to win the whole Western World."[35] And London has since become the site of the largest mosque in Western Europe. It is situated in Regents Park, along with an Islamic University.[36]

In August 1994, Britain allowed 8,000 Moslem fundamentalists to hold a conference in London's Wembley stadium. The Moslems came from all over the world, and the conference was described as "the biggest gathering of Moslems outside the Middle East."[37] The conference "backed calls by its organizers for the establishment of a single global Islamic state and the demolition of the state of Israel."[38] The resolutions found great favor with the delegates and they "stood up from their seats, raising their fists, stamping their feet and shouting "'*Allahu Akbar.*'"[39]

New Zealand is strategically valuable to Islam, as it is geographically situated at the "ends of the earth," and Islam believes that "praise to Allah will come from the ends of the earth." New Zealand's Moslem population is growing rapidly, and mosques are being established throughout the land. But, there was contention between Christians and Moslems in 1988 over the proposal to build a mosque at New Zealand's longitudinal southernmost point which would have been a fulfillment of Islamic aspirations.

Moslems also began using the Auckland University's Maclaurin Chapel for Friday prayers at the beginning of 1994. The university's ecumenical chaplain, a Presbyterian minister, made a typical Christian statement when he said in justification of the Moslem's use of the Chapel, "Christians and Moslems have much in common, we worship together the God of Abraham and follow Abraham on the journey of faith. Christians may also be surprised to learn that Moslems see Jesus as expressing the Word of God."[40] Well, the minister will "be surprised to learn," as I have already made clear, that we do not "worship together the God of Abraham." As Robert Morey so aptly says: "It is not enough to say there is only one God, if you have the wrong God!"[41]

Islamic beliefs and writings contain many outrageous statements—a mixture of *Arabian Nights* and *Mein Kampf.* Christians may "be surprised to learn" that Moslems deny Isaac

The Great Satan

was Abraham's heir, and have substituted Ishmael[42] as the one that was to be offered by Abraham at Mount Moriah, celebrating this annually with the feast of *El-Dahiya* (Feast of Sacrifice). Christians "may also be surprised to learn" that Islam teaches that "Abraham was an 'upright Moslem,'"[43] as was Adam, Isaac, Jacob, Joseph and Moses. Jesus and the 12 apostles were also Moslem prophets, "whose books were forged by the unworthy Jews and Christians."[44] Moslem doctrine teaches that every child is born with a Moslem disposition, but his parents may make him a Jew, a Christian or a Zoroastrian.[45] The Moslems therefore believe that the advance of Islam throughout the world liberates this "divine" implantation.

Christians may "be surprised to learn," too, that Moslems see Jesus not only as "expressing the Word of God," but also believe Him to have been "a Palestinian freedom fighter [*fedayi*–assassin] who led the Palestinian revolt against Rome."[46] They believe Jesus cried out "Allah, Allah," and not "Eli, Eli," when He was on the cross,[47] and they also deny His divinity, death and resurrection.

The President of the Islamic Club of the Auckland University, Mr. Yaseen Dobson said that the Moslem students, "who number about 200, had wanted to use a place that was prominent and dedicated to a religious purpose."[48] Of course they wanted a "prominent" place "dedicated to religious purposes." Islam wants all of the West's prominent churches and holy places—it is a another stride along the path toward accomplishing "mastery over the earth."

First Israel, then the West

Islam is solidly entrenched in the Arab and Iranian psyches. It "faces no risk at all"[49] of being supplanted by the dominant religion of the West in its current state—Islam is growing at almost twice the annual rate for Christianity.[50] And the "proportion of devout Moslems is much higher than that of devout Christians or Jews. Moreover, Islam has a political content and a political message."[51] Islam is well on its way to achieving its objective of world subjugation, and it will achieve it unless remedial actions are taken now to stop its dangerous forward thrust.

But is a comfortable, apathetic Church or self-seeking humanist governments capable of stopping or even derailing this runaway religious locomotive? Only time will give us the answer, but for many it will be too late. The missile technologies acquired, or soon to be acquired, by Moslem states, together with their chemical and biological warfare potential, will shortly threaten large areas of Western Europe. Even the diplomatic pouches of Moslem states, "exempt from search and seizure or customs inspection"[52] have been used to "transport arms and explosives into Europe or wherever they want them to go."[53] Western targets are lined up in the sights of the Islamic "warriors of *jihad*;" all that restrains the itching fingers is Israel. And Israel has just signed a "Peace Accord" with one of those "warriors of *jihad*," Yasser Arafat, the leader of one of the worlds largest, most active and murderous Islamic terror organizations.

5
Arafat and the PLO

On September 9, 1993, Yitzhak Rabin's ultra left-wing Israeli government formally recognized the PLO (Palestine Liberation Organization) as the "sole legitimate representative of the Palestinian people." This followed its bloody 29-year terrorist war against civilians of the State of Israel, Israeli embassies abroad, and all Jews—Israeli or otherwise—anywhere in the world. And in secret negotiations held in Oslo, Norway, Israelis met with PLO officials to iron out a formula for "peace."

September 13, 1993, on the White House lawn in Washington D.C., Israel's Foreign Minister, Shimon Peres, signed a "Declaration of Principles"—an agreement stating the terms under which Israel and the PLO would conduct their "peace negotiations." At his side sat the other signatory to the agreement—Yasser Arafat, chairman of the PLO. After Arafat had signed the DOP, Yitzhak Rabin took his hand and shook it. And on what has been described as another "landmark day,"[1] May 4, 1994—this time in Cairo, Egypt, before 2,500 spectators and millions watching on television[2]—Rabin and Arafat signed the "Gaza-Jericho First" Peace Accord which created a Palestinian autonomous area in Gaza and Jericho, over which the PLO would have control after Israel withdrew its military forces.

The world sighed with relief. Most felt the 100-year-old Arab-Israeli conflict—the obstacle to world peace—had ended. Shimon Peres, the architect and driving force of the "peace initiative" said in Cairo: "Today we have ended the Israeli-Arab conflict—Utopia is coming!"[3] And as Norwegian, United States and radical leftist Israeli politicians slapped each other's backs and sipped glasses of champagne—toasting the success of their diplomatic coup—others mourned over the absurdity of such actions.

Yasser Arafat

Arafat came into this world on August 27, 1929, in Cairo. He was born Abd al-Rahman Abd al-Rauf Arafat al-Qudwa al-Husseini.[4] His maternal grandfather was Mahmoud al-Husseini, cousin to Haj Amin al-Husseini,[5] the Grand Mufti of Jerusalem—confidant of Adolf Hitler and a Nazi collaborator during World War II. He was Arafat's "mentor and guide."[6] Arafat avoids mention of his full name as it reveals his blood relationship to the former, virulently anti-Semitic Grand Mufti. Arafat took the name Yasser in memory of Yasser al-Birah, a leader of the Grand Mufti's reign of terror in the 1930s."[7]

Acquaintances of Arafat in his youth describe him as "fanatical, ruthless, and particularly brutal."[8] Arafat was 20 years old when he committed his first murder.[9] He shot an innocent Palestinian living in Cairo—Rork Hamid.[10] A former friend of Arafat recalls:

> "The shooting of the Hamid boy put an end to any temptations we might have had not to take him [Arafat] seriously. It was like an initiation rite for him...after that our guerrilla activities became a deadly serious business."[11]

Another former friend of Arafat relates the following:

> "There was a student whose parents had sent him out of Palestine in the '48 war to live with relatives in Cairo. When the war ended...the Israelis would not allow the boy to return to his parents...He had no sense of himself, but would follow the lead of anyone who showed any friendliness towards him. Yasser had recruited him...He worshipped Yasser.
>
> "Then – oh, a year later – Yasser discovered the boy's parents were living in Israel [and] were apparently satisfied there. Yasser tried to get the boy to publicly denounce his parents. The boy would have done just about anything for Yasser. But this! This he could not do.
>
> "Yasser...really loved the boy. He was delicate, sensitive, a flower. He was very much a part of Yasser's inner circle – four or five boys who lived in the same place and, well, you can imagine what I mean. And what did Yasser do?
>
> "There was another boy – we used to call him The Scimitar – who came from Bedouin people. He was totally ruthless. Yasser...pointed to the boy, he said, 'My heart aches for Ahmed...'. It was very dramatic. And then he said 'But

Arafat and the PLO

my Arab brother Ahmed cannot bring himself to be a true *feday* [terrorist], so he must be taught.

"Thereupon the boy we called The Scimitar appeared with a knife...The Scimitar proceeded to castrate the boy. The next day the boy was dead. He had killed himself."[12]

In 1951, Arafat joined the extremist Moslem Brotherhood which later assassinated Anwar Sadat, government officials, numerous tourists and Egyptian Coptic Christians.[13] During the Suez crisis in 1956, Arafat became an Egyptian Army junior officer in demolitions. His unimportant command was reduced from 40 to 3 persons,[14] and later he mistakenly blew up an ammunition dump—"an act that cost the Egyptian army several million dollars."[15]

In 1957, Arafat fled from Egypt to Kuwait to avoid arrest when the Moslem Brotherhood was outlawed. He remained on the Egyptian wanted list until 1968.[16] Arafat joined the fledgling *Fatah* terror organization and later became its leader. He became chairman of the PLO in 1969 and must take credit for some of the "most vicious and bloody terrorist attacks on record."[17] Under his leadership, *Fatah* and other PLO splinter terror groups carried out hundreds of attacks around the world—"bombings, shootings, hijackings, rocket attacks and kidnappings in 26 countries."[18] Most of the victims and more than 90 percent of the thousands of hostages were not Israelis.[19]

Arafat's natural cunning notched up record after record in the field of terrorism: the largest hijacking (four aircraft in a single operation); the largest number of hostages held at one time (300 passengers); the largest number of victims killed and wounded by a single booby-trap bomb (15 killed, 87 wounded); the largest number of casualties in a terrorist raid (38 killed, 70 wounded); the largest number of people shot at an airport (31 people); the largest ransoms ($5 million paid by Lufthansa; 15 million dollar ransom demanded but not paid due to armed intervention by special forces in Mogadishu). The greatest variety of targets—two-thirds of the terrorist attacks were against countries other than Israel—(40 civilian passenger aircraft, five passenger ships, 30 embassies or diplomatic missions, and about the same number of economic targets, including fuel depots and factories[20]). Israelis especially remember Arafat for the massacre of 11 members of their sports team at the Munich Olympics in 1972, and the massacre of their children at a Maalot school in 1974.

With an annual income of over $1.2 billion,[21] Arafat commanded the wealthiest terror organization in the world. But in addition to fleeing Egypt, Arafat also fled Jordan in 1970, was evicted from Lebanon in 1982, and expelled from Syria in 1983.[22]

Today, **the world's politicians and news media have changed Arafat the unrepentant killer into Arafat the conquering hero.** The man who virtually invented international terrorism—the one who "personally dispatched hundreds of murderers to commit thousands of murders"[23]—has become the recipient of prestigious peace prizes. Arafat has been given respectability—a man directly responsible for the brutal murder of tens of thousands of people. A vicious, cold-blooded, murderous leader of one of the world's most brutal terrorist organizations has been turned into a world statesman. In the eyes of the world, the Biblical tables have been turned—the valiant Philistine has now vanquished the circumcised Israeli giant.

After 30 years of pulling the strings, Arafat's bombs and hand grenades have ripped innocent people apart around the world; his bullets have torn into Jews and Gentiles on land, on seas and in the skies; his knives have slashed the throats of men and women, the old, the young and the babes-in-arms. And he has spawned an enormous brood of demoniacal offspring that seeks to outdo each other in sheer repulsive deeds. The PLO flag now flutters over 82 embassies located in major cities of the world, and after murdering a team of athletes at the Munich Olympics, the PLO has been invited to send their own athletes to the 1996 Olympic Games in Atlanta.[24] We are told that crime does not pay. Who is kidding whom?

Arafat made his first visit to the new Gaza-Jericho enclave on July 1, 1994, as part of the process of establishing a PLO state there. Arafat had planned to celebrate his entry into the area on June 5, the anniversary of the outbreak of the Six Day War, but Israel's Foreign Minister, Shimon Peres, apparently understood the significance of Arafat's symbolic entry and persuaded him to

Arafat and the PLO

postpone his visit.[25]

For more than a month,[26] foreign and local journalists were sitting in line, eagerly awaiting an opportunity to interview Arafat. They will find out soon enough that they must learn to choose their words with care or join the thousands who have been "dispatched to a better world by PLO death squads in Lebanon and the [Israeli-administered] territories."[27] Arafat does not suffer being asked questions that he does not want to hear. He is "unaccustomed to anything less than groveling obsequiousness from journalists."[28] A recently recorded reaction to an Arab reporter's question was: "How dare you ask me such a question? Don't you know who I am? I am Yasser Arafat, the leader of the mighty Palestinian people."[29] An even more recent reaction came when Arafat was "incensed"[30] by a question from Jane Wendt, the Australian television's *60 Minutes* interviewer:

> "[Arafat] jumped from his seat, shouted something in Arabic and stalked out.
>
> "His henchmen promptly declared the interview over, tore the films out of the still cameras, pulled the cassettes out of the video cameras and destroyed the tape, and bodily ushered out Wendt and her crew.[31]

A Western journalist, who frequently interviews Arafat, said:

> "I learned the technique many years ago. You cannot provoke this man. You have to remind him constantly that he is the greatest leader in the world and that the world would have been destroyed long ago if not for him. He expects questions like: 'Mister President of the State of Palestine: As a great and mighty man, as the undisputed leader of a nation no less mighty, as a man beloved by his people and the world, a man who has neither competitor nor substitute, as a distinguished president, generous and democratic, as a veteran and honored freedom fighter, what is your response Mister President, to...'."[32]

And a senior Arab journalist wrote about what the Arab press can expect in their new PLO state:

"We, the journalistic community, must prepare for the next phase, when we live in a democracy under the government in Gaza and Jericho. Every journalist who wishes to interview a senior Palestinian official must be equipped with the following items: a casket, a burial plot for himself and his family, and a will prepared well in advance."[33]

On the very day of the historic handshake on the White House lawn, Arafat's name appeared near the top "in a list of world terrorists released by a [United States] congressional committee."[34] Barring unforeseen health problems or assassination by an irate Israeli, Yitzhak Rabin will, even at his present age of 75 years, live to rue that fateful day he took Arafat's hand.

The PLO

The PLO was not created by the Palestinian Arabs, but by Egypt's president Nasser.[35] Neither was the PLO created in order to regain territory lost to Israel in the Arab's abortive war upon the Jewish state in 1967. The PLO was created in Cairo in January 1964, three full years before the outbreak of the Six Day War. And Nasser established the PLO for the express purpose of continuing his unsuccessful war against Israel, and the stated goal was "to obtain the objective of liquidating Israel."[36] The terrible punishment suffered by the Arab armies at Israel's hands in the June 1967 war, and the consequential loss of large tracts of territory from which they had boasted they were going to throw the Jews into the sea, gave rise to the widespread myth that the PLO was formed to liberate the lands "stolen from the Palestinians in 1967."

The Six Day War came as a result of the closure of the Tiran Straits to Israeli shipping by an Egyptian naval blockade, and the mobilizing of several Arab armies along each of Israel's land borders—all designed to crush Israel in a vice. The flags of the PLO, bearing the skull and crossbones,[37] were unfurled, and the PLO's leader at that time, Ahmed Shukeiry, was asked what would happen to the Israelis if the Arab attack succeeded? He replied: "Those who survive will remain in Palestine. I estimate that none of them will survive."[38] The days immediately preceding the Six Day War was, according to Howard Sachar, "one of the gravest moments—perhaps the gravest—of Israel's existence."[39] But Israel did not wait for the Arab noose to be tightened around her neck; she struck out with: "An aerial thunderbolt, a mailed fist."[40] In ensuing years military academies throughout the world would study what came to be known as "a classic of tactics."[41]

Members of the various PLO terror factions, including Arafat, fled to Jordan "to avoid capture by the Israelis."[42] Continued PLO terror attacks against Israelis from Jordan, however, brought forth further Israeli responses, and on March 21, 1968, combined forces of Israeli paratroopers, commandos and tank units crossed into Jordan and attacked Arafat's main *Fatah* training base in Karameh (Arafat had established his Karameh headquarters "in the primary school for girls).[43] The IDF destroyed 171 buildings, killed 200 fighters and captured another 141 terrorists.[44] The Jordanian army took part in the fighting, and siding with Israel, launched "a heavy tank and artillery barrage onto the besieged Palestinian facility."[45] This Israeli action, code named "Operation Inferno," was the first of her many operations against the PLO in Jordan between 1968 and early 1970.

By 1970, some 55 PLO terrorist bases formed a virtual ministate within Jordan. The PLO set up roadblocks throughout and "extracted 'fees' and 'donations' from businessmen."[46] Hundreds of lawless acts of murder, brutality, robbery and rape by PLO forces against Jordanian civilians[47] finally became too unbearable for Jordan's King Hussein. That year he unleashed his Bedouin troops in a bloody war against the PLO in what became known as the "Black September." Each side appeared to compete with the other to commit "heinous atrocities to prisoners, wounded personnel, and civilians,"[48] which "surpassed all the imagined horrors of infracticide."[49] After several weeks of particularly brutal fighting, which wrongfully became known as the "Jordanian civil war,"[50] Hussein's troops flushed the PLO terrorists out of their protective lairs and drove them out of Jordan and into "an operational exile in Lebanon."[51]

The Rape of Lebanon

An old dog does not learn new tricks. The "world's most wanted terrorists,"[52] the members of the various PLO factions—

Fatah, commanded by Yasser Arafat;
Democratic Front for the Liberation of Palestine (DFLP), commanded by Nayif Hawatmeh;
National Front for the Liberation of Palestine (NFLP);
Popular Front for the liberation of Palestine (PFLP), commanded by George Habash;
Popular Front for the liberation of Palestine—Special Command (PFLP–SC);
Popular Front for the liberation of Palestine—General Command (PFLP–GC), commanded by Ahmed Jibril;
Palestine National Liberation Front (PNLF), commanded by Abu Nidal;
Palestine Liberation Front (PLF); Popular Struggle Front (PSF) and National Salvation Front (NSF)

—simply took up in Lebanon from where they had been forced to leave off in Jordan.

The PLO's reign of terror in Lebanon lies almost beyond human description. Some have tried to document PLO barbarity, but few have succeeded. Lebanese journalists compiled a document which they called "An Album of Terrorist Atrocities." It was published clandestinely in 1978 but was quickly suppressed in Lebanon and never saw the light of day abroad. Thus, the outside world "remained in ignorance of the true nature of the PLO."[53] Similarly, David Aikman, *Time* magazine's Jerusalem Bureau Chief during Israel's 1982 "Operation Peace For Galilee"—the Israeli invasion of Lebanon—wrote an article which he himself had documented on PLO atrocities in Lebanon. But *Time*, known for biased reporting and antagonism toward Israel, did not print the article. Shortly after submitting the article, Aikman was "transferred" to China.

But some did manage to inform the outside world of the horror of Palestinian oppression in Lebanon. After reading some of the documentation, it is not at all surprising that the Lebanese expressed to Western reporters "how happy they were that Israel had liberated them."[54] Walid Azzi, 27, whose house had been destroyed said: "The Israelis are our friends, and I hope they stay for some time with us."[55] American columnists Rowland Evans and Robert Novak—who hate to have to say anything good about Israel and who have earned the distinction of being called "the patriarchs of all Israel-bashers"[56]—were forced to declare after touring Lebanon, that the facts "tend to support Israel's claim that the PLO has become permeated with thugs and adventurers."[57] They interviewed a Lebanese doctor whose farm had been taken over without compensation by the PLO, and turned into a military depot. "'You ask me how do we like the Israelis,' he said. 'Compared to the hell we have had in Lebanon, the Israelis are brothers.'"[58]

Thousands of homes were taken over by the PLO. They would enter apartment complexes and "forcefully evict the occupants of the most centrally situated apartments."[59] These would be used for "the storing of ammunition and explosives"[60] in order to lessen the risk of Israeli raids, and if they were attacked by the IAF, Israel would be reported by the world's news media as "indiscriminately bombing civilian areas."[61] Lebanese protests against PLO orders to "immediately vacate"[62] their homes were met by killing the father with "a burst of gunfire in front of the assembled family,"[63] and the "systematic rape of all the females."[64] The lowest estimate of Lebanese victims massacred by the PLO during their reign of terror in a country of two million people appears to be 100,000,[65] but Peter Grace says that it could be "as high as 300,000."[66] Grace says that the number of young girls pregnant to PLO mobsters at the time of the Israeli invasion "exceeded 100,000."[67]

A distinguished Lebanese surgeon, Dr. Khalil Torbey, told an American journalist that he was often called in the middle of the night to attend to PLO torture victims:

> "I treated men whose testicles had been cut off in torture sessions. I saw men—live men—dragged through the streets by fast-moving cars to which they were tied by the feet."[68]
> "'I know of cases,' Dr. Torbey said, 'of people being thrown into acid tanks and reduced to unrecognizable masses of porous bone. Many young girls came to me for abortions

after being raped by PLO gangsters."[69]

Dr. Ghassen Hamoud, owner-director of one of the largest, best equipped of Sidon's 11 hospitals tells of his dealings with the PLO:

> "The PLO made me hate them, not because they demanded their wounded be treated free of charge, nor because they behaved as if my hospital belonged to them. It was when they broke into the operating theater and forced us to stop surgery and treat their wounded instead...and badly beat one of our doctors who refused to obey them...that I realized they were beasts from the jungle."[70]

The PLO fighters were badly mauled by the Israeli troops and were in need of blood for transfusions. Lebanese civilians were rounded up and brought to hospitals and clinics[71] where they were tied to a bed "until the last drop of blood had drained from their veins."[72] The corpses were later "stacked like railway sleepers against the wall or in a corridor."[73]

Devilish forms of amusement were devised by the PLO for the person they wished to punish:

> "[The victim's] hands and legs were chained to the fenders of four vehicles. When a *Fatah* officer signaled with his pistol, the four cars raced away, tearing his body apart while the horrified spectators screamed. The cars raced through the streets with the bloody limbs dangling. People fainted."[74]

Another favorite was to slowly dismember live human beings with chain saws. "First the fingers, joint by joint; the toes; hands; feet; lower arm; lower leg; and so on."[75] A witness to the barbarity is still tortured by the terrible screams of her 21-year-old friend. "'Why don't you kill me,' she screamed. 'We will, we will,' the animals replied."[76]

Susan, a young Christian girl, is a mutilated survivor of PLO depravity. A number of PLO fighters broke into her home:

> "The PLO men killed Susan's father and her brother, and

raped her mother who suffered a hemorrhage and died. They raped Susan 'many times.' They cut off her breasts and shot her. Hours later she was found alive, but with all four limbs so badly broken and torn from gunshot that they had to be surgically amputated. She now has only the upper part of one arm. Nuns take care of her in a hospital north of Beirut, high in the mountains. She has asked them to let her die, but they have consistently replied that they cannot do that...."[77]

Countless Lebanese told "harrowing tales of rape, mutilation and murders"[78] committed by the PLO forces:

"'[They] killed people and threw their corpses in the courtyards. Some of them were mutilated and their limbs were cut off. We did not go out for fear we would end up like them,' said two Arab women from Sidon. 'We did not dare go to the beach, because they molested us, weapons in hand.' The women spoke of an incident, which occurred shortly before the Israeli invasion, in which PLO men raped and murdered a woman, dumping her body near a famous statue. A picture of the mangled corpse had been printed in a local newspaper."[79]

The question needs to be raised as to how it became possible for the PLO to keep such heinous outrages under such a complete wrap of silence for more than seven years? Where were all the journalists during those years—those people who are always ready to criticize Israel's every action and crucify her for the smallest misdemeanor? "Where were they when their colleagues were being murdered in Lebanon—Larry Buchman and Sean Toolan of *ABC TV*; Mark Tryon, for *Free Belgium Radio*; Robert Pfeffer, *Der Spiegel* and *Unita* correspondent; Tony Italo and Graciella Difaco, Italian journalists; Jean Lougeau, correspondent for French *TFI*—all murdered because they failed to report in accordance with Arafat's wishes?"[80]

The media has an inherent ability to uncover and publish the sordid and the sensational. It likes stories with a murder and mutilation content, because they put bread on the journalists' tables and millions of dollars in the corporations' bank accounts. The long, loud silence on PLO activities in Lebanon can only mean the foreign media purposefully looked the other way. And by doing so, it totally deceived the world's masses.

After the Israelis had driven Arafat and his trigger-happy followers from Beirut, knowledgeable Lebanese newsmen said that most of the capital's press corps—national and foreign—entered into a "'conspiracy of silence' during the long occupation by 'the Palestinian Mafia'"[81]

A prominent Lebanese industrialist, 54 year-old Frederick El-Murr, voices the same opinion as other leading Lebanese when he says that the events in Lebanon from 1975 onward, "following Arafat's triumphal return from the United Nations, was not a civil war,' as the press hastened to characterize it, but a conquest of my country by the PLO and Syria."[82] El-Murr says that "the PLO had 'plenty of money' with which to 'persuade' Lebanese editors and journalists to write favorably about the PLO's so-called 'revolution,' or to remain silent."[83]

One editor whom the PLO could not "buy" was Salim El-Lawzi.[84] El-Lawzi was a Lebanese patriot from one of the wealthiest Moslem families in West Beirut. He began "warning his countrymen against the Palestinian terrorist organizations back in the 1970s, when he saw that their ultimate goal was the creation of a state-within-a-state."[85] The PLO began making threats which El-Lawzi ignored until two bombs went off in the building that housed the presses, editorial rooms and administrative offices of his newspaper—the whole building collapsed. El-Lawzi went to England, revived the paper and continued his work. After three years the longing to see members of his family enticed him to make a return visit to Lebanon. At the end of his visit, the car in which he was traveling was stopped at a roadblock where El-Lawzi was dragged out of the car and taken to the PLO mountain village of Armoun:

> "[He was] held for three days in the torture chambers. The fingers of his hands were cut off joint by joint. He was subsequently dismembered and his remains turned up

Arafat and the PLO

scattered about the village. Horrifying photographs of El-Lawzi's mutilated body spread terror throughout the capital's journalistic colony."[86]

Other journalists in Lebanon who were not carrying out PLO directions found packages on their doorsteps—"human limbs in plastic containers with warnings that unless they toed the mark editorially, they too would 'wind up wrapped in plastic.'"[87] Western journalists were fearful of incurring the wrath of the terrorists and developed a quasi pro-PLO policy while continuing their anti-Israel tirades. And they still remain silent on PLO atrocities in Lebanon even today.

In June 1982, Israel decided it had had enough of Arafat and his minions killing Israeli women and children, and the IDF (Israel Defense Force) invaded Lebanon and drove the PLO out. The foreign media then turned its full attention on Israel again, crucifying her for besieging West Beirut where the IDF had caught the PLO in a finely meshed net. The only means of escape for the PLO was by way of the open sea, and Israel was about to eradicate this nest of vipers. El-Murr said the PLO had destroyed "many cities with artillery and Katyusha rockets and in West Beirut, hardly a building remained untouched."[88] But the anti-Israel media portrayed Israel as the terrorist that destroyed West Beirut and brought misery on its inhabitants!

There is ample documentation that even "the Shi'ite Moslems there greeted the Israeli soldiers as liberators,"[89] showering them with flowers. But this was not the message the media wanted the world to see and hear. As they are wont to do (see chapter 9), they initiated no small amount of deception:

> "American networks would pay Arab women to demonstrate and yell anti-Israel and anti-American slogans. The minute the camera stopped rolling, the women would stop shrieking and calmly stand in line to collect their fees."[90]

And during the intensive Israeli assault on the last PLO stronghold in West Beirut, *United Press International* (UPI)—

from which many newspapers obtain much of their foreign news—ran an article including a photograph, about a seven-month old Lebanese baby girl who had been badly burned and had lost her arms in the Israeli bombardment.[91] A touching photograph of a little baby swathed in bandages made front page news everywhere, making the Israelis look like cold-blooded killers. President Reagan was handed a copy of the photograph and he placed it on his desk. Reagan was extremely angry with Israel and "picked up the telephone and told the Israeli prime minister Menachem Begin that the bombardment had to stop. Begin complied."[92]

After a thorough investigation which lasted several days, the baby was located. She had not suffered burns, neither had she lost her arms, but had suffered injuries to the wrists. Her injuries, however, were the result of a shell from a PLO battery in West Beirut![93] UPI confirmed that the article was "inacurate,"[94] but whereas the article and photograph were splashed on the front pages, the apology was buried inside—the *New York Times* printed it on page 14![95] The malicious reporting accomplished its purpose—the impression of "Israel's brutality had penetrated a notch deeper into the consciousness of the American leadership and public."[96]

The media's pressure was relentless upon Israel to effect a release of the PLO from her grip. And finally, under the watchful eyes of a multinational force made up of "American marines, French paratroops, and Italian infantrymen,"[97] a total of 14,938[98] PLO terrorists were evacuated from West Beirut by sea. They boarded the evacuating ships holding their guns aloft and firing them into the air, giving the impression that they were the victors rather than the vanquished. It must have been a bitter pill for Arafat to swallow, he who had vowed to throw the Jews into the sea, was himself "forced into the Mediterranian."[99]

The PLO was, and still is, the world's premier terror organization. It has also been responsible for the training of practically all other terror organizations. So many terrorists came to the PLO in Lebanon that Binyamin Netanyahu poses the question, "Who *didn't* come to the PLO bases in Beirut and Sidon?"

"The Italian Red Brigades, the German Baader-Meinhof

gang, the IRA, the Japanese Red Army, the French Action Directe, the Turkish Liberation Army, the Armenian Asala group, the Iranian Revolutionary Guards, the terrorists from all over Latin America as well as the neo-Nazis from Germany—all were there."[100]

Another well informed source confirms the above:

"The PLO is organizing terrorism all over the world. They are behind the Italian terrorists, the Irish terrorists, the Baader-Meinhof gang in West Germany. They train Africans, South Americans, North Americans. They are the heart of international terrorism, a thing that will destroy civilization if it is not stopped."[101]

But the PLO were not limiting their activities to Lebanon. During the same period, they were also busy training murderers abroad, especially Idi Amin's killers:

"Arafat maintained training camps in Uganda, where Idi Amin's murder gangs were trained in the fine art of killing black Christians – an estimated 300,000 in the case of Uganda."[102]

Several years prior to the Israeli invasion of Lebanon, the President of Lebanon, Suleiman Franjieh, had publicly expressed his resentment for the way in which the PLO had returned Lebanese hospitality:

"The Lebanese had given them a refuge, and our reward was the destruction of Lebanon and killing of its people. I have served the Palestinian cause for thirty-five years. I never expected the day would come when I would ask God to forgive my sins because I served a people who did not deserve to be served or supported."[103]

This same PLO, headed by the same Arafat, is today establishing a state within the Biblical heritage of Israel. Chased out of Jordan and then out of Lebanon, thousands of cold-blooded, bestial murderers are finding their way back to "Palestine." And in 1984, British customs officials ambushed a yacht and seized 4.3 metric tons of hashish—the drugs had been purchased from the PLO.[104] In April 1994, Halil Abu Ma'alek, a senior PLO official, was assassinated in the center of Tunis as he emerged from his "limousine."[105] Tunisian authorities said the killing "was a dispute over a drug deal."[106] The proceeds from its many drug deals helps finance the PLO's continuing murder activities.

The PLO orchestrated *intifada* in the Israeli administered territories has already extracted a terrible price from the local Arab inhabitants—"thousands of people tortured and over 900 murdered"[107] by PLO "death squads."[108] Many of these were victims of "personal rivalries and clan feuds."[109] The *intifada* has devoured its own people:

> "The bodies of scores of Arabs were discovered covered with burns, swollen from beatings, disemboweled, dismembered, decapitated. Wives of 'collaborators' were raped, and their children molested and beaten as warnings."[110]

Yasser Arafat has publicly admitted his complicity in the bestial murders and tortures of his own people:

> "Arafat announced in a television interview and on other occasions that he routinely inspected every file of every person accused of collaboration, and approved the punishment 'if not before it is implemented, then after.'"[111]

Nothing has changed. The PLO is the PLO and Arafat is Arafat—satanic incarnations from the pit of hell. A former Israeli Knesset member actually refers to the Peace Accord as "the pact with the Devil."[112]

Those that make up the membership of the PLO are descendants of Arabs who have lived in the Middle East for thousands of years. The Hebrew Bible only refers to demons on two occasions (Deuteronomy 32:17; Psalms 106:37)—both are direct references to the idols in the land of Canaan, and both refer to human sacrifice and the shedding of blood. And this is the area from where most of the PLO members are recruited. Perhaps this helps the reader understand why the PLO is so cruel, twisted and depraved. And perhaps it also helps us to understand why Arafat "telegrammed his congratulations to the Chinese leadership"[113] when China used tanks to physically crush thousands of students so that "their blood spurted onto the walls"[114] of Tiananmen Square in June 1989.

Some 4,600 experienced PLO fighters have arrived in the Jericho-Gaza enclave from Lebanon thus far, and they comprise the nucleus of the new "Palestinian Police Force." The Palestinian Police Force will be made up of current PLO gunmen and those Palestinians who have either been jailed for violent acts (including murder) against Israel or have proven their courage by having been involved in violent acts. It must be the only police force in the world where answering "yes" to the question, "Did you serve time in prison?,"[115] earns points for the applicant.

The distraught widow of David Rosenfeld, a PLO victim who was stabbed over 100 times[116] by three *Fatah* members in July 1982, wrote to the Editor of *The Jerusalem Post* protesting that her husband's killers (released in a prisoner exchange in 1985) were, because of their status as "heroes in *Fatah*," now "eligible to serve in the Palestinian Police."[117]

Among the graduates from the PLO's "security training school"[118] in Jericho, are many convicted murderers. One of the graduates, Jawad Shahawan, is "a former prisoner convicted of murdering five Palestinians."[119] Another released prisoner and graduate of the PLO school, Nasser Nadji Abu Khmeid—a "convicted *Fatah* death-squad leader sentenced to 11 life sentences for murdering nine Arabs (he boasts the real number is 13)"[120]— was recently caught by Israeli police outside of the autonomous areas near Jerusalem. He was carrying a Kalasnikov assault rifle.

The employment of convicted murderers in the PLO security services is a flagrant violation of the agreement made with Israel. The agreement is blatantly violated, but Ahmed Tibi, Arafat's advisor, blithely says: "Israel simply did not understand the place these convicted killers, the leaders of the *intifada*, have in Palestinian society. They are heroes."[121] And so are the leaders of the PLO "security forces" heroes. In less than a month in his new position as boss of the PLO "security forces," Jibril Rajoub is known to have ordered the murders of at least 11 Arabs.[122] The killings were carried out by members of Arafat's *Fatah*, and were done "at Arafat's behest."[123] Another senior head in the "security forces," Amin Hindi, planned the massacre of the 11 Israeli athletes at the Munich Olympics in 1972.[124] Hindi is described as "one of the most obscene murderers of all."[125] And Fatmeh Birnawi commands the Palestinian women's police force. Birnawi was sentenced to "two life terms in October 1967 for bombing a cinema in Jerusalem."[126]

At a graduation ceremony from the Jericho "security school," Palestinian policemen were photographed giving the Nazi '*Seig Heil*' salute.[127] And the PLO police also use Nazi tactics. They murder their fellow Arabs; are already known to have tortured at least one to death;[128] and kidnap men in areas under Israeli control, "transporting them to Jericho for interrogation and brutal torture."[129]

In May 1994, two Palestinian "policemen" were apprehended with a stolen Israeli car. They said that they were "trying to return the car to its owner."[130] In September 1994, one of Arafat's bodyguards was arrested for driving a stolen Israeli car.[131] In April 1995, it was admitted by the PLO Police chief, Brigadier-General Ghazi al-Jabali, that "**some 25,000 Gazans**, among them political and security officials,"[132] are driving stolen Israeli vehicles. Al-Jabali said that the PLO was giving the drivers until April 8, 1995, to pay a $32 license fee.[133]

On a number of occasions, Palestinian "policemen" have openly attacked—even ambushed—Israeli soldiers and opened fire. Palestinians, fortunately, as John Laffin remarks, "are poor shots and many cannot hit a stationary bus at 400 yards."[134] The results from these attacks thus far are two wounded Israelis and several dead or wounded PLO gunmen. In one of the most publicized attacks, on January 2, 1995, a number of PLO "police" opened fire on an Israeli patrol east of the Erez checkpoint between Israel and the new Gaza autonomous area.[135] The unsubtle PLO gunmen, dressed in camouflage fatigues, fired from official "police" positions and had the element of surprise and the cover of darkness, but the Israelis, however, suffered no casualties. Israeli soldiers returned fire killing three PLO men, wounding another and severely damaging the "police" building. In a press interview, the PLO Economics Minister, Nabil Sha'ath, called the Israeli killing of the PLO gunmen, "deliberate murder."[136] And Arafat eulogized his dead men as "martyrs of Palestine...killed while defending Palestinian land."[137] The funeral was "turned into a state ceremony with a 21 gun salute."[138]

The "peace agreement" allows for up to 9,000 Palestinian "policemen." At the time of writing there are more than 20,000, of whom most are former terrorists. Two weeks prior to the actual signing of the DOP, a PLO official made no secret of the fact that the PLO would use the agreement to assemble it's murderous "army" together again, dressed up as "policemen":

"Under the new interim period arrangements, **the Palestine Liberation Army forces will be transformed into security police, with an aim of bringing in thousands of PLO guerillas outside the camp in stages.**"[139]

When all the gunmen have assembled from the different countries—where many have been actively involved in international terrorism—the strength of the "Palestinian Police Force" will be boosted to around 30,000. The "policemen" were equipped by Israel with Russian Kalashnikov assault rifles, 120 big machine guns, and instead of patrol cars, "they will have 45 armored personnel carriers!"[140]

But the land and sea smuggling routes are now bustling with activity, and the Gaza Strip has been turned into "a huge arms cache.[141] The area has become a free market for weapons—"a 14mm gun goes for $2,400 to $3,000; a Karlo machine gun for $3,250; a Kalashnikov or M-16 machine gun for $5,200."[142] On September 20, 1994, a *Voice of Israel Radio* news broadcast reported that a ship was sailing in the Red Sea carrying 30 tons of South African weapons, mainly machine guns, destined for the PLO. The cargo was to be unloaded in South Yemen, but the ship's Master refused to go there or to Lebanon. And at the February 1995 summit meeting in Cairo between Rabin, Arafat, Mubarak and King Hussein, Arafat told Rabin that he should "give him more guns."[143]

And there seems little doubt in the minds of local Arabs that the armed force signals "a new repressive authority of PLO chief Yasser Arafat."[144] The expectation of Arafat's rule has caused apprehension to form in many Palestinian hearts. The Dehaishe refugee camp outside Bethlehem, in particular, has been set "on edge."[145] Local Arabs fear that he will "first target his Palestinian critics,"[146] and they also "fear the force will be used as Arafat's private army."[147]

The Arabs' fears are justified. Israeli intelligence experts now confirm that the 20,000 strong "police force" "has become Yasser Arafat's militia."[148]

The Peace Accord

There were over 90 terrorist attacks[149] against Israelis in the immediate 31 weeks following the signing of the DOP in September 1993. Of these attacks, 37 were known to have been directly carried out by Arafat's *Fatah*. Three were "initiation rights for joining *Fatah*,"[150] which included axing a 70 year-old man to death[151] and beating a 65 year-old to death with iron pipes.[152] And one of the murders, in which the victim's body was burnt, was carried out by two members of the new "Palestinian Police Force."[153] **In 1994, with Jericho and Gaza under Arafat's rule, Israel suffered more terrorism than in any year "since the founding of the state in 1948.**"[154]

The basic principle of the Israeli-PLO Peace Accord is this: In exchange for PLO renunciation of terror and the amendment of the PLO's Palestine National Covenant which calls for Israel's destruction, Israel will hand over the cities of Jericho and Gaza and some of the surrounding lands to the control of the PLO. They will become autonomous "Palestinian" areas. The agreement is called the "Gaza-Jericho First" agreement, because if the autonomy principal is found to be workable, Israel will also grant autonomy to the PLO over most of the West Bank areas. Yitzhak Rabin signed the accord on behalf of the government of Israel,

Arafat and the PLO

and Yasser Arafat signed for the PLO.

The Israelis have honored the agreement—fulfilling their pledges to dismantle their military installations and government infrastructure, and to withdraw Israeli troops from the autonomous areas. Israel has completed the formalities of handing over these areas to the control of the PLO, and have also handed over government buildings and police stations. But they have only released about two-thirds of the 5,000 Palestinian prisoners which they are to release according to the terms of the Peace Accord.

As the majority of Arabs in Israeli prisons are murderers or accomplices to murder, the Israeli security services require the prisoners to sign a pledge, before they are released, that they will not return to terrorism. Most are refusing to sign the statement and are consequently still held in a prison. Many who signed and have been released have immediately returned to terrorism, nevertheless. Two such prisoners were involved in the murder of an Israeli just two days after being released.[155] The PLO considers the requirement for prisoners to sign a pledge against returning to terrorism to be a breach of the Peace Accord, terming it "Israeli blackmail."[156]

To date, however, **the PLO has not fulfilled a single pledge it made.** Yes, Arafat did publicly "renounce terrorism" by saying: "I, as chairman of the Palestine Liberation Organization, hereby once more declare that I condemn terrorism in all its forms...."[157] He went on to qualify his remarkable statement:

> "I also offer a reverent salute to the martyrs who have fallen at the hands of terrorism and terrorists, foremost among whom is my lifelong companion and deputy, the martyr-symbol Khalil al-Wazir [Abu Jihad—who planned and directed some of the worst massacres of Israeli civilians], and the martyrs who fell in the massacres to which our people have been subjected in the various cities, villages and camps of the West Bank, the Gaza Strip and South Lebanon."[158]

Terrorism, as defined by Arafat, is what Israel has done to the PLO! The PLO's "armed struggle"—the murderous onslaught against Israel and the world in general—is a euphemism for what all the Western world refers to and understands as terrorism. And Arafat's deputy, Abu Iyad, said: "We have never interpreted [renouncing] 'terror' as meaning a suspension of military operations."[159] And to clarify the point further he said: "The PLO has never obligated itself to stop the armed struggle, and it will not renounce it."[160]

In a letter to prime minister Rabin, Arafat stated that the PLO "will assume responsibility over all PLO elements and personnel."[161] But terrorist attacks have increased in both frequency and intensity, and Arafat has boldly stated "The *intifada* will continue, continue, continue... ."[162] And he has also said: "Whoever thinks of stopping the *intifada* before it achieves its goals, I will give him ten bullets in the chest."[163]

The majority (63 percent) of Israelis are opposed to further self-rule negotiations with the PLO,[164] and almost 66 percent want to see Arafat and the senior PLO officials "put on trial."[165] "They kill the innocent who have done nothing," said an Israeli man whose 15 year-old daughter was stabbed to death as she waited for a school bus. The terrorist then "cut out her left breast and heart."[166]

Arafat has not stopped the brutal terrorism. On the contrary, he has created an escalation in violence. And on May 10, 1994, just six days after signing the "Peace Accord," Arafat called for *jihad* (holy war) to liberate Jerusalem.[167] And the rise in violence in Jerusalem has been recorded at 30 percent.[168]

As shown earlier, Arafat's *Fatah* has been proven to be still carrying out terror attacks. In April 1994, the Egyptian daily *Al-Ahram* stated that *Hamas* and other Palestinian terror groups "take credit for terrorist acts committed by *Fatah* so as not to undermine the negotiations process." According to the paper, Palestinian sources in Gaza say there is "full cooperation between the organizations on terrorist operations and an exchange of intelligence on Israeli army activities." Indeed, every report coming in bears out the truth of this. Israeli intelligence sources say *Hamas* terrorists have recently been training in PLO bases in Tunisia."[169] And Dr. Dore Gold of the prestigious Jaffee Center for Strategic Studies says *Fatah* leaders are openly collaborating with *Hamas*.[170] When Israel warned the PLO that turning a blind eye to *Hamas* attacks against Israelis could annul the Israel-PLO agreement, *Fatah* leaders angrily retorted that "an agreement with *Hamas* is an inter-Palestinian affair...and does not concern Israel."[171]

And it is a fact that large numbers of both *Fatah* and *Hamas* gunmen have joined the "Palestinian Police Force," as this legitimatizes them and enables them to legally "hold on to their weapons."[172] It is also fact that *Fatah* gunmen only agreed to join the "police" "on condition they could choose to which branch they would belong."[173] Also, a recent *Hamas* video shows a Palestinian "policeman" riding on the shoulders of *Hamas* members, he is "brandishing his rifle in one hand and a Koran in the other – a common expression of devotion to *jihad*".[174] And when reports were released that the Palestinian "police" were selling ammunition to *Hamas* terrorists in Gaza, even Western diplomats were alarmed.[175]

Due to the unprecedented wave of terrorist attacks on Israelis, Arafat was forced—for political reasons—to offer condolences to the Israeli families of the bereaved. Perhaps it is hard for most readers who live in Western countries to imagine the results of a terrorist bomb. When an Arab terrorist detonated a bomb aboard a crowded bus in downtown Tel Aviv in October, 1994, the blast lifted the bus half a meter (20 in.) into the air, and "hurled bodies up to 50 meters (165 ft.)[176] Twenty-two people died and 47 more were injured. (It would hardly be accurate to say that the people died, or that some were injured.) Pieces of bodies—severed limbs, a head, and the remains of human liver and intestines—were found on rooftops and balconies across the street. Twenty-four hours later they were still collecting the remains of the victims, and scraping parts of a brain from the wall of a second floor apartment.[177] Arafat called President Ezer Weizman to express his "regret," because he had discovered that simply expressing regret was enough to placate the entire world. But, Ezer Weizman saw through Arafat's pretense of virtue and refused to take the call.[178]

Another bomb attack took place in January 1995, at the busy Beit Lid junction in central Israel, killing 21 and injuring 62 others. One eyewitness said: "I saw parts of people's bodies—heads, arms, legs—and there was blood, lots of blood, everywhere."[179]

Another said: "Like a slaughterhouse, people were butchered like pieces of meat."[180]

After the Beit Lid attack, some 1,000 Gazan Arabs gathered to celebrate at the home of one of the "martyrs" who carried out the attack. They pitched tents around the home and had a huge 24-hour-long party. One Arab shouted through a microphone: "The Islamic movement gives its condolences to the hero of the attack which led to the killing of 20 pigs and the injuring of 60 monkeys."[181] Neither Arafat nor his PLO "police" did anything at all to prevent the celebration nor to break it up. President Clinton said that he was "sickened" by the sight of Palestinians "indecently celebrating outside the house in Gaza."[182]

A young soldier was kidnapped in October 1994, and a video was soon circulated by *Hamas* showing him pleading for his life—appealing to the Rabin government to meet the terrorists' demands. Days went by without his whereabouts being known, and fears for his safety mounted. Arafat's advisor, Ahmed Tibi, informed the soldier's parents that their son was "alive and well."[183] No one, apparently, felt to press Tibi on the question where he got his information. A few days later the soldier was shot through the head by his captors as an élite Israeli army unit stormed the located terrorist hideout and tried to free him.

Arafat has expressed his "regret" over some murderous Arab outrage on two or three occasions, and the PLO goes through the motions of arresting dozens of Arabs who are known "to have no knowledge of terrorist attacks,"[184] and then quietly frees them again. The Islamic Jihad terrorist group claimed responsibility for the Beit Lid massacre. And in order to appease the world, the PLO "police" rounded up more than a 100 Islamic Jihad activists, closed its office in Gaza and banned its newspaper. The activists were slowly released over a period of weeks, and by February 1995, the leader had been released, the office reopened, and the newspaper republished.[185] Likewise, the "police" have displayed a few rifles, hand grenades and explosives deemed to have been "captured" from terrorist groups, and have even handed over a couple of hundred stolen Israeli cars "discovered" in the autonomous Jericho area. These comedies are nothing more than charades undertaken for political reasons, but which incredibly

Arafat and the PLO

gullible politicians and newsmen take to be indicative of Arafat's real intent.

And when Israel demanded from Arafat the extradition of the two killers who "slashed the throats of two elevator technicians"[186] on a building site, Arafat said the men had fled to Egypt. The murderers, however, were sighted in Gaza by Israelis. The terror groups, under Arafat's protection, can carry out their activities under the most favorable conditions. A few regrets and a few arrests keeps the world happy. The PLO is laughing! Feisal al-Husseini, one of the PLO's top men—directly descended from Hitler's confidant and ally, Haj Amin al-Husseini, the former Grand Mufti of Jerusalem, and also blood related to Arafat—gave a speech to the Arab students of Bir Zeit University, a breeding ground for terrorism. Due to the "official press releases" from the PLO, the students were concerned that the PLO had actually given up the fight against Israel. Husseini was reassuring and put them at ease: **"Everything you see and hear today is for tactical and strategic reasons. We have not given up the rifle."**[187]

Arafat has no more intention of stopping the murder and mutilation of Israelis as he has of implementing changes to the Palestine National Covenant calling for Israel's destruction.

Palestine National Covenant

The PNC (Palestine National Covenant) was formulated and adopted in 1964 and revised in 1968. It contains 33 articles which define the goals of the PLO, the rules by which it operates, and provides the motive, the power, that drives the PLO machine. Article 2 of the PNC allows no room for a Jewish State in the Middle East; Article 20 denies that Jews have ever had any "historical or religious ties" to the area; Article 9 informs us that "armed struggle is the only way to liberate Palestine," and that this armed struggle "is the overall strategy, not merely a tactical phase." Article 10 states that "commando action constitutes the nucleus of the Palestinian popular liberation war;" Article 15, that the PLO's aim is "the elimination of Zionism in Palestine," and Article 21 rejects "all solutions which are substitutes for the total liberation of Palestine." The Covenant also states in Article 22 that Israel is a constant threat to peace "in the Middle East and the whole world," etc.

The Israeli-PLO Accord requires the canceling of clauses in the Covenant that Israel finds offensive, especially those calling for the destruction of Israel. They have not been. To amend the Covenant requires a two-thirds majority of the Palestine National Council, the governing body of the PLO. And "Arafat has not even bothered to call a meeting of the Council"[188] in the **nineteen months** since the signing of the DOP in September 1993.

There is no intention of changing the PNC. On the day that Arafat signed the agreement on the White House lawn—**on the very same day**—he made an address to the Palestinian Arabs on Jordan TV in which he said *inter alia*:

> "Since we cannot defeat Israel in war we do this in stages. We take any and every territory that we can of Palestine, and establish a sovereignty there, and we use it as a springboard to take more. When the time comes, we can get the Arab nations to join us for the final blow against Israel."[189]

Arafat also personally sent a letter to Israel's neighboring Arab states saying that if they cooperated, his agreement with Israel "will lead to a Palestinian state which will be **a jumping off point 'to remove the enemy from all Palestinian lands.**"[190]

And in arguing for the acceptance of the Israel-PLO agreement in the eyes of the Moslem world, PLO's Abu al-Aynayn stated:

> "**The agreement is in the framework of our National Covenant. We have to accept the deal and wait for a change in the circumstances that could lead to the elimination of Israel.**"[191]

Arafat's signing of the "Peace Accord" was a change in tactics, not a change in intent. And Arafat's unchanged habit of wearing only an army uniform is an expression of his resolve. If Arafat has truly had a change of heart and the PLO has really given up its dream of driving the Jews into sea, then the moon is truly made of blue cheese, and the earth is really flat. The PLO continues to plan and scheme its genocidal war against the Jews. And the aim of its war is, "**not to impose our will on the enemy but to destroy him in order to take his place.**"[192]

Since the signing of the Accord, there has been a horrific rise in the number of murdered and maimed Israelis. Arafat has made a call for an Islamic *jihad* in Jerusalem which brought an escalation of violence in the capital. And he has not attempted to amend the PNC. Arafat is humiliating the entire Israeli nation, and Binyamin Netanyahu says the Israeli government has been "constantly debased, spat at, and slapped in the face."[193] Arafat "is obviously treating *any* written commitment – whether the obligation to amend the PLO covenant or to punish dissident PLO factions – with unmitigated contempt."[194] But terror is the tactic that has brought Arafat to center stage in world attention. Only fools would believe that a handshake with Rabin would change anything.

The PLO (Palestinian Liberation Organization) as the very name implies was created for a single purpose—the total destruction of the State of Israel. This is the sole reason for the PLO's existence. Take away that purpose, and it has no other reason to exist. And any change to the PNC is an admission that the goals of the PLO have changed, which despite the fact of a signed Peace Accord, they have not.

The Purpose

We saw previously that the Moslems have an all-consuming passion to annihilate Israel from the Middle East—from the heartland of Islam. We have seen that Israeli victory over the Moslem nations, most especially the 1948 defeat, is considered to be the greatest shame in modern Arab history. And we have seen, too, that the above provided the motivation for the exception to the rule that Arabs always substitute words for actions.

And so the question arises, "Why is Arafat making peace with Israel?" And the answer is that Arafat is not making peace with Israel. He is going through some motions that look and sound like peace but are, in reality, a prelude to war.

We dare not make the mistake of divorcing Arafat from Islam. Arafat's refusal to amend the PNC, like his call for *jihad* over

Jerusalem, is the true reflection of the Islamic heart. We must remember that Islam regulates every activity for the Moslem—every thought and every feeling. We should remember, too, that lying is a not only a way of life, but also a duty in order to secure favorable results. And what is a favorable result? The destruction of Israel and the eradication of Jewish history in the Middle East.

Arafat is a Moslem, and lying is as natural to him as breathing. But he was not lying when he said: "I want all of Palestine, all of it entirely—Palestine is indivisible."[195] Even if Israel's present government does seem to possess a lot less acumen than what is expected from the nation's leadership, it certainly does not intentionally plan to vacate the homeland by sending the Jewish people back into the exile. That it is willing to relinquish strategic military terrain in its bid to secure a lasting peace with her Moslem-Arab neighbors by first offering Jericho and Gaza to Arafat's PLO is admirable, but futile, nevertheless.

This foothold into "Palestine" is what the PLO has been dreaming of for years! And getting both feet into Jericho first is the ultimate in dream realization. Jericho was the first city to be captured in the 15th century B.C. conquest of Canaan by the Israelites. Jericho's location made it the key to the capture of the central hill country—the heartland of modern Israel. Arafat realizes both the spiritual and strategic value of the city, and General Hajj Ismail, the PLO military commander in the Jericho district, says Jericho is "the gateway to Jerusalem."[196]

Getting its feet into Jericho and Gaza is the second stage of the "Phased Plan" that was approved by the PLO on June 8, 1974.[197] The Phased Plan's second stage is the securing of a platform in "Palestine" from which the PLO can continue its terrorist war against Israel. An eventual full-scale, united Arab war would be launched against a weakened Israel to accomplish total destruction of the state. The Phased Plan is too long to reprint in full, but some selections from the numbered paragraphs are as follows:

2. **The PLO is fighting by every means, and primarily by the armed struggle, to free the Palestinian land** and establish

a national, independent and fighting government over every part of the soil of Palestine to be freed.
4. Any step of liberation is a link in realizing the strategy of the PLO for the establishment of a Palestinian-democratic State, as resolved by previous Councils.
8. **After its establishment, the national Palestinian government will fight for the unity of the countries of confrontation, to complete the liberation of all the Palestinian land... .**
10. On the basis of this plan, the leadership of the revolution will formulate tactics that will enable these objectives to be realized.

And just so the reader can understand that the total destruction of Israel is, indeed, the real PLO objective in the Israeli-PLO Peace Accord, listen to the voice of the PLO:

"It is our right that we should have a state, and not just on paper, because this state will be an independent Palestinian state **that will function as a base from which to liberate Jaffa, Akko, and all of Palestine.**"[198]

"The establishment of a Palestinian state in the West Bank and Gaza will be the beginning of the downfall of the Zionist enterprise. We will be able **to rely on this defeat in order to complete the struggle to realize our entire goal.**"[199]

"If we achieve part of our territory, **we shall not relinquish our dream to establish one democratic state on all of Palestine.**"[200]

"The victory march will continue **until the Palestinian flag flies in Jerusalem and in all of Palestine—from the Jordan River to the Mediterranean Sea and from Rosh Hanikra to Eilat.**"[201]

"There are two phases to our return: **the first phase to the 1967 lines, and the second to the 1948 lines.**"[202]

> "Recovery of our occupied territories **is only the first stage toward the total liberation of Palestine.**"[203]
>
> "Our first objective is to return to Nablus [a town in the West Bank], **and then move on to Tel Aviv.**"[204]
>
> "We seek to establish a state **which we can use in order to liberate the other part of the Palestinian state**"[205]
>
> "The struggle with the Zionist enemy **is not a struggle about Israel's borders, but about Israel's existence.**"[206]
>
> "We have not abandoned the gun. The *Fatah* **still has armed bands, they continue to exist, and anything you hear** [to the contrary] **is purely for strategic purposes.**"[207]
>
> "[The Peace Accord] **is only a cease-fire until the next stage in the armed struggle. There is no decision in** *Fatah* **to cease the armed struggle** against the occupation."[208]

Listen well to those voices. The PLO leaders, even those currently negotiating the Peace Accord, are today saying the Accord is just the first concrete step to the complete annihilation of Israel. They are openly saying that terrorism, Peace Accord notwithstanding, will continue until Israel no longer exists:

> "All Palestinian liberation groups—*Fatah*, *Saika*, the PLF, the PLFP, the PLFP–GC, the DFLP and the PLO—have stated their aims clearly: **The formation of a Palestinian state is only the first step toward driving the Jews completely out of the Land.**"[209]

Accepting a peace which allows an Israeli presence in the Middle East and gives recognition to Israel's right to exist will never remove the shame of military defeat from the face of the Arab Moslem world. "Are we to leave a legacy of Israeli conquest to future generations?"[210] "Did we shed our blood for 50 square kilometers in Jericho?"[211] Of course not! But when will the

Chamberlains currently leading Israel, the United States and the European nations wake up to the fact that the peace offered by Arafat is the exact same peace that Hitler offered in Munich!

The PLO are today establishing a sovereign Palestinian state which is the very foundation of both the PNC and the Phased Plan. The PLO-Israel Accord sets out Jericho and Gaza as "Autonomous Areas," but Arafat has already declared himself "President of Palestine" and is also referred to as such. He has his own police force, flag, anthem, broadcasting corporation, postage stamps, telephone codes, border guards and territorial waters. Custom agents at the borders issue travel documents; official delegates are sent to the United Nations and many countries, and the Palestinian flag is currently flying over 82 foreign embassies. The sovereign Palestinian state only lacks formal recognition from the nations of the world. And this recognition is sure to be granted within a year or two after Arafat takes up official residence in the autonomous areas.

Arafat's Peace

Adolf Hitler convinced Britain's Neville Chamberlain that peace in Europe could only be assured by forcing Czechoslovakia to give up the Sudentenland, which according to Hitler, "rightfully belonged to Germany." Diplomatic pressure was applied, and the Czechs were forced to relinquish a rugged mountain range that formed an almost impregnable line of defense against a German invasion.

The rest of the story is history. With control of the mountain passes, the German army destroyed what remained of Czechoslovakia by occupying Bohemia-Moravia and making Slovakia a German protectorate. Hitler continued his military aggression by invading Poland on September 1, 1939, which was the spark that ignited World War II. Forty-seven million people lost their lives as a result.

Arafat, like most Moslem Arabs, is a keen admirer of Hitler. The PLO strategy for Israeli annihilation is based upon Hitler's dealings with Czechoslovakia. By his use of terror and a highly sophisticated propaganda machine, Arafat has succeeded in convincing the whole world that "peace" can only be assured by forcing Israel to return land that "rightfully belongs to the 'Palestinians.'"

The military and propaganda strategy is a copy of Hitler's, but Arafat's peace strategy is copied from Islamic history. Arabs hold to a strong belief in the proverb that they can "remedy the present only with the remedies of the past."[212] And Arafat looks to the past—not only to Hitler, but also to the two most famous figures in Islam's long history of warfare, Mohammed and Saladin—in order to remedy the present. And Arafat's concept of peace is the same as that of Mohammed and Saladin—a coin that one must pay to achieve something else:

> **"Peace for us means the destruction of Israel.** We are preparing for an all-out war, a war which will last for generations. Since January 1965, when *Fatah* was born, we have become the most dangerous enemy that Israel has. We shall not rest until the day when we return to our home, and **until we destroy Israel**."[213]

Arafat was even more pragmatic when he defined the peace he offers Israel: "The PLO offers not the peace of the weak, but the peace of Saladin."[214] Saladin was the great Moslem warrior of the 12th century. His capture of Jerusalem in 1187 sparked the Third Crusade. But Saladin is also "famous" for the "peace" which he made with the Crusaders, before he attacked with ferocity and drove the Crusaders from the Holy Land.

It was Mohammed himself who laid the foundation for Islam to build a history of making peace with an enemy in order to attack at a later, more opportune time. In 628, Mohammed made a "peace treaty" with the Kuraish tribe in Mecca in order for Moslems to worship at the Ka'abah. Two years later, when he had gained more followers and was considerably stronger, he abrogated the treaty and attacked the Kuraish people, slaughtering every male among them. This agreement between Mohammed and the infidels of Mecca is known as the "Truce of Hudaybiyyah."

"This truce became a model and a precedent in Islamic law for all agreements with infidels: never permanent, never lasting more than 10 years (with the possibility of another 10 years extension, no more). **Islam is not permitted to stop its war against non-Moslems for more than this period.**"[215]

"In the Arab-Islamic teaching concerning peace with non-Moslems, the peace is an entirely Islamic affair: it is initiated by the Moslems when they feel it is a necessity, and anticipate its practical benefits; and they end it at their will whenever they feel they should or can. Even when peace treaties are entered into by the Islamic people with non-Moslems, the enemy remains an enemy. **In the Islamic thought and teaching, it is permissible to conclude peace treaties for practical reasons, on the road to ultimate Islamic victory. The Islamic concept of peace is therefore the cessation of hostilities until such time the conditions favor resumption of hostilities that will ultimately lead to Islamic victory.**"[216]

The truce is part of Islam's long-term policy of war—it is an integral facet of Islam's drive to bring the world into complete subjection. According to Islamic law books, "war could be interrupted, when expedient, by an armistice or truce of limited duration. It could not be terminated by a peace, but only by victory."[217] The reason should now be very clear why, in one of the above quotes, a PLO leader refers to the Peace Accord as a "cease-fire." Only an "armistice" or "truce" is permissible in Islam, and that is "not to last for more than 10 years."[218] When the enemy is too strong, as Israel has proven again and again, a truce may be made for a limited time. The enemy understands such a truce as peace, and thus Arafat and all Arabs see peace as "a weakness to exploit."[219]

The Israeli-PLO Peace Accord, therefore, is a tactical move in an overall plan. We should not be surprised if pressure is brought upon Arafat to amend the PNC, or that he even appears to change it in order to complete the duplicity.

Jerusalem

There is a powerful rallying cry for Moslems—*Al Quds*—Jerusalem! And down through the ages that cry has been used to rally the "warriors of *jihad*"—from Mohammed's use in the 7th century to Saladin's in the 12th to Arafat's in the 20th. Arafat is remedying "the present" with "the remedies of the past."

Six days after signing the Peace Accord, Arafat called for a *jihad* to liberate Jerusalem. The following extracts are taken from his speech in a Johannesburg mosque:

> "In the name of Allah...believe me there is a lot to be done. The *jihad* will continue...Our main battle is Jerusalem. Jerusalem...And, here we are, I can't—and I have to speak frankly, I can't do it alone without the support of the Islamic nation. I can't do it alone...**No, you have to come and fight and to start the *jihad* to liberate Jerusalem**...no, it is not their [Jews] capital. It is our capital. It is your capital...This agreement [Israeli-PLO Peace Accord]—**I am not considering it more than the agreement signed between our prophet Mohammed and the Kuraish tribe—a despicable truce.** The same way Mohammed had accepted it we are accepting now this peace effort...From my heart, and I am telling you frankly from brother to brother, we are in need of you. **We are in need of you as Moslems, as warriors of *jihad*...Again I have to say...onward to victory, onward to Jerusalem!** 'They will enter the mosque as they entered it before.'"[220]

Could Arafat's intentions be made any clearer? Mohammed's Truce of *Hudaybiyyah* is the model for Arafat's peace with Israel! He thought he was confiding to the Islamic faithful, but his speech was secretly recorded by a journalist who had managed to slip into the mosque uninvited.

Consider:
a) Arafat speaks as a Moslem in the name of Allah.
b) Although he has signed an agreement that calls for the end of violence and terror, he pledges that it will continue.

c) He makes absolutely clear that Jerusalem is the real prize and that it is not the Jewish capital, but the capital of the Palestinian state and an Islamic capital.
d) He boasts that he will treat the Israeli-PLO Accord just as Mohammed treated his agreement with the Kuraish people—it is a "despicable truce."
e) He uses Mohammed's and Saladin's rallying cry of Jerusalem to invite South African Moslems to wage *jihad* in Jerusalem against the Jews.
f) Arafat ends his speech by quoting the Koran[221]—a verse that refers to the Roman Army entering the Jewish temple like the Babylonian Army had done previously: "utterly destroying all that they laid their hands on"—implying that he would do the same.

The Israeli-PLO Peace Accord is a sham—a tactical Islamic military maneuver designed to bring about the Jewish state's destruction. And Arafat has made no bones about the PLO's view of the Accord's objective. During his "triumphant" return to Gaza in early July 1993, an area from which Israelis were barred, he "stirred the crowd by shouting with them, 'In blood and spirit we will liberate Palestine.'"[222] He took delight in informing the Arab world of his success: "From here, from the land of Palestine, I say to the world, I say to my brothers the Arab leaders, that we will keep our promise...."[223] And then he clarified the "promise":

> "From here in Gaza, we will go to the Ibrahim mosque [the Machpelah Cave in Hebron], we will go to Nablus, Jenin, Tulkarm, Kalkilya, Bethlehem, Ramallah and then, after Hebron, Jerusalem, Jerusalem, Jerusalem."[224]

And the emotionally charged crowds joined Arafat in chanting the Islamic battle cry—"*Allahu Akbar.*"[225] It was a true expression of the aspirations in every Moslem's heart:

> "Millions of Moslems, from Iran in the east to Libya in the west, vow with raised fists and holy fervor to redeem Jerusalem by the sword. They swear that the Jews, whom

the second Sura of the Koran calls 'sly, cruel and treacherous,' will be driven out of the occupied land."[226]

The message to Israel is loud and clear: The PLO wants Jerusalem for its capital—"all of Jerusalem."[227] And the commander of the new "Palestinian Police" also asserted: "This is the first step toward the restoration of Jerusalem and the entire occupied land to their owners."[228] He also said: "The door is open to [those]...who wish to escalate the armed struggle."[229]

Jerusalem is history, power and God. Her daily events have become real-life drama to hundreds of millions throughout the world. Jerusalem has become home to the second largest press bureau in the world—hundreds of foreign journalists and dozens of TV crews. The world waits for the coming clash over the Holy City. Some see it as the end of time, others as a decisive battle in the struggle between Islam and the West.

The battle for Jerusalem is not a struggle for Palestinian rights nor is it a struggle between men, that is, between Jew and Arab. It is a spiritual battle—an attempt by the forces of Satan to unseat God from the city where He chose to establish His throne. It is a battle that will ultimately end in a nuclear and chemical holocaust. The earthly protagonists are the Jews, a despised, minority people who have been a major source of blessing to the whole world,[230] and the Palestinians—a conglomerate of Arab people who recently created an identity by using the ingredients of murder and terror freely mixed with the usurping, recreating and rewriting of history.

6

Palestinian Refugees

The Palestinian refugee problem is an integral part of Arab strategy in their war with Israel. For nearly half a century the world has been incessantly and increasingly bombarded about the plight of Palestinian refugees. It is high time Western people blew the dust from history books sitting on their shelves and started searching out the truth for themselves. By doing so they would be able to put the subject into perspective. But, unfortunately, the average Westerner now relies completely on the news media to keep him informed, and here lies the root of the problem. Those that control the information of the masses will, ultimately, control their judgments and opinions. Still, with such an abundance of material available to anyone who wishes to be properly informed about the refugee situation, it is difficult to understand why (apart from anti-Semitism and Arab oil) the media continues to propagate the myth that the refugee problem only affected the Arabs. And this myth, says Joan Peters, has become "perhaps the most pervasively misconceived image of any political situation in the world."[1]

The Myth

On May 15, 1948, the day following Israel's declaration of statehood, seven[2] Arab armies launched an attack against Israel in a bid to snuff out the life of the newborn state. Although vastly outnumbered and outgunned, tiny Israel with the help of her God emerged victorious from the war.

But the Arab attack created two concurrent refugee problems. Arabs fled from every area of Palestine and found refuge in Arab lands, and Jews fled from their ancient Arab homelands and found refuge mainly in Israel.

The Arab's flight was due to two different reasons:

a) "The Arab States encouraged Palestinian Arabs to leave their homes temporarily in order to be out of the way of the Arab invasion armies."[3] The "'majority' of the Arab refugees in 1948 were not expelled, and '68 percent' left without seeing an Israeli soldier."[4] A Palestinian refugee succinctly summed up the situation six years later: "The Arab governments told us: 'Get out so that we can get in.' So we got out, but they did not get in."[5]

b) "For the flight—it is our leaders who are responsible. They instilled fear and terror into the hearts of the Arabs of Palestine until they fled, leaving their homes and their properties to the enemy."[6]

Both of these reasons are put into perspective by the records of William Hull who was in Palestine throughout the war:

"The Arabs fled because their leaders had left and because God put fear in their hearts. In Bakaa and some other parts of Jerusalem they left food on the tables; silverware, jewelry, money and other valuables in their drawers. Their leaders told them that they should leave now and that they would be able to come back in a few days, after the Arab armies had defeated the Jews. These Arabs had laid in large supplies of oil, food and other supplies in anticipation of the war. Each Arab house had a large cement cistern under it, full of water. These supplies and water were literally a God-send to the starved and thirsty Jews in Jerusalem. It almost seemed as though God had provided all this to meet their need.

"We sympathize with the Arabs; it was a tragic disaster for them; it was their misfortune to be living at the time that God decreed Israel should return to their own land. The Arabs themselves were almost entirely to blame for their flight, for their leaders so multiplied the Deir Yassin massacre and concocted so many other tales without any foundation of fact that the Arabs were terrified of the *terrible* Jews. These were the 'hornets of fear' released by the Arabs themselves. The purpose of these exaggerated or false reports was to discredit the Jews in the eyes of the world. But the result was to create a panic flight of their own people."[7]

More than 60 percent of Israel's population today—nearly three million people—are Jews or offspring of Jews who lived in Arab countries and have fled from "Arab brutality."[8] Most of the people currently living in Israel consist of refugees and their descendants from two oppressions: European-Nazi and Arab.[9]

Considerably more Jews from Arab lands became penniless refugees at the time of the 1948 war than did Arabs leaving the newly established Jewish state. Hundreds of thousands of Jews fled from Arabs lands due to the accelerated massacres that were taking place in their communities. Arab pogroms against Jews had been taking place continually since the time of Mohammed, but as a way of revenge for Israel's declared statehood, the Arabs stepped up their brutality until life for the Jew in Arabia became unbearable.

"Clearly the massive exodus of Jewish refugees from the Arab countries was triggered largely by the Arab's own Nazi-like bursts of brutality, which had become the lot of the Jewish communities. But the history is long of persecution against Jews by the Arabs, a chronicle of 'intolerable pressure' that had it beginnings in and took its inspiration from the seventh-century book of the creator of Islam."[10]

In an unusually candid article written for an Arab journal, Sabri Jiryis, a researcher, author and member of the Palestine National Council—the PLO governing body—stated that: "Jews of the Arab states were **driven out of their ancient homes...shamefully deported** after their property had been commandeered or taken over at the lowest possible valuation."[11]

Evidence of the Arabs' injustice to Jews—who in many cases had lived in Arab lands since before the advent of Islam, and in some instances even more than a thousand years earlier than that—is so overwhelming that even some of Israel's declared enemies were compelled by conscience to acknowledge the truth of it. The Jews were stripped of their possessions and property and driven from the Arab lands. The Arabs, on the other hand, left their homes either on their own accord or at the request of their leaders. There is **no valid comparison between the flights** of the two peoples—one forced, the other voluntary—nor is there a valid comparison between their personal losses:

> "The losses by the expropriated Jews who left Arab countries were sudden and total; the Jews took next to nothing. In the Arab exodus, the rich Palestinians went in early waves, taking as much of their property as they could. No one was prevented from taking anything.
>
> "By the most conservative estimates, the value of homes, businesses, banks, real estate and other assets owned by the Jews of Iraq and Egypt alone amounted to billions of dollars. (In 1952, financial expert, Dr. Edmund Roth, dispatched by the Jewish Agency, calculated Jewish losses in just the Maghreb countries as reaching $7 billion, which obviously would be much more today). There is **no valid comparison in value with property abandoned by local Arabs** in the wars (and duly registered by the authorities concerned)."[12]

The Western world has been brainwashed into believing the false notion that several million Palestinian refugees are living either in squalid camps, or eking out an existence somewhere in exile. The Arabs and the PLO propagate this lie strongly, and the anti-Israel Western news media is only too happy to broadcast it. Statistical figures from the United Nations Relief and Work Agency (UNRWA) are often given in an effort to bolster the believability of the lie, but no reliance can be placed upon such "facts" when less than 18 months after war's end the UNRWA director himself declares that **hundreds of thousands of their "hungry Arabs" were not refugees!**[13] In 1961 **another UNRWA director admitted that their refugee counts included other Arabs** and said that it would be "wrong to deny them aid merely because they weren't legally qualified."[14] And by 1970, that same director was admitting that **he himself had proven the refugee figures were "erroneous and grossly inflated."**[15]

United Nations refugee figures are based upon the number of ration books distributed. And after a United States investigation in 1960, it was reported that: "Ration cards have become chattel for sale, for rent or bargain by any Jordanian, whether refugee or

Palestinian Refugees

not, needy or wealthy."[16] As far back as 1955, Cairo's Arab News Agency reported that **there are "refugees who hold as many as 500 ration cards.**"[17] Forty years later statisticians readily acknowledge that documenting deaths in the refugee camps is an impossibility, "**since reporting a death means losing a valuable UNRWA ration cared.**"[18] Obviously, UNRWA figures on Palestinian refugees today are even more grossly inflated than they were 40 years ago, so false in fact that they cannot even begin to bear scrutiny. And so we must go back to 1948 where the problem began.

According to the *British Survey of Palestine,* known for its tendency to inflate Arab numbers, the total number of Arabs living in the area, which became Israel after the 1948 war, was 561,000. Of these, 140,000 stayed in Israel. The number of refugees, then, "could not have been more than 420,000."[19]

The most exhaustive research into the refugee problem comes from Joan Peters who spent seven years producing her monumental work *From Time Immemorial: The Origins of The Arab-Jewish Conflict Over Palestine.* Peters and her assistants painstakingly sifted through boxes of British governmental data that literally filled rooms from floor to ceiling, and she searched the entire archives of some of the world's largest Public Libraries.

In her book, Peters strips away the thousands of nomads that were included with the settled population figures in official statistics. She carefully documents the thousands of government-recorded Arab immigrants and also 170,000 *in-migrants* from the Arab Areas of Western Palestine (non-Jewish settled areas).[20] This 170,000 could not be categorized as refugees because they simply went home to their villages and towns outside of the truce lines. With the "non-settled" Arabs removed from the population totals along with the 140,000 that remained in Israel, Peters concludes that the maximum number possible of genuine refugees could have been no more that 340,000.[21] And Peters says:

> "It should especially be noted that the maximum figure of 343,000 is *less than half* the number of refugees claimed by the Arabs immediately after their leaving,

before the numbers were...further 'inflated' in the refugee camps."[22]

Peters also adds: "What the population study could not calculate is how many among the 343,000 Arab 'settled population' were in fact **illegal immigrants**."[23] She maintains: "...illegal Arab immigrants could account for a **very substantial number** among the Arabs included in the 343,000 refugee figure."[24] Peters's documentation of populations and population movements is so exhaustive, so detailed, that if it were published without any other data, it would in itself be a hefty volume!

Both of our Arab refugee totals come from official sources, but Peters's tally should be awarded highest credence due to her unbiased, painstaking research. Still, to be absolutely fair to Arabs, we can obtain a virtually indisputable maximum figure by adding the totals together and then dividing them equally. Thus, we arrive at an absolutely unshakable maximum 1948 refugee total of 381,500 Palestinian Arabs—a far cry indeed from the ridiculously absurd "'four million' Arab people who were said to have lived on their farms in the Holy Land 'from time immemorial.'"[25] And now these refugees, of whom the great majority were children in 1948, have supposedly burgeoned into many millions. The swollen refugee figures have never been verified **because the Arabs "refused official censuses to be completed** among the refugees."[26] The Arab purpose is to seek "greater world attention through an exaggerated population figure and thereby induce the UN to put heavier pressures upon Israel."[27] With known high infant mortality rates, low Arab life-expectancy levels and increased trafficking in UNRWA ration cards, less than half of current Palestinian refugee estimates would still not be credible.

Fairly accurate figures for Jewish refugees from Arab lands are available from several sources: Netanyahu in *A Place Among The Nations* gives the lowest number of 800,000;[28] Bard and Himelfarb in *Myths and Facts* give 820,000;[29] Joan Peters in *From Time Immemorial* sets her total at 821,000;[30] and Yosef Yaakov of the editorial staff of *The Jerusalem Post* places his at 850,000[31] as do most other sources. Applying the aggregate rule as we did

Palestinian Refugees 111

previously, we arrive at 822,750 Jewish refugees—well over double the amount of Arab refugees.

When we consider the true facts of the matter, it is very obvious that for every Arab refugee—adult or child—who elicits our sympathy, there were more than two Jewish refugees who were also deserving of our stirred emotions. And, it is also fact that most Arab refugees never traveled more than a few miles from their home to the other side of the truce line, where they remained "linguistically, culturally and ethnically"[32] part of the greater Arab nation. Conversely and also paradoxically, the Jews fled from the communities that had been home to them and their ancestors for thousands of years, to an even more ancient homeland where their roots are yet older.

An irrevocable defacto exchange of population took place to the overwhelming benefit of the Arab countries. The seven pronged Arab attack in 1948 created two concurrent refugee problems, but due to the Western news media, everyone in the world knows only about Arab refugees. The refugees flowed in two directions, but justice is demanded only for the Arab. Arab "justice," however, does not demand only that the Arabs be compensated for loss of property, but also that Israel be replaced by an Islamic state.

The Egyptian naval blockade of the Tiran Straits and the massive mobilizing of the armies of five Arab nations in 1967 ignited the June Six Day War in which a further 230,000 Arabs became refugees. As in the 1948 debacle, most of these 1967 "fugitives departed voluntarily; no attempts were made to influence them to leave."[33] Israel subsequently allowed 54,000 Arabs to gradually return to their homes for the sake of family reunification, and their "homes, land, and other property at all times were maintained intact."[34]

It behooves us to remember that when the world speaks of the inalienable rights of the Arab refugees that fled Israel in 1948 and 1967, it irrationally forgets that more than double the amount of Jewish refugees fled Arab nations from 1948–1973. Of the more than 820,000 Jewish refugees from 10 Arab nations, not a one has received a penny in return for the inestimable properties left behind. While the Arabs who left their homes were, on the whole, peasants from primitive and underdeveloped areas, some of the Jewish refugees left fortunes, businesses and lands in the countries from which they fled. When sources are researched for world refugee figures, one fact stands out beyond all others: Millions of Palestinian refugees are currently shown living in "Gaza, Jordan, Lebanon, Syria and the West Bank,"[35] but not a single, solitary Jewish refugee is shown to exist in any known source. Does it not strike the reader as a little odd that a tiny country like Israel with a 1948 population of only 650,000 and a crushing defense burden, could successfully absorb over 820,000 refugees, while the Arab nations with a combined land mass exactly 690 times that of Israel and untold billions of oil dollars, have not absorbed more than a handful of Arab refugees?

Arabs in Israel

Nearly a quarter of a million Palestinian Arabs chose to stay in the Jewish state during and after the 1948 and 1967 wars. These Arabs have equal rights with Israeli Jews, and they enjoy Israeli citizenship and "rights beyond that enjoyed by nationals of Arab lands. Today, they represent more than 16% of the voting population of this democracy."[36]

Jews in Arab Lands

Arabs have always made extravagant claims of a tradition of Arab tolerance and just treatment for all Jews that have lived in Arab lands. These claims are not just false—they are sheer fantasy and delusion! Many volumes of works by various historians have recorded Arab persecutions against Jews throughout the entire Arab world for over 1,300 years—since the founding of Islam. Arab hatred of Jews did not begin with the founding of the Jewish state in 1948; it began in the 7th century with the founding of the religion of Islam. Nearly a thousand years ago, the great Jewish philosopher Moses Maimonides wrote concerning Arab treatment of Jews: "Never did a nation molest, degrade, debase, and hate us as much as they."[37] But for propaganda purposes some Arab leaders will even make elaborate invitations for "their Jews" to come back "home." They promise that "the Moslem community will treat them generously and tolerantly as it has always done,"[38] while in the very same breath, saying that Jewish wickedness is "incurable unless they are subdued by force."[39]

It may be fairly claimed by some that numbers of Jews have fond memories of life in Arab lands, that life under Arab rule could not have been all bad. Some Jews had pleasant memories of life in Germany, too, despite the fact that six million of their people were murdered by the Nazis. And let us not forget that many Israelites, so recently freed from extreme persecution and bondage in Egypt, also had fond memories of *"the fish which we ate freely in Egypt, the cucumbers, the melons, the leeks, the onions, and the garlic"* (Numbers 11:5).

Most Jews do not carry happy memories of their years of being *dhimmi*—subjugated infidel inferiors—in Arab lands. Instead they remember the daily humiliation and constant cruelty of their "superiors." They remember that everywhere they were compelled to pay the *dhimmi* poll tax to the Moslem authorities. They remember, too, that they had to wear special hats and badges and that the building of synagogues was barred while existing ones had to be lowered beneath the level of Islamic buildings.[40] They remember the prohibition on riding horses, camels and asses in the presence of an Arab. They well remember that upon seeing an Arab coming, they had to quickly dismount and go on foot, leading their mount until the Arab disappeared. If they forgot or took too long to dismount, the Arabs brutally reminded them of their inferior status by throwing them to the ground.[41] They remember that when a Jew walked among Moslems in the market, "one would throw a stone at him," another would "pull his beard and a third his ear lock," and yet another would "spit on his face."[42] They remember having to always pass Moslems on their left side, because that was the side of Satan.[43] And they remember having to step off the pavement to let the Arab go by, making sure not to touch him in passing as this could bring a violent response.[44] And among a myriad of other things, they remember that one of their tasks was to "clean the city latrines while another was to clear the streets of animal carcasses—without pay, often on their Sabbath."[45]

Throughout the Arab world, from the 7th century until today, Jews have constantly lived in fear of attack by Moslems, and many of these attacks were and are "premeditated and coldly murderous in intent."[46] Down through the ages, hundreds of thousands of Jews have died horribly at the hands of Moslem Arabs. *New York Times'* Clifton Daniel filed the following report after Libyan attacks on Jews in 1945:

> "Babies were beaten to death with iron bars. Old men were hacked to pieces where they fell. Expectant mothers were disemboweled. Whole families were burnt alive in their houses. Two brothers lost 27 relatives in one attack."[47]

Normal life for Jews in Arab lands meant beatings, humiliation, forced conversion to Islam and girls being raped with their families looking on.[48] And under Arab rule, even the Holy Land—the Jew's own ancient homeland—offered no improvements:

> "In towns where Jews lived for hundreds of years, those Jews were periodically robbed, raped, in some places massacred, and, in many instances, the survivors were obliged to abandon their possessions and run."[49]

The British consul in Jerusalem reported in 1839 that "the Jew in Jerusalem is not estimated in value much above a dog."[50] And the High Commissioner and Commander-in-Chief in Palestine in 1929 wrote:

> "I have learned with horror of the atrocious acts committed by bodies of ruthless and blood-thirsty evil-doers, of savage murders perpetuated upon defenseless members of the Jewish population, regardless of age or sex—acts of unspeakable savagery."[51]

But Moslem leaders continue even today to make their outrageous statements concerning the kindly nature and gentleness of the Arab people toward the Jews, deluding even themselves and lying to all their listening, viewing and reading audiences:

Palestinian Refugees 115

"Moslem rule has always been known for its tolerance...according to history Jews had a most quiet and peaceful residence under Arab rule."[52]

"Islamic tolerance is in complete contrast to Jewish intolerance and cruelty."[53]

"Arabs and the Moslems throughout their long history were not the aggressors...they always initiate good deeds and spread peace."[54]

Such expressions of fantasy will not lure a single Jew to return to the place they have escaped. Too many of Israel's ex-refugees from Arab lands recall their bitter years under Moslem rule:

"They waited for us in the square, close to the bus stop. Not one, not two, hundreds of Arabs on the street. I'm not exaggerating. They knew we were walking down, and they gathered hundreds, hundreds, honestly.

"I was able to slip away. But they caught one of my friends and beat him and beat him on the head. And I couldn't move. I saw him. I just froze. An Arab Moslem religious man said to me, 'Come here my boy, poor boy,' and then he took his stick and he hit me on the head, and they threw me into the street. There was no transportation anymore; cars couldn't move, and they started to hit me, kick me—soldiers in their big shoes....."[55]

"I was four years old; I remember. They closed the Jewish ghetto. Arabs came and killed one hundred and eighty Jews and took everything. We escaped from one roof to another for a couple of days."[56]

"Sure, there was nothing to complain about. We came back alive from school...And many times I had incidents, as I was ten, eleven years old—this was in 1946 to 1948 or '49. It was a fact of life. Nothing to complain about. I mean just to say, well it was raining today. So what? Nothing extraordinary. It was part of everyday life to be beaten for being a Jew; you could expect it."[57]

"Killings, it happened once in every two years, about. You should expect that too. Every now and then, for one reason or another, though you have done nothing—I mean nothing concerning you directly—you must expect it, in every two years, something like that. You try to avoid it. The same as cholera and typhoid and malaria."[58]

Girls suffered most at the hands of Arabs. Shoshana escaped from Syria where her family still "lives." Weeping, she is ashamed to tell what the Arabs did to her:

"They destroyed me for life because what I have gone through has become part of my life and I can't get rid of it. I can't believe my family is there and they live this kind of life."[59]

More than 820,000 of the 850,000 Jews in 10 Arab lands fled between 1948–1973 taking none of the fruit of their labors from many centuries. No amount of Arab soliloquies expressing "traditional Moslem tolerance and gentleness toward their Jews" will convince a sane mind that Jews lived anything but an abysmal, persecuted and intolerable life under Islam.

The Weapon of Non-Absorption

Israel absorbed all of her thousands of refugees from Arab lands at an enormous cost to the young country. And since that invasion of Oriental Jews, Israel has literally absorbed millions of Jews from the four corners of the world. Some Jews were just wanting to go "home," some were survivors from the death camps of the Nazi Holocaust, another half million fled from the anti-Semitic Soviet Union where they had been forcibly detained for decades. Besides absorbing her own people, Israel has successfully built housing and resettled over 60,000 of the Palestinian refugees—something not done by "the Arab states, the United

Palestinian Refugees

Nations or any Western power."[60] Israel has also contributed over $12 million[61] to the United Nations and other relief funds—more than most Arab countries.[62] The Arab countries have contributed only a tiny fraction to UNWRA's funds for the support of refugees—the entire Arab world contributes less than one percent—less than the donation made by the Swedish Save the Children Fund![63]

Concerning Israel's treatment of Palestinian refugees, one is constantly subjected to television film clips and newspaper and magazine photographs (some completely faked—see chapter 9) of the squalid living conditions of the refugees. Many refugees living in camps do, indeed, live in squalid rat-infested conditions, but that is not the fault of Israel.

First, many Middle Eastern Arabs have little concept of health or sanitation, and open or no sewerage has been a way of life for decades of centuries. Second, Israel did not build the refugee camps—the Arabs did! When Israel entered Judea, Samaria and the Gaza Strip in 1967, the inhabitants in the camps were found, after 19 years of Arab rule, to be living in the same abject squalor and misery as had existed in 1949. Third, Israel has tried repeatedly to re-house Palestinian refugees into better conditions, but has met with powerfully strong opposition from the United Nations.

Since 1970, Israel has been engaged in a consistent effort to improve the living conditions of the Palestinian refugees. Beginning in that year, plans were drawn up and steps were taken to improve the situation of the refugees, and provide them with proper housing and an infrastructure of services. Nine residential projects were built, housing some 10,000 families who chose to leave the camps. Each family was given a plot of land, and more than 70 percent of the families built their own homes according to their needs and preferences. The new neighborhoods were built on state land within municipal areas near the camps, and each was provided with its own network of electricity, water, sanitation, roads, paved sidewalks and developed surroundings. In each neighborhood, public buildings—schools, healthclinics, shopping centers and mosques—were built.

The policy continues today. Any refugee who wishes to leave

a camp is given a plot of land, chooses his own type of dwelling and construction plan, and receives a building permit from the municipal authorities who are responsible for supervising construction. He becomes the full property owner once the building is completed, and his property is registered in the Land Register.

With the limited means and resources at its disposal, Israel has not been able to resolve this most difficult problem on her own. However, by initiating and going ahead with this refugee rehabilitation program, Israel seeks to show that a solution to the problem is feasible.[64]

Since 1971, however, a little-noticed United Nations Resolution on the Gaza Strip has been annually adopted. The resolution states *inter alia*:

> "The General Assembly...reiterates strongly its demand that Israel desist from the removal and resettlement of Palestine refugees in the Gaza Strip....."[65]

A typical year's vote (October 30, 1987) was: 150 in favor; 2 against (Israel and the United States); 3 abstentions (Costa Rica, Liberia and Zaire).[66]

A similar annual Resolution on the West Bank states *inter alia*:

> "The General Assembly...alarmed...by Israel's plans to remove and resettle the Palestine refugees of the West Bank and to destroy their camps...calls once again upon Israel to abandon those plans and to refrain from any action that leads to the removal and resettlement of Palestine refugees in the West Bank....."[67]

On this resolution the typical year's vote (October 30, 1987) was: 145 in favor; 2 against (Israel and the United States); 7 abstentions (Costa Rica, El Salvador, Equatorial Guinea, Central African Republic, Ivory Coast, Liberia and Zaire).[68]

Those who preach about the need to overcome the plight in

the Palestinian camps and who castigate Israel for not improving the refugees' lot, are the very ones who lend their hands to United Nations Resolutions specifically designed to perpetuate the miserable condition of the refugees. The United Nations does not want the refugees out of the camps; it wants Israel out of the land. The Palestinian refugee problem is strictly political. It is a powerful weapon used against Israel, and the suffering of refugees is of no concern to those who use that weapon. In 1958, before the United Nations established its anti-Israel bias, a former director of UNRWA angrily declared:

> "The Arab states do not want to solve the refugee problem. They want to keep it as an open sore...as a weapon against Israel. **Arab leaders do not give a damn whether Arab refugees live or die.**"[69]

In 1972, the Mayor of Gaza, Rashad Ashawa, refused to allow Israel to install sewage, water and cleaning facilities for the 40,000 residents of the Shatti refugee camp. Ashawa said that "granting services to the Palestinians in the camp would make them fully-fledged citizens and make them forget they were refugees."[70] And an eminent expert on the Palestinian refugee problem said in a 1978 interview concerning the refugees: "You must remember—well—**these people are simply pawns.**"[71]

The 19 Arab nations—Algeria, Bahrain, Egypt, Iraq, Jordan, Kuwait, Lebanon, Libya, Mauritania, Morocco, Oman, Qatar, Saudi Arabia, Somalia, Sudan, Syria, Tunisia, United Arab Emirates and Yemen have "for over a thousand years inhabited a larger geographical area than any comparable ethnic group,"[72] but despite all this land, and despite all their massive combined oil wealth, they have refused to settle their Arab brothers. This is the cause of the Palestinian problem. It is high time the West leaned as heavily on the Arabs, in proportion to their land and financial holdings, as it has done upon Israel. And it is beyond time that Western politicians and mediacrats stop kowtowing to Arab oil and petro-dollars, and started to act righteously.

From time to time, Arab leaders have twinges of conscience

and actually publicly acknowledge their part in the conspiracy of refugee suffering:

> "Since 1948 it is we who have demanded the return of the refugees while it is we who have made them leave. We have rendered them dispossessed. We have accustomed them to begging. We have participated in lowering their moral and social level. Then **we exploited them in executing crimes of murder, arson and throwing bombs at men, women and children.**"[73]

> "We have brought destruction upon a million Arab refugees by calling upon them and pleading with them to leave their land, their homes, their work and their business, and we have caused them to be barren and unemployed though each one of them had been working and qualified in a trade from which he could make a living. In addition we accustomed them to begging for hand-outs and to suffice with what little the United Nations organization would allocate them."[74]

> "Since 1948 Arab leaders have approached the Palestine problem in an irresponsible manner..... They have used the Palestinian people for selfish political purposes. This is ridiculous and, I could say, even criminal."[75]

And the refugees themselves also know why they remain in the rat-infested camps:

> "We, the refugees, have the right to address the members of the Arab League and to declare: **We left our homeland on the strength of false promises by crooked leaders of the Arab States.**"[76]

That appeal fell on deaf ears. And a representative of the Jewish refugees from Arab lands also sent the following message to the Arab nations:

"We, the Jewish refugees from Arab lands whose history in those countries goes back more than 2,000 years, long before Islam—suggest that the Arab governments finance the welfare of their own brothers instead of using them as political pawns, while they spend huge amounts for **hypocritical propaganda, half truths and outright lies.**"[77]

The refugees, meanwhile, have been callously allowed to rot in their camps by Arab decree, while offers by Israel to rehouse them more suitably have been rejected.

The Third Stage of The Phased Plan

The refusal to absorb the Arab refugees from the Arab-inspired wars of 1948 and 1967 has been a major Arab weapon against Israel. But it is more than a weapon, it is an integral part of the plan to annihilate Israel by stages; it is the third stage of the Phased Plan mentioned previously. The first stage will be dealt with in the next chapter, the second was dealt with in the last chapter, and the others we will come to in due time.

The third stage of the Phased Plan is to overwhelm Israel by the return of Palestinian refugees—not just the refugees that actually left the area because of the wars, but the millions of Arabs whom the PLO claim as refugees. With a foothold in Israel, the goal of the second stage of the Phased Plan is to gradually force Israel to indefensible borders by demanding the "return" of more and more areas, while continuing their war of terror to "soften" the Israelis into accommodating the demands. The third stage is to introduce millions of Arab "refugees" into Israel until Arabs far outnumber Israel's current 4.6 million Jews.

As an integral part of the "peace initiative" the PLO had to "recognize Israel." The accepted meaning of "the recognition of Israel" is to recognize her legitimacy and right to exist within the Middle East. When Yasser Arafat was asked by journalists, "Do you recognize Israel?" he replied: "Israel exists, it is a fact that everyone can see."[78] This, of course, was not a recognition of Israel's legitimacy or of her right to exist in the Middle East, but the Western media and politicians accept that it is. This *"recognition of Israel* as a strategy"[79] was proposed years ago to obtain the return of the Palestinian refugees, which would virtually guarantee Israel's destruction:

> "The return of all the refugees would create a large Arab majority that would serve as the most effective means of forming **a powerful fifth column for the day of revenge** and reckoning."[80]

Just as the "recognition" of the Jewish state is a strategy, so is the plight of the Palestinian refugees. The direct extent of the Arab leaders' interest in the refugees is clearly related to the degree this group can contribute to the ultimate Arab objective of destroying Israel. The PLO understands full well the truth of the words spoken by Nasser of Egypt: "If refugees return to Israel, Israel will cease to exist."[81] And thus, this became the third stage of the Phased Plan—a noose around Israel's throat:

> "Any discussion aimed at a solution of the Palestine problem, which will not be based on ensuring **the refugees' right to annihilate Israel**, will be regarded as a desecration of the Arab people and an act of treason."[82]

> "It is well-known and understood that the Arabs, in demanding **the return of the refugees** to Palestine, means their return as masters of the Homeland and not as slaves. With greater clarity, they mean **the liquidation of the State of Israel**."[83]

The PLO's theme song—the time-worn phrase, "the right of Palestinian return"—is further imbedded into the minds of the Western masses each day by the news media. It has been like a battering ram at the walls of the Jewish state. Israel cannot withstand the incessant pounding and large, gaping cracks are evident in the nation's fortitude. The media is merciless. It portrays Israel as the brutal overlord of the suffering Palestinians and has done more for the PLO than the thousands of mangled corpses from Arafat's 29 years of terrorism.

To see the discrepancy in the media's presentation of Israel, one needs to take a drive through the Israeli "occupied territories." Unbelievable prosperity will be found among those employed by Israel. Many large multi-storied homes have been built that only the most well-to-do Israeli could afford. The abundance of Mercedes Benz and BMW cars parked on the streets proves that the news media lies when it represents those living in the Israeli administered territories as poor and oppressed. One wealthy Arab contractor, who actually had $10,000 cash in his pocket at the time, remarked to me that, "Under the Turks it was awful, under the Jordanians it was not much better, but under the Israelis we make money." A high-ranking Russian politician who spent some time in both Israel and Arab countries, made statements to the press that: "Arabs in Jerusalem had the best conditions anywhere in the Arab world."[84]

The press portrays Israel as oppressive, repressive and brutal. But even during the *intifada* and the continued murder of Jews in their own country, the Israelis showed many acts of compassion towards the Arab people. For example: Facing the threat of missiles containing poison gas from Saddam Hussein of Iraq in 1991, Israel distributed gas masks to the Arab people who were urging Iraq to attack and "burn up Israel." Many who had actually murdered or attacked Israelis received gas masks before large numbers of Jews did! After the Gulf War, Israel freely allowed 50,000 Palestinians deported from Kuwait to settle in Israel, in the areas of Judea and Samaria.[85] And Israel also opened her doors to Moslem refugees from the war in Croatia.[86]

The Israeli-Arab leadership had themselves refused to take in orphans from the war-ravaged country, and they also made a decision "not to help with the absorption of the refugees."[87] The government of Israel opened the doors, and the Jews of Israel opened their hearts. The Bezek telephone company installed telephones for the refugees to call their relatives overseas, gave them all telecards, and also cash gifts to every family and individual. Other Israeli companies donated televisions, chocolates, baby bottles and other items.[88] Some of the would-be-refugees canceled their flight plans at the last minute when they heard that the Arabs refused to welcome them, but those that came spoke to their relatives about the "warm welcome" they had received in Israel.[89] Such actions are not those of a cruel and heartless oppressor.

Another important fact the foreign press keeps from its audience is that the large majority of Israel's current 800,000 Arab citizens prefer Israeli rule to that of fellow Arabs. Even in the midst of the *intifada* madness, threatened both by PLO death squads and radical Moslem fundamentalists, over half of them still voted for Jewish parties rather than for their own Arab parties.[90]

The Palestinian refugee problem is a weapon of human suffering used by the Arabs against Israel. The warhead of this missile has been primed by an unprincipled, anti-Semitic news media that has played upon the heartstrings of the Western people in order to bring pressure upon the Jewish state. The information disseminated by the news media—the real "spokesman" of the world—concerning the refugees is as false as the lies told about the history of Palestine.

7
Palestine

There has been an aggressive attempt to usurp the entire history of the ancient Jewish nation. This usurping—the rewriting of history—has been undertaken by a collaboration of Arabs, the news media and the academe. This is a three-tiered deceitful manipulation of facts sponsored by a collusion between powerful, motivating forces—religion and hate, whose respective names are Islam and anti-Semitism.

Thucydides, the eminent Greek historian of the 5th century B.C., wrote in his *History of the Peloponnesian War*: "Most people will not take pains to get at the truth of things, and are much more inclined to accept the first story they hear." The observation of Thucydides is as true today as it was 2,500 years ago. I cannot repeat often enough that those who control the people's information will, ultimately, control their judgments, opinions and actions. And this has proven so true in Israel's case.

Islamic hatred of the Jews motivates the Arabs to rewrite the history of the Middle East. Anti-Semitism motivates the news media to delegitimatize the Jewish presence in the Middle East by publishing falsified facts and even outright lies. And inherent anti-Semitism also motivates the Western academe to rewrite the historical records and falsify scholastic textbooks.

Those responsible for the collection, editing and dissemination of news are intelligent people, just as those who write scholastic articles are. The distorting and manipulating of facts is deliberate. Their aim is to rewrite the history of the Middle East.

A news media favorite for falsifying facts is known as "turnspeak." Turnspeak is defined as "the cynical inverting or distorting of facts, which for example, makes the victim appear as the culprit."[1] And, regarding the academe: "All historians select from that 'pile of detritus of past facts' what suits their object, obscuring the remainder."[2] Thus, for example, "A history of World War II could be written focusing on the suffering of Germans from Allied bombings and invasions – all based on facts. All one need do is distort proportions."[3] What is given here as an example has today become reality—Jewish victims have become Jewish culprits, and their wars of defense have become Jewish wars of aggression.

A Brief History of Israel According to the Bible and Other Unimpeachable Sources

Being some 4,000 years old, the Jewish nation is one of the most ancient peoples in history. Abraham, the father of the Jewish people, was born around the year 2011 B.C. He was a God-fearing man, and God made an eternal covenant with Abraham to give him and his descendants all the land of Canaan for posterity. And according to the manner of ratifying covenants in those days, the LORD God said to Abraham, while he was yet called Abram:

> "'Bring Me a three-year-old heifer, a three-year-old female goat, a three-year-old ram, a turtle-dove, and a young pigeon.' Then he brought all these to Him and cut them in two, down the middle, and placed each piece opposite the other; but he did not cut the birds in two...And it came to pass, when the sun went down and it was dark, that behold, there appeared a smoking oven and a burning torch that passed between those pieces. On the same day the LORD made a covenant with Abram, saying: 'To your descendants I have given this land, from the river of Egypt to the great river, the River Euphrates—the Kenites, the Kenezzites, and the Kadmonites, the Hittites, the Perizzites, and the Rephaim, the Amorites, the Canaanites, the Girgashites, and the Jebusites'" (Genesis 15:9,10,17–21).

The LORD God manifested Himself in the form of smoke and fire, much like He did at the burning bush (Exodus 3:2), and in the pillars of cloud and fire (Exodus 13:21). He then passed between the pieces of the cut animals and sealed the promise made to Abraham. The carcasses were not consumed because it was not a sacrifice offered, but a covenant made. The two parts of the animals represented the two parties to the covenant. The parties would walk down the aisle flanked by the pieces of the slaughtered animals which signified the following oath: "May it be so done to me if I do not keep my oath and pledge."[4] Abraham did not walk between the pieces because he did not make a covenant with God—God was ratifying His covenant made with Abraham.

When Abraham was 100 years old (Genesis 21:5)—approximately 25 years after the sealing of the covenant—Abraham's wife Sarah gave birth to a son named Isaac. Isaac was 60 years old when his wife, Rebekah, gave birth to Jacob (Genesis 25:26). Jacob's name was later changed to Israel (Genesis 35:10), and the descendants of his 12 sons were called Israelites before emerging finally as the nation of Israel.

In the late 19th century B.C., Israel and his family, which now numbered 70 members, (Genesis 46:27) went down into Egypt and sojourned there for 430 years (Exodus 12:40). The Israelites increased mightily in numbers, and the Egyptians grew fearful of their strength. In time a cruel Pharaoh subjected them to severe bondage and issued a decree that, henceforth, all new-born male Hebrew babies were to be thrown into the Nile and drowned (Exodus 1:22).

A baby boy was hidden by his mother for three months, and when it was no longer possible to conceal him in the house, she made a little waterproof ark and hid him in some bulrushes growing on the banks of the Nile (Exodus 2:3). Pharaoh's daughter came to the river to bathe one day, and because of the baby's cries, the ark was discovered. Having compassion on the infant, Pharaoh's daughter named him Moses, which means "drawn out from the water," and raised him in the Egyptian court.

At the age of 40 years (Acts 2:23), Moses, knowing that he was himself an Israelite, became enraged upon seeing an Egyptian beating one of his Israelite brethren. He then killed the Egyptian and buried the body in the sand, but his act became known to Pharaoh and he had to flee Egypt. At age 80, after tending sheep in the desert for 40 years (Acts 7:30), Moses was confronted by God in a burning bush (Exodus 3:2–12). God instructed Moses to return to Egypt where He would use him to deliver the Israelites from Egyptian bondage and bring them into the land promised to Abraham over 600 years earlier. Moses obeyed.

Ten times Pharaoh refused Moses' request to let the Israelites emigrate from Egypt, and in demonstrations of His power, God systematically brought upon the Egyptians ten terrible disasters that physically destroyed the nation. The catastrophes were retributive action for the afflicting of His chosen people, and they were promised by God at the time He made the covenant with Abraham (Genesis 15:13,14). After the 10th catastrophe, Moses led the children of Israel out of Egypt toward the Promised Land.

Twelve Israelite spies were sent into the Promised Land to gather intelligence prior to the upcoming conquest. Some of the inhabitants of the land were giants, and ten of the spies brought back a negative report which discouraged the entire camp of upwards of 2.4 million souls.[5] Disobedience and grumbling on the part of the Israelites kept them out of the Promised Land. They wandered in the wilderness for another 40 years—until the whole generation that grumbled had passed away. And disobedience and anger on Moses' part also caused him to die in the desert without entering the Promised Land.

Joshua, one of the two spies who brought back a positive report from Canaan, led the Israelites across the Jordan River and into the Promised Land early in the 15th century B.C. The conquest of Canaan was all but completed within five years. The Israelites became the nation of Israel, and the land of Canaan became the land of Israel.

The land promised by God to Abraham is referred to as the land of Israel 29 times in the Old Testament beginning in 1 Samuel 13:9, which was written in the 10th century B.C., and twice in the New Testament (Matthew 2:20,21), which was written in the first century A.D. King David, Israel's most famous king, made Jerusalem his capital in the 11th century B.C., and Jerusalem was also the city where the God of Israel placed His name forever (2 Kings 21:7; 2 Chronicles 33:7).

The Jews (as the Israelites were wont to become universally known) became disobedient and faithless again, which prompted God to bring the Assyrians and, later, the Babylonians against them as judgments. Israel succumbed to their armies, and the great majority of Israelites were either killed or taken captive to Assyria and Babylon. The city of Jerusalem and the majestic temple that it contained were both destroyed. God, however, had decreed a limited captivity of only 70 years (Jeremiah 25:11) for the inhabitants of Judah and Jerusalem, and true to His word, He brought the captives back at the end of the stipulated term. They then rebuilt their nation and the temple.

Apparently, nations do not learn from the lessons of history, because given time the Jewish nation committed further abominations, became no less disobedient than before, and was equally as faithless. God then brought the might of the Roman empire against the land. The Romans subjugated it, making it a province of the Roman empire in 6 A.D.

A Jewish rebellion against Roman rule began in 66 A.D. which culminated in the second razing of Jerusalem in 70 A.D. The magnificent, new temple that had taken Herod the Great 46 years to build (John 2:20) was burnt, and not a single stone was left standing upon another, because the Romans tore them apart to get at the gold that had melted and ran down between the cracks.

The rebellion had been nationwide, but from the siege of Jerusalem alone, 1,100,000[6] Jews died either by starvation or by the sword, and 97,000[7] were carried away captive. In 130 A.D. the Romans renamed Jerusalem *Ælia Capitolina,* after the emperor Hadrian (*Ælias Hadrianus*) and the god *Jupiter Capitolinus,*[8] and also built a temple to Jupiter on the site of the Jewish temple.

This desecration of their most holy place stirred the large Jewish population to once again take up arms. The Roman Army took three and a half years to quell this revolt, and there was great loss of life on both sides. At the end of the war in 135 A.D., Rome entirely banished Jews from Jerusalem and its environs, ending its more than 1,100 years of uninterrupted sovereignty as Israel's capital.

The Romans kept *Ælia Capitolina* as their name for Jerusalem, and renamed the Promised Land *"Syria Palæstina."* The indomitable Jews had brought no small humiliation to the might of the Roman Army over the years, and the renaming of the land was an overt effort to eradicate the Jewish connection.

Dozens of small Jewish communities continued to exist throughout the land, and a continual physical Jewish presence remained until it burgeoned into the Israel that exists today. The

Jews are "indigenous people on the land they never left."[9] They survived "for millennia"[10]—against every obstacle, every discouragement—the only people who have continuously inhabited the land for 3,000 years.[11] And this has been no mean feat considering the number of conquering hordes that have ravished the degraded country since Roman times.

After the Moslem conquest of *Palæstina* in the 7th century A.D., the name *Ælia Capitolina* gradually faded from use. The Arabs called the city *Al Quds*, and Christians and Jews reverted back to Jerusalem. And in due process of time *Palæstina*, the Latin form of Philistia—the land of the ancient Philistines—was Anglicized into Palestine, the name that is daily placed before our eyes and in our ears by the news media.

The Roman slaughters in the two rebellions had taken a high toll of Jewish lives—in excess of 2.5 million in the first and a further 500,000 in the second.[12] And another 100,000 were taken to Rome to be made sport of by gladiators. Jewish life in the land, although active, was minimal. And those that remained, together with those that gradually returned after having fled the might of Rome, were brutally and systematically persecuted and murdered—first by the Christians for the supposed "killing of God," and then by the Moslems because Mohammed had made them out to be the enemies of Allah.

The Christian persecution turned into Moslem persecution after the 7th century Islamic conquest. The Moslem victory raised the ire of Christendom which sparked the Crusades that brought about the defeat of the Moslems and another holocaust of the Jews. The Crusader conquest was subsequently overthrown by the Islamic armies under Saladin, and the Jews suffered yet again. The land had no rest—a succession of conquering armies: Moslem, Christian, Mongol, Turkish, etc. kept the blood flowing, and each new master brought a different brutality to the Jew living there.

Many Jews started life afresh in other lands where they fled to escape the wrath of the Romans. These Jews, however, fared no better than their kinfolk who had remained in the land. Unrelenting persecution haunted them in practically every country they entered. Their hopes of finding refuge from the storm were dashed upon the rocks of Jew-hatred. The waves of anti-Semitism reached

Palestine

their crest in the Nazi Holocaust during World War II, which took the lives of some six million Jewish people—one third of all world Jewry.

Jews fleeing from the Nazis were even stopped from entering Palestine by the British, who after they had captured it from the Turks during World War I, had been given a mandate by the allies to govern the country. The British were to have set up a Jewish national home in the whole of Palestine in accordance with the Balfour Declaration of 1917. But the British turned justice on its head by reneging on their obligations and promises. With one stroke of a pen in 1922, they cut off a whopping 77 percent of the entire area and gave it to King Abdullah who formed the Kingdom of Transjordan (now Jordan), from which the Jews were and still are barred from settlement. The British not only gave away more than three-quarters of the promised Jewish homeland, but proceeded to restrict Jewish immigration into the balance of Palestine. Later, they even denied them entry to the ancient land in their hour of greatest need. British hostility against the Jews became so intense that no effort was spared in their attempts to prevent the Jews from ever establishing the National Home in Palestine.

In 1947, the United Nations voted to partition between the Jews and the Arabs the 23 percent that remained of the once vast tract of land that comprised Palestine. Today, the world believes this remaining 23 percent to actually be the entire 100 percent of Palestine, but in fact, it is less than one-quarter of the whole—more than three-quarters was cut off and made into a sovereign Palestinian Arab state in 1922.

The Jews, however, were willing to settle for what had been allotted to them in the partition plan—less than half of the remaining 23 percent. Their desire was to again establish a sovereign Jewish state where Jews would be free from anti-Semitism. But the Arabs refused to accept the result of the United Nations partition vote. They demanded instead to have the whole of the remaining area of Palestine—to establish yet another Arab state. Meanwhile, Britain was on the side of the Arabs—training and arming them and preventing the Jews from returning to their land. It ruled with an iron-fist and gallows to prevent the very thing it had been commissioned to effect.

Thousands of Jews, however, escaped the British nets and slipped into Palestine. A violent guerrilla war broke out between the British forces and the somewhat motley band of Palestinian Jews. And, as in the days of yesteryear, the little band of Jews fought tenaciously—humiliating the British imperial lion—forcing it to give up its mandate and withdraw from Palestine to lick its wounds.

On May 14, 1948, one day before the final termination of the British mandate and the withdrawal of the last troops, the Palestinian Jews officially declared that their recreated homeland was to be called the State of Israel. The following day, the last day of the British presence, seven Arab armies launched an all-out war to annihilate the new state. The end result of that aggressive action became for the Arab world, "the greatest shame in modern Arab history"—Israel won the war. And they won the next war. And the next. And the next.

Hasbara

Unable to defeat Israel militarily on physical battlefields, new strategies became necessary for the Arabs. A new battlefield was chosen, a new defense, a new weapon, and new terms. In Hebrew its called *hasbara*—propaganda. And the Arabs had oil—petrodollars—with which to buy both the nations' leaders and the world's major news medias.

There was a great deal of support for the courageous Jews in 1948. The impossible odds of seven trained, fully equipped Arab armies against 18,000 Jews[13]—of whom thousands did not even have a gun[14]—found much of the world praying for Jewish success and cheering them on to victory. And facing annihilation from the Arab world again in 1967, Israel's incredible, lightening victory left the world gasping and military academies entering new battle tactics into their journals of warfare. Then came Arab *hasbara*. Israel entered the new arena of warfare and even opened an official Department of *Hasbara*, but the Israelis were never successful on the new battlefield. Oil and anti-Semitism defeated them again and again.

Palestine 133

Israel was savagely attacked again in October 1973 on *Yom Kippur* (The Day of Atonement), the holiest and most solemn day of the Jewish calendar. On this day the Jewish nation fasts and conducts five-hour synagogue services. Television and radio stations are off the air, newspapers are not printed, buses and cars do not run, and if a telephone rings, most people would not answer it. On this day the Arab armies invaded Israel, and many hundreds of Israelis were dead, dying or injured before the country even knew itself to be at war.

It took Israel three days to fully mobilize its fighting forces, and 300,000 Israelis fought against more than 1.2 million Arabs.[15] Some Israeli units fought to the last man, but in ten days Israel had driven the Arabs out. Israeli tanks were only short distances from both Cairo and Damascus when it was forced by non-combatant nations to stop the war. The *Yom Kippur* War took the greatest toll of Israeli lives of all of the Arab-Israeli wars—there was terrible mourning throughout Israel. But at the war's end, 61 nations broke diplomatic relations with Israel![16] Arab oil and *hasbara* had "proven" to the world that the victim was in fact the aggressor.

Israel finally closed the Department of *Hasbara* in 1993 after having lost every round of every battle in the propaganda war. The Arabs' vast, abundantly funded propaganda machine has convinced most of the world's literate masses that the Jews poured into Palestine during the first half of this century and displaced millions of indigenous Arabs, who had been living there for thousands of years. And they have also convinced them that Israel is a wanton, brutal, heartless aggressor that has an insatiable lust for Arab lands. It is perhaps the greatest deception in the history of mankind.

Bogus Claims

Even the most outrageous lie will be believed if repeated often enough. Consider the Nazi propaganda against the Jews that began in the 1930s and culminated in the Holocaust. Repetition of outrageous lies was so successful that extermination camps were built throughout Europe to facilitate the eradication of Europe's Jewish population. With the exception of Sundays, when gas chamber operators would attend church services (often with their families),[17] the death camps operated around the clock at maximum capacity. The camps were responsible for the great majority of the six million Jews murdered in Europe. One of the saddest moments in the history of modern Israel was when the remains of 200,000 Austrian Jews were brought to Israel for burial in June 1949. For them the State of Israel had risen too late, and Hitler's gas chambers had claimed their own. The ashes of 200,000 Jews was preserved in 30 jars and contained in one large glass casket. And William Hull, who watched the funeral cortege pass through Jerusalem's streets, wrote:

> "These ashes, the cakes of soap which Germans had made from Jewish bodies, the lamp shades and coats made from skin stripped from Jewish bodies, these were all that remained...."[18]

The Jewish people personally experienced the bestial fruit of German hatred which sprang solely from the repetition of outrageous lies. Paul Josef Goebbels, the Nazi propaganda minister, rightly argued that "a lie spreads in proportion to its size."[19] Today the Arabs with the help of the news media and the academe are emulating the Nazis and working toward a similar goal—the eradication of the Jewish population in the Middle East.

Some weeks ago, I was handed a clipping from an unidentified English language publication which contained a short article entitled "Palestinians," written by an Israeli tour guide. The article says:

> "Every day I hear about Palestinians, and as it was not clear to me who they are, I decided to try and discover at least one of them. In East Jerusalem I met a man who identified himself as a Palestinian. I asked him if he spoke Palestinian. He answered that he spoke Arabic. Then I asked him if he writes with Palestinian letters. 'No, I write with Arabic letters and numerals.' I continued questioning him, and he answered that he did not know of any Palestinian king, president or prime minister. Finally I asked him if his

religion was Palestinian, and he replied that he was a Moslem.

"I gave up, and now I am convinced that there is not and never has been a 'Palestinian' people. (There were Philistines until 300 B.C., but that is another matter.) Nevertheless, there are those that want to create a 'Palestinian' people in order to eradicate the people of Israel from the land of Israel."

Millions of Palestinians now claim their ancestry goes back thousands of years—to the Philistines and beyond, even to the Canaanites and Jebusites. And yet the Palestinian people have no history, artifacts, language or culture. Claims of an ancient Palestinian history is another Arab myth—until 1948 the only Palestinians in existence were Jews! Until the 20th century, "the name *Palestine* referred exclusively to the ancient land of the Jews."[20]

During Britain's mandatory period, the Jews of Palestine were always carefully referred to as Palestinian Jews by the British. This was done in order not to offend the Arabs. The Arabs, who came mainly from Syria, Egypt and what is now known as Jordan, scorned the name Palestinian and were simply referred to as Arabs. After the recreation of a sovereign Jewish state in 1948, the "Palestinian Jews" became "Israeli Jews," and the name "Palestinian" became almost defunct. The current Arab pretension of possessing a Palestinian nationality is the Arabs' way of laying claim to the land.

Arab defeat on the military battlefields caused a quantum shift in Arab strategy and *hasbara*—propaganda entered the arena. A definite point of attack needed to be established if the Arabs were to successfully deliver a mortal thrust to the soft underbelly of the new Jewish state. An Arab activist, Musa Alami, proposed that the Arab people were "in great need of a 'myth' to fill their consciousness and imaginiation."[21] According to Alami, an "indoctrination of the 'myth' of Palestinian nationality would create 'identity' and 'self-respect.'"[22] As no such Palestinian history existed, the Arabs simply sat down and created one—a mythical history of a Palestinian Arab nation with roots that thread their way through the desert sands for thousands of years.

A strongly defined Palestinian identity did not emerge until after 1968—two decades after the myth was prescribed by Alami. It took 20 years of propaganda to establish a myth that is now deeply embedded into the hearts and minds of both the Arab and non-Arab worlds. It is now a self-perpetuating myth. By successfully influencing some of the world's most prestigious reference books to promote a bogus Middle East history, the Arabs have already affected our academic world for generations to come. The distinguished historian and Arabist, Bernard Lewis of Princeton University, says: "The mythopoeic faculty is the ability to create myths, to believe in them, and to make others believe."[23] Arabs have scored incredible successes in each of these three areas. But, if you remember, Moslem *jihad* does not limit war to the use of swords, it also means to fight with "speech" and with the "pen."

In 1986 Lewis wrote: "The rewriting of the past is usually undertaken to achieve specific political aims."[24] The political aim of the Arabs is to bypass the Biblical Israelites and claim kinship with the Canaanites, the pre-Israelite inhabitants of the land. Then it becomes possible to assert an historical claim antedating the Biblical promise and the subsequent possession of the land by the Jews. The Moslems intend to disconnect the Jewish people from their history in their homeland and have them appear as recent interlopers, thus providing the rationale for their removal or annihilation.

The mythical claim of Palestinian identity is simply another tactical maneuver in the Islamic war waged against Israel to effect her destruction. This has been admitted by a member of the executive council of the PLO and late head of its Military Department:

> "Yes, **the existence of a separate Palestinian identity serves only tactical purposes.** The founding of a Palestinian state is a new tool in the continuing battle against Israel."[25]

> "In fact, **there is no Palestinian people...Only for political reasons do we speak of a Palestinian identity.**"[26]

Prof. Philip K. Hitti, the leading Arab historian, decried the use of the word Palestine even in maps. He said that it was associated "in the mind of the average American—and perhaps the Englishman, too—with the Jews."[27] And testifying under oath Hitti stated unequivocally: "Sir, **there is no such thing as Palestine in Arab history; absolutely not.**"[28] But Arabs persevere in stating their false claims, the news media keeps on airing them, and the public continues to believe them. It has been proven time and again that when words are used to create false realities, people begin to live with these false realities.

One of the strongly propagated lies of Yasser Arafat and other Arabs is that today's Palestinian Arabs are the descendants of the ancient Philistines, and that the Philistines were Arabs no less. Anwar Sadat, the former president of Egypt, said:

> "The assassination of Arab brethren like Goliath, by Jewish sheep-herders like David, is the sort of shameful ignomy that we must yet set aright in the domain of the occupied Palestinian homeland."[29]

It is not surprising that the Arabs believe such nonsense, but it is utterly incredible that an educated world would swallow it. *Webster's Unabridged Dictionary* defines "Philistine" as: "a member of **non-Semitic people** who lived in southwestern Palestine from c. 1200 B.C. on."[30] If there is one thing that Arabs are very proud of it is being Arab, but Arabs are Semites—Philistines were non-Semites!

That Philistines were non-Semitic (non-Arab, non-Jewish races) people is also borne out by the *Encyclopædia Britannica*:

> "Philistines, a people **of Aegean origin** who settled on the southern coast of Palestine in the 12th century BC shortly before the arrival of the Israelites...they occupied the coastal plain of Palestine."[31]

And also by the *Random House Encyclopedia*:

> "Philistines, a **non-Semitic people** who probably came to Philistia from Crete in about the 12th century BC."[32]

Another part of the lie of Palestinian ancestry is that they are also the descendants of the Jebusites, the original occupants of Jerusalem when it was called Jebus (Judges 19:10) during the Canaanite period. Western scholars are in agreement that the Canaanites and Jebusites are Hamitic peoples who predate Arab existence by at least five centuries! The Egyptian Copts are also an Hamitic people. The Copts are the original Egyptians and their numbers today are around two million (the name Copt is derived from the Arabic *qubt*, a corruption of the Greek *Aigyptikos*, meaning Egyptian).[33] Copts have distinctly different features and skin coloring from those of Egyptian Arabs. The Copts also have their own language, but the Moslems banned the use of the Coptic language in 997,[34] forcing the Copts to use Arabic as the Egyptian vernacular. Another surviving Hamitic people is the black skinned Ethiopians. Palestinian Arabs are Arabs in every sense of the word, both physically and culturally—they bear little resemblance to Hamitic peoples.

The Palestinian Arabs boast of thousands of years of rich Arab history, and Yasser Arafat maintains that: "Our nation is the Arab nation, extending from the Atlantic to the Red Sea and beyond."[35] But at the same time, they declare themselves not to be Arabs by claiming descent from a non-Semitic Aegean Sea People that disappeared from history during the 2nd and 3rd centuries B.C., and also from another race with whom the Arabs had no connection nor share any physical characteristics. With one breath the "Palestinians" are claiming to be Arabs, and with the next, they refute it. Perhaps someone would like to point this out to Arafat? (If that person is tired of living, that is).

We have heard from Arab lips that there never was an Arab Palestinian state nor an Arab Palestinian identity, and that these claims are made only for political and tactical purposes. We have also seen that Palestinian claims of descent from ancient peoples is as bogus as previous claims, and made for the same reasons. And we earlier saw that the number of Jewish refugees fleeing from Arab lands were twice that of Arab refugees fleeing from Palestine, and that they left many times more property and wealth behind than did the Arabs. We saw, too, that the Arab refugee figures were, and still are, grossly exaggerated, and that these

Palestine

inflated figures are used as yet another weapon in the Moslem war against Israel. There are many more similar bogus claims and distortions of history used by the Arabs to delegitimatize Israel's right to her land, but we can only give space to a few.

The Arabs now living in scattered portions of the remaining 23 percent of original Palestine are demanding an "independent Palestinian state." They are wanting to create yet another sovereign Arab state out of half of the less than one-quarter left of Palestine. All of Palestine had been promised to the Jews to be made back into a Jewish national homeland. But Britain, wanting to protect its oil supply in Mosul, Kirkuk and other parts of the Moslem world,[36] sliced off 77 percent of Palestine and gave it to Abdullah of Mecca who was piqued because his younger brother Feisal had been given Iraq. This 77 percent, however, was and is a Palestinian state, and the Arabs are acutely aware of this fact both then and now.

Abdullah originally wanted to call his 77 percent of Palestine the "Hashemite Kingdom of Palestine,"[37] but he gave in to British opposition and called it "Transjordan." It was later renamed to the official name it still carries—the "Hashemite Kingdom of Jordan," but more commonly known as Jordan. In 1981 King Hussein (Abdullah's grandson and current ruler of Jordan) stated in an interview with an Arab newspaper: **"The truth is that Jordan is Palestine and Palestine is Jordan."**[38] And even later, in 1984, in another interview with an Arab newspaper, he said: **"Jordan is Palestine...Jordan in itself is Palestine."**[39] Crown Prince Hassan, heir to Jordan's throne, also stated the same thing: **"Palestine is Jordan and Jordan is Palestine. There is one people and one land, with one history and one destiny."**[40] And the PLO leadership declare it also:

Yasser Arafat: "What you call Jordan is actually Palestine."[41]
Chafiq el Hout: "Jordan is an integral part of Palestine."[42]
Abu Iyad: "We are one and the same people."[43]

Never were truer words spoken. The country of Jordan comprises most of the land of Palestine. The great majority of

Jordan's population is Palestinian, the Jordanian army is comprised of a majority of Palestinians, and most of the Arabs living in the Israeli administered territories hold Jordanian passports. And the 1970 Jordanian-PLO war was considered a civil war and recorded as such.

The evidence is overwhelming. An independent Palestinian-Arab state already exists in the Middle East in the form of Jordan—nearly 80 percent of the whole of Palestine. So why do politicians and the news media keep beating on Israel to withdraw to indefensible boundaries? Why do they not turn the screws and apply some pressure to Jordan who backed Saddam Hussein in the Gulf War? Because the Arabs hold more than 50 percent of the world's known oil reserves, and they have billions of dollars to spend with countries who toe the Arab line—that is why.

The PLO leadership, together with many other Arab leaders, maintain that the Jews were newcomers to Palestine who displaced "millions" of Palestinian Arabs by forcing them from the land they had farmed for thousands of years. Yasser Arafat told the world:

> "Arab people were engaged in farming and building, spreading culture throughout the land for thousands of years, setting an example in the practice of freedom of worship, acting as faithful guardians of the holy places of all nations."[44]

Four bald-faced lies in a single sentence! The final statement that Arabs were "faithful guardians of the holy places of all nations" would be laughable if it were not so tragic. Arabs did guard the holy sites of Moslem nations, but treated Jewish and Christian holy sites with utter contempt—those that they did not make into mosques. The Arabs even denied that the last remains of the western wall of the Jewish temple, the most holiest of all Jewish places, was part of the temple[45] and refused to allow the Jews to pray there.[46] And after the 1948 war when the Old City of Jerusalem was entirely in Arab hands, they completely destroyed 58[47] Jewish synagogues—including the magnificent Hurva synagogue—by blowing them up. All Jewish cemeteries were destroyed, and the tombstones were used to cobble streets or for building urinals for Jordanian soldiers.[48]

The Arabs were truly "an example in the practice of freedom of worship" in Palestine, too. The Arabs, who also claim to have always "treated the Jews kindly and graciously,"[49] robbed, raped and murdered the Jews who had "less value than a dog."[50] Christians as well as Jews were *dhimmi*—subjugated inferiors—in Palestine, and a pilgrim to the land wrote: "Christians and Jews go about in Jerusalem in clothes considered fit only for wandering beggars."[51]

The Arab conquest took place in the 7th century, and since that time, they claim to have been busy "spreading culture throughout the land for thousands of years." A single quotation from Philip Hitti, the leading Arab historian, will suffice: "...the invaders from the desert brought with them no tradition of learning, no heritage of culture, to the lands they conquered."[52]

The Arab claim of having lived and farmed in Palestine for thousands of years is the foundation upon which they have based their mythical Palestinian identity. And it has been one of the most potent weapons used against Israel during the Arabs' propaganda war. Even those who believe in the Bible, and those who are conversant with Israel's ancient history, cannot help but feel sorry for a people deprived of their lands after so long a time. But the claim is not only as false as other Arab pretensions, it is also utterly impossible by reason of the fact that Arabs never came into the area until the 7th century Moslem conquest. Subtracting 638 (the year of the Islamic victory over the Byzantine Christians) from 1948 (the year the Arabs launched their first attack against the Jews) does not result in "thousands of years," but 1,310 years. Had the Arabs remained in possession of the land from the time of the Moslem conquest, they would now have a solid, legitimate claim to the land. The Arabs, however, did not remain in control for very long. A succession of conquerors came—Christian, Moslem and Mongol—and the land saw such massacres that it was said, "if blood were indelible, Old Jerusalem would be red, all red."[53] Christian Crusaders defeated the Arab Moslems, and they in turn were defeated by Kurdish Moslems. Arabs would have everyone believe that the great Moslem warrior, Saladin, was an Arab, but in fact he was a Kurd,[54] and Kurds are not Arabs, neither is their language Arabic.[55] After an interval of time, the Kurds were attacked by more Crusaders. But the Crusaders were unable to defeat the Moslems, and Jerusalem ended up being divided between the Christian and Moslem forces.

The 13th century saw the Mongol conquest of Palestine, and within the space of 50 years, the Mongols were themselves conquered by Moslem Mamluks. Like the Kurds before them, the Mamluks destroyed many Palestinian towns out of fear that other Crusaders might use them in a campaign against the Moslems. Early in the 16th century, Moslem Turks conquered the land, and they remained in control until Palestine was captured by the British during World War I.

Far from Palestine being an Arab land for "thousands of years," the Arabs actually had an extremely short tenure in the land. Western historians are agreed that the Arab empire "lasted **less than a century**."[56] David George Hogarth, described by eminent Arab writers as "one of the greatest authorities of his time on Arabian history,"[57] wrote that sovereign Arab rule lasted "for **much less than a century**."[58] And a Moslem leader even attested in 1919 that: "The only Arab domination since the Conquest in 635 A.D. **hardly lasted, as such, 22 years**."[59]

The Arabs that came with the 7th century Islamic invasion were, according to Joan Peters, "small in number"[60] and were "wiped out by disease."[61] Another reliable source confirms that Arab numbers "were small" and were "decimated by epidemics within two years after the capture of Jerusalem."[62] Thus the voice of history indicates that the actual Arab conquerors were wiped out by disease by mid-640 A.D. Other Moslems were brought in to replenish the decimated Arab ranks, but they, too, suffered the same fate.

Cruel and harsh was the climate of Palestine—what disease did not claim, other catastrophes did. The population was continually ravished by the "endemic massacres, disease, famine and wars."[63] The constant decline of the population caused one Moslem ruler to bring in "Turks and Negroes. Another had Berbers, Slavs, Greeks and Dailamites.

The Kurdish conqueror, Saladin, introduced more Turks, and

some Kurds."[64] The Arabs and their recruits, the Kurds and their recruits, the Turks and others with theirs, made Palestine a melting pot of ethnological chaos. The Arabs are claiming as "pure Arab stock" such imports as "Balkans, Greeks, Syrians, Latins, Egyptians, Turks, Armenians, Italians, Persians, Kurds, Germans, Afghans, Circassians, Bosnians, Sudanese, Samaritans, Algerians, Motawila and Tartars."[65] Another source, John of Wurzburg, adds the following to the above list: Hungarians, Scots, Navarese, Bretons, English, Franks, Ruthenians, Bohemians, Bulgarians, Georgians, Armenians, Indians, Norsemen, Danes, Frisians, Russians and Nubians.[66] And the *Encyclopædia Britannica 1911 edition* (before the British encouraged a more chauvinist Arab history) records that early in the 20th century the divergence of nationalities in Palestine brought an equally diverse list of tongues—"no less than fifty languages."[67] The claim that pure Arab peoples have inhabited Palestine for "thousands of years," is yet another myth—"a romanticized notion discredited by serious scholars."[68]

The Arabization of Jesus

In chapter 2 it was mentioned that Hanan Ashrawi, the spokeswoman for the PLO negotiating team and the "darling of the news media," sidestepped a legitimate question from a Christian journalist and went on to speak about her direct descent from the first Christians in the world—Palestinians. We have spoken much about Palestinian Moslem-Arabs, but I need to speak a little here about Palestinian Christian-Arabs.

When we speak of Palestinian Christian-Arabs, we are using general terms. We are referring to those non-Moslem Arabs who have a Christian background, but who might never have set foot inside a church nor opened a Bible in their lives. With these people we lump together those Arabs who do attend church and Bible studies regularly, and who might or might not have had a Biblical born-again Christian experience. There are a number of the latter group personally known to me, most of whom I would describe as very fine people. But of the Palestinian Christian-Arabs that I **know well**, there is not even one that I could call truthful.

My personal experience has been that they have all "lied

through their teeth" when the occasion necessitated. And from personal experience, and also from the numerous statements I have read, the great majority of Palestinian Christian-Arabs are very pro-PLO. It might seem totally ludicrous to my readers, but a prominent evangelical Palestinian Christian-Arab involved in reconciliation work between Christian-Arabs and believing Jews, privately said to my wife and me: "Terror is the only answer to Israel—we will beat you in the end." The reader, therefore, should treat as suspect any statement made by Palestinian Christian-Arabs, until it has been thoroughly verified.

The question asked of Hanan Ashrawi by the Christian journalist at a Madrid press conference was:

"How can you expect Israel to give up Judea and Samaria after they have served as launching pads for attacks against Israel at least twice."[69]

Unable to answer the question without incriminating both herself and the PLO of which she is the spokesman, Ashrawi cleverly counter-attacked—she plucked the emotional heartstrings of the world's press by claiming that she was a Palestinian Christian descended from the very first Christians in the world. It had nothing at all to do with the question, but the correspondents of the anti-Semitic British press wildly applauded her answer. And a delighted American syndicated columnist, Mary McGrory, reported Ashrawi's rejoinder as: "It was pretty much game, set and match."[70]

Appalling ignorance! **All the first Christians were Jews**—Arabs (and Ashrawi **is** an Arab) did not come into the land until the 7th century—her claim is just another huge Palestinian hoax. Ashrawi, who looks to television viewers more like a headmistress of a British finishing school, is a PLO proxy, and her father was one of the founders of the PLO! She supports "Saddam Hussein, terrorist attacks on Jewish civilians, and death-squad executions of Palestinian Arabs."[71] Moshe Arens, a former Israeli Minister of Defense, designated Ashrawi as "the authority who sanctions murderous raids."[72]

Ashrawi also said to the Christian journalist: "There is no Judea and Samaria—Jesus was born in **my** country."[73] Most readers are probably aware that for part of Israel's ancient history the land was divided into two kingdoms—the larger, northern kingdom of Israel, and the smaller, southern kingdom of Judah. The boundaries between the two kingdoms ran almost straight across from the Great Sea (Mediterranean) to the top center of the Salt Sea (Dead Sea), and then southwards down through the middle of the Dead Sea. Judah contained Jerusalem, and Israel contained Samaria. In Roman times, the land was determined by three main geographical areas, Galilee, Judea and Samaria—Judea being the Latin form of Judah. The Romans referred to the whole colony as Judea until they renamed it *Syria–Palæstina* in 135 A.D.

Ashrawi says that "Jesus was born in **my** country"—**Palestine**. The Bible tells us in the Old Testament (Micah 5:2), and also in the New Testament (Matthew 2:6—where it refers to Micah's prophecy), that Jesus was to be born in Bethlehem, and that Bethlehem is in the land of Judah. The New Testament, which was written while the Jews were under Roman occupation, mentions Judea 45 times and Samaria 12 times. And, sure enough, it records that *"Jesus was born in **Bethlehem of Judea**"* (Matthew 2:1). And speaking of Jesus in John's gospel (4:3-4), the Bible says: *"He left **Judea** and departed again to Galilee. But He needed to go through **Samaria**."* Jesus even told his disciples (Acts 1:8) that they would be his witnesses in *"Jerusalem, and in all **Judea** and **Samaria**."* The same gospels that link Jesus to the Biblical areas of Judea and Samaria, also tell us that Jesus came out of Egypt *"into the **land of Israel**"* (Matthew 2:20,21). Jesus was born in **Judea**, in **Israel**—not in Palestine—it did not exist in Biblical times.

As they have done for millennia, the Jews today still refer to the hilly interior regions as Judea and Samaria. In 1948, King Abdullah of Jordan followed the Roman example and disconnected the historic Jewish connection to Judea—he simply renamed it. Just as the Romans coined the name *Palæstina*, so Abdullah coined the name "West Bank." And now the whole world happily refers to Judea by this name. Almost 3,500 years of continual Jewish presence in their ancient land is buried beneath consecutive layers of Arab propaganda and lies.

Ashrawi is not alone in remaking Jesus—"King of the Jews" (Matthew 27:37; Mark 15:26; Luke 23:38; John 19:19)—into an Arabian king and his disciples into Arabs. Most Palestinian Christian-Arabs parrot the same fairy tale. And Ashrawi's illustrious boss, Yasser Arafat, has described the Apostle Peter as "a Palestinian who defied Rome."[74] The Jews are also blamed by them for murdering Jesus, "the Palestinian prophet."[75]

The hostility toward Israel of many Palestinian Christian-Arabs is apparently matched only by their zeal for the PLO. Another Palestinian Christian-Arab, Dr. Geries Khoury, has written a book entitled: *The Intifada of Heaven and Earth: A Palestinian Theology*. Khoury propounds that the PLO orchestrated *intifada* (which has thus far claimed well over 1,200 deaths and many, many thousands of injuries and disfigurements) is divine, a God-inspired "glorious time." Khoury's divine *intifada* doctrine also states: "Any believer who tries to justify through his theology the religious right of Israel in Palestine is an infidel who denies God and Christ."[76] And, believe it or not, he even "excommunicates Christian Zionists"![77]

An Anglican priest, Elias Khoury, was convicted for transporting explosive devices in his car that killed two people and injured 11 others at the British Consulate in Jerusalem and at a city supermarket. Khoury is now on the executive council of the PLO in Amman, Jordan.[78] Archbishop Hilarion Cappucci was also caught gun-running for the PLO terrorists—large quantities of weapons and explosives were hidden in his Mercedes. Cappucci said: "Jesus Christ was the first *fedayi* [terrorist]. I am just following His example."[79]

Jesus was born a Jew in a Jewish town called Bethlehem in the Jewish homeland. But now even Christmas cards from Bethlehem have more Moslem content than Christian.[80]

Jewish Displacement of Arabs

The Arabs claim that Jews forced "millions" of Palestinian Arabs from the lands they had farmed for "thousands of years." They also claim that the Arabs have always been in the majority. We know that prior to modern times "millions" of Arabs have

Palestine 147

never lived in Palestine. And we also know that Arabs have not been around for "thousands of years," and that only Jews have ever had a continual presence in the land. This raises a question: From where did the 381,500 refugees of 1948 come if not from the land?

Before we attempt to answer the question, we should address a point concerning the Arab refugees that was not dealt with in chapter 6. The problem of refugees has been with us since time immemorial and will no doubt remain with us until the End of Days. The human traffic that is driven to escape wars, famines and other catastrophes runs into countless millions. But for the Arab refugees of the 1948 war, the United Nations redefined the general definition of refugee eligibility[81] and broadened it "to include as 'refugees' any persons who had been in 'Palestine' for only *two years* before Israel's statehood in 1948."[82] The United Nations knew that the Arabs neither had permanent nor habitual homes in Palestine and, therefore, found it necessary to amend the Arab refugee definition. In answering the question: "Where did the Arab refugees come from?" we also find the reason for the United Nations amendment of the definition for Arab refugees.

Rather than being farmed by Arabs for "thousands of years," Palestine was a wasteland. Eminent writers and pilgrims to the Holy Land throughout the ages have left many, many written testimonies of the empty, barren wilderness. And one historian after another report the same findings:

> "In the twelve and a half centuries between the Arab conquest in the seventh century and the beginnings of the Jewish return in the 1880's, Palestine was laid waste. Its ancient canal and irrigation systems were destroyed and the wondrous fertility of which the Bible spoke vanished into desert and desolation."[83]

In the late 16th century a "simple English visitor" wrote of Jerusalem:

> "Nothing there to be scene but a little of the old walls, which is yet Remayning and all the rest is grasse, mosse and Weedes much like to a piece of Rank or moist Grounde."[84]

Other parts of Palestine at that time were described thus: "We saw nothing more stony, full of thorns and desert...a vast and spacious ruin"[85] In the 18th century a French author and historian wrote of Palestine as "the ruined and desolate land...The traveler meets with nothing but houses in ruins, cisterns rendered useless, and fields abandoned."[86] And a British archaeologist wrote that Palestine was "lacking people to till its fertile soil."[87]

A German encyclopedia published early in the 19th century depicted Palestine as "desolate and roamed through by Arab bands of robbers."[88] A few years later, the French Poet Alphonse de Lamartine gave this description:

> "Outside the gates of Jerusalem, we saw, indeed, no living object, heard no living sound. We found the same void, the same silence as we should have found before the entombed gates of Pompeii or Herculaneum...a complete, eternal silence reigns in the town, the highways, in the country."[89]

The middle of the 19th century saw Palestine's British Consul write: "The country is in a considerable degree empty of inhabitants and therefore its greatest need is that of a body of population."[90] And Mark Twain, the celebrated American writer who toured Palestine in 1867, wrote:

> "Come to Galilee...these unpeopled deserts, these rusty mounds of barrenness, that never, never, never do shake the glare from their harsh outlines...that melancholy ruin of Capernaum...We reached Tabor safely...we never saw a human being on the whole route.
>
> "Bethlehem and Bethany, in their poverty and their humiliation, have nothing about them now...the hallowed spot where the shepherds watched their flocks by night, and where the angels sang, 'Peace on earth, good will to men,' is untenanted by any living creature...Bethsaida and Chorzin have vanished from the earth, and the 'desert places' round about them...sleep in the hush of a solitude that is inhabited only by birds of prey and skulking foxes.
>
> "Stirring scenes...occur in the valley of Jezreel no more.

There is not a solitary village throughout its whole extent—not for thirty miles in either direction.
"Palestine sits in sackcloth and ashes...desolate and unlovely...it is a dreamland."[91]

Other writers of the same period echoed Twain's gloom: "How melancholy is this utter desolation! Not a house, not a trace of inhabitants, not even shepherds...to relieve the dull monotony."[92] "Jericho, once renowned for its famous palm and balsam plantations was, in 1850, treeless and deserted. Wells were choked with rubbish and erosion was rife."[93] And in the latter years of the 19th century visitors to the land continued writing of its desolation:

"I traveled through sad Galilee in the spring, and I found it silent...As elsewhere, as everywhere in Palestine, city and palaces have returned to dust...This melancholy of abandonment...weighs on all the Holy Land."[94]

Over and over again the same words are used to describe Palestine through the ages—empty, silent, barren, abandoned, deserted, melancholy, desolate, ruined, unlovely, void and useless. Compare this with Yasser Arafat's November 1974 speech at the United Nations:

"The Jewish invasion began in 1881...**Palestine was then a verdant area,** inhabited mainly by an Arab people in the course of building its life and **dynamically enriching its indigenous culture.**"[95]

Clearly, the description of Palestine given by historians, writers and pilgrims, is the exact opposite of Arafat's verdant—green, flourishing, forested, lush land. And apparently the only indigenous culture the Arabs enriched Palestine with was robbery, thievery and murder. The few peasant Arab farmers that did work the land were at the mercy of the nomads—the Bedouin tent dwellers. With the Bedouin "came lawlessness and the uprooting of all authority,"[96] and the Bedouin "always sought to thrust into the settled areas, terrorizing and exploiting the villagers and eventually causing them to give up cultivation and flee."[97]

The barren, emptiness of the land that contained so few Arab farmers leads us to the inevitable conclusion that the 140,000 Arabs that remained in Jewish occupied areas after Israel declared statehood in 1948 were, in fact, the only Arabs who had permanent roots.

Jews were always to be found in small communities throughout Palestine, but in the 1880's the Jews began to migrate back to the land. Claims that Arabs were always in the majority holds as much truth as does Arafat's claim that Palestine was a lush, thriving, culturally rich country under Arab rule.

Jews began again to visit Jerusalem around 250 A.D., and shortly thereafter, they were allowed to take up full residence. As in former times, the city soon became the seat of Jewish religious studies, and the spell of Jerusalem, their ancient, holy city, drew many pious Jews. The American newspaper *Pittsburgh Dispatch* of July 15, 1889, reported: "Thirty thousand out of 40,000 people in Jerusalem are Jews."[98] And, lest we forget, a great many of the 10,000 non-Jews were Christians and Armenians, not Moslems.

In the area where organized Jewish settlement began—the area where 98 percent of the Jews would live until Israel's independence—the entire non-Jewish population, Moslems, Christians and "others" was, in 1893, "little more than 92,000,"[99] of which "nearly 38,000 were Christians."[100] Despite the restrictions against Jewish immigration, which the Turkish government had been enforcing for years, the Jewish population numbered nearly 60,000. These figures are validated by Vital Cuinet's 1895 survey of 93,600 non-Jews (37,853 Christians and 55,823 Moslems) against 59,431 Jews, in the Jewish-settled areas.[101]

Thus we have reliable figures showing a small Jewish majority during the period of restrictions on Jewish immigration, and at the time when Arabs from other areas were enjoying almost free access which considerably boosted their numbers. This confirms what I have written elsewhere,[102] that with the exception of the 7th century Arab conquest, it is a dubious point whether the Arabs have ever held a majority in Palestine.

A phenomenal rise in Arab numbers came as Jewish settlement increased, and the Arab population in Palestine increased out of

Palestine   151

all proportion to the Jewish settlement. Arabs swarmed around the Jewish settlers like bees around a honey-pot. The Arabs in Palestine and neighboring countries were poor, and they came looking for the jobs that were being created by the Jewish agriculture and industry. So great was the influx of Arabs into Palestine, that in May, 1939, President Franklin D. Roosevelt was moved to note in a memo to his Secretary of State: "Arab immigration into Palestine since 1921 has **vastly exceeded the total Jewish immigration** during this whole period.[103]

This spectacular rise in Arab population between 1893 and 1947—a 400 percent increase[104]—has been claimed as "natural increase." If this were true, it would arguably have been the world's highest population explosion, but the claim can be dismissed completely out of hand. Just as Arab numbers increased in direct proportion to Jewish settlement, so the percentage of increase was in direct proportion to Arab proximity to Jewish settlement. A 400 percent Arab increase was recorded **inside** Jewish-settled areas, 150 percent **adjacent** to Jewish-settled areas, and 100 percent **outside** the Jewish-settled areas. Arabs poured into Palestine and most sought to find work among the Jews themselves.

An example of the tremendous surge into Palestine to take advantage of Jewish expertise can be found in the Jewish settlement of Rishon l'Tzion (First in Zion) that was founded in 1882. By the year 1889, "the 'forty Jewish families' settled there had attracted '**more than four hundred Arab families**,'"[105] which settled around the settlement itself. Many other Arab villages sprouted in the same fashion. Jewish settlement brought "a ten-to-one ratio of Arab migrants and immigrants to the Jews in the Jewish-settled areas."[106] It should also be pointed out that the above dramatic increase in Arab population took place **well before the census of 1893**, which even then showed a Jewish majority in Jewish-settled areas. The Jews did not displace a settled Arab population—the exact opposite has happened with Arabs having displaced Jews. If any guilt at all is to be laid on the Jewish doorstep, it can only be for bringing Arabs **into** Palestine.

The Jews purchased tracts of land from those few Arabs who actually owned land, and only **three percent** of Palestine was owned by Arabs in 1948—nine percent was owned by Jews, 17 percent was abandoned land, and the remaining 71 percent was empty Crown or State Land vested in the British Mandatory government.[107] Often the Jews paid exorbitant sums of money for what was considered useless land—malaria infested swamps, for example. The tenacity of the Jewish settlers overcame every obstacle, and once more sank their roots deep into their ancient home. The dramatic change brought to the face of Palestine by the Jews forced a distinguished Biblical encyclopedia to applaud them:

"Altogether, these determined settlers have produced **the most marked advance of cultivation over waste that has occurred since Roman times**, bridging centuries of misuse and neglect."[108]

The Jewish development of agriculture, together with the influx of Jewish industry and commerce, brought a giant leap to Arab incomes that was unparalleled in any neighboring Arab country. The wages of an Arab worker in Haifa, for example, "were twice what his counterpart was receiving in Nablus, where there was no Jewish presence."[109]

From the immense inrush of Arabs from Western Palestine (where there was no Jewish settlement), Syria, Egypt and Libya, came the refugees that left again in 1948. The great majority of the refugees were, in fact, newcomers, taking advantage of the prosperity the Jews had brought to Palestine. For this reason, the United Nations had to redefine the definition of an Arab refugee to that of any person having been in the land for two years or more.

Jewish employment of Arabs continues until today despite the fact that numbers of Arabs attack, murder or maim either those that employ them or some other innocent, defenseless person. The Israeli government allows tens of thousands of Arabs to enter the Jewish state each day for employment, and on July 17, 1994, 10,000 Arabs rioted at Israel's Erez checkpoint near the Gaza Strip.

Israeli authorities had warned the new "Palestinian policemen" that they were taking too long in checking Arab identity papers and work permits before allowing them to enter Israel for their day's work. Arabs, frustrated at the delays, threw rocks at the Israelis manning the Israeli side of the checkpoint, injuring 18 border policemen, one critically. They then stormed through the checkpoint, looted and set a gas station afire and destroyed 152 new buses, parked at a bus parking lot, causing millions of dollars in damages.[110]

The following day found the checkpoint closed to all Arab workers for an undetermined period due to the riots. The Arabs grumbled because they were now forced to find work among their Arab brothers—in Israel the Arabs "worked less hours and earned triple the wage."[111]

Jewish Roots in Palestine

We saw earlier that Article 20 of the PLO's charter, the PNC (Palestine National Covenant), denies that Jews have **ever** had an historical or religious tie to Palestine. And we have just seen that even some Palestinian Christian-Arabs would have us to understand that Christians who believe Jews have a Biblical, historical or religious right to possess their ancient land are infidels—unbelievers, heretics, "who deny God and Christ."

It might come as a shock to many to find that the Jews not only have roots that precede the Arabs by thousands of years in Palestine, but they have roots even in Arabia, in Medina—the second holiest city of Islam—that precede the Arabs! Arabs boast of their "pure Arab lands," but the facts of the matter are that "Jews originally settled the city of Medina, or as it was known before Islam, Yathrib."[112] Mohammed's invasion of Medina, situated some 280 miles (450 kilometers.) north of Mecca, was the beginning of the 7th century "Arab conquest of Arabia"[113]—the Jews were completely overrun and eliminated.

For Arabs to claim that Jews have no historical or religious ties to Palestine is almost too ridiculous for words. If more people (including evangelical Christians) were to read more of the Bible, less of the populace would be misinformed. Nearly 4,000 years ago Abraham purchased the Cave of Machpelah in Kiryat

Arba—Hebron (Genesis 23:2) for 400 shekels of silver (Genesis 23:15-16). He bought the Cave as a burial site, and in it he buried his wife Sarah. Abraham was later buried there also, as were Isaac, Rebekah, Jacob and Leah—all of the Jewish Patriarchs and Matriarchs.[114]

At the time of the conquest of Canaan, Caleb, one of the two faithful spies, was given the entire area of Kiryat Arba because he was loyal to God (Joshua 14:14). The city was later renamed Hebron after the great, great-grandchild of Caleb. And Hebron was from where King David ruled the kingdom of Judah for *"seven years and six months"* (2 Samuel 5:5). Around 1,000 B.C. David captured the fortress of Zion (the City of David, 2 Samuel 5:7) in Jerusalem, and from there he ruled all of Israel for 33 years (2 Samuel 5:5). Jerusalem remained the capital of Israel until the Jews were expelled in 135 A.D.—over 1,100 years of sovereign rule. But Arab revised history would have the world believe that Jerusalem has remained under Arab control "from the time of its establishment until today."[115]

Hebron has always been an especially holy place for Jews because it contains the Tomb of the Patriarchs—the Machpelah Cave. For 700 years the Moslems would not allow Jews to approach beyond the seventh step leading to the Cave. Not until Israel captured Hebron in the 1967 war were Jews able to enter the Cave again and pray as before.

The Moslems make much of Hebron and Jerusalem being part of the "cradle of Islam." But neither Hebron or Jerusalem were ever capitals of any Arab entity, and Mohammed attached no Islamic importance to the cities, as neither city was deemed worthy of even a single mention in the Koran.

Hanan Ashrawi has told the world that Bethlehem is a Palestinian Arab town. But Bethlehem was Caleb's grandson who was born to Ephrathah (1 Chronicles 4:4). From this combination we get Micah's prophecy:

> *"But you, **Bethlehem Ephrathah**, though you are little among the thousands of Judah, yet out of you shall come forth to Me the One to be ruler in Israel, whose goings forth have been from of old, from everlasting"* (Micah 5:2).

Palestine

It was Bethlehem who founded the town that still bears his name today. We could go on and on, but all one needs do to dissolve a multitude of other Arab myths is read the Bible.

History Rewritten

Arab myths have taken hold of the minds of the educated masses. So much undue publicity has been given to Arafat and other top PLO officials that the whole world has become their oyster. But almost anything they have to say on any subject is a lie—including the "ands" and the "buts."[116] Arafat claims to be descended from the Philistines; Ashrawi avows her descent is from the first Christians; and Feisal al-Husseini, the top official in Jerusalem and another member of the PLO negotiating team, professes Saladin to be his forefather.[117] All swear to being "pure Arab," but none claims Arab decent! The Philistines were non-Semites, the first Christians were Jews, and Saladin was a Kurd!

Feisal al-Husseini's family has indeed been around in Palestine for a good number of years. The al-Husseinis were part of the elite ruling class that helped force the peasant farmers from their lands through the imposition of exorbitant rents, dues and interest. Peasant farmers in the 19th century were paying as much as 200 to 300 percent interest![118] Joan Peters describes the al-Husseini family as members of the "parasitic landlord class."[119] Feisal al-Husseini is directly related to Haj al-Husseini, the former Moslem Mufti of Jerusalem and confidant of Adolf Hitler. Faisal is a cousin of Yasser Arafat.

Like other top PLO officials, al-Husseini strongly propagates mythical Palestinian-Arab history. His Palestine Academic Society for the Study of International Affairs (Passia) is merely a front for a formidable distribution of PLO propaganda. An example of Passia's "academic" contribution to revised history is found in an appointment calendar distributed largely to journalists, politicians and other influential members of society. Following are short excerpts from the PLO version of the history of the Arabs of Palestine as it appears (spelling errors included) in *The Land, its People and History*:

> "In the **middle of the Third Millenium (3000 BC)**, after the wave of drought and dessication that struck the Arabian peninsular, the **Canaanites, tribes of Arab Semites**, came to and settled in the territories east of the Mediterranean Sea that consist of present day Syria, Lebanon, Jordan and Palestine.
>
> "About the year **4,000 BC, the Jebusites, a Canaanite subgroup founded Jebus—Jerusalem...** .
>
> "The **Philistines** gave [the land of Canaan] the name Philistin or '**Palestine.**'
>
> "About the year **1900 BC**, Abraham (Ibrahim)...settled somewhere in the Jordan valley.
>
> "Around the **fourteenth century BC**, the twelve sons of Jacob (Israel) **fled to Egypt**...they multiplied and gained strength during **500 years** in Egypt... .
>
> "Moses, along with his people (Banu Israel), left Egypt around the **thirteenth century BC (1290 BC).**
>
> "Around **330 AD**...the relationship the Jews had with the city and the Temple were severed.
>
> "But although Palestine became part of the **Byzantine** and Hellenic cultures, **Arab life** was never dissociated from it or Jerusalem... .
>
> "In the seventh century AD, Palestine and the rest of Syria (The Land of Canaan) **emerged from the rule of the Romans and entered the sphere of the Arab-Islamic Empire.**"[120]

The mythical Arabs are subtlety introduced in the form of Canaanites—as Arabs from Arabia! And Arab life in Jerusalem, indeed, throughout all of Israel's ancient homeland, was never even disrupted by the Romans! This is true—a non-existent entity cannot be disrupted even if the world itself ceased to exist! And al-Husseini's Academic Society disguises the 7th century Moslem invasion and massacre of practically all Jews and Christians in the land as simply: "emerging from the rule of the Romans and entering the sphere of the Arab-Islamic Empire."

It is also interesting to note that the Canaanites arrived in the year 3000 B.C.—described here as the "**Middle** of the Third millenium"—but the Jebusites, a Canaanite subgroup arrived more than 1,000 years earlier!

Abraham arrived in the 19th century B.C.; his great-grandchildren fled to Egypt in the 14th, stayed there for 500 years, and left in the 13th century—within 60 years after their arrival! It is a pathetic story that has more holes than a fine-mesh sieve. It is just an example of how Arab academicians rewrite the history of the ancient land of the Jews.

Prestigious Reference Works

The wealthy Arab propaganda machine has done immense harm to the real, ancient history of the Jewish people. But the long-term, almost irreparable damage will come from the extra hands willingly being lent to the Arabs by the academe. Numbers of reference works are including misleading or falsified information concerning Jewish history in their volumes, and it is from these works that many nation's extract information for inclusion into their educational systems.

Individuals who expend a great deal of money for expensive reference books for their private libraries, usually do not replace these books for decades—if ever. It is common to see 20 and 30 year-old sets of *Encyclopædia Britannica* being offered for sale in a newspaper's classified advertisements. False information included—knowingly or unknowingly—in any reference work will continue having an impact upon minds several generations after it is first published. Arabs are very much aware of this fact and are aggressively and successfully implanting their warped version of history into some of the world's most prestigious publications. Many articles in today's encyclopedias—those having a bearing on Jewish history and their presence in the ancient land are, unbelievingly, being written by Arabs! Someone has pointed out that this is like keeping score in a game of cricket by counting the runs of only one side.

Space will never permit us an extensive coverage of falsified or incorrect information in encyclopedias, dictionaries and text books. Information contained in articles pertaining to the same subject in the same work will vary greatly according to the particular author or authors. Only a few examples from some of the more prominent publications can be given here.

In a nutshell, the condensed history of Israel and Palestine is as presented in an excerpt from an article in *The Random House Encyclopedia*:

> "Once the land of Canaan, then Israel, then Palestine, the modern state of Israel was born on May 14, 1948, after 2,000 years of Jewish statelessness and half a century of efforts by Zionists."[121]

At least we know that what I have maintained since the beginning is correct—Palestine was originally called Canaan before it became known as Israel, and only after that did it become Palestine. In a different portion from another article in the same encyclopedia we read: "Moses led the Jews out of Egypt and into **Palestine**."[122] Whatever happened to Canaan? It is completely omitted and upholds the Arab version of history.

Another scrap from an article from the same source: "The Philistines, a trading people, conquered the Jews who had settled in **Palestine**."[123] Again, no Canaan mentioned, and the Arab version of history is upheld.

Once again from the same source:

> "Gaza...One of the five city-kingdoms of Philistines, it was under frequent attack because of its strategic position between **Palestine** and Egypt."[124]

No Canaan—Arab version upheld again. And yet another excerpt from the same source in an article concerning Sennacherib, King of Assyria (704–681 B.C.): "He led another major campaign

Palestine

against, Phoenecia, **Palestine**, and **Philistia** in 701."[125] The simple fact that the name Palestine originates from Philistia—the land of the Philistines seems to be of no account whatever to this "historian," he just replaced "Israel" with "Palestine." It is an absolute impossibility to have Palestine and Philistia in existence at one and the same time—perhaps Arafat himself authored this article?

Groliers Illustrated Encyclopedia provides much the same distorted information as *Random House*. In an article on the Philistines we find: "The Philistines were one of a number of Sea Peoples who penetrated Egypt and **Syro-Palestine** coastal areas during 1225–1050 BC."[126] Here we have an Anglicized version of the Roman name that was given to the land of Israel—some 1,200 years before the Romans actually gave it! Another extract from *Groliers*:

> "Although some scholars date the arrival of the Hebrews earlier, the principal influx of Hebrew tribes (see JEWS) from the desert into **Palestine** occurred between the 14th and 12th centuries BC."[127]

The same old story. The Jews came from Egypt, wandered around in the desert before going straight into Palestine. *Groliers* is another major reference work that supports an Arab revision of Palestinian history.

Earlier we had three quotations concerning the Philistines. Only *Random House* had theirs entirely correct: "Philistines, a non-Semitic people who probably came to **Philistia** from Crete in about the 12th century BC."[128] The Philistines were one of the Sea Peoples—their name derived from having settled in Philistia.

Webster's Unabridged Dictionary followed the crowd and defined "Philistine" as: "a member of non Semitic people who lived in southwestern **Palestine** from c. 1200 B.C. on."[129] Revised history is enforced by having the Philistines live in Palestine more than 1,300 years before it existed.

The authoritative *Encyclopædia Britannica* also misinforms people with its article on the Philistines:

"Philistines, a people of Aegean origin who settled on the southern coast of **Palestine** in the 12th century BC shortly before the arrival of the Israelites...they occupied the coastal plain of **Palestine**."[130]

Here the *Britannica* also upholds Arab revisionist history and delegitimatizes Jewish claims to their homeland by having Palestine in existence 1,250 years prior to the entry of the Israelites. I am most fortunate to possess a rather large and comprehensive personal library (which includes the *Britannica* and five other major encyclopedias), but not a single book or article consulted corroborates the 12th century date given for the entry of the Jews into Canaan. The most reliable authorities place the date between early and mid-15th century B.C.

In the text concerning the modern history of Palestine, the *Britannica* takes an apparent pro-Arab stance by depicting Israel as racist, aggressive and expansionist. An example:

"In 1950 the Kingdom of Jordan annexed the West Bank of the Jordan River; this was seized and occupied by Israel in 1967, along with the Gaza Strip, the Sinai Peninsula (Egyptian), and the Golan Heights (Syrian)."[131]

Not a mention anywhere in the whole article of an Arab blockade of the Tiran Straits. Not a mention of the massing of Arab troops on each of Israel's land borders, nor of the Arab contemplation of there being "no Jewish survivors" in the inevitable war that was to follow. And no mention at all of the Six Day War and Israel's miraculous victory over five Arab nations—each of which had larger and better equipped armies than that of the Jewish state. For absolutely no reason and without any provocation, Israel simply "seized and occupied" Jordanian, Egyptian and Syrian territory. Is it any wonder that the world is on the side of the "downtrodden" Arabs?

The *Encyclopædia Britannica* has been taken to task of late by better informed readers objecting to the publishing of radically slanted information in the 1992 edition that completely redefines

Palestine 161

Jewish history. To his credit *Britannica*'s current editor-in-chief, Robert McHenry, has agreed to make some changes, but the 1992 edition will still be in constant use by the year 2025, and still doing inestimable damage. Arabs from the American University of Beirut contributed to both the "Israel" and modern "Palestine" articles.[132] And Palestine National Council (the PNC is the PLO's governing body) member Walid Khalidi is a co-author of the post-1900 "Palestine" article.[133] The "blitzkrieg" of Arab propaganda efforts are paying off handsomely. By rewriting the history of the Middle East, it will ultimately threaten the very existence of the modern State of Israel.

The distinguished *Encyclopædia Britannica*—arguably the world's pre-eminent reference work—might have actually set the standard for the widespread revisionism that is now the vogue in other reference works, both major and minor. Check the entry under "Palestine" in *Webster's New World Encyclopedia* published by Prentice Hall. It says Palestine:

> "...was in ancient times dominated in turn by Egypt, Assyria, Babylonia, Persia, Macedonia, the Ptolemies, the Seleucids, and the Roman and Byzantine empires. Today it forms part of Israel. The Palestinian people...are descendants of the People of Canaan."[134]

An entire 3,000 years of Jewish domination and presence is deliberately left out, and the last line is a dead giveaway that Arab fingers have been in the till again. A bogus Middle East history with an equally bogus claim made of Arabs being descended from the Canaanites. But that is not all. *Webster's* included a historical chronology under their entry of "Palestine" that begins not with the Canaanites, but with the Islamic conquest in the 7th century A.D. This allows the "historian" to delete thousands of years of Jewish history without even blushing. And under the entry for the year 1948, readers are informed that a series of Arab-Israeli wars "resulted in the total loss of the Palestinian state."[135] There has never been a Palestinian state in existence from the time of Adam and Eve until the present day. But how will the tens of thousands of unsuspecting people who will search *Webster's New World Encyclopedia* for information know that?

Colliers Encyclopedia has teamed up with *Britannica* and *Webster's* in the race to present biased and falsified accounts of Jewish and Israeli history. In *Colliers'* "Palestine, Modern" section, Rashid Khalidi, another Arab "historian" begins with a passage averring the prior existence of "a sovereign Palestinian state."[136] A reviewer of the work says "Khalidi flatly misrepresents facts."[137] I wonder why he did that?

The American Heritage Publishing Company has also been penetrated. The description of the town of Bethlehem in *The American Heritage Dictionary* is quite something:

> "A town in **Israeli-occupied Jordan**, five miles south of Jerusalem, and the **Palestinian village** of Biblical times where David lived and Jesus was born."[138]

Jordan's annexing of the West Bank in 1950 was never recognized by the United Nations, nor even by the Arab League. And there was never any Palestinian anything in Biblical times. David Bar-Illan says that the above quote reminds him of the old joke about spelling Noah (a two-letter word in Hebrew) with seven mistakes.[139]

In June 1992 the venerable *National Geographic* ran a story entitled, *Who are the Palestinians?* The article written by Ted Szulc asserted that today's Palestinian Arabs are descended from the ancient Canaanites, and that the Jews were simply one of the waves of regional invaders that have afflicted them. Many and strong were the protests against the article that was chock-full of misinformation. The protesters of the fake history published by *National Geographic* were referred to one Phillip Mattar, associate editor of *The Journal of Palestine Studies* which is headed by Hisham Sharabi—friend and advisor of Yasser Arafat.[140]

The rewriting of Israel's history even spills over into Christian Bibles. For Example: The *New King James* version published by Thomas Nelson, arguably the world's largest Christian publisher (owned by two Lebanese Arabs), defines the *shulamite* bride in the Song of Solomon as: "A Palestinian young woman."[141]

Palestine

Sadly—libraries, schools and homes will soon be filled with this type of poisonous revision of history. It is fully designed to turn the world against the Jews on the immoral charges of having ill-treated the Arabs of Palestine, and for insidiously stealing the land on which they have lived for thousands of years. But the revision of history is a lie. And a lie is a lie, no matter which prestigious publication prints it. And the sad fact is that they are printing what they must know to be false. Shame on you America! For it is you who are publishing the most distorted and patently false information, and that without a single twinge of conscience.

Take revisionist history to its logical conclusion, and we have the stage set for the world's final battle—Armageddon, *"the great day of God Almighty"* (Revelation 16:14,16). All the kings of the earth—the whole world coming against the Jews in the valley of Megiddo in northern Israel. When *"the cities of the nations fall"*—destroyed in a nuclear holocaust—who will be left to mourn over the lies that destroyed them?

8
The United Nations

The Arab-Islamic front attacks Israel through every channel, every medium, at every gathering, and from every platform. And the cynical rewriting of history cannot even be compared to another powerful weapon available to the Arab cause—the United Nations. The United Nations was once a creditable and respected body that enjoyed the trust of vast numbers around the world. Today, this same instrument that encouraged and helped birth the Jewish state, spends much of its time trying to destroy it. David Bar-Illan writes: "A visitor from another planet could hardly be blamed for assuming that the organization was established for no other purpose than to damn Israel."[1] The headquarters of the United Nations in Israel is located in Jerusalem on the site known as the "Hill of Evil Counsel"—where Ahithophel advised Absalom on how to wrest the kingdom from David (2 Sam 16:21,17:2). It is doubtful that the organization's possession of this site is coincidental.

The United Nations has been deeply penetrated by the Arabs and their propaganda. It has become a devoted Arab ally—a tool that applies considerable pressure to Israel, often forcing it to comply with Arab demands under the threat of sanctions. The combined power of the Arab and Soviet blocs (a former powerful, virulently anti-Semitic opponent of Israel) gave them "complete control of the United Nations, its microphones, and its printing presses."[2] It was once said that if the Arabs had proposed a United Nations resolution "decreeing that the earth was flat, it would pass."[3]

Anti-Semitism and Double Standards

An anti-Semite is "one who is hostile or opposed to the Jews"[4]—one who "discriminates against Jews."[5] Being anti-Semitic is "having or showing prejudice against Jews."[6] And anti-Semitism is defined as: "the hatred of Jews and the application of a double standard in treating Jews."[7] And it has been stated that, "Nowhere is raw anti-Semitism more blatant than in the United

Nations itself"[8]—the truth of which can readily be seen by the perusal of a few facts.

The United Nations holds itself to be "impartial" in its mediating role toward Israel, but the measure of its anti-Semitic venom can be perceived by the actions of its staff and members. In March 1993, for example, a senior United Nations official witnessed the stoning and murder of Rabbi Yehoshua Weissbrod in Gaza. Arabs threw stones at Weissbrod's car causing him to lose control and crash into a wall. An Arab mob then "beat him with iron bars and building blocks, and later gunmen fired several shots from a Kalashnikov assault rifle into him."[9] After that Weissbrod's car was set on fire. Katharine Striker,[10] the United Nations official, "did nothing—neither tried to stop the stoning or reported the incident to the military authorities."[11]

The amount of time that the United Nations actually spends discussing and condemning the Jewish state is incredible. It is a fact that the Security Council has targeted Israel—devoting "30 percent of all its meetings, and a full one-third of all its resolutions"[12] to a country that contains "less than one-thousandth of the world's population."[13] And this is in "an era of totalitarian repressions, wholesale massacres, expulsions of vast populations, expanding slavery and unspeakable acts of genocide."[14] The Security Council has issued "31 expressions of concern, seven warnings, and 49 condemnations against Israel."[15] But not until Saddam Hussein invaded Kuwait was there ever a resolution made against an Arab country, not even in 1982 when Hafez Assad of Syria personally ordered the slaughter of 20,000 people in the city of Hama, who were from a rival sect. Syrian soldiers systematically sealed the occupants inside the houses and pumped in cyanide gas[16] before bulldozing the city under a mound of dirt.[17] Numerous wars, indescribable atrocities and hundreds of terrorist acts that have taken thousands of lives have been carried out by Arab states, but until the time of the Gulf War the United Nations Security Council never once warned, censured or condemned a single Arab state.[18] The United Nations looked the other way when Syria used the cyanide gas against its civilians in 1983, just as it had done when Egypt used mustard gas[19] against the Yemenis in 1966. It stared glassy-eyed in the opposite direction when Iran

The United Nations

and Iraq used some 1,000 tons of nerve gas[20] against each other during their eight-year war, and also when Iraq killed thousands of its Kurdish people with chemical weapons in 1988.[21] Chemical weapons and poison gas are banned from use in warfare, but the same United Nations that issued the ban[22] freely allows Arab states to defy it without uttering one word of protest.

In June 1981, the Israeli Airforce conducted a hazardous journey across enemy airspace—refueling during flight—and with surgical precision, reduced Iraq's Osiraq nuclear reactor to a mound of rubble. The Iraqis were using the reactor to produce a nuclear bomb, and the operation set Iraq's nuclear program back by a decade or more. The Israeli attack against an enemy target (Iraq is in a declared state of war with Israel) brought vehement condemnation from the world's press and another condemnation from the United Nations. Use of poison gas against unarmed civilians is obviously permissible when used by Arab states, but for Jews to even attack an enemy target is not permissible—especially when the target is Arab. As a direct consequence of the 1991 Gulf War, the United Nations is itself spending millions of dollars today, sending teams to destroy all of Iraq's chemical and nuclear capabilities! But the condemnation of Israel still remains on the books.

Just prior to the Gulf War, Syria invaded the Christian enclave in Lebanon with some 2,000 tanks and 40,000 troops and virtually wiped it out. The bodies of about 600 Christian army officers were shown on Israeli television and also published in the Israeli press—the men had been bound hand and foot and shot through the back of the head.[23] The White House turned a convenient blind-eye to the activities of its new found ally; the American news media omitted any mention of the atrocity, and the United Nations also remained true to its form by not raising a peep of protest either.

When Israel deported 12 Palestinian terrorists in early January 1992, the United Nations "strongly condemned" Israel for doing so. A denunciatory resolution by the PLO was not considered sufficiently strong enough by the United Nations American delegate, Thomas Pickering,[24] who proposed the much more stinging resolution—"strongly condemned"—which was passed.

And concerning the term "strongly condemn," a Washington political consultant points out:

> "The phrase (strongly condemn), **the most severe of diplomatic terms**, was not used against totalitarian states which sponsor international terrorism, nor when an outlaw nation invaded a neighbor and plundered it, nor when Arab terrorists murder Jews, Israelis or any other nationality, indiscriminately in airports, nursery schools or city streets."[25]

The Syrian army can invade a neighboring country, kill thousands and execute hundreds of helpless, bound prisoners without a single American or United Nations' voice being raised in protest. But when Israel simply deported 12 terrorists, it was "strongly condemned" by the same hypocrites that keep silent over atrocities committed by their "friends." It was perhaps poetic justice that Pickering fell from grace and was removed from his position one month later.

The strongest, most severe political condemnation possible was laid upon Israel by the United Nations for deporting 12 terrorists who planned the murders of innocent Israelis. Yet, when the Soviet Union shot down a Korean civilian airliner in 1983, killing all 269 passengers, the United Nations was merely "gravely disturbed."[26]

The storm that raged over 12 deported terrorists was a glassy calm compared to the hurricane that blew in over 400 *Hamas* and Islamic Jihad terrorists that Israel deported for the same reasons—masterminding the murders of innocent Israelis, including women and children. The terrorists were to be deported to Lebanon for a maximum term of two years, after which time they would be allowed to enter Israel again. The world's news media made heroes out of the murderers and, true to form, "virtually ignored the reasons for the expulsion and concentrated on pictures of 400 plus men relegated to 'yet another refugee camp' in the cold Lebanon hills."[27]

The United Nations was furious—most probably because "15 percent of the deported terrorists were salaried workers of the organization."[28] Together with the "immediate and unanimous condemnation,"[29] Israel received "thinly veiled threats for the imposition of sanctions"[30] from the secretary-general himself. The media's presentation of the terrorists as "suffering" heroes of the Palestinian cause, the United Nations condemnation coupled together with threats of sanctions (which had the full backing of the Clinton administration), eventually forced Israel to bring the murderers back to Israel where they immediately continued with their foul deeds. The media's portrayal of the terrorists "suffering" so badly in their camp in the cold Lebanon hills caused a Lebanese newspaper to satirize them in an editorial:

> "Anybody visiting their camp in South Lebanon can't help but notice the rich variety of drinks and luxuries they are enjoying, unlike most Lebanese.
> "They are in much better shape than many Lebanese, and probably better off than some Palestinians in the territories.
> "They have fresh meat and all kinds of fruits and vegetables, gas stoves, televisions and telephones, while the majority of Lebanese have been dreaming of hearing a telephone ring in their home for the past 20 years.
> "Moreover, these people are getting more publicity than the Lebanese prime minister and his government. Their spokesman, Abdul-Aziz Rantisi, is no longer satisfied to talk about conditions in the camp, but is sending messages to the United Nations Security Council, the White House and the Arab League."[31]

The newspaper intimated that the deportees were also traveling freely in Lebanon, saying some of them had been "vacationing far from their camp."[32]

The early return of the deportees was another huge Arab political success. This success could not have been achieved without the overly generous help of the anti-Semitic United Nations and an equally anti-Semitic news media, which gave the deportees—"terrorist inciters, organizers and executioners"[33]— wide, sympathetic coverage. But when 300,000 Palestinians—the vast majority of whom were "innocent victims of base, vindictive revenge"[34]—were deported from Kuwait after the Gulf War because Yasser Arafat embraced Saddam Hussein, the United Nations and the media responded with a "thunderous silence."[35] In fact, the United Nations "never saw fit to even discuss it"![36]

On April 11, 1974, three Arabs crossed into Israel from Lebanon and engaged themselves in an "orgy of carnage"[37] in Kiryat Shmoneh. They went from apartment to apartment killing whoever they came across—"it didn't matter if the hapless victim was an old man taking his dog out for a walk or a three-year-old girl playing with her dolls on the staircase—all received a close-quarters burst of 7.62-mm death to the head."[38] Eighteen Israelis were slaughtered and 25 injured before Israeli commandos arrived and killed the murderers. The dead included eight children and five women[39]—and "an entire family was butchered as they sat around the breakfast table."[40] The sight of small childrens' bloody bodies caused some of the commandos—seasoned veterans who had fought in Israel's toughest battles—to weep openly,[41] and many "threw up in disgust."[42]

On the day that Israel buried the bodies of the victims of the massacre, IDF units retaliated and attacked Lebanese terrorist bases, killing several gunmen. The United Nations condemned Israel again, this time for "violating Lebanese territorial integrity and sovereignty"[43]—no mention of the massacre was made, nor was the terrorism condemned.[44] One month later three more Arabs entered Israel from Lebanon, seized a school house in Maalot and killed 25,[45] including 20 schoolchildren (mainly girls)—an additional 70 were "critically wounded."[46] Hundreds of such attacks against Israelis have taken place over the years and are still taking place today, but the United Nations never condemned a single attack until Israeli outrage finally forced it to do so in April 1994. The United Nations has consistently shown total indifference to the shedding of Jewish blood, whether by Arab armies attacking the Jewish state or by state-sponsored terrorists attacking Jewish targets in Israel or overseas.

The whole nation of Israel mourned the murder of their 11 Olympic team athletes after the terrible PLO massacre at the Games Village in Munich in 1972, but the United Nations stayed silent, and the Olympic Games played on. Another massacre in

The United Nations

March 1978, that took the lives of 37 Israeli men, women and children and injured 87 others, also failed to disturb the agenda of the United Nations or raise a debate. But when a severely provoked Israeli shot 29 Arabs in the Cave of the Jewish Patriarchs in February 1994,[47] the United Nations literally spent weeks discussing it. It then condemned the entire nation for the act of one man, called for an international presence in the Israeli administered territories, and also called for "action to disarm" all Israelis living in the administered areas.[48] It was a true-to-type manifestation of the United Nation's chronic anti-Israel reflex. Condemnation of Israel for the lone man's action was axiomatic—condemning Israel is the only thing the United Nations ever gets excited or united about.

A United Nations' contingent of 120 Italians, Norwegians and Danes duly arrived in Israel—all adorned in splendid white uniforms. Within "minutes"[49] of their arrival, Arabs began throwing rocks at Israeli soldiers in full view of the brand-new observer force. The Israeli soldiers responded by firing tear gas to disperse the mob, and the coordinator of the observer force upheld the United Nations' "impartiality"—he blamed the soldiers for "provoking the incident."[50]

Within the United Nations

According to the Charter of the United Nations, Chapter V, Article 23–1, the Security Council shall consist of 11 members of the United Nations—the United States, the United Kingdom, the Union of Soviet Socialist Republics (now the C.I.S.), the Republic of China, and France. These are all permanent members of the Security Council, and with the exception of the U.S., are all aggressively anti-Israel. The Charter was conveniently laid aside and a permanent PLO representative was also appointed and took his place alongside the major powers. Six non-permanent members are elected by the General Assembly to serve on the Security Council for two-year terms.

The United Nations' discrimination against Israel is reflected in the make-up of the Security Council—Israel has never once been asked to serve even though it joined the United Nations in

1949 when there was only about 50 member countries. Today there are some 160 member countries, and with few exceptions, they are all "prepared in return for favors to support the Arab cause."[51] At least 15 Arab states[52] have already served on the Council, and Arab states are elected as members of the Council almost every year—sometimes two Arab states serve at the same time. Boutros Boutros-Ghali, the present secretary-general—the head of the United Nations—is an Arab, and today's Security Council has two Arab members as well as the PLO representative!

And no one should have the slightest doubt about where United Nations secretary-general Boutros-Ghali's interests lie. As a Moslem, he totally rejects Israel's right to self-determination, the maintaining of its Jewish character, and the development of its political orientation. He has made it perfectly clear that he envisions peace in the Middle East only after the Jewish people turn their backs on their state and accept *dhimmi* status according to Islamic tradition. At a symposium of the Egyptian intelligentsia Boutros-Ghali said: "The Jews must give up their status as a nation and Israel as a state, and assimilate as a community in the Arab world."[53] The alternative, he predicted, would be "repeated wars."[54]

U Thant, Burma's United Nations delegate who rose to become vice president of the General Assembly before serving as secretary-general from 1962 to 1971, was a Marxist. U Thant praised Lenin, the leader of the Bolshevik Revolution and founder of Communist ideology, and saw Lenin's ideals as fully in line "with the aims of the United Nations Charter."[55] Kurt Waldheim served as secretary-general from 1972 to 1982—a period when many of the worst slaughters of Israelis took place both inside and outside of Israel. Waldheim, who later became president of Austria, was barred from entering the United States in 1987 when a 3,000 page[56] documented report of his Nazi wartime activities was analyzed by the United States government. It was proven that Waldheim participated in the "Nazi murder machine"[57] which exterminated six million Jews.

The PLO and the United Nations

In late October 1974, the United Nations General Assembly

voted "to disregard the provisions of the Charter"[58] and to invite Yasser Arafat, the head of the PLO terrorist organization, to address the General Assembly. The man elected as "president of the General Assembly during the session in which Arafat was to speak was himself a former Algerian terrorist."[59]

"Escorted, beaming, to the rostrum of the General Assembly on November 13, a pistol visible in his belt, the *Fatah* leader immediately made clear that he was **demanding a state for all of Palestine and that the very existence of the Israeli republic had no place in his scheme.**"[60]

He was "rapturously received."[61] Indeed, he received a standing ovation, and "nobody seemed to object to his wearing a pistol into the chamber."[62]

Arafat's "status and that of the PLO were enhanced by the United Nations recognition."[63] The United Nations recognized not only the PLO terror organization, but also recognized the "legality of the armed struggle against Israel."[64] And in 1992 the United Nations Human Rights Commission "affirmed the right of the Palestinians to **resist the Israeli occupation by all means.**"[65]

The United Nations in Lebanon

In Lebanon, due to constant PLO attacks against Israel and Israel's subsequent reprisal raids, an "impartial" United Nations force was deployed on Lebanese soil to act as a buffer zone, ostensibly to keep the "peace." This "peace keeping" force is known as UNIFIL (United Nations Interim Force in Lebanon). The UNIFIL force was initially deployed in Lebanon in April, 1978, and is still operating there at an annual cost of many millions of dollars. It has proven to be as effective as an umbrella in a Force 7 hurricane. Major Saad Haddad, the leader of the Lebanese Christian army and a friend of Israel, said of UNIFIL:

> "The United Nations is doing nothing. They are just there for a show. Worse than that, sometimes they are covering for the PLO. The area where the United Nations troops moved in used to be clean of PLO, but not any more. **The**

PLO moved in and they have camps inside the United Nations area from which the PLO make terrorist actions."[66]

By June 1978—just two months after the initial deployment of UNIFIL troops—"at least 300 PLO terrorists had reoccupied UNIFIL-controlled areas of south Lebanon."[67] And within six months of UNIFIL's arrival, "more than 700 PLO terrorists had returned to the area under its jurisdiction and **established 42 bases** there."[68] Moshe Dayan, Israel's Foreign Minister at that time, complained that UNIFIL was not only permitting PLO terrorists to infiltrate southern Lebanon but, in fact, allowed them to supply the southern terrorist groups from their bases in north Lebanon.

"Dayan's charge was rebuffed by United Nations secretary-general **Kurt Waldheim**, who said he saw nothing wrong with UNIFIL permitting the delivery of 'supplies' to 'limited Palestinian groups still in its area of operations.'"[69]

By July, Israeli intelligence reports coming in from south Lebanon revealed that UNIFIL units were actually making direct deals with the PLO terrorists—the PLO would be allowed to infiltrate the south in exchange for "refraining from attacking UNIFIL outposts."[70] The direct collaboration between many UNIFIL units and the PLO terrorists facilitated easy penetration of Israel's northern border. The "impartial" United Nations' peace keepers "more often than not openly assisted armed Palestinians heading toward Israel."[71] Many UNIFIL soldiers were actually recruited as "operational agents,"[72] and a "Nigerian major who had commanded a UNIFIL contingent was arrested inside Israel with a trunkload of weapons destined for terrorist cells on the West Bank."[73] An officer from the Sengalese unit was also caught attempting to smuggle "a large quantity of explosives from Lebanon to PLO cells in Israel."[74]

Soldiers from UNIFIL were observed taking part in a funeral and rally held in honor of a terrorist who had been killed by Israeli troops.[75] More than 40 soldiers "of the Iranian UNIFIL contingent deserted their unit to join the terrorists"![76] And Nepalese UNIFIL soldiers were seen posing for photographs with Hizbullah terrorists in 1992![77] Israelis continued to be murdered as a result of the terrorists' frequent excursions into Israeli border towns, and the populations of some towns would spend days shut up in bomb shelters—kept under constant siege from Katyusha rockets fired from within UNIFIL territory.[78]

A French UNIFIL officer and a Swedish UNIFIL soldier were arrested by Lebanese Christian forces for "photographing Israeli military installations."[79] And a captured PLO terrorist revealed that the PLO had paid $25,000 to a senior Irish UNIFIL officer to provide photographs and data concerning Israeli military positions in northern Israel and southern Lebanon.[80] The same terrorist revealed that the PLO had purchased missiles from the Irish unit![81]

In June 1982, Israel invaded Lebanon with the intention of clearing southern Lebanon from the PLO terrorist presence.[82] UNIFIL troops were collaborating heavily with the PLO against Israel and did their best to prevent Israel's advance and eradication of the terrorists. The UNIFIL troops were to be a neutral force, but the Dutch planted obstacles in the path of an advancing Israeli tank column, and the Irish turned off the night spotlights to help PLO terrorists evade the Israelis.[83] Israeli forces had orders not to open fire at all—even on the PLO—if UNIFIL troops were in danger of being hit. But numbers of Israelis got into fist fights with the multinational force before proceeding with the "Peace for Galilee" operation.

The Israelis searched UNIFIL's area and found PLO terrorists being given shelter in UNIFIL tents. They also located "entire United Nations' facilities that were routinely used as PLO training bases."[84] A United Nations Relief and Works Agency (UNRWA) **school** in Siblin had also been turned into a terrorist training center. Among the decorations on the walls was a picture of PLO chief Yasser Arafat and a Nazi swastika:

> "It took more than three days for Israel Defense Forces engineers to defuse bombs, remove booby traps and load the enormous quantities of arms found: crates of RPG launchers and missiles, hundreds of Kalashnikov rifles, anti-

aircraft and anti-tank missiles, hand grenades and mines. The school boarded 600 boys and girls aged 18–19 who trained to become PLO officers. Chemistry and electronics labs were used to manufacture mines and booby traps."[85]

None of the UNRWA staff was able to explain the PLO's use of their school over the years, but when we take into account that Palestinian Arabs comprise 99 percent[86] of the UNRWA staff, explanations become unnecessary. Israel charged UNRWA with having threatened to withhold ration books from "refugees" if certain men did not join terrorist organizations, and that UNRWA trucks have been used to transport weapons.[87]

The continuing Israeli advance in Lebanon unearthed numerous treasures. In a captured PLO bunker inside the United Nations area the Israelis discovered:

> "A written agreement between the commander of the Norwegian UNIFIL unit and the PLO that promised non-interference by the Norwegians in any terrorist activity that took place in their zone."[88]

The Chief of Staff of the Israeli Army revealed that other captured documents included:

> "PLO intelligence reports that quoted UNIFIL sources for estimates of Israeli troop strengths and movements—evidence that high-ranking UNIFIL officers have been passing intelligence information on the Israeli Army to the PLO."[89]

The PLO presence and infrastructure in southern Lebanon was enormous—even including submarine bays in Sidon.[90] And so colossal were the arms caches that it literally took Israel months to transport the captured weapons back to Israel—"4,330 truckloads—sufficient to sustain a million man invasion of Israel."[91] And the United Nations was supposedly there to "keep the peace"!

Guarantees of Security

The whole concept of the United Nations or America providing security for Israel against its hostile neighbors is an utter delusion. As Israel today moves ahead with huge territorial concessions to the Arabs—conceding territory from which Arabs have already launched three invasions of Israel—the government looks toward the United Nations and the United States to provide "guarantees" that the agreements will be upheld. Considering the past and present performances of the United Nations to fulfill its undertakings, any reliance put upon its "guarantees" is naiveté of the worst form.

The thousands of UNIFIL troops in Lebanon have not only been incapable of protecting Israeli populations from terrorist attacks, they have been unwilling to protect them—siding with the terrorists against Israel. UNIFIL's record in Lebanon is not the archetype of a multinational force's inability to protect Israel—the total abandonment of its responsibilities in Sinai paved the way for the June 1967 war.

Israel's 1957 retreat from Sinai was based on the emplacement of a United Nations multinational force and the "guarantee" of free navigation through Suez and the Gulf of Eilat. Israel withdrew from Sinai, the United Nations Emergency Force (UNEF) took up its positions, and America "guaranteed" to uphold Israel's right of free navigation through Suez and the Gulf of Eilat. In May 1967, Egypt decided to "challenge Israel in war."[92] Egypt's Chief of Staff sent a message to the commander of UNEF, Major General Rikhye, of the Indian Army, requesting withdrawal of all United Nations troops along Egypt's borders. The reason given was that "the Egyptian armed forces had been ordered 'to prepare to go into action against Israel.'"[93]

The Egyptian Foreign Minister, Mahmoud Riad, sent a letter to the secretary-general of the United Nations, **U Thant**, telling him that the Egyptian government "had decided to 'terminate the presence of the United Nations emergency force in Egypt and the Gaza Strip.'"[94] U Thant's reply to the Egyptian letter was **delivered within 75 minutes**[95] **of receiving it**! His reply constituted an agreement for a "complete withdrawal,"[96] and his decision was made before consultation with Israel or with governments that contributed troops to the force.[97]

America's record of fulfilling its guarantees of security is absolutely appalling—no better at all than the United Nations. Such a statement might shock some American people, but it is the truth, nevertheless. Unless American economic or political interests are threatened, all guarantees made by the White House are virtually worthless due to the simple fact that succeeding administrations do not feel honor bound to fulfill pledges made by previous administrations. And Israel has found itself holding the dirty end of the stick a number of times. An American explains:

> "Commitments made with all good intentions by one administration may fall by the wayside when a different administration, with different goals and a different worldview, assumes power. The history of **American guarantees to its small allies is not a laundry list of betrayals but** rather a manifestation of the simple reality that in a democracy, voters, Congressmen and presidents often change their minds about commitments made by their prececessors."[98]

But is it just and honorable to make a commitment upon which a government stakes both its country's security and also the very lives of its people, and then renege on the "guarantee" when it is needed? For example, the Eisenhower administration's "guarantee" to uphold Israel's right of free navigation through Suez and the Gulf of Eilat made on February 20, 1957,[99] was just another worthless scrap of American paper when the time came to honor it during the Johnson administration.

The United Nations reneged on its commitment and the multinational force was pulled out of Sinai; the Americans reneged on their guarantee (the lame excuse given was that they "could not find a copy of the commitment"[100]), and Israel was embroiled in a military holocaust as a result. Israel won hands down, but hundreds of Israeli and thousands of Egyptian, Syrian, Jordanian, Iraqi and Libyan soldiers were killed, while many more thousands were maimed and injured. Who in the United Nations or in the Johnson administration lost any sleep over the causalities? All

The United Nations

the deaths, disfigurements, pain and suffering could have been avoided if the "guarantees" really had been guarantees instead of useless pieces of paper.

The United Nations' multinational forces are supposed to be neutral bodies that keep warring factions apart, thereby maintaining a peace in that particular region. But when it comes to Israel, the United Nations either sides with the enemies of Israel, or acts like a fire brigade that flees at the "first smell of smoke and the first sight of fire."[101] And after running away at the first whiff of smoke, the United Nations then adopts cease-fire resolutions easily when they are "designed to stop Israeli advances."[102]

The current Israeli government is foolishly looking toward the United Nations to provide guarantees that peace agreements made with the PLO will be upheld. But the United Nations is "the PLO's sponsor"![103] And the United Nations' anti-Semitic make-up and pathetic peace-keeping record speak for themselves. The Israeli government would indeed be wise to carefully note the statement made by Lebanon's Major Haddad: "If we trusted the United Nations' forces to protect us, we would all be dead."[104]

9

The News Media

Perhaps the most formidable weapon available to the Arabs for use against Israel has been the foreign news media—the American media in particular. Anti-Semitism has moved from the "wandering Jew" to the Jewish state as a whole. By vilifying Israel the news media can express its displeasure at all Jews and all things Jewish.

Currently there are around 200 press bureaus in Israel—now the second largest concentration of journalists in the world. Israel is not a Western country, it is a Middle Eastern country. Israeli culture and thinking is "foreign and exasperating"[1] to American and other Western journalists. Most foreign journalists know little or no Hebrew (Israel's official language), and this only adds to their "anger,"[2] "confusion, disappointment and disorientation."[3] This reflects in their reporting which, "for the most part, is biased and inaccurate."[4] And some journalists "do not report Israel, they are at war with Israel."[5]

> "Most foreign journalists in Israel during the past decade are not just charter members of the 'blame Israel first' crowd; they are spiritual heirs of Walter Duranty, the first *New York Times* Pulitzer Prize winner. One of the most distinguished journalists of his time, Duranty almost single-handedly changed Western opinion on the Soviet Union with his reports from the USSR in the 1930s. His stories were monstrous lies and deceptive half-truths, whose full extent was discovered only with the fall of the Soviet empire."[6]

The generation of American reporters that have come to Israel "matured during the period of the civil rights struggle in the United States."[7] At the back of their minds, the Arabs in the Israeli administered territories are "viewed as the Middle East equivalents of the blacks in the United States,"[8] and the reporters and editors are on the side of those they consider to be the underdog.

Again, Israel is not a Western country, but it is a democracy—the only democracy in a totalitarian Middle East. But it is a democracy at war. Being a democracy, however, the central question in the American reporter's mind becomes "If they are like us, why don't they behave like us?"[9] Those that pose the question choose to ignore the disgraceful facts that America in peace time has a crime rate that is unprecedented anywhere else in the world, and has as a consequence, the highest incarceration rate in the world; that America has the largest pornographic industry in the world—bigger than both its film and music industries combined—warping the minds of countless millions around the globe; and that during the five years of Israel's war to put down the *intifada* in which some 350 Arabs were killed by Israeli troops (for which Israel was publicly crucified by the American media), around 125,000 Americans were brutally murdered at the hands of their own countrymen.[10] Apparently this is fully acceptable, democratic American behavior.

Most foreign journalists know less Israeli history than the average bell-boy in a Midwestern hotel. Thus Thomas Friedman, winner of two Pulitzer prizes, wrote about Arafat and "biblical Palestine."[11] There is no such thing as "biblical Palestine" and never has been, but journalistic ignorance continually usurps Israel's right to its ancient land in the minds of readers and television viewers around the world.

The inability to speak Hebrew forces most foreign journalists to rely on other ways to obtain "news." This means that many only air "facts" provided directly or indirectly by Arabs—whether these are untruths, half-truths or outright lies. The Arab capacity for sheer fabrication is absolutely amazing. Arab "eye witness accounts of Israeli atrocities" can be similar to this account televised on March 13, 1992: "I saw it with my own eyes, with my own eyes, how the three [Israeli] soldiers who killed him bent over on the ground and drank his blood."[12]

Another primary source of information for foreign journalists are the officers of UNRWA (United Nations Relief and Works Agency).[13] Earlier, we saw just how biased and anti-Semitic this organization is. Information obtained by journalists from UNRWA officers is direct Arab propaganda. But, as will become clear, the

The News Media   183

media is fully adept at fabricating its own lies and deceptions without having to rely upon Arabs or the United Nations.

The free publicity given by an international army of television cameramen to the PLO terrorist organization has been worth billions of dollars to Arafat. The video camera, the VCR and the satellite dish have been no less powerful than tanks, guns and bullets. Every attack on an Israeli town, every murder of an Israeli civilian, every scene of carnage after a bus attack or car-bomb was like an unpaid advertisement on TV for the Arab "cause." It has placed the Arab-Israeli conflict on the front pages of the world's major newspapers and magazines and also on the prime-time slots of television news programs. But the minds of the world's population are fed a pre-packaged, pre-digested diet of "poor Arab-nasty Israeli" meals, and "brave David brings down Goliath the giant Philistine" has long since been replaced by "Jewish bully beats up Arab kid!"

The news media is the real spokesman of the world, and it manipulates the mass of humanity by controlling what it is fed in terms of information and, thereby, controls its judgment and reactions. The anti-Israel media plays along with the Arab cause and gives the Arab-Israeli conflict constant coverage according to Arab dictates—this has affected practically every nation in the world. Nation after nation distanced themselves further from Israel, because it was clear that Israel was "dispossessing" and "oppressing" the Arabs. After all, they had seen them doing it on television night after night, month after month and year after year. When Israeli authorities tried to counteract the damage being done during the *intifada* by restricting the access of television camera crews in the administered territories, the major American television networks distributed "dozens"[14] of "Super-8 video cameras"[15] to the Arabs for them to do their own filming. Obviously, nothing factual or balanced was beamed into millions of homes around the world, but only that which put Arabs in a positive light and Israelis in a negative one.

The foreign press, especially television, bears heavy responsibility for encouraging the murderous deeds perpetrated against

Israelis by members of terrorist organizations, by surreptitiously providing terrorists with cameras. The murderers film their attacks and then pass on the videos to television companies looking for scoops. In some instances, news cameramen have actually been involved in the making of these insidious films. And what vile code of journalistic ethics does a cameraman operate under when he accepts an invitation to photograph the public murder of an Arab by a fellow Arab, and afterward distribute the photos to a news agency for pay? This happened in December 1992 when Yasser Abu Samahdaneh was photographed as he placed a gun to the head of Jamal Fadda and pulled the trigger. The cameraman then photographed Abu Samahdaneh standing on Fadda's corpse "jubilantly proclaiming what he had done."[16] Jim Lederman, a senior American journalist with over 20 years of experience in living and reporting in the Middle East, writes:

> "Media news coverage is a market place. Those who participate in it behave no differently from farmers who come to town on Thursdays to sell their produce or brokers who work on Wall Street. **Each is out to buy, sell, beg, barter, invest, or steal for his or her own defense or gain.**"[17]

Little close attention is paid by viewers to the news coverage of violent clashes between Arabs and Israelis and the numbers of young children, teenagers, women and the elderly involved go almost unnoticed. But it is this continual involvement of young children, teenagers, women and the elderly that has brought sympathy for the Arabs and animosity toward Israelis.

An observant American television viewer commented to me that she had seen the same Arab woman on television three times! The reason for this is that many television crews are not at all embarrassed to treat the world's news as a cheap show by paying all-too-willing "actors and actresses" in order to produce "news" for their employers. The reporters and cameramen produce and direct their own "scenes of violent protest":

> "First it was CBS's *60 Minutes* crew, an ingenious bunch. Back in the 1970s, years before the *intifada*, they were

The News Media 185

accused by Israeli police of paying Arab boys to set tires on fire for the cameras."[18]

And we saw back in chapter 5[19] how American networks in Lebanon in 1982 paid Arab women to demonstrate and yell anti-Israel and anti-American slogans. The minute the cameras stopped rolling, the women would stop shrieking and calmly stand in line to collect their fees." During the *intifada*, "Japanese television crews in Gaza were caught staging a rock-throwing assault on passing jeeps. They paid even more than the German crews in Judea-Samaria."[20] An Australian television crew was also observed asking young Arabs not to throw rocks until they had their cameras in place.

Numbers of crews from all over the world are guilty of the same things. Concocting anti-Israel "news" is no new phenomenon. We have already seen how United Press International (UPI)[21] published something so patently false that it bordered on the criminal, and which effectively ended Israel's bid to rid the world of the murderous PLO terrorist organization in Lebanon in 1982. The news media unblushingly manipulates world leaders including the President of the United States—arguably the most powerful man in the world.

Statistical studies have proven that no national-ethic strife in the world has ever been subjected to such intense coverage as has that of the *intifada* in Israel.[22] The obsession with Israel can be seen by the way the news media gives coverage to other national-ethnic struggles. When the Iraqis gassed and killed 5,000 Kurds in March 1988, for example, the *Boston Globe* ran one front page story, three stories on the inside, published two photographs, and printed one editorial.[23] The coverage of Israel in the same newspaper for the same month produced 13 front page stories, 60 stories on the inside, 15 photographs and six editorials![24] Five thousand lives were taken in Iraq and just a handful in Israel, but Israel received 15 times the amount of coverage! The coverage given to Israel by the media spurred the *intifada* on and fanned the flames of anti-Semitism worldwide. World opinion was manipulated while the media filled up its coffers with billions of dollars. And newsmen gave vent to their latent anti-Semitic feelings while satisfying their huge egos—one American television personality even used to declare before his broadcasts: "I am going to create the Palestinian state right from this studio."[25]

And just as the news media has the power to drive events like the *intifada*, so it has the power to completely blackout events and hide them from the eyes of the world, if it is in their interest to do so. The Syrian annihilation of thousands of General Aoun's Christian militia in Lebanon just prior to the Gulf War (see page 167) was one example. Another blackout, effective since 1993, covers up Egypt's invasion of the Sudan. Egypt invaded the Sudan's strategic Hala'ib triangle with the goal of attaining control of the Persian Gulf.[26] Egypt attempted to invade the Sudan in 1958, but was thwarted by the United Nations. Being confident of its "American umbrella,"[27] Egypt successfully carried out the invasion in 1993. Sudanese officials reported that "Egypt has cut electricity and water supplies, as well as telephone connections to Sudan's Embassy in Cairo."[28] But the media has chosen to keep all this from the eyes of the public.

There was a lot of support for the establishment of a Jewish national home back in yesteryear. But with increased Arab blackmail pressure upon nations to boycott Israel or lose their supply of oil imports, support for Israel dwindled. The Arabs not only forbade trade between Israel and themselves, but also blacklisted Western businesses with links to Israel, and sometimes, even "companies that do business with companies that do business with Israel."[29] Hundreds of European companies regularly honor requests to abandon all Israeli links.[30] European companies have utterly debased themselves in their slavish attempts to placate the Arabs. Hundreds of companies regularly certify that they have no Jewish employees![31] And it is not only Europe that complies to Arab blackmail. Japanese companies also have histories of capitulating to the Arabs.[32] It is expressly against the law for American companies to comply with the Arab boycott, but some do, nevertheless. And *Time* and *Newsweek*, the magazine giants, directly appease the Arabs by including Israel in their European editions rather than their Middle East editions![33] They then print

The News Media

special European ex-Israeli editions (editions that carry no Israeli advertising and are not circulated within Israel).[34] These editions:

> "Cater to companies that wish to avoid the taint of having even pictures of their wares seen by Israeli eyes. And, though it is impossible to put an exact figure on it, the boycott has cost the Israeli economy billions of dollars in lost trade and foreign investment."[35]

These two mammoths—the most powerful and influential in the magazine business—are no more beyond misleading their readers than the big television networks are beyond misleading their viewers. Both *Time* and *Newsweek* have been exposed in their publishing of faked pictures used to illustrate the Israeli "oppression" of the Arabs in the administered territories.[36] Pictures are powerful weapons that can immediately misinform the reader. Readers gets their first impressions of a story from the pictures that accompany the text. Like the television networks, *Time* and *Newsweek* well know the power of the visual image and that, "one picture is worth a thousand words."

Israel has suffered compounded insults to her integrity from the foreign media. The question, "Does the media deliberately mislead the public?" can only be answered in the affirmative—Yes! Often! The media, especially American television networks, are both aware and proud of their immense power to influence the decisions and policy making of their nation's government. Big budgets, massive salaries (senior American television reporters receive salaries equivalent to that of movie actors[37]) and equally hefty egos are involved—these "obscenely overpaid superstars of the American media are often far more famous than the politicians they interview."[38]

These "actors" manipulate the information on which the world makes its decisions. Both the politicians and the people are manipulated by carefully chosen subliminal and background pictures, lighting and sound effects shown at hours when people are hungry or tired and only partially attentive. Events can be created, manipulated or totally falsified,[39] but there are no factual errors or lies as such in the individual segments that make up the film. Therefore the media is almost beyond judicial proceedings, (those that attempt to bring a communications organization to account can spend several years and millions of dollars doing so).[40] But when individual segments—which can sometimes be separated by the space of several years—are spliced together and viewed as a whole, the viewer can be manipulated perceptually to react emotionally at the whim of those responsible for the program.

For example, the reporting by Dean Reynolds—chief correspondent for ABC-TV, one of America's major networks, on the "Temple Mount" episode in October 1990—helped cause negative repercussions to fall upon Israel from both the White House and the United Nations, by the deliberate joining together of two separately filmed events to make them appear as one. With a false visual view of events, and in this case, an equally false audio story to match the visual, the viewers reacted negatively to Israel, which was a prime intention. Reynolds's reporting was vehemently criticized in the Israeli press as "Unadorned, blatant fabrications...lies...."[41]

Splicing film to control the viewer's perception of events is an old trick. The Nazis made full use of it in many of their 1,400 anti-Semitic propaganda films produced between 1939 and 1945 to maintain support for "The Final Solution"—the extermination of the Jewish people.

Mike Wallace, star of CBS-TV *60 Minutes* (CBS is another of America's major networks, and *60 Minutes* has been one of the most popular shows for years), also reported on the "Temple Mount" incident and used the same technique to further discredit Israel in the eyes of the Americans. Wallace deliberately used a segment of an old press conference with former Israeli Deputy Foreign Minister Benjamin Netanyahu, purporting it to have been made at the time. He spliced portions of an interview with Jerusalem's former mayor Teddy Kollek, out of context and out of sequence. Wallace also led Kollek to believe that he was being interviewed for something entirely different, which in itself is a breach of television's rules. Kollek protested to CBS and stated *inter alia*: "Mike Wallace deliberately used me."[42]

Wallace's main production consultant was a well known PLO propagandist,[43] and between the two of them, they gave a grossly distorted and untruthful version of events which not only influenced the White House and American television audiences, but also further inflamed Moslem hatred against Israel. Concerning this screening of events, a noted Israeli newspaper editor condemned both Wallace and CBS in a series of three articles. The third article had a postscript which ended with:

"Innocent Jewish victims of Islamic knifers have paid with their lives for this lie. But we can hardly expect Wallace and his colleagues to think about such matters when making a sensational television show."[44]

ABC-TV's influential and popular anchorman, Peter Jennings, said in an interview: "I am against having a Jewish or Israeli correspondent serving ABC in Israel."[45] Jennings feels that Jews and Israelis cannot be objective in their reporting on Israel. Yet ABC continues to supply "the most distorted coverage of the Middle East of any major TV network, and as senior editor and anchorman, Peter Jennings wields direct influence on the content, tone and prominence of stories aired."[46]

Would his "apparent pro-Arab tilt"[47] and the fact that he "parrots Arab propaganda"[48] have anything to do with the fact that he served in Lebanon as ABC's Beirut bureau chief,[49] and was married to an Arab?[50] Also he had a dating relationship with Hanan Ashrawi, the PLO proxy and Palestinian spokeswoman.[51] An example of Jennings's perception of "objective" reporting was seen on December 14, 1990, when he took a whole 20 seconds to report on the murder of three Jews at a factory in Tel Aviv. He never felt to mention that the Arab killers "quartered one of the victims, beheaded the second and eviscerated [disemboweled] the third."[52] But when in response to the murders, Israel expelled four terrorist leaders, Jennings felt justified in taking eight times as long to report on their expulsion.[53]

As Jennings feels Jews and Israelis simply cannot be objective when reporting on Israel, ABC finds genuinely "impartial," "unbiased" and "objective" people for their programs on Israel. For example, when ABC's Dean Reynolds reported on the somewhat touchy subject of Jerusalem on July 25, 1991, he painstakingly searched out three eminently "impartial, unbiased and objective" people—"**an Arab named Mufid Khaladi, an Arab named Hanan Ashrawi and an Arab named Unir Elyan.**"[54]

Cable News Network (CNN) is the most influential television network, and world leaders often get their information from CNN before their own intelligence agencies provide it. Government leaders are actually "known to have made decisions based on such information."[55] CNN and Peter Arnett still propagate the myth that Arnett was the only Western correspondent left in Baghdad during the Gulf War. But Alfonso Rojo of *El Mundo* was there before the start of the conflict and remained until all Western correspondents, including Arnett, were expelled.[56] Rojo insists that the "powdered milk factory" which Arnett displayed on the CNN screen after it had been destroyed by allied bombing, was in fact "a center for nuclear weapons research and development."[57] An *El Mundo* editorial also asserted that "Arnett's behavior implied that CNN might have been in connivance with Baghdad."[58] And world leaders actually make decisions that affect their nations according to what they see on the CNN screen!

The CNN network is as anti-Israel as other television networks. In November 1993, for instance, an Arab plunged a knife into the back of an Israeli garage mechanic and then lunged at the Israeli's heart. The man managed to intercept the knife with his hand, but lost a finger in the process. Despite his injury, the Israeli managed to pull out his gun and shoot the would be murderer dead. CNN World News "fairly" summed up the event: "Last week a Palestinian was killed in a dispute with an Israeli."[59] And on March 4, 1994, when it was already known that Arabs were the prime suspects in the bombing of the World Trade Center, CNN chose to show Arabs in Gaza declaring that they were going to kill Jews, rather than breathe a word about Arabs having bombed New York.[60]

In all matters related to the Arab-Israeli conflict, the British Broadcasting Corporation (BBC) long ago stopped being a news medium. It has become a public-relations agency in the service of the PLO. David Bar-Illan, Executive Editor of *The Jerusalem Post*, writes that "to wait for the BBC to present a program from an Israeli perspective is to wait for hell to freeze over."[61] Dr. Gerald M. Steinberg, a political scientist who heads the Division of Journalism and Public Communications at Bar-Ilan University, wrote the Director General of BBC radio in late 1993 concerning their coverage of Israel:

> "The reports of Mr. Tim Llewelyn, the BBC's Middle East correspondent, violate the elementary norms and ethics of a professional journalist. Day after day, Mr. Llewelyn feeds the BBC audience with simplistic Palestinian propaganda and slogans."[62]

Dr. Steinberg goes on to say that Llewelyn's reports are "racist propaganda" and insinuates that Llewelyn is an accessory to terror and racism.[63] Five weeks later one of Checkland's assistants replied to Dr. Steinberg's letter stating that Mr. Llewelyn was attempting to present the "Palestinian point of view."[64]

The Palestinian point of view" is also woven into how the BBC views murderous attacks on Israelis. In late 1993 for example, an Israeli civilian was attacked by two Arabs wielding axes. They hacked his head, hands and legs so severely that he required nine hours of continuous surgery. During the attack, badly wounded as he was, he managed to draw his gun and shoot one of the attackers dead while the other ran off. This attack was described by the BBC as: "A Jewish settler shot to death a Palestinian on the West Bank."[65]

Scenes of the shooting of 29 Arabs by Dr. Goldstein in February 1994, was aired on BBC television every hour for days on end and intermittently for two full weeks. But when Moslem terrorists blew up the Jewish cultural center in Buenos Aires on July 18, 1994, demolishing a seven-floor building, killing more than 100, and injuring over 250, the BBC never saw fit to even mention it on its news programs at all that day. That terrible attack all but destroyed Jewish cultural life in the city, but it was "almost ignored by the foreign media."[66]

The prejudice in the BBC's reporting on Israel can be seen in the way it always called IRA gunmen "terrorists," but PLO killers of Israeli women and children are "commandos" or "guerillas."[67] And the pro-Arab-anti-Israel stance of BBC television's reporting from Israel is also made plain in the likes of the interview with masked members of the Black Eagles terrorist group in late 1993. When asked what they think of Israel, the leader of the murder gang (the Black Eagles are affiliated to Arafat's *Fatah*) replied: "For us, Israel doesn't exist."[68] The BBC editors apparently felt that only Israel's enemies would understand Arabic, because this English subtitle appeared: "We have nothing against the Jews."[69]

Britain's Channel 4 follows hard in the footsteps of its BBC patriarch with its airing of *The Big Battalions*, a series dealing with religious conflicts. In its portrayal of the Arab-Israeli conflict, an Israeli sign in Hebrew which read, "Welcome to the Allenby Bridge border station" was reinterpreted as "Allenby Bridge—checkpoint for Arabs."[70] But harder for Israelis to swallow was the translation of the lyrical Hebrew lines, "There's stones, stones, stones. I'll teach you how to throw." The English subtitles appeared as, "This is how we deal with Arab scum."[71]

Of all the British newspapers, *The Guardian* is perhaps the most obnoxious toward Israel. In August 1992, it listed a television show, *Heart of the Matter*, about the trials and tribulations of women soldiers in the Gulf War. Now, most everybody in the entire world knew that Israel stayed out of the war at America's request, but that did not stop the *Guardian* from describing the television program as "the story of a brave American woman: an army major who was 'sexually assaulted by Israeli guards.'"[72] After three days of protests the paper did print a correction—on page 30: "The guards were of course Iraqis. We apologise for the error"[73]

And what sort of pus festers in the heart of *Guardian* writer, Edward Pearce, for him to write about Israeli civilians as "racist, oppressive and arrogant;"[74] "conscious, get-out-of-my-way intruders;"[75] "riding around in swagger-wagons cowing local Arabs."[76] Pearce describes Israel itself as "a diminished, ugly place...garnished by know-nothing zealotry, a flourish of phylacteries worthy of the Christian Middle Ages."[77] That a handful of determined Jews drove tens of thousands of British troops from the Middle East must really be irking Pearce and company.

According to Derek Brown, the *Guardian*'s Israel correspondent, Gaza Arabs are nothing but ducks at an Israeli shooting gallery. He relates how Israeli soldiers simply shoot a boy "just coming out of his house;"[78] how they shoot another "just getting into a car;"[79] and how soldiers are stationed on roofs "shooting when they like. They do this every day. There is no confrontation. They only shoot."[80] The column that contains Brown's insidious report is called "**Eyewitness.**" But Brown saw not a single event that he presents as gospel truth. He got it all "**by listening to stories at the United Nations health center in Gaza.**"[81]

Not all foreign journalists or news editors are unethical or anti-Israel. One honest reporter[82] spoke out against what he called "unfair" and "biased" reporting on Israel. His article correctly evaluated the media's reason for its anti-Israel presentations by posing the question, "So what causes this bias—esteem for Jewish ethics or for Arab oil?"[83]

It is a known fact that those who own the media determine when and what the media will broadcast or publish. In 1988, while ministering in New Zealand, I was informed via the person then in charge of incoming news for the government-owned New Zealand Broadcasting Corporation, that only items portraying Israel in a poor light could be broadcast on the single channel television network—all else was consigned to the trash can. But the American media is by far the world's most powerful media and has been the most damaging to Israel. American television, as a whole, "holds a near monopoly on the presentation and dissemination of moving images of events taking place in foreign lands."[84] And with the American media wielding so much power, we should ask, "Who owns the American media?" Consider the following:

"Ten financial and business corporations control three of the four major television and radio networks, 59 magazines, including *Time* and *Newsweek*, 58 newspapers, including the *New York Times*, the *Washington Post* and the *Los Angeles Times*. Three-quarters of the major stockholders of ABC, CBS and NBC are banks like Chase Manhattan, Morgan Guarantee Trust, Citibank and Bank of America... some corporate owners intervene directly to control the news and public information."[85]

But what is not made clear in the above is that all ten corporations and each of the four banks are all, in turn, owned by a single conglomerate—the Rockerfeller family. And it is an alarming fact that the Rockerfellers "control every facet of the information industry, from television to public education."[86] It is widely believed and often stated that the Jews control the media. But the Rockerfellers are not Jews, and this should put that lie to rest. The Rockerfellers not only control the information industry, but practically all media personalities are members or past members of the Rockerfeller controlled Council on Foreign Relations and the Trilateral Commission.[87] And, according to Gary H. Kah, a high ranking government liaison, it is not unfair to say that the Council on Foreign Relations and the Trilateral Commission actually run the United States government.[88] The Council on Foreign Relations is also the driving force behind the establishment of the New World Order (One World Government) which seeks to bring the whole world under Satan's government[89]

It is also fact that "Oil representatives sit on the boards of the most powerful news media."[90] Each of these directors is legally obligated to act in the best interest of each corporation on whose board he sits, thus:

"In the Arab-Israeli conflict, where hundreds of billions of petrodollars are involved, it requires little imagination to guess where the interests of the oil-banking-investment directors lie."[91]

It should now come as no surprise that at least four of the

world's seven largest oil companies are known to be under the control of the Rockerfellers.[92] And just one of those companies known to be controlled by the Rockerfeller family—Standard Oil of New Jersey (Exxon)—controls 321 other oil companies, some of which are "themselves among the largest corporations in the world."[93] Thus, we clearly see a twofold thrust in the media's crucifying of Israel: Satan wants to dethrone the *"God of Israel"* and seeks to rule the world himself from Jerusalem—sitting *"as God in the temple of God, showing himself that he is God"* (2 Thessalonians 2:4); Israel has absolutely no oil deposits worth anything in terms of real money, whereas the Arabs and Moslem Iran control two-thirds of the world's supply. And the easiest and simplest way to continue siphoning billions of petro-dollars from the Arab and Iranian oil owners into the pocket of the coming One World Government is to appease them by maligning Israel.

The second highest concentration of journalists in the whole world reside in Jerusalem, and they are all looking for a story that might keep their employers happy. To do this many journalists are forced to compromise their personal and moral ethics in order to provide for themselves and their families:

"In the normal hiring and firing of reporters, editors, writers and producers, the owning corporations quietly eliminate those who do not conform to corporate wishes...Anyone who believes that writers have complete freedom also believe in the tooth fairy."[94]

Faked, fraudulent and biased reporting against Israel emanates from the same demonic spirit and the same black ooze that brings economic and political bias against Israel. And the acquisition by a Saudi Arab of United Press International (UPI) in June 1992, can only fuel anti-Israel sentiments throughout the world—even worse than its effort concerning the seven-month-old baby in Lebanon. United Press International is one of the major wire services of the world, and most local newspapers in the West get their Middle East news from wire services. Within a few short weeks after Walid Ibrahim, owner of the London-registered Middle East Broadcasting Center, bought the bankrupt UPI for

$4 million, Israel felt the sting of its new ownership. After the publication of an anti-Israel article dispatched from Jerusalem and printed in *The Toronto Sun*, David Bar-Illan took UPI to task and publicly charged them with publishing "an unmitigated, vicious lie."[95]

But for all of it's shortcomings, UPI is not the worst of the wire services. Reuters is far more "virulent and openly anti-Israel,"[96] and cannot show a single story from Israel "even remotely favorable to the state in the past decade."[97] "Reuters has made a policy never to present the Israeli view."[98] Reuters employs Daoud Kuttab, the PLO propagandist[99] (CBS-TV's consultant mentioned above), as well as PLO and *Hamas* operatives.[100]

One of Reuters Gaza correspondents was arrested and spent time in jail for his help in distributing a Hamas leaflet calling for attacks on Israelis.[101] Four other Reuters journalists were arrested for circulating videos showing a masked *Hamas* terrorist holding a bound, kidnapped Israeli soldier pleading for his life[102]—the video was made by a Reuters cameraman.[103] Two weeks later yet another Reuters correspondent—who has been arrested in the past by both Israeli and Arab police—"together with his brother who works for CBS"[104] was arrested after another Reuters cameraman "filmed a masked man in Gaza reading the *Hamas* ransom demand"[105] for the release of the kidnapped soldier. The soldier, sergeant Nahshon Wachsman, was later murdered—shot in the head at close range—while still bound hand and foot.

With such an employ of terrorists and terrorist sympathizers, the reader might now understand why, like the BBC, Reuters correspondents portray Arab murderers as "guerillas," "freedom fighters" or "militant activists," instead of what they really are—terrorists and murders. As Reuters reporter, Jack Reddon, wrote in February 1993: "One man's terrorist is another man's freedom fighter."[106] And it helps us to understand why Arafat, responsible for the murder of thousands, is glowingly written up as the "Symbol of struggle"[107]: "...secretive guerrilla leader and charismatic politician, he rose to be a world statesman, eventually sharing the stage with President Clinton... ."[108]

Reuters reports sent out around the world from Israel contain biased and incorrect information. The report concerning the July

The News Media   197

1994 riot at the Erez checkpoint, for example, printed in New Zealand's leading newspaper, stated that "workers burned a gas station and a bus terminal...Twenty buses were destroyed."[109] Rampaging Arabs looted both the gas station and bus terminal before setting them on fire, and it was not only 22 buses that were destroyed, but "152 new buses."[110]

Space has allowed us but a few brief examples out of the hundreds and hundreds available—hateful reports, fabrications and misinformative news items concerning Israel. Suffice it to say that all over the world—from east to west, from north to south—from the Americas to Europe, from the Far East to Australia and New Zealand, television networks, radio networks, newspapers and magazines are maligning Israel and the Jewish people.

Tempted by reward, the corrupt prophet Balaam was willing to curse the Jewish people (Numbers 22:5–24:25). Many today, for the same reason, are willing to curse those whom God has blessed. The Soviet people learned to treat anything published in *Pravda* as a lie until proven otherwise. We would all do well to imitate the former Soviets and adopt the same attitude toward the Western media.

10
The Israeli Connection

Israel is a unique nation: The *"Maker"* and *"Creator of Israel"* is its *"King—the LORD of hosts, the Holy One of Israel"* (Isaiah 43:15,45:11,54:5). And *"the LORD"* elected Israel to adoption as a son—*"Israel is My son, My firstborn"* (Exodus 4:22). Israel was created and elected to God's purposes, and all attempts to create its own purpose brought home the terrible truth that God's name is *"Jealous,"* and that He is *"a jealous God"* and *"a consuming fire"* (Exodus 34:14; Deuteronomy 4:24).

Israel has a long, long history accompanied by miraculous interventions of Almighty God which raised it to a position of unsurpassed glory when it contemplated His ways and acted accordingly. Antithetically, it was reduced to the deepest depths of misery and despair—to destruction and servitude—when it determined to walk the way of the nations. And Prime Minister Yitzhak Rabin's statement at the Cairo signing ceremony in May 1994, that Israel simply wants "to be like all other nations,"[1] bodes ill for today's people of Israel.

The terrible distresses that befell Israel in the past were due entirely to forgetting God. Israel forgot God, but could not escape Him. Planning for a secure and peaceful future for the Israel of the 21st century must factor in God's presence and will, if further distress of catastrophic proportions is to be avoided—vision which fails to include God is practical blindness. The Israeli-PLO accord is more than a step toward further distress, it is a giant leap to embrace it. As Israel basks in the plaudits of the nations for making "peace" with its enemies, an Israeli proudly reveals how so much apparent progress has been made: **"We succeeded because for the first time the government took God out of the equation."**[2]

The modern, reestablished state of Israel is a direct fulfillment of Biblical prophecy concerning ancient Israel, and so is the ingathering of God's elect people from the four corners of the earth. Israel's leaders of today are God's people, but not God-people. And here lies Israel's problem.

The current Israeli government led by Prime Minister Yitzhak Rabin and Foreign Minister Shimon Peres is a humanist government—perhaps even the most ungodly government ever to be in power during Israel's entire 4,000 years of history. It has no belief in God, no belief in His Word, no belief in His covenants, and no belief in the coming of the Messiah. Its belief is in man and in man's capabilities. Members of this government even quote the Bible and the Prayer Book on occasions, but that does not alter the fact that they do not believe it. Shulamit Aloni, for example, (former Minister of Education and Culture, now Minister of Communications) speaks about the "beauty of the Bible,"[3] but stresses that "the Bible is not a religious book."[4] She has also suggested that the word "God" should be dropped from the *Yizkor* prayer used at IDF ceremonies[5] to make it "acceptable" to Israelis. As Shakespeare is to the British, so the Bible is to Rabin's government.

The June Elections

Yitzhak Rabin successfully wrested the leadership of the Labor party from his arch rival Shimon Peres, and led it into the seats of Israeli power as a result of the June 1992 elections. Labor ran a campaign that branded the ruling Likud party as corrupt. The Likud had ruled for 15 years and its overthrow was seen and described by some as a "landslide"[6] victory for Labor. But in actuality Labor crept in "just by the skin of its teeth"[7] managing only to create a 61 seat blocking majority.

Abba Eban, a former Israeli Foreign Minister and fellow humanist, along with most other Labor party members, wrote: "I was more enthused by the decline of Likud than by the rise of my own party."[8] But when the dust had settled, it became clear exactly how thin teeth skin actually is—"**a shift in fewer than 100 votes**"[9] could have created a 60–60 tie which would have effectively left the Likud in power. At worst, there would have been a Likud-Labor unity government.

Seven months after the elections, however, after Labor had become firmly entrenched in office, the state comptroller released the results of an investigation into the running of the election campaigns. The Labor party, which had "yelled 'corruption' and slung mud at the Likud,"[10] now stood "accused of dirty dealings as no other party in this country ever was."[11] What was revealed was "a dire conspiracy by the highest Labor echelons to bring down the Shamir government."[12]

Among illegal acts carried out by the Labor party was the paying out of enormous sums of taxpayers' money to influential heads of large organizations to "persuade" their members to vote for Labor. Even bigger sums were paid to induce other political parties to give Labor their support in any coalition necessary for Labor to rule. The state comptroller fined the Labor party NIS 844,236 ($285,000).[13] for its unlawful and underhanded activities. The Shas religious party had benefited by a "transfer of NIS 1.5 million ($506,000)"[14] to its coffers, and duly lent its support to Rabin and the ensuing Labor coalition. But the comptroller found the Shas party to be even more corrupt in its dealings than Labor and subsequently fined it NIS 3 million ($1 million).[15] Five other political parties were fined a total of "more than NIS 900,000 ($304,000)"[16]

Meanwhile, the Likud party, ousted through a smear campaign after 15 years of government, "emerged from the comptroller's scrutiny without blemish."[17] The party that was daubed "corrupt" was in actual fact found to be "spotless."[18] After the comptroller's report was released the Knesset (Israel's Parliament) control committee head Dan Tichon (Likud) said: "This calls into question the results of the June elections...the Likud failed, because it was not dirty and did not buy power."[19] The leader of the Tsomet party, Raphael Eitan, whose own party also came away spotless, said the comptroller's report "unmasks Labor's true ugly face. It is a corrupt party with corrupt norms, which stopped at no dirty deal to assume power and hold on to it."[20]

In March 1995, another scandal involving Labor's 1992 election campaign hit the headlines. Police investigations showed that millions of dollars were illegally siphoned from the *Histadrut*—the giant, cash-strapped, Labor controlled trade union federation—to finance the political campaigns of senior Labor figures in 1992.[21] An Israeli journalist succinctly described Israel's Labor government as "the best government money can buy.[22]

No Mandate

In truth, Rabin and his Labor coalition government has no mandate at all from the people to rush ahead with its "trading territory for peace," because it came to power via an election that was not democratic in the true sense of the word. Labor used a huge outlay of taxpayers' money to grease the palms of people in high places, and by other sleights of hand, gained enough Arab votes to secure "four or five Knesset seats."[23] Also, there is "evidence to suggest that the decision to betray Jordan and embrace the PLO was taken by Shimon Peres before the 1992 election in Israel **in return for a promise from Arafat to mobilize Arab votes for the Labor Party and its potential coalition partners.**"[24]

And much to the chagrin of many Israelis, Rabin does in fact rely on Arabs to not only keep his government from falling, but to ensure the passing of the controversial agreements in the peace process. One of Rabin's vital Arab coalition partners, Abdul Wahab Darawshe, leader of the Democratic Arab Party, speaks "approvingly of the *intifada*"[25] that has taken such a brutal toll of Israeli lives. To gain Darawshe's support for his coalition, Rabin pledged **NIS 1.7 billion** ($573 million) **a year** in National Insurance Institute funds[26] to Arabs holding Israeli citizenship but who refuse to serve in the Israeli army, making their benefits equal to those who serve. Another Arab member, Hashem Mahameed of the Democratic Front for Peace and Equality (a euphemism for the Communist Party), was filmed by Israel Television inciting Arabs to violence against Israel—calling for "armed struggle against the nation."[27] He was cheered as he told his Gaza audience, which included masked *intifada* "activists": "So long as the occupation continues, so will the struggle, and by struggle we don't mean only stones, but a battle with all the means at our disposal."[28] Later, in an interview with the Israeli newspaper *Yediot Aharonot*, he clearly made his point that in the struggle against Israel "any weapons are justified."[29] Former Chief Rabbi Shlomo Goren has stated:

> "As long as the government does not rest on a Jewish majority but rather on Arab Knesset members—among them

Arab MKs who hate Zion and are willing to lend their hand in destroying the country and who deny our historical and national rights to *Eretz Yisrael*—its decisions have no validity."[30]

Rabin: the Juggler

Rabin, at the time of writing, holds the posts of Prime Minister, Defense Minister, Minister of Religious Affairs and Interior Minister. It is impossible for any one man to do justice to four extremely important government posts and every one of the four ministries are suffering—each portfolio requires a full-time minister. Rabin prides himself on his military capabilities and simply refuses to entertain the idea of another holding the reins of the defense ministry, although he knows he cannot give it the attention that it so desperately requires. But Rabin holds the religious and interior ministries for very different reasons.

The carrot for which the Shas party was induced to join Rabin's coalition was for them to gain the powerful religious and interior portfolios. These posts had been the traditional domain of the National Religious Party for many years, but the NRP refused to join Rabin's coalition. Ariyeh Deri, the leader of Shas, duly became Minister of Religious Affairs and also Minister of the Interior. Deri, however, was forced to resign in September 1994, due to numerous charges of fraud, theft, corruption, breach of public trust, etc. brought against him by the state. His trial, heralded as promising to be "Israel's most spectacular trial,"[31] has drawn much attention due to the virtual mountain of evidence presented by the police against Deri—"2,500 cassette tapes and 115,000 typewritten pages."[32]

Rabin unsuccessfully tried to prevent Deri's forced resignation and even appeared in court to argue on his behalf. After Deri stepped down, Rabin took over his portfolios to keep the positions open, thereby ensuring that Shas would not vote against the coalition on vital issues and bring down the government. Rabin even offered to personally fund Deri's defense.[33] Rabin somehow manages to continually shore-up his house of cards that exists in the guise of a Labor–left-wing–Arab coalition government—much to the sorrow of most Israelis.

Lies and Deceit

After holding office for only a short while, it became obvious that the Rabin-Peres duo has few qualms about lying—either to the public or to the Knesset. In fact, they have lied on so many occasions that few Israelis now give much credence to anything either of them say at all. Tens of thousands of Israelis had voted for Rabin on the strength of promises he had made prior to the elections, but which he "changed his mind"[34] about after taking office. And issues that now threaten to split the nation and engulf it in civil war—such as withdrawal from the Golan Heights—were issues that were going to determine the outcome of the elections. Rabin knew this only too well. He made fine speeches mixed with many firm, unambiguous promises and allayed the fears that filled the hearts of hundreds of thousands, if not millions, of Israelis.

On June 10, 1992, just 13 days before the people cast their votes, Rabin visited the Golan and assured those living on the Heights (and through them the rest of the nation), that if he was elected, he would on no account give up the Golan. The time and place were dramatic—it was the 25th anniversary of the capture of the Golan Heights during the Six Day War. Rabin spoke about the "terrible nightmare"[35]—the murderous rain of shells on Israel's northern Galilee towns from the Syrian-held Golan which had been the norm before the war. (In 1966, in a single day, 300 Katyusha rockets fell[36]).

Rabin recalled the heavy cost the IDF had paid in casualties to capture the towering heights, but it had put an end to that threat "forever," he said, "forever."[37] He showered praise on those who lived in the 32 communities on the Golan, and who had invested years of their lives building up the towns and villages. He proudly mentioned that the town of Katzrin where they were gathered, was founded during his previous tenure as Prime Minister. He claimed to be "filled with hope that Katzrin would become a great Israeli city,"[38] and cried:

> "Let us all invest, invest, here in Katzrin, in the villages and kibbutzim, let us help them live in dignity, maintain their families, absorb immigrants, absorb settlers."[39]

And he spoke especially of the future:

> "As for the future, it is **inconceivable** that even in peacetime we should come down from the Golan. **Whoever even thinks of leaving the Golan wantonly abandons, wantonly abandons, the security of Israel.**"[40]

Less than two weeks later, "71 percent of the Height's 13,500 residents voted for Rabin's Labor Party"[41] on the strength of his reassuring speech—without those votes Rabin and Peres could not have gained power. But within just a few weeks of taking office, Rabin made it known that he was prepared to "compromise" on the issue of retaining all of the Golan Heights. And as the months ticked by, Israel braced itself for Rabin's real "compromise." Although he had denied the rumors a hundred times his "compromise" finally became public: "Israel was prepared to withdraw totally and absolutely from the Golan Heights."[42] Israel would "give up every last inch of the Golan."[43] "Rabin does not think that lying to the public to win an election is a crime. He does not try to cover it up. On the contrary, he practically boasts about it."[44]

The great majority of the people on the Golan were, and still are, devastated at Rabin's betrayal—the total disregard of his clear promises. After being encouraged to pioneer settlements on the strategic, formerly barren Golan; after investing 25 years of their lives building homes, schools, synagogues and community centers; after establishing Israel's most prestigious vineyards, they are callously told in a round-about way that they are soon to be uprooted—their towns, villages, and vineyards razed.

The people reacted. The same Golan residents that cheered Rabin during his election campaign are today burning tires and holding anti-government demonstrations—along with tens of thousands of other Israelis. One year later, the same Rabin, who showered praise on the Golan's inhabitants and promised never to come down from the Heights, said of the people he duped: "The Golan settlers can spin around in their demonstrations like propellers. It won't do them any good."[45] Completely unmoved by their mass demonstrations, 12 residents of the Golan entered into an open-ended hunger strike. As many as 200,000 Israelis made a "pilgrimage" up to the Golan "in a massive display of solidarity with the hunger strikers."[46] That fact got hold of Rabin's attention. He "lashed out at the Golan hunger strikers"[47] and declared: "**I do not accept hunger strikes as proper behavior in a democracy**"![48]

Israeli Opposition

The term "Israeli-PLO accord" is often replaced with "Rabin-Arafat pact," because "**polls show that most Israelis oppose the agreement**"[49] and reject the handing over of "130,000[50] of their fellow citizens to the mercies of the nation's worst enemies."[51] Demonstrations are everywhere—protesters sit down in the middle of busy intersections and completely disrupt traffic just to let the government know that they oppose its policies. Massive demonstrations have taken place—the largest political protests in the history of the recreated state, and possibly, in Israel's entire history. Rabin sweeps all the chaos aside and dismisses these immense demonstrations as "nothing more than a nuisance to be ignored."[52] Other settlers, from Judea and Samaria—the heartland of Biblical Israel—demonstrated as well. They were also encouraged to build their lives under pioneer conditions, and have "exercised Job-like patience throughout the past six years of incessant stonings, petrol bombings, stabbings and shootings by Arab terrorists of every stripe."[53] Like the Golan settlers, they feel abandoned, and fear for their future also. Rabin called them "cry-babies"[54] and said they were "not real Israelis,"[55] and that "they don't move me."[56]

On December 8, 1993, as Shimon Peres arrived at a Jerusalem hotel to attend a Shas banquet, he was greeted by about a dozen demonstrators. Peres turned to the leader of the group, an Austrian-born Holocaust survivor who came to live in Jerusalem with her husband and four children 18 years ago, and demanded angrily:

"Where do you live?"

"Jerusalem," she said in Hebrew.

Apparently noticing her accented Hebrew, Peres switched to his

Polish accented English and said insultingly:
"You don't belong here! Go back where you came from!"[57]

"Give It To Them"

A "get-tough" policy is advocated against those disagreeing with government policies. Environment Minister Yossi Sarid is quoted as admonishing the security forces to "'**stop treating settlers with kid gloves. Give it to them**,' he urged."[58]

Almost a quarter of a million protesters gathered together on September 6, 1993. They arrived in thousands of vehicles (including 2,000 buses),[59] and on foot. It was to be a passive demonstration, symbolically laying siege to the seat of power—the Knesset complex. The "get tough" policy and government contempt of the peoples' opinions were demonstrated by the Police Commissioner Rafi Peled, who "**ordered excessive force to disperse the crowd**, as jails were too full to accommodate mass arrests."[60] "Police clubbed demonstrators with batons, dragged, kicked and beat people. After 45 minutes, the area was clear. Dozens were removed by ambulance...."[61]

The settlers were once the heroes of Israel, now they have been delegitimatized by their own government. And the "Give it to them" suggested by Yossi Sarid, has been taken seriously. Netty Gross, a Jerusalem based journalist, happened to be in the emergency room of the *Shaare Zedek* hospital the night Anat Cohen was brought in by a "contingent of at least five police officers of various ranks, including a powerfully built female cop."[62] Cohen, a mother of eight children, had "resisted arrest" and had been, according to settlers, "brutalized by the police."[63] Gross wrote that Cohen's face seemed puffy; she spoke haltingly, and she could barely walk."[64] The reason given by police for using their version of "reasonable force"[65] against Cohen to induce her to accompany them to the police station, "was due to her insistence upon taking her two-month old infant with her to nurse."[66] Gross was taken aback by Cohen's condition and said: "I don't know what sort of force was used against this mother of eight for the crime of wanting to nurse her baby. But whatever it was, it didn't seem 'reasonable'...it wasn't a pretty picture."[67]

And the police "get tough" violence is not just restricted to "dangerous" nursing mothers, but also to other women posing a dire threat to Israel's security—for example, the "handicapped 60-year-old"[68] who was "roughed up,"[69] and the arrested "82-year-old winner of the Jerusalem award for voluntarism."[70] The police defy regulations by not wearing their identity tags,[71] which effectively prevents their victims from identifying them. The police bullies are also flinging "women to the ground,"[72] and throwing "housewives in jail for no reason."[73]

The whole country is seething at the actions of the Rabin government. Even the prayer for the welfare of the state, recited on Sabbath and holiday mornings, has become a point of sharp contention in many Israeli synagogues. The peace of Sabbath services is "shattered by shouting matches"[74] over whether Rabin's government deserves the prayer. Former chief rabbi Shlomo Goren says, "There is no need to pray for a government that is handing over half the country to the dean of murderers."[75] And in just one synagogue in the Jewish New Year service, as the cantor began the phrase calling on God to enlighten government ministers, one man shouted out: "It's a shame and disgrace that we should pray for divine blessing for the likes of Shulamit Aloni."[76] Another yelled, "We should curse the government."[77] And this goes on throughout all of Israel.

An Israeli visiting the memorial to Mordechai Lipkin, one of the victims "offered up on the altar of a false peace"[78] who was brutally murdered by Arab terrorists, was asked if she had watched the Cairo signing ceremony. She replied: "I watched the signing because I hoped I would see them get killed."[79]

While in Washington for talks with President Clinton, Rabin was asked by the American news media about the widespread Israeli opposition to his leadership. He blithely answered: "I don't care what they think, when I make up my mind to do something, I do it."[80] His minority government is accused of "lip service, insulting remarks and blatant lies,"[81] and opposition MKs are presenting bills to the Knesset in an endeavor to stop Rabin from ceding the Golan Heights and Jerusalem by simple majority votes from his Labor–left-wing–Arab coalition. If passed into Israeli law, the bills would require a majority vote of 80 Knesset members out of the total of 120, to cede all or part of the Golan, and also to cede all or part of Jerusalem.

Rabin promised he would not "sign a peace treaty without first calling new elections or going to the people in the form of a national referendum,"[82] but he totally ignored public opinion and simply signed the agreement with the PLO. Few trust him to keep his word concerning any referendum, and the shallowness of Rabin's commitment of "going to the people" is expressed by Labor Party secretary-general Nissim Zvilli: "There is no logic on earth for Labor today to say it must ask the people...**Labor can cede whatever territories it wants to without asking anybody.**"[83]

In submitting the bill for a change in the present law concerning the necessary majority for ceding the Golan, Yitzhak Levy of the National Religious Party said his bill was necessary "because Rabin could not be trusted to keep his promise. The Prime Minister is the biggest penitent in the nation—he repents of every statement he makes."[84] Few trust Rabin because he unequivocally promised not to withdraw from the Golan, and now he is willing to withdraw from "every last inch" of it. Few trust him because he has "violated his commitment to the electorate not to recognize or negotiate with the PLO."[85] Not only has he negotiated with the terror organization, but he has legitimatized it, signed an agreement with it, and is preparing the way for an independent state of Palestine with Arafat as president on a full one-third of Israel's land.[86]

Rabin has also repeatedly sworn that Jerusalem would forever remain Israel's undivided capital. In July 1992 he said: "United Jerusalem has been and will forever be the capital of the Jewish people under Israel sovereignty, a focus of the dreams and longings of every Jew."[87] He reaffirmed this in June 1994 when he said: "Jerusalem, our eternal capital, will remain united and no one will change this."[88] But now Rabin "mocks" the very notion that Jerusalem's Jews and Arabs can mix, and speaks of "complete separation."[89]

Labor MKs have already met with PLO leaders to discuss dividing the city's authority between them,[90] and Rabin is "strongly against the Landau Bill"[91] which proposes to change the existing law to require an 80 member majority vote before ceding any part of Jerusalem. The bill would make it more difficult for the government to make concessions on the city, but Rabin says the bill "would establish preconditions in the negotiations."[92]

But if Jerusalem really is "non-negotiable"[93]—not "open to negotiation"[94]—as Rabin repeatedly states, then preconditions surely need to be established, unless of course he has already formulated "secret" plans to divide the city and cede the eastern sector to the PLO. It is very apparent that the emperor is naked even in the eyes of Israeli high school students. A girl student, skeptical of Rabin's intentions, asks: "How is Jerusalem's status permanent if the [Rabin-Arafat] agreement says it will be discussed at a later date? Why discuss something unchangeable?"[95]

In many speeches over a period of several months, Arafat made mention of a letter he purported to have received concerning the status of Jerusalem. Rabin's government made equally firm denials of the alleged letter's existence as Arafat did of it being in his possession. Finally, however, in June, 1994, the government gave in to the mounting pressure, and Rabin acknowledged that Peres, with his authorization, had indeed written a letter "encouraging" PLO institutions in Jerusalem and had "pledged" to preserve them.[96] Feisal al-Husseini, a top PLO official, said in an interview that the PLO received other letters in February, 1994[97]—this has also been denied by Rabin.

During an August 1994 Knesset session, an MK protested that the government had promised the PLO it could build a "resort on the shores of the Dead Sea"[98]—opening up the area to the Arab terrorism that has plagued every place on which they have set foot thus far. Rabin called the MK "a liar," and said there was no such agreement. The MK subsequently produced a copy of a letter granting the PLO permission for the Dead Sea resort—it was signed by Shimon Peres.[99] Rafael Eitan, leader of the Tsomet Party, said, "Rabin and Peres are liars; they lied to the people; they lied to their voters; and they've signed an agreement with the greatest murderer of Jews since Hitler."[100] Arafat, the man they refer to, is, says Shimon Peres, **our ally**."[101]

The Rabin-Peres government has tried to fool the world into believing that the peace process is the will of the Israeli people.

The Israeli Connection

Nothing could be further from the truth. The majority of Israeli people are not with Rabin and Peres despite the government's attempt to brainwash them into accepting its disastrous actions. Massive amounts of taxpayers' money is being spent to rent advertising space on hundreds of street signs, bus shelters and walls of buildings to promote the peace agreement.

There also is a collusion of deceit between the Israeli government and the overwhelming majority of Israeli and foreign medias. Completely false crowd numbers are published about demonstrations in order to play down the extent of public opposition. Thus, the huge gathering of more than 200,000 Israelis opposed to the signing of the agreement with Arafat in September 1993, was presented in the foreign media as "an unruly mob gathered outside PM's office."[102] And when some 100,000 Israelis swarmed into Jerusalem to protest Arafat's arrival in July 1994, the news medias gave the figure of 5,000 for the seething mass that filled the streets and pedestrian malls of the city's downtown area.

Conversely, when 300 Peace Now activists gathered in support of the Rabin-Arafat agreement, the media gave it wide coverage. Obviously, they were desperately searching for something to print, because one featured story was a **16-year-old** Israeli who said of the accord's signing: **"It's the highlight of my political life** so far."[103] The high school student was described as having "always been politically active."[104] The distinguished *Wall Street Journal* published a similar piece of inane "representative Israeli opinion" on the subject of Jerusalem's division when it published a pro-peace interview with an Israeli mother and 17-year-old son.[105] When researchers from the Hebrew University's education and psychology departments actually conducted a poll among the Israeli youth, however, they found that 70 percent[106] were against the PLO agreement and 78 percent[107] were against withdrawal from the Golan Heights. And, it should be remembered that those interviewed are the very ones who must fight to defend their country when Rabin's "peace" is found to be what it is—a hoax.

According to a Gallup poll, the majority of Israelis actually want the senior PLO officials put on trial for murder! Far from embracing the Israeli-PLO agreement, almost 66 percent of the population—including 59 percent of Labor voters[108]—want the PLO officials put on trial. In a similar poll conducted by the Dahaf Institute, 63 percent[109] of the Israeli public were found to be against any further negotiations with the PLO, and 27 percent of those surveyed said that they had shifted from support of the peace process to "outright opposition."[110] Another Gallup poll showed that even if Syria really aspired to a full peace—cessation of hostilities, open borders, establishing of diplomatic embassies, etc.—57 percent[111] of all Israelis would still oppose a full withdrawal from the Golan. And on the question of Jerusalem, yet another Gallup poll showed a staggering 89 percent[112] of Israelis are opposed to any "change in the status of any part of Jerusalem"[113]

A real, tangible expression of the Israeli people's opposition to the Rabin-Arafat agreement was apparent on November 2, 1993, the day Israel held its municipal elections. Municipal elections should have nothing to do with national politics, but Rabin made them political when he campaigned for MK Avigdor Kahalani, the Labor candidate in the Tel Aviv mayoral election, and said: "The world will view the results of next week's Tel Aviv mayoral election as a measure of Israel's support for the peace process."[114] Rabin then went up to Jerusalem to back Jerusalem's beloved incumbent mayor Teddy Kollek, a Labor party member who had been mayor for 28 consecutive years. Rabin said: "I came here to say that the Jewish people, the State of Israel, the residents of Israel, and residents of Jerusalem are in debt to a great man, who since 1966 has been mayor of Jerusalem."[115] Kollek, without doubt, was one of the world's most distinguished and best loved mayors, but Rabin made Kollek's reelection "a referendum for the agreement with the PLO."[116] A Likud candidate, Ehud Olmert, contested the mayoralty along with Shas candidate Nissim Ze'ev. Olmert's subsequent victory was "stunning in its proportions, with the new mayor registering a massive 56.8 percent of the vote."[117] Kollek's defeat was described as "sad and shocking,"[118] but Jerusalem voters let Rabin know exactly where he stood. And so did the voters in other cities. In Tel Aviv, "Kahalani didn't have a chance,"[119] and the Likud's Ronni Milo swept into power. With only two or three exceptions, the Labor candidates were trounced in much the same fashion throughout all of Israel by the Likud. And in early January 1995, *Time* magazine released a report about a secret poll conducted by the Labor Party itself. The results of the poll showed "the Labor party would be soundly defeated"[120] if national elections were to be held at that time. The report created a furor within the Labor Party, and the party "intimated it would sue *Time* for libel."[121]

Muzzling the Media

When public demonstrations against the government's "peace initiative" first began, Israel Television gave the sort of coverage the demonstrations warranted. Rabin, however, was furious and "chastised Communications Minister Shulamit Aloni for 'not controlling' television."[122] The message went out and the head of the Broadcasting Authority "read the signals with perfect perception"[123]—Israel Radio and TV news now follows the directive of the government. Thus, soon after Rabin's rebuke, a program on the Golan featured two local residents who "avidly agreed that they would readily leave the Golan,"[124] and one even "volunteered that she would vote for Rabin in the next election."[125] None of the "90 percent of the Golan residents who regularly tell pollsters they oppose withdrawal"[126] were interviewed.

Practically all of the media has bowed to the government's intention of presenting the Rabin-Arafat agreements as the will of the people. But *The Jerusalem Post* has not complied with government directorates and has been critical of government policies, although it has been more than fair in giving equal space to both the left and right camps of the peace process. In December 1993, however, it published an investigative story by Steve Rodan entitled "Government plans to withdraw to 1967 borders," and was punished by the government's immediate cancellation of 1,110 copies of the Post's English and French international editions distributed to representations of the Israeli Foreign Ministry abroad.[127]

Almost simultaneously, the government doubled its purchases of a Spanish-language newspaper (*Aurora*) for distribution in Spanish-speaking countries. The *Aurora's* editor is "super-dovish and enthusiastically supportive of government policies."[128] The government cited "budgetary reasons" for the Post's cancellation, but Yehuda Levy, the publisher of *The Jerusalem Post* accused the government of "lying,"[129] not only because of the doubling of the purchases of *Aurora*, but also due to the fact that he had offered to continue supplying copies of the Post free of charge which the government had "flatly rejected."[130]

Shimon Peres was reported to be "furious"[131] with the Post and "angered by the antagonistic attitude taken by the paper to Israel's deal with the Palestine Liberation Organization."[132] And an Israel Radio news magazine editor, Eliyahu Ben-On, was even suspended for quoting from the Post's story![133]

No one is allowed to criticize the Rabin/Peres-Arafat/Assad peace process. Disagreeing with the government is illegitimate. If Israelis support it unreservedly, they are "for the peace."[134] But if they have any reservations; if they think it might guarantee another war under the most unfavorable conditions, they are "against the peace."[135]

Having done its utmost to gag or control the media and plaster the country with pro-peace signs and billboards, the government also brought in a law against "unnecessary use of a car's horn," in an overt attempt to stop passing motorists from honking in support of anti-government demonstrations.[136] A substantial police force is on hand at demonstrations to apprehend drivers who "dare to honk in solidarity"[137] and a fine of NIS 160 ($53) is imposed."[138]

The Likud has also filed complaints with the state comptroller, because the Labor Party has even stooped to hiring people to participate in rallies in Tel Aviv and at the Ben Gurion airport, welcoming Rabin home after the signing ceremony in Cairo. They also hired people to stand on street corners holding placards supportive of Rabin.[139] A number of people who went to private employment agencies to find a job were offered work "standing on assigned street corners and major road junctions with placards for NIS 11 ($3.65) an hour plus transportation costs."[140] They were supplied with placards which read: "Rabin, we are with you."[141]

Treason

The deceit entered into by the Rabin government to hoodwink the Israeli people would fill an entire volume on its own. The deception began well before the election campaign and has since gathered momentum. Until the Rabin government voted to lift the ban on meetings with the PLO in January 1993 contact with PLO officials was classified as treason. But Labor Party members and top officials had been meeting with them for two decades or more! Even when Rabin was prime minister in the mid-1970s, he received reports from Major-General (reserve) Matityahu Peled of his private meetings with Arafat![142] And Deputy Foreign Minister Yossi Beilin, the protégé of Shimon Peres—whom Rabin once called "Peres's poodle,"[143] but whom others believe to be the architect behind the entire peace process (it is an established fact today that "Rabin prefers to get his advice from Yossi Beilin"[144])—met with Nabil Sha'ath, now Arafat's top aide, in Cairo on January 19, 1992, and promised him that if Labor won the elections, "it would stop settlements" and "lift the ban on meeting the PLO."[145] Beilin and Peres began their own contacts with the PLO in the mid-1980s,[146] and another Labor MK, Yael Dayan, has met with the PLO in Tunis, Europe and the United States.[147]

Labor members had vehemently denied allegations of meeting with the PLO, but the lies were exposed when Abu Mazen, chief PLO negotiator of the DOP, published his book *The Road to Oslo* in 1993. In it he gave names of Labor Party members who had met with the PLO, the dates of the meetings, and the PLO officials with whom they met. And even worse, Mazen said the meetings prior to the 1992 elections were an attempt by Labor to "torpedo the Likud's Madrid peace talks."[148] After the storm created by Mazen had died down, senior Labor Party sources asked: "What was Labor's crime?"[149] The Likud called it "the most terrible, treasonable conspiracy ever."[150]

There have been too many denials—first of contacts with the PLO and later of concessions—that have all proved to be false. Then the secret letter to Arafat concerning Jerusalem and another concerning a resort at the dead sea—both denied, both proven true. And an assertion by Tsomet MK Moshe Peled that there are in fact "five secret appendices"[151] to the Cairo agreement with the PLO cannot be ignored either. One of these appendices is said to include "a promise to negotiate the fate of Jerusalem, just as Arafat has said."[152]

Rabin repeatedly denied as "baseless"[153] reports that secret talks were being held with Syria, and that an agreement had been reached. But Steve Rodan of *The Jerusalem Post* again did some in-depth investigating, and a three and a half page feature story entitled "Behind Closed Doors" was the result. Discussions had apparently been underway "for the past two years,"[154] and Rabin has indeed arrived at an understanding with Syria over the Golan—to the detriment of Israel, naturally. Yossi Beilin was again one of the envoys, and it was disconcerting to many to know for sure that the Rabin government is "ready to uproot and dismantle settlements."[155]

Communications Minister Shulamit Aloni raised another storm in April 1994 when she said, "It is time Israelis begin saying their farewell to the Golan...The Golan is part of Syria and will be returned to it."[156] And on July 14, 1994, Peres himself said: "The government of Israel has recognized Syrian sovereignty over the Golan Heights."[157] After *Time* magazine reported that Labor would be "soundly defeated," Beilin told the Labor Party: "Labor ought to pursue the peace process as if it had less than two years to carry out its aims...We must not lose sight of the fact that we might not have much time to further our goals... ."[158]

Israel's Knesset opposition is effectively frustrated by the government's Labor–left-wing–Arab blocking majority. And when it loudly voices its objections to Rabin's policies in the Knesset forum, Rabin simply leaves the podium without concluding his remarks or gets up out of his seat and leaves altogether.

IDF and Politics

Lieutenant-General Ehud Barak, Israel's 14th Chief of General Staff, ended his four-year term of duty on December 31, 1994. During his tenure, he often spoke publicly against withdrawing from the Golan which brought rebukes from Rabin. In June 1993, Barak said: "As long as we still have a situation in which war is possible between us and Syria, we need every meter of the Golan

Heights.[159] Just four months before his term was completed—long after Rabin announced that Israel was prepared to "give up every last inch" of the Golan—Barak said: "From a military standpoint, the IDF must retain control of the Golan Heights, **even in peace time.**"[160] And in June 1993, Israel's chief negotiator with Syria, Itamar Rabinovitch, said: "Israel doesn't base its claims to the Golan Heights on the Bible. The Israeli claims to the future of the Golan Heights are based solely on the need for security."[161]

Israel's current Chief of General Staff, Major-General Amnon Lipkin-Shahak, however, believes Israel can survive without the Golan. Shahak was selected by Rabin to be Barak's successor because Shahak had been the chief negotiator of the Cairo accord with the PLO.[162] The position of Chief of General Staff is the highest office in the Israeli Defense Force, but Shahak is a left-wing, pro-peace, Rabin appointee who will be in charge of an army that will likely be ordered to uproot Jewish settlements. And the politically picked IDF High Command is deliberately "distancing itself from the majority of soldiers and lower-rank and middle-rank officers."[163]

Rabin's policies have created conditions that are ripe for civil war. Israelis—especially the 140,000 settlers—have a "growing feeling of betrayal by a government to which promises, and even court decisions, are meaningless."[164] Many settlers have said that they will resist being forced from their homes by the army, and this could be the reason the High Command is distancing itself from the soldiers. And it is extremely disturbing to learn that the IDF is prepared to wage war against the settlers:

> "A special unit established to evacuate settlers was receiving training in sniping and house-to-house fighting. **Applicants had to prove they had no religious friends or relatives, no friends or relatives in Jewish settlements in Judea-Samaria, the Gaza strip or the Golan Heights, and held left-wing views.**"[165]

Premature publication of the above caused yet another uproar and brought the inevitable denials from those responsible. But it is shocking to realize that the Jews—God's elect people—would even consider forming an anti-religious, élite IDF unit for the express purpose of forcefully evicting their brethren who have settled the land in accordance with God's wishes and with the help and encouragement of previous governments. It was Yitzhak Rabin himself, as Prime Minister of Israel in 1976, "who laid the cornerstone of what became the first permanent settlement in Gush Etzion (the area between Bethlehem and Hebron)."[166]

Bid Farewell!

With the number of deceitful and secret deals already coming to light, it will not come as much of a surprise to find that other secret deals have also been made with the PLO, Syria, and other enemies sworn to the annihilation of Israel. Given the track record already established by the Rabin-Peres-Beilin trio (all three truly belong together—in 1988 Beilin signed a document behind the back of Rabin and the Labor Party[167]), other plans must have already hatched while others are yet in the incubation stage. In May 1994, for example, Yael Dayan (a Labor MK who met with Arafat and other PLO officials when it was still a crime of treason to do so) wrote an article for *The Jerusalem Post* entitled "Good riddance to Gaza." Her article states *inter alia*:

> "Farewell Gaza and satellites, and Jericho—and the rest of the occupied West Bank that will be included in the interim agreement that follows this first one...Farewell and an easy parting...everyone knows that it is impossible to give Gaza without Jericho and without the rest of the West Bank after it."[168]

Dayan, a humanist MK who fights tooth-and-nail for homosexual rights, was telling the Israelis what they were already fearful of hearing. After Gaza and Jericho, the government intends to give the PLO all of the territories captured by Israel in the 1967 war—the same strategic areas from which the Arabs have launched their horrendous wars. But, of course, the government denies that it plans to give it all away. Israelis, however, are being psyched into ultimately accepting the government's plan by individual ministers telling them to begin bidding "farewell" to the Golan Heights, to Gaza, Jericho and the entire West Bank.

At the same time Foreign Minister Peres is engaging in transparent lies trying to hide the plans for Jerusalem. Peres's close friend, the French intellectual Mark Halter, told the Israeli weekly *Shishi* that in May 1993, he personally delivered a letter from Peres to the Pope outlining the Foreign Minister's plans for Jerusalem. Peres offered to hand over the sovereignty of Jerusalem to the Vatican. According to Halter: "The city will stay the capital of Israel but will be administered by the Vatican. The city will have an Israeli mayor and a Palestinian mayor, both under orders from the Holy See."[169] And it is now an established fact that after 46 years of refusing to even recognize the Jewish state, the Vatican announced on June 15, 1994, an agreement reached between itself and Israel—"establishing full diplomatic relations, **with the Catholic Church being allowed to participate in efforts to determine the future of Jerusalem.**"[170]

Henry Kissinger wrote some 30 years ago (unrelated to Israel, but poignantly relevant): "Those ages which in retrospect seem most peaceful were least in search of peace."[171] Therefore, in the age in which we live, when only a militarily powerful Israel dwelling within secure, defensible boundaries can deter further Arab aggression, we might well ask what particular brands of madness possess Rabin and Peres? What forces them to rush headlong into "peace" agreements with enemies who are currently planning the annihilation of the Jewish state? What insanity drives them into adopting a defeated nation status—Israel, the victor in defensive wars of blatant Arab aggression, suing for peace while the vanquished aggressors call for unconditional surrender? What possesses them to ignore the warnings of "every single intelligence agency"[172] and blindly forge ahead with giving away Israel's strategic defense areas? What convinces Rabin that at 70 he is wiser than the IDF generals? And not only IDF generals, but also generals from other nations.

Retired American colonel Irving Kett, for example, wrote in the name of **100 American admirals and generals**—all joining the **United States chairman of the Joint Chiefs of Staff** in determining that:

"From the viewpoint of military security, **Israel is the only country in the world which, in a comprehensive war, has no margin for error**; the smallest mistake could cause her downfall and bring disaster."[173]

Foreign Minister Peres and Deputy Foreign Minister Beilin pushed hard to reach agreement for a rapid IDF withdrawal from Gaza and Jericho, but the "IDF's reservations about security"[174] delayed the signing. And although he denied it, Peres was reported to have said in the United States that "the military keeps throwing monkey wrenches into the negotiations."[175]

Another piece of sheer lunacy is the giving away the control of more than 80 percent—yes, more than 80 percent—of Israel's already deficient water supply! Forty percent of Israel's water supply is drawn directly from aquifers "wholly or partially under Judea and Samaria"[176]—the areas being given over to the PLO! Another 40 percent comes down from the Golan Heights "which dominates the headwaters of the Jordan River and the Sea of Galilee."[177] And if this were yet not enough, in its peace treaty signed with Jordan on October 26, 1994, Rabin's government agreed to annually transfer 150 million cubic meters of Israel's best water to Jordan![178]

Consider the implications of the above. Even with all current water supplies intact, Israel is already forecasted to suffer an annual shortage of some 400 million cubic meters of water within a little more than a decade. Yet Rabin and Peres are willing to give up more than 80 percent of all of Israel's water resources, which is as close to committing suicide as any nation can possibly get. The ominous words of the prophet find fulfillment in the actions of Israel's current leadership: *"We have made a covenant with death, and with hell we are in agreement...we have made lies our refuge, and under falsehood we have hidden ourselves"* (Isaiah 28:15).

Fear and Pride

Fear and pride has lent a firm hand to driving the government's peace train. Pride, because Rabin regards himself "as more capable of assessing Arab intentions than Intelligence commanders who are young enough to be his children."[179] Fear, because Shulamit Aloni voiced exactly that when she said: "The god of the Moslems has many more troops than the God of the Jews."[180] Humanism only recognizes man's strength and scoffs at the mere thought of the existence of God, let alone that He had a part in Israeli victories in six terrible wars with neighboring Arab states.

The 13th Knesset was sworn in on July 13, 1992, and Yitzhak Rabin officially took office as Israel's Prime Minister. A little more than one week later, Syria gave Israel a no-nonsense notice of its intentions—it test-launched two Scud-C missiles that it had purchased from North Korea.[181] The Scud-C "can hit any target in Israel with double the accuracy of the older Scud-Bs [used by Iraq against Israel in the Gulf War]."[182]

The timing of the missile launches spoke volumes to the new government. Two weeks later, Shimon Peres said: "Neither Israel nor the Arabs have a better alternative than to reach a peace. To carry on now with the missile race would endanger the whole of the Middle East."[183] And Yitzhak Rabin subsequently prepared the nation for a retreat from the Golan by saying, "whoever is not prepared to make peace with Syria could expect a war within five to eight years."[184] Yes, fear is a major factor in the Rabin-Peres rush to placate their most deadly of enemies—fear that Israel might not survive in the age of technological warfare.

Rabin: the Warrior

Rabin is usually portrayed as a military man, an exceptionally astute military man, and often affectionately called an "old warrior."[185] But does this profile match his record?

It has been mentioned that Rabin had previously held the post of Prime Minister. He first held the position in 1974. Three years after taking office he was "forced to resign in a cloud of scandal"[186] after it was discovered that his wife (with Rabin's full knowledge) held an illegal bank account in the United States,[187] and the backlash brought about his party's downfall in the ensuing elections.[188]

Rabin's military career is indeed widely lauded, and even Rabin himself hardly fails to mention it when he addresses his audiences, be they Jewish audiences, or Christian. And in almost every biographical sketch of Rabin's life, it is mentioned that he "commanded," or was the "Commander of the Harel Brigade"[189] during the 1948 War of Independence. But the ignominious fact that he was relieved of his duties on May 17, 1948, just 33 days after assuming command,[190] and only two days after the Arab nations launched their concentrated, coordinated attack upon Israel, is not mentioned! It is a documented fact that Joseph Tabenkin replaced Rabin after he became the target of the anger of those in the Harel Brigade due to the unusually high number of casualties—220 men dead and another 617 wounded—more than "half of the 1,500-man brigade."[191]

Rabin was the IDF Chief of General Staff during the Six Day War, a war that is recorded as a classic in the annals of history, and whose tactics are now studied by the nations' war experts. But how many know that due to the mounting pressure leading up to the war, Rabin "**suffered a nervous breakdown**"[192] a few days prior to the outbreak of hostilities? To cover for him at such a crucial time, his breakdown was "charitably defined as nicotine poisoning."[193] General Ezer Weizman (President of Israel, today) wrote in his book, *On Eagles' Wings*, that "on May 23, 1967, during the crisis preceding the outbreak of the Six Day War, this man was broken and depressed, begging to be relieved of his duties."[194] Rabin told Weizman, "I have involved Israel through a series of mistakes I've made...I want to resign. You take over as chief of staff."[195]

Defense Minister Moshe Dayan received and accepted all the credit, and subsequently became famous. Abba Eban—Israel's Foreign Minister at the time—writes concerning Dayan:

> "In cold truth, he had not been the architect of Israel's military victory. He came out of the obscurity of parliamentary opposition a few days before the war at a time when the battle plans had been formulated, the commanders appointed, the equipment efficiently accumulated.
>
> "Prime Minister Eshkol deeply resented what he regarded as a successful effort to steal the credit of our victory from him. After all, it was Eshkol who had prepared the defense

system for its ordeal, and it was he who had fixed the timing of our fight."[196]

In October 1973, on *Yom Kippur* (The Day of Atonement), the holiest and most solemn day in the Jewish calendar, Egypt and Syria together launched a war against Israel that is regarded as "the greatest trauma ever to have hit Israel."[197] The *Yom Kippur* War was, next to the 1948 War of Independence, "the bloodiest war in Israel's history."[198] Until six hours before the war erupted on October 6, military and political leaders had "adopted the assessment termed 'the Concept'—that the Arabs would not launch a war against Israel."[199]

Rabin was a Lieutenant-General (reserve) at the time, having completed his term as Chief of General Staff. On July 13, 1973, three months before Egypt and Syria launched their catastrophic war, Rabin wrote an article that appeared in the Israeli newspaper *Ma'ariv*. In the article he stated: **"There is no need to call up our forces even when the enemy makes threats and deploys its forces along the cease-fire line."**[200] And prior to the same war he wrote: **"The Arab states' ability to coordinate their diplomatic or military moves has diminished. Even before, this ability was not great—now it has been reduced even more."**[201]

Israel was taken by almost total surprise when thousands of Egyptian tanks powered over bridges placed across the Suez Canal, and thousands of Syrian tanks poured across the Golan Heights. Nearly one million Arab troops took part in the initial assault—thousands of Israelis died. Israel, through a series of divine miracles, prevailed, even though it went along with Rabin's advice not to mobilize.

Rabin has already proven with the Israel-PLO accord that he is no more capable of assessing Arab intentions today than he was before the disastrous war of 1973. It is agonizing for Israelis to realize that not only is the same party in power with many of the same personalities, but that they are also making the same tragic mistakes. Indeed, Syrian president Hafez Assad "has correctly evaluated Rabin as a weak man in Washington's pocket."[202]

"Mene, Mene, Tekel Upharsin"

Shimon Peres did not fare at all well during the 1991 Gulf War. While the United States led coalition forces pounded Iraq, Saddam Hussein launched 39 Scud missiles at Israel and registered 31 hits on Israeli population centers. Some 5,000 homes were damaged or destroyed, and the repair bill was around $2 billion. Iraq's missiles carried only conventional warheads, but they served to remind the Israelis "that it had been Peres who had opposed Menachem Begin's decision to destroy the Iraqi nuclear reactor in June 1981."[203] Had Peres's advice been taken in 1981, as Rabin's was in 1973, there might well have been no Jewish state in existence today.

Shimon Peres, whose original name was Perski, was born in Poland and emigrated to Palestine in 1934. A 1991 biographical sketch of Peres says: "While his talents are undoubted, many see him as **a shifty politician** and have no confidence in him."[204] And Rabin in his autobiography described Peres as an "**indefatigable conniver**."[205] Far more condemnatory is an extract from the personal diary of Moshe Sharett, a former Minister of Foreign Affairs under Prime Minister David Ben Gurion and Ben Gurion's successor: "I have stated that **I totally and utterly reject Peres and consider his rise to prominence a malignant, immoral disgrace**. I will rend my clothes in mourning for the State if I see him become a minister in the Israeli government."[206] Also, this writer was informed by a reliable source who knew Peres's father, that conniving ran in the family—Peres's father made secret deals with the British during the Mandate period!

Following the signing of the DOP on the lawn of the White House, Henry Kissinger told British television: "Peres is on an emotional bender. He thinks the millennium has arrived and that the Palestinians and Israel are going to live together like Belgium and Holland."[207] The actual hard, cold, facts are this: Since the signing of the DOP in Oslo on September 13, 1993, terrorism has taken a greater and greater toll of Israeli lives—greater than the worst years of the *intifada*.[208] And 1994 actually became "the worst for terrorism **since the founding of the state in 1948**."[209]

After Rabin and Arafat signed the Israel-PLO "Peace Accord" on May 4, 1994, in Cairo, Peres (still on his "emotional bender"), exclaimed at the ceremony: "Today we have ended the Arab-Israeli conflict—Utopia is coming."[210] Perhaps someone should bring to his attention that the word "Utopia" comes from two Greek words: *ou* (not), and *topos* (place).[211] The literal meaning of Utopia is, therefore, "not a place." It is **an imaginary place or situation.**"[212] And this learned and established definition exactly describes Shimon Peres's fantasy of a Middle Eastern Utopia.

In the 6th century B.C., when Belshazzar, king of Babylon, mocked the LORD and profaned His holy things (Daniel 5:3–4) the fingers of a man's hand appeared and wrote upon the wall, *mene, mene, tekel, upharsin* (Daniel 5:25). The translation of those words are found in Daniel 5:26–28: *mene* (*"God has numbered your kingdom, and finished it"*); *tekel* (*"you have been weighed in the balances and found wanting"*); *peres*—singular of *pharsin*; *u* is simply "and"—(*"your kingdom is divided and given to the Medes and Persians"*). As Shimon Peres is the driving power behind the agreements with Arafat and the PLO, it is not coincidental that his name is "Peres"—for he has indeed "divided" Israel's "kingdom" and given it to its enemies. And the days of Peres's kingdom and the reign of the government of which he is a part, has been numbered and brought to an end. At this stage of events it is highly unlikely that it could be reelected for a further term.

A Place in History

There has been an evident desire on the part of Rabin and Peres to receive world recognition as "peace makers." Peres, especially, has been overt in his quest to get entered into history books. The "peace" agreement has seen to be not working, but both leaders are continually defending both Arafat and the PLO against charges of not keeping the Oslo Accords, even to the extent of making excuses for non-compliance. It has been proven beyond any doubt that Arafat's own *Fatah* has been involved in numerous murders of Israelis since the accord was signed, but Rabin and Peres jump to Arafat's defense and deny it again and again. And when Likud MK Benny Begin demanded that the government "release a report listing violations of the Oslo

Accords,"[213] Peres denied that such a report existed. Begin immediately "pulled a copy from his briefcase and charged the government with trying to hide it and its secret clauses on Jerusalem."[214]

Noted co-authors, Uri Dan and Dennis Eisenberg, of *The Mossad: Secrets of the Israeli Secret Service* and other books on the Middle East, wrote the following observations: "Rabin has swallowed the breaking of every promise the PLO made in Oslo."[215] And of Peres: "Arafat is like a puppet-master skillfully manipulating Peres, his ambitions of dislodging Rabin from the premiership and his dream of being the man who gets the Nobel Peace Prize...."[216] It is indeed a sad fact that Arafat knows of the rivalry between Peres and Rabin, that has existed for longer than 20 years, and exploits their weaknesses to the full.

As the prime-mover of the peace initiative, Peres considered that he should sign the DOP on behalf of Israel at the White House, thereby receiving the credit and getting into the world's spotlight. But reports began to circulate that Peres had considered resigning because he heard from a radio report of Rabin's plans to go to Washington. And sources in the Prime Minister's Office said that "while there had been tension between the two, all disagreements between them had been smoothed out."[217] The "smoothing" resulted in Peres signing the DOP and Rabin shaking Arafat's hand!

The Washington summit with Jordan's King Hussein brought yet another eruption. The news media gave accounts of "tension and even hostility"[218] between Peres and Rabin. In a television interview after returning home, Peres admitted to "being 'hurt' by Rabin's treatment of him in Washington."[219] Coalition ministers tried to ease the tension, and Police Minister Moshe Shahal later told how he had turned to both of the men and told them: "...this tension was totally redundant and that **there is plenty of room in history for the two of them, for their deeds and accomplishments.**"[220]

Rabin, Peres and Arafat have been jetting around receiving the plaudits of the nations and collecting their "peace prizes"—in Paris, Hollywood, Madrid and Oslo. Peres did not fully realize his ambition in getting the Nobel Peace Prize—he had to share it

The Israeli Connection

with Rabin, his rival, and Arafat the terrorist. And on the day they and their wives were in Oslo collecting their respective shares of the prestigious prize (with protesting Israelis present), the man who resigned in protest from the Nobel Peace Prize Committee was being accorded a tumultuous welcome in Jerusalem.

Kaare Kristiansen, a former Norwegian Minister of Energy and Parliament Speaker, resigned from the Committee because he could not agree to honoring Arafat with the Prize. Kristiansen had been invited to a reception in his honor by the International Coalition for Missing Israeli Soldiers. He was given a silver dog tag on behalf of the soldier's families, and he was presented with a prize for "Excellence in Leadership."[221] In the same hour when Rabin, Peres and Arafat were receiving the Nobel Prize, Israelis were honoring the man whom they considered the real prize winner, and had the privilege of hearing him.

A little over 2,000 people overflowed the hotel ballroom designed to hold fractionally more than half that number, and hundreds "crammed the foyer and almost climbed the walls—there has never been an event like it in Israel before."[222] Only *The Jerusalem Post* covered the event—no other representation from the media was present! Two television film crews entered the hotel, and the hotel staff spontaneously directed them toward the ballroom—the cameramen replied that they had been "**expressly ordered not to cover the Kristiansen assembly.**"[223]

Many Israelis feel that Rabin and Peres should never have accepted the prize when it was known that Arafat was co-laureate. One writer[224] suggested that they refuse the Nobel Peace Prize "in the name of truth and self-respect" on two grounds: "The first is that they are to share it with that man whose sole success has been in orchestrating the murder of Jews," and the second is that "there is no peace" to celebrate. Kristiansen apparently agrees, and so do at least five members of the Norwegian Parliament who also planned to boycott the awards ceremony.[225]

Kristiansen says that he evaluates "the Oslo Agreement more realistic and less enthusiastic than many other politicians in Norway and in Israel."[226] He said the Oslo Agreement "turned upside down"[227] the peace initiative that was begun by the Likud government in Madrid. He said there was no provision in the Nobel stipulations for terrorists to receive the prestigious prize—"up until this year, I'm sorry to say."[228] And he spoke about Arafat, about "the man's terrorism and blind violence during so many years,"[229] and that "the arguments used for giving him the prize really said that his only qualification was that he, at the moment, does not kill so many people as before!"[230] Rather than promoting peace, Kristiansen felt that honoring Arafat would "likely give a stimulant to more bloodshed in the world."[231] Ovation after ovation greeted Kristiansen's discourse on honor and integrity.

Kaare Kristiansen, a twice born Christian, attended Friday evening services at the Jerusalem Great Synagogue before he spoke the following evening. At the conclusion of the service, he was warmly welcomed from the pulpit. And then the unexpected happened—"for the first time in the history of the Synagogue; spontaneous applause broke out."[232]

Kristiansen resigned from the Nobel Committee by presenting his application to leave the parliament that had elected him. And Israelis paid homage to a man whom they considered to personify honor, integrity and other related qualities.

Godless Leaders

The current leaders of Israel have fallen victim to deception. And it is their very godlessness that has both caused the deception and bred their fears. Fear can only be beneficial when the fear is of God—*"the LORD your God you shall fear; and He will deliver you from the hand of your enemies"* (2 Kings 17:39). The answer to the question of what madness possesses Rabin and Peres, impelling them to blindly rush in where even the unintelligent would fear to tread, is their avowed godlessness.

We would do well to remember that God is firmly in control of history, and that history and prophecy are the same to Him. Also, throughout Israel's four millennia of history, God has often used godless leaders as the means to fulfill prophecies of unutterable distress. It should not come as any surprise, therefore, to realize that God is using today's leaders to position the Jewish nation for a massive war and the further fulfillment of prophecy.

In January 1995, the government stopped all expansion in Jewish satellite cities that are incorporated in greater (metropolitan) Jerusalem. Peres later spoke about the 1967 boundaries, which intimates the government intends to at least cede the eastern sector of Jerusalem and possibly destroy the satellite cities which are home to tens of thousands of Israelis. He said that "greater (metropolitan) Jerusalem was a 'literary,' not a political expression."[233] There is no appreciation of the fact that for 3,000 unbroken years Jews have prayed daily for Jerusalem, their holy city and symbol of everything Jewish. There is no appreciation for the fact that October 1996, sees the beginning of the planned massive celebrations commemorating the 3,000th anniversary of the founding of Jerusalem as the capital of Israel under King David. There is no appreciation because their hearts are humanist, not Jewish.

For the same reason neither Rabin or Peres or the majority of the government has any appreciation for the fact that Hebron is the site of the Cave of Machpelah—the burial place of the Patriarchs, Abraham, Isaac, Jacob, Sarah, Rebekah and Leah—Judaism's second holiest shrine and place of substantial pilgrimage. In a March 1994 cabinet meeting only two ministers opposed the immediate forced removal of Hebron's entire Jewish community.[234] Technicalities have prevented the "evacuation" from being carried out at the time of writing. It is from these cities that the Jews came, it is these places of which they dreamt, and it is these cities to which they returned. And godless Jewish leaders will now prevent them from living in them?

Peres believes he is creating a "New Middle East," but violence is rising rapidly and scores of Israelis are being stabbed, axed or shot to death. Scores more are blown to pieces—their brains being scraped from walls 100 meters from the explosion. Rabin's "peace" is "ultimately aimed at bringing about a separation between Israelis and Palestinians."[235] And he has actually spoken about "establishing a fence that would separate Jews from Palestinians."[236]

Establishing a security fence around Israel is diametrically opposed to any concept of peace. Even during 20 years of cruel terror attacks taking place within an existing state of war, Israel did not need such a thing! And in his November 1994 speech before Tansu Ciller, Turkey's prime minister, Peres made it clear that his "New Middle East" envisions an "integration of Israel into the Moslem Middle East."[237] Rabin's vision of a "peaceful" Middle East, and Peres's vision of a "New Middle East," have both replaced the vision of the prophets. As we stated earlier, vision which fails to include God is practical blindness.

While Rabin and Peres busy themselves with dotting the i's and crossing the t's of the peace accords, the Moslems will, at the appropriate time, strike a line through all the words. Rabin is playing the type of music Moslems want to hear. He told the military industries to beat their weapons into plowshares: "The country has to convert military industries into commercial enterprises."[238] And it has also been announced that: "Compulsory military service for men could be shortened by as much as six months by the end of 1996, and reserve service can be cut in half."[239] And all because Arafat promised... Assad said... Mubarak smiled... .

History repeats itself. We now have Israeli Chamberlains preaching "Peace in our time." As Chamberlain did in 1939, so Rabin and Peres have come waving meaningless scraps of paper that will also be torn up at will by Israel's enemies. On January 22, 1995, after another terrorist attack that blew 21 Israelis to pieces and injured more than 60 others,[240] Israel's president Ezer Weizman told the nation: "We can't go on like this,"[241] and advised Rabin to suspend the peace talks with the PLO. On the same day Rabin told the nation: "Ours is the only way,"[242] and "made it clear that he will not adopt President Ezer Weizman's advice."[243] How perfectly does the Scripture find its fulfillment in the Rabin government: *"They have also healed the hurt of My people slightly, saying, 'Peace, peace!' When there is no peace"* (Jeremiah 6:14).

Rabin and Peres desire to be remembered in history for their accomplishments, and they will be—in its hall of eternal shame. They will not be forgotten like most of the dead—what they have done and the resulting distress will be spoken of and will perpetuate their memory.

11

Peace: the Road that Leads to War

Rabin's Labor–left-wing–Arab coalition government calls Israel's capitulation to its enemies, "the peace process." The nations' governments and the news media refer to it as, "the Middle East peace process." But those that are reading the signs call it, "the **piece** process." Because it is, in fact, a formulated plan of attack drawn up by the repeatedly defeated, but who are now making significant advances in the battle for the destruction of Israel—piece by piece.

The foundations of the Israel-PLO "peace" are the shifting sands of Israeli godlessness upon which the PLO, and other unappeasable Moslem enemies, are building a substantial house of deception as the prelude to war. One of Mohammed's oft-quoted sayings is, "War is deception."[1] And in his book *Protracted Warfare*, the Master Communist, Mao Tse-tung, wrote: "There never can be too much deception in war." Also, one of the PLO's favorite slogans is the Mao doctrine that, "Justice and peace comes from the cannon's mouth."[2]

The engineers, designers and supervisors of the "peace house" are some of the world's most prominent statesmen—professional politicians seeking prestige for themselves, higher popularity ratings in the polls, and preeminence for their nation. But that which they are helping to construct—the house of illusion and deceit with a peace facade—will collapse with the first wind of realism; with the first flood of truth, that will come with the rumbling of tanks and the launching of missiles.

Six times Israel has found itself embroiled in bloody wars of wanton aggression by its Arab neighbors. The Israeli presence in southern Lebanon today is solely to prevent its northern towns from having to suffer continual violence from indiscriminate rocket and terror attacks. Each subsequent war grew in intensity, and each war saw Israel emerge victorious and, ultimately, stronger through its capture of higher and more defensible ground. Consider the following political philosophy:

> "A people which has been attacked, has defended itself and wins wars, is bound by sacred duty to establish for itself in perpetuity a political situation which will ensure the liquidation of the sources of aggression. It is entitled to maintain this state of affairs as long as the danger of aggression does not cease.
>
> A nation which has attained security at the cost of numerous victims, will never agree to the restoration of the previous borders. No territories are to be returned as long as the danger of aggression still prevails."[3]

No, the above philosophy was not formulated by Israel to justify its occupation of lands won in 1967, but by the Supreme Soviet and published in *Pravda* almost three years before Israel's Six Day War. Israeli "peace doves," however, are willing to sacrifice their nation's security on the strength of promises—promises from people who had no intention of honoring them or from nations intending to honor them, but who have histories of not doing so.

It is true that Israel genuinely seeks peace—an end to 50 years of war and terror attacks—but the Arab nations see the desire for peace only as a weakness to exploit. Thirty years ago, Tunisian president Habib Bourguiba said: "**The only way to destroy Israel is through 'peace.'**"[4] What they have not been able to accomplish with Israel on the battlefield, the Arab nations are seeking to do around the "peace" table through deception, and with the willing help of self-seeking, power-hungry leaders and nations.

The two "brokers" in the peace process are the United States and Russia. The former Soviet Union supplied more arms to the Arab Middle East than any nation in the world. Following hard on its heels was the United States, who since the collapse of the Soviet Union, has not only taken first place, but also greatly increased its input. Russia is now seeking to reassume the former Soviet Union's position as an influential power in the Middle East[5] and is stepping up its involvement.

Peace: The Road that Leads to War 233

Both the Soviet Union and the United States grew fat on the billions from the sale of weapons to the Arab states—the weapons that have been used against Israel. Now these two nations act as "brokers" in the "peace process," forcing Israel into suicidal pacts, while they themselves step up their arms sales to Shimon Peres's Utopia—the "New Middle East."

In Rabin's "New Middle East," Jews and Arabs will be totally separated. In Peres's "New Middle East," the Jewish state is absorbed "into the Moslem Middle East." But the "New Middle East" of the Arab dream is a Middle East entirely cleared of any sovereign Jewish presence. The only change in Arab hearts is a renewed belief "of their cherished hope of Israel's disappearance appearing over the horizon."[6]

In the decade 1984–94, Saudi Arabia alone spent the staggering sum of $130 billion[7] on weapons of war, some of which have been passed on to Syria and other Arab states. Today, while everyone is talking "peace," the "Arab countries are arming at an unprecedented pace. Over a 30 month period—January 1991 to July 1993—they accumulated conventional weapons to the tune of $58 billion."[8] Also, in this age of "peace," not a single country—including those bordering Israel—has dissociated itself from the frequent Islamic conferences in which multitudes of nations unanimously proclaim their intention of annihilating Israel. The latest three-day conference began on March 30, 1995, in Khartoum, Sudan, where **delegates from more than 80 countries** gathered and "resolved to support armed struggle against Israel."[9]

The Arab states are arming for another massive war against Israel, and despite the current peace negotiations and three signed agreements—Egypt, Jordan and the PLO—Ya'akov Ami Dror, head of the IDF military intelligence research division, said in September 1994: "**Not one Arab leader** has accepted the concept of peace with Israel[10]...**not one of the rulers—not Arafat, not Assad—has accepted peace.**"[11] It was Ami Dror who warned his superior hours before the October 1973 *Yom Kippur* War of an impending Arab attack—but then, as now, his warning was ignored.[12]

Ami Dror's professional opinion—based on information gathered by his intelligence officers—directly opposes what politicians and news medias are telling the world. Whom should we believe, politicians, the TV news, or the head of IDF intelligence? Let us look at some recent actions, statements and situations of those who have signed peace agreements with Israel; of those who could be close to signing; of those of other Arab states and Iran; and of those of the two "broker" powers.

Egypt

Egypt's 15-year-old peace agreement with Israel is touted to be the role model for all other Arab-Israeli agreements. Without firing a shot, Egypt received the huge Sinai Peninsular in which Israel had invested $10 billion building flourishing cities, military and naval installations, as well as developing oil fields that would have made it energy independent for the foreseeable future. In addition, Egypt has received to date some $40 billion in direct United States grants, while Israel continues to pay millions of dollars to the United States every year in interest on the loans used to develop the Sinai and afterwards to dismantle it all!

In return for what it gave Egypt, Israel received from Egypt a "peace treaty"—a piece of paper covering some 50 items relating to "normal relations between states."[13] Since that piece of paper was signed 15 years ago, Egypt has failed **"to implement any of those agreements—except for those that could be actively violated."**[14] The entire agreement, according to Egyptian president Hosni Mubarak, **"will fall away the minute another war breaks out** between Israel and an Arab country."[15] Mubarak has also vowed **"to support any Arab state in a war against Israel."**[16]

The Egyptian president has a "self-imposed ban on visiting Israel"[17]—having never once stepped foot on Israeli soil despite the fact that Israeli prime ministers have gone to Egypt on a number of occasions. After President Weizman's visit to Cairo in December 1994, Egyptian foreign minister Amr Moussa said that a reciprocal visit by Mubarak to Jerusalem was "out of the question."[18]

The Egyptian-Israeli peace treaty is not exactly the miracle that it is hailed to be. It is "not peace,"[19] says Israeli Defense Ministry director-general Major-General David Ivri, "It is actually a cease-fire that has continued for 15 years."[20] Numbers of Israelis

Peace: The Road that Leads to War 235

have been killed on the border or in Egypt proper, and an Egyptian police officer machine-gunned seven Israeli tourists including four children. The Egyptian government-controlled media hailed the killer as "a national hero."[21] Israelis have been arrested and tortured by the Egyptian police. A 17-year-old Israeli-Arab girl described her ordeal: "They would beat me, put electric shocks in my mouth. They would say '**There is no peace between Israel and Egypt and you are Jews and you are dirt.**'"[22]

The Israeli ambassador in Cairo is "isolated and blacklisted and does not participate in any official functions of the Egyptian government."[23] Israeli scientists, who were to have taken part in a 1994 International Conference on Mathematical Analysis and Signal Processing in Cairo, were told by the Egyptian organizers "to stay home."[24] Egyptian officials have also been preventing Israel from participating in the International Book Fair that takes place each year in Cairo. Egyptian delegates to the world conference for air traffic controllers, held in Jerusalem in March 1995, cancelled their participation, because it was to be held in Jerusalem.[25] An Israeli spokesman says: "Egyptian attitudes to Israel in every international forum goes **beyond the bounds of decency.**"[26] At the recent Casablanca conference—heralded as the dawning of the "New Middle East"—"maps of the Middle East distributed by an official Egyptian agency neither mentioned Israel's name nor demarcated its borders."[27]

Egyptian relations with Israel have been hostile since the time of Moses and the Pharaohs, and after 15 years of the coldest peace possible, normalization of relations has still not taken place. In December 1994, it was even reported that the Egyptian finance minister had "ordered the normalization with Israel **be slowed.**"[28] That minister has also "refused to visit Israel."[29]

Not content with its own non-compliance in normalizing relations with Israel, Egypt actively seeks to prevent Israel from "establishing relations with more countries."[30] And, recently, its pressure successfully prevented the Comoro Islands (an Arab archipelago in the Indian Ocean officially known as the Federal Islamic Republic of the Comoros) from establishing relations with Israel.[31] Egypt was also "angered by the signing of the Israel-Jordan peace treaty."[32]

One of the agreements that make up the Egypt-Israel peace treaty is a ban on "hostile propaganda." The government controlled Cairo press is the mouthpiece for the ruling party and prints nothing that Mubarak does not want printed. The Cairo press is described as being "full of anti-Israel and anti-Jewish venom, preaching hatred and prejudice."[33] The very real hatred can be perceived in the way former Israeli prime minister Yitzhak Shamir is depicted in Cairo's *Al Mussawar*. Apparently flattered by Israeli protests against previous insults to Shamir, the newspaper printed an apology—not to Shamir, but to people **and animals** who "may have been insulted by associating them with the Israeli leader."[34] The writer, Mahmud a-Sa'adani, confessed to describing Shamir inappropriately. By calling him a butcher, Sa'adani says, he "insulted butchers."[35] Sa'adani continues: "Shamir is also upset by my calling him a monkey, and I must apologize to all monkeys, from gorillas to the tiniest specimens, for monkeys are pretty and make people laugh...The monkey can be useful: its hair is used for brushes and blankets, its meat makes a luxurious meal, and eating its brain is a cure for memory-loss."[36] But Shamir, apparently, is good only for "opening the bellies of pregnant women...and skinning their fetuses with joy as if he were dancing with a beautiful girl on a cruise ship on the Danube."[37] Other examples of anti-Israel "niceties" would fill an entire book.

Comparatively few Egyptians have visited Israel during the 15-year-old peace treaty. Those who wish to do so undergo lengthy interrogations by the security police.[38] A prominent Egyptian who did visit Israel, stated: "In order to come to Israel and receive a visa on my passport, I have to make a commitment that I will not visit any other Arab country as long as this passport is valid."[39]

An opinion poll, the first of its kind taken in Egypt, conducted at the end of 1994 by the mass circulation weekly *Al-Ahram*, showed that nearly 16 years after Egypt made peace with Israel: 71 percent of people said they would not buy Israeli goods; 75 percent did not want Israeli factories in Egypt; 63 percent did not want to visit Israel; and 53 percent did not want Israelis to visit Egypt.[40] And in a May 1995, public opinion poll conducted in Egypt, 98 percent[41] were opposed to having full relations with

Peace: The Road that Leads to War   237

Israel, and 91 percent[42] want Egypt to have nuclear capability "to confront Israel."[43]

After being at "peace" with Israel for more than a decade and a half, every night at the close of its broadcast Egypt Television screens footage of the zenith of Egyptian military might—the opening hours of its treacherous 1973 invasion of Israel on *Yom Kippur*. It should be remembered that Egypt was the initiator of all three of the major Arab-Israeli wars—the 1948 War of Independence, the 1967 Six Day War, and the 1973 *Yom Kippur* War. Egypt today is "modernizing its army, introducing Western military doctrine and integrating **massive amounts of Western equipment.**"[44] "United States financial aid and the United States' consent to sell Egypt top-of-the-line weapons systems, has transformed the Egyptian military from a predominantly Soviet war machine."[45] Egypt's foreign minister Amr Moussa acknowledges that Egypt's goal "is to achieve military parity with Israel."[46] Israeli Air Force General (retired) Avihu Bin-Nun wrote:

"...the Egyptians are receiving from the Americans every weapons system Israel receives...Worse, **sometimes Israel refrains from requesting a certain weapon system lest the Arabs be supplied with it...All the U.S. talk about 'maintaining Israel's qualitative military edge' is nonsense... .**"[47]

A senior Israel intelligence officer says: "The Egyptians are building their military forces aimed at Israel—there is no doubt about this."[48] Many IDF generals also "find the evidence that Egypt is arming against Israel overwhelming."[49] Israeli concern over the buildup has led to a decrease in Israeli military cooperation with the United States. The Airforce, for example, has turned down several United States offers for joint exercises. The reason is that Israel does not want the Americans to "relay its methods to the Egyptians."[50]

Like Syria, Egypt was impressed with Iraqi missile hits on Israeli population centers—"Israeli life came to a halt."[51] Egypt is currently preparing to buy and also manufacture the enhanced

Scud-C missile from North Korea.[52] It is also building a 300 megawatt Chinese-made nuclear reactor, which "once on line, will be capable of making four nuclear warheads a month."[53] There is also a great deal of speculation about just what Egypt's Mubarak and Syria's Assad discuss at their many meetings—often "held in a jet out of range of Israel's electronic 'ears.'"[54]

Egypt is also demanding that Israel sign the Nuclear Non-Proliferation Treaty (NPT) and open all its facilities to international inspection. Egypt has the largest arsenal of chemical weapons in the Middle East, and it "adamantly refuses to sign a treaty against the proliferation of non-conventional biological and chemical weapons [banned in warfare]. It also rejects the very idea of international inspection."[55] It never protested Iraq's use of poison gas against the Kurds, nor of Syria's use of it in Hama, and it used it itself against Yemen in 1966. Neither has it protested against the development of nuclear weapons by Iraq, Iran or Pakistan—Mubarak simply wants to make Israel indefensible by depriving it of "its nuclear deterrent."[56] Political and military analysts point out: "The Egyptian military threat to Israel has never been greater,"[57] and that "Egypt is Israel's most dangerous potential enemy."[58] Egypt is accused of "playing a risky double game—simultaneously discussing peace and pursuing 'an expedited and dangerous arming policy.'"[59] An opposition MK has warned the government against "missing or ignoring the signals of war with Egypt, as happened in 1973."[60]

After its 15 years of "peace" with Israel, Egypt's Brigadier-General Morad Dessouki, a military expert at the Al-Ahram Center for Political and Strategic Studies, was asked why Egypt needs such a large army, and just who is the enemy? He answered: "**The Israelis...they are our enemy.**"[61] And in the January 29, 1995 edition of the Egyptian weekly *Rous el Yusef*—the contents of which are dictated directly from Mubarak's office—the former Egyptian minister of war, Amin el-Huwaidi, was quoted as saying: "The war with Israel is a certainty, and we are ready."[62] In that same edition the present minister of war, Field Marshall Ani Tantawi, was quoted as saying: "In spite of the fact Israel has atomic weapons, Egypt will know how to cut off the arm of the enemy when it comes."[63] And this, they say, is the role model for all Middle East peace agreements.

The PLO

In January 1995, sixteen months after the signing of the DOP in Oslo and just eight months after the signing of the peace agreement in Cairo, Yasser Arafat gave a speech on *"Fatah Day"*—the PLO's annual celebration commemorating the start of its 30-year-long war with Israel. Arafat said:

> "And I say to the martyrs who died, in the name of the martyrs who are still living: We stand by our oath and hold to our commitment...to continue...the revolution."[64]

He also told them again of Mohammed's temporary agreement in 627 A.D. with the Kuraish people of Mecca,[65] and alluding both to Israel and the Arab proverb "We can remedy the present only with the remedies of the past,"[66] went on to say: "But there are people **who will not learn from history. As for us, our history is our best teacher.**"[67]

Arafat is blatant in his proclamations that the PLO's war against Israel will continue. He is also arrogant in declaring that the peace accord is temporary until such time like his mentor, Mohammed, he believes that he is sufficiently strong enough to destroy an indefensible Israel. But, Arafat can afford to be arrogant. He knows that Rabin and Peres, together with the entire Israeli coalition government, are now locked into the peace process—prisoners of their own policies. To reverse the course of the peace process now will be equally as disastrous as going further ahead. The PLO's plan of stages—the phased plan—is progressing beyond its expectations. Prior to the signing of the Oslo accords, Arafat's "Foreign Minister" Farouk Khadoumi said:

> **"We shall pitch our tent in those places which our bullets can reach...This tent shall then form the base from which we shall later pursue the next phase."**[68]

And in 1994, after the signing of the Cairo peace agreement, Khadoumi said:

"Everyone in the world should know there is no way that we will relinquish one grain of sand of Palestinian land. **We carry our weapons and there is no way we will stop...We will not rest until the occupiers have been thrown out.**"[69]

Terrorist attacks against Israelis are increasing daily. After the suicide bombing in January 1995, which left 21 Israelis dead and more than 60 injured, an Arab poll revealed that 53 percent of Palestinian Arabs "would like to see more '**military actions**'"[70] against Israelis. A similar survey conducted by *The Voice of Israel Radio* found 60 percent wanted more attacks.[71] A "scientifically"[72] conducted poll among Arabs on November 17, 1994, showed that "more than two-thirds supported continued attacks on Jews."[73] Arab terrorist "military actions" are nearly all attacks against the innocent—against civilians, against women and children and schools. A Gazan Arab explained that such attacks are "legitimate operations against military targets"[74]: "Of course, **we have no civilians on the other side, Israel is a military state.**"[75] And Arafat has vowed "in the name of the martyrs who are still living," that this bloody war will continue, and often declares his intention of establishing "**the peace of the brave**"[76]— the same peace that Mohammed made with the Kuraish tribe before he annihilated it.

Jordan

Of all the Arabs surrounding Israel, Jordan's King Hussein is the exception—he has genuinely wanted to cooperate with Israel for years. But the king remembers that his grandfather, King Abdullah, moved to make peace with Israel and was assassinated on the Temple Mount in Jerusalem, in July 1951. From the 1967 Six Day War onwards, Hussein has met secretly with every Israeli leader since Golda Meir, and twice provided former Israeli prime minister Yitzhak Shamir with *kosher* Shabbat meals in one of his English homes where Shamir actually slept over.[77] The King needs peace with Israel in order to axe the cost of maintaining a large and unquestionably the best Arab fighting force in existence. Jordan's army and air force is leeching a large portion of his kingdom's somewhat meager annual budget, and the military exists

Peace: The Road that Leads to War   241

largely to confront Israel.

King Hussein recognizes Israel's substantial military and economic powers and desires cooperation in both fields. After the devastating Six Day War in which Jordan fared worse than all other Arab invaders, Jordan has not taken any meaningful part in subsequent Arab-Israeli conflicts. Of the Six Day War Hussein claimed he was forced to go in and said: "I believe I'm damned if I do and I'm damned if I don't—but more damned if I don't."[78] This was a hint that he was more frightened of Iraq and Saddam Hussein, his immense neighbor who "could swallow him for breakfast,"[79] and he was, in effect, saying that he "lost half of his kingdom, but otherwise he would have lost his throne."[80] For the same reasons he spoke for Iraq in the Gulf War.

Israel and Jordan, however, not only cooperated together against the PLO in 1968's Operation Inferno,[81] but they have also been cooperating together for years in the fields of irrigation technology, agriculture, mining Dead Sea minerals, etc., and their "de facto peace" has been far more effective and beneficial than has Israel's formal peace with Egypt signed in 1979.

After the signing of the Israeli-PLO accord, Hussein seized his opportunity and signed a formal peace treaty with Israel. The PLO, however, protested, and enforced a complete strike throughout all Israeli administered territories![82] Arafat and the PLO plan on destroying Israel, and signed a pseudo peace agreement to effect that plan. Jordan's king Hussein walked in and not only signed a bona fide agreement, but immediately opened his borders to Israelis and established a Jordanian Embassy in Tel Aviv.

King Hussein killed more than the two proverbial birds with one stone. He formally made peace with Israel, ending the official state of war between them—accomplishing what he had feared to do for more than forty years. And, as compensation for doing what he was more than happy to do, the American House of Representatives immediately wrote off $220 million from Jordan's United States debt, and the whole of the remaining $474 million is expected to be written off over the next three years.[83] In addition, by opening its borders to Israel, tens of thousands of Israeli tourists poured hundreds of thousands of dollars into Jordan within a few short weeks—seeing the sights, tasting the foods, and buying the souvenirs forbidden to them for nearly 50 years. The future, however, will not be without pain—the days of Hussein's Hashemite kingdom are numbered.

King Hussein has been battling with cancer for some time, and Arab sources close to the king say that he is still quite ill and "only expected to live for another year or so."[84]

The king is a Hashemite, the descendant of Arabian rulers driven out by the Saud clan in the early 1920s. The king's forefathers, right down to his grandfather Abdullah Ibn Hussein, were born in Mecca, and from there the Hashemites also administered the Islamic shrines in Jerusalem. (The king claims direct descent from Mohammed, but generated ire in the hearts of many Moslems by marrying Elizabeth Halaby, an American who assumed the name Nur el Hussein in 1978, and by being a 33rd degree Freemason—the highest degree in Freemasonry). His great-grandfather, Sharif Hussein Ibn 'Ali, was Emir of Mecca under the Ottoman Turks and launched the British-aided Arab revolt in June 1916. The rebellion was successful and Sharif Hussein assumed the title King of Hijaz. Abdullah his son was his political advisor and Foreign Minister.

In 1921, Abdullah gathered troops together and marched on Syria to restore Arab-Hashemite rule from under the French. He entered Amman in June, but the British, who had been given the mandate to establish the Jewish national home in Palestine, wanted to avoid a clash between their Hashemite allies and the French. The British proposed to slice off a whopping 77 percent of the designated Jewish homeland and give it to Abdullah for appeasement. Abdullah duly accepted the British offer and became the Emir of Transjordan. He later assumed the title of King and renamed his realm the Hashemite Kingdom of Jordan. Today, Jordan without the West Bank is three and a half times the size of Israel with the West Bank. Jordan, including 1993's estimated 960,200 "Palestinian refugees,"[85] only supports a little more that 60 percent of Israel's current population of 5.5 million, which does not include the Arab population figures for the West Bank.

Unfortunately for today's King Hussein, only a tiny minority of Jordanians are Hashemites. His "subjects" are nearly 75 percent Palestinian (remember, "Palestine is Jordan, and Jordan is Palestine"[86]), and the remainder is mostly nomadic Bedouins. Many Jordanians, therefore, regard the king as a foreigner, owe him no loyalty, and see him merely as an undemocratically elected leader. When he hastily signed a formal peace treaty with Israel, "Jordan reeled in shock."[87]

Unlike Israel's overwhelming majority Knesset vote in favor of the peace treaty—105 for the treaty, 3 against, and 6 abstentions—Jordan's parliament only ratified it by a vote of 55 for, 23 against and 2 abstentions. And that vote only came "after many members attacked the accord as a total sellout of the Arab-Moslem cause."[88] Also, unlike the sea of Israeli flags waving furiously in Israel's warm welcome to King Hussein as he became the second Arab leader to set foot in Israel (Egypt's president Sadat came in November 1977—he was duly assassinated in October 1981), not a solitary flag was to be seen as the Israeli leaders made their reciprocal visit to the Hashemiyeh Royal Palace in Amman.[89] And thousands[90] of Jordanians defied a government ban on protests and demonstrated in the center of the Jordanian capital—"the king's armored personnel carriers patrolled to ensure calm."[91]

Israeli journalists were for the first time permitted to operate from Amman, but they reported widespread Jordanian opposition to accepting the king's peace. On the day the border crossings were opened, a lady interviewed by *Voice of Israel Radio* spoke for many: "The King gives us an order—this is what he wants. Am I supposed to stop hating you now? Are my sons supposed to stop hating you?"[92] Jordanian security forces escorted the Israeli tour buses, and "police even went so far as to block off all intersections through which the buses passed!"[93] One Jewish visitor was stabbed and slightly injured on a bus near Amman, and Jordanian terror groups pledged to launch more attacks against the "unwelcome Zionists."[94]

In December 1994, 11 Jordanians were sentence to death for their part in trying to overthrow the government.[95] And, while the Jordanians opened their embassy almost immediately, Israel has not been able to establish its embassy in Jordan—it is operating from a hotel in Amman at the time of writing. Israeli Embassy staff have found several suitable properties, but the "landlords refuse to allow Israel to use their properties."[96] In February 1995, King Hussein hosted a group of 28 Israeli MKs in his palace, but it was hard for the Israelis to ignore a front page article in the *Jordan Times* which said the visit "offended the feelings of the Jordanian people, who will **see the enemies of the nation, the occupiers and the war criminals on their national soil.**"[97]

The king is hoping that Israel will in some way help to prolong the life of the Hashemite Kingdom. Fundamental Islam is growing at a rapid rate in Jordan as in all other Arab states, and the king knows that it is in the interests of the Israelis to extend Hashemite rule in Jordan after his death in the near future. But an unidentified "very senior source"[98] said in an interview that: "Developments in Jordan will 'sooner of later' bring about 'the end' of the Hashemite regime. I am not saying that Jordan will disappear as a state. But Jordan as a kingdom, as a country ruled by a king [will disappear]...'the mood in the street is irreversible.'"[99]

Sooner or later, Palestinian Islamic fundamentalists will topple Hussein's government or that of heir-apparent, Crown Prince Hassan, Hussein's brother. When that takes place, Israel will face a PLO-Islamic state four times its own size that is ready to go to war at the first opportunity. Arafat has already rejected the Hashemite administration of Jerusalem's Islamic shrines even though he has no authority in Jerusalem whatsoever. When Jerusalem's supreme Moslem Mufti Suliman Jabari died in October 1994, King Hussein speedily appointed a successor. But Arafat rejected Hussein's authority and appointed a PLO Moslem Mufti, Ikrema Sabri, who on the Temple Mount before 10,000 Moslem worshipers, said: "Moslems, I am sure that Israel will eventually be destroyed and that the settlements will be your spoils."[100] And, in May 1995, Sabri called for *jihad* and stated that Jerusalem must be "liberated from Israeli occupation and turned into Jerusalem, the capital of Palestine."[101] Currently there is a stand-off between Hussein and Arafat. Jerusalem now has two Moslem Muftis, and the Moslem holy places have two administrative bodies.

Syria

For many months the news media has carried reports of "a change in mood"[102] among the Syrians. Egypt's President Hosni Mubarak has said that Syria is now "keen to have peace."[103] United States Secretary of State Warren Christopher has also said that President Hafez Assad "is ready for 'normalization with Israel.'"[104] Even President Clinton has said that Assad is willing to "normalize relations with Israel."[105] Along with "normal relations," Syrian Foreign Minister Farouk Sha'ara says that Syria wants a "comprehensive, just and lasting peace."[106] But after a two-hour session with United States Senator Hank Brown, Sha'ara refused to commit Syria to an actual peace treaty with Israel after retrieving the Golan Heights. He merely said that "Syria must get back all the territory, **and then we'll see**."[107] In an unprecedented interview on Israel television in October 1994, Sha'ara even "rejected Israel's right to exist."[108] And when President Clinton requested from Syria's President Hafez Assad a clarification of the meaning of the "full peace" he says he is willing to make with Israel, Assad "rejected Clinton's request."[109] Six months later, Assad stated that, like the PLO, he, too, was offering Israel the "**peace of the brave**."[110]

Westerners do not seem to understand that Arabs use code phrases that have more to do with the diplomatic meaning of the words than with their literal meaning. Thus, "normal relations" with Israel is a virtual continuation of the existing state of war. A "just peace" means obtaining every Arab demand. A "comprehensive peace" is the elimination of Israel from the Middle East. So, when Clinton met with Assad in Geneva in January 1994, Clinton painted a rosy picture of his understanding of their talks. He said Assad had "expressed a willingness to normalize relations" with Israel, which Clinton obviously understood to be "an exchange of ambassadors, open borders with free movement of people and goods, and all components of neighborly relations."[111] But Assad meant nothing of the sort, and when pressed by a CNN correspondent to say if Clinton was quoting him correctly, "**Assad pointedly declined to answer**."[112] Assad was reported to have come out of the meeting, "smiling."[113] The current lack of progress between Syria and Israel in achieving a "full and comprehensive peace" is, according to Syria, "**because Israel is making unjustified demands**, such as **normal relations between countries, open borders and an end to the Arab economic boycott.**"[114]

Assad can afford to "smile"—the world actually believes that an Ethiopian can change his skin and a leopard its spots (Jeremiah 13:23). One of the Israeli tank commanders whose divisions threw the Syrians off the Golan Heights in 1967 says: "I do not believe Assad has changed his skin. He can change the color but not the nature of it."[115] And Assad's skin is infamous for its brutal, sadistic nature, but now these characteristics apparently find favor in the eyes of the leaders of the New World Order. United States President Bill Clinton was "fascinated to be meeting with this somewhat notorious character"[116]

Clinton, like other prominent Western leaders, ignores the fact that Assad is one of the world's cruelest dictators, and that his regime uses diabolical methods of torture to stay in power. Assad's secret police routinely use horrible methods of torture, many of which are simply too gruesome to describe. It is perhaps hard for readers to imagine that in the last days of the 20th century that torture devices such as *al-khursi al-almani*—the German chair—are in use in Syria. This particular instrument brings excruciating pain as "knives cut into the victim's flesh as the chair is revolved."[117] And can Western people really understand the Syrian regime's use of *al-abd al-aswad*—the black slave—whereby "a prisoner is strapped down while a heated metal skewer is thrust into his anus"?[118] These and many others are the normal methods of "questioning" undertaken by Assad's police.

The method Assad uses to muzzle the press against publishing stories considered by Damascus as "unfriendly to Syria,"[119] is by shooting the journalists.[120] *Reuter* correspondent Bernd Debusman was shot in the back four times as he walked home in Beirut. His crime was that he mentioned that Assad belonged to the minority Alawite Moslem sect. The Alawites comprise only 12 percent of Syria's population, but hold 100 percent of the power. Syrian journalists—Salim Lawzi, Ali Jundi, Riyad Taha, Salah Bitar and Michel Nimri—serving as foreign correspondents, wrote about Assad's tight control and about the ruling Alawite minority. They were "**all subsequently murdered** in Beirut, Paris, and Athens."[121]

The world's leaders, the United Nations and the news media, also overlook the Syrian army's killing of the 20,000 people in Hama with cyanide gas before bulldozing the city under a mound of dirt.[122] They also choose to overlook the Syrian murder-by-execution of hundreds of bound Christian army officers in Lebanon.[123] And they choose to overlook the fact that Syria hosts 10 terror groups which it allows to operate openly and freely. Ahmed Jibril—"the father of techno-terrorism"[124]—"commander of one of the most lethal terrorist organizations to emerge on the international scene,"[125] "is a Syrian army officer and part of Syrian intelligence, a branch of Mr. Assad's presidency."[126] Jibril's office is not far from the Damascus office of Islamic Jihad, the terror group responsible for catastrophic bombing of Israeli civilians. After its latest bombing in January 1995, which left 21 Israelis dead and more than 60 wounded, Damascus admitted that Islamic Jihad was based in Syria, but said its intention is to "**just let them let off a little steam.**"[127]

Overlooked is the Syrian war-by-proxy against Israel. Via its proxy, Hizbullah, together with other terror groups operating against Israel in Lebanon, Syria wages war. The terror groups "are almost totally dependent on their Syrian 'host' which provides training, logistics and weapons."[128] Syria, which also allows Iranian weapons to pass freely through Damascus airport on their way to terror groups in Lebanon, says, "Armed resistance to Israel is a legitimate act that will continue until Israel withdraws from all occupied Arab land."[129] And Assad told Israel in January 1995, that Rabin's concept of "building a fence around the occupied territories will not stop the violence, neither will individual peace agreements with Arab states—they are timebombs waiting to explode."[130] Syria "totally rejected Egypt's peace treaty with Israel,"[131] and "vehemently objected"[132] to Jordan's.

Also overlooked is Syria's multi-billion dollar drug trade. A 1992 report by the United States House of Representatives Subcommittee on Crime and Criminal Justice detailed the Syrian drug connection. Under Syrian military rule, the area in the Lebanese Beka'a valley devoted to drug cultivation has risen **from 10 percent to 90 percent.**[133] "**Almost 20 percent of the heroin**

consumed in America originates in Lebanon."[134] Cocaine and heroin paste "are shipped through Damascus airport to the Beka'a valley, where refineries have cropped up like poppies."[135] At least "four tons of heroin and large quantities of cocaine found their way last year [1991] from these refineries to Europe, adding **billions of dollars** of revenues to support terrorism."[136] Assad's own brother, Rifaat, is "intimately connected with drug traffickers,"[137] as is Assad's "Defense Minister Mustafa Tlass; General Ali Dubah, Commander of Syrian Military Intelligence; and General Ghazi Kenaan, Commander of Syrian Military Intelligence in Lebanon."[138] Assad's drug production directly kills "over 35,000 young Americans every year,"[139] but President Clinton, fully aware of the facts, was "**fascinated** to be meeting with this somewhat **notorious character**."

Syria's President Hafez Assad says he wants peace with Israel, but gives sanctuary to 10 terror groups dedicated to Israel's destruction. Assad wants peace, but controls one of the world's largest drug organizations providing funds for international terrorism against Jews. Assad wants peace, but is currently producing thousands of chemical warheads."[140] Assad wants peace, but is manufacturing biological weapons *en masse* in a factory near Haleb.[141] Assad wants peace, but is constructing factories to produce and assemble his own advanced Scud missiles.[142] Assad wants peace, but has signed "a strategic cooperation agreement with Iran for developing and producing nuclear weapons."[143] Assad wants peace, but builds an enormous military machine parallel with his "peace talks" with Israel.

Major-General Yitzhak Mordechai, head of IDF Northern Command, notes that Syria has "doubled and in some cases tripled it armor, artillery and helicopter forces"[144] since its surprise 1973 *Yom Kippur* attack upon Israel. Mordechai is also recorded as stating: "Assad's army is three times larger" than when it launched its 1973 attack. He said, "Assad has amassed over 4,000 tanks compared to 1,680 at the time of the *Yom Kippur* War, and now has a **vast array of missiles** such as advanced Scuds which can strike deep into Israel with chemical warheads."[145] He also added that since 1982, Assad has acquired advanced warplanes and air-

Peace: The Road that Leads to War 249

defense systems that are among the most sophisticated in the world."[146]

Does Assad want true peace? Never! Assad is offering Mohammed's peace in order to regain the strategic Golan Heights. After that comes war. Brigadier-General Ya'akov Ami Dror, head of the IDF military intelligence research division, bears this out when he says Assad is "employing the peace option to regain the Golan Heights while preparing through rearmament for eventual war."[147] Major-General Yitzhak Mordechai, head of IDF Northern Command, also fears that Assad is "talking peace while preparing for war."[148]

Assad exposes his hand when he says that his war against the Jewish state will last "as long as time,"[149] and that once Israel has withdrawn from the Golan Heights, there must be no "observation posts at the strategic plateau."[150] Syria's long term strategy, like that of Egypt, Iraq and Iran, aspires to being the predominant power in the Middle East, and Israel blocks its way. Israel's liquidation is essential to both the Moslem cause and Assad's realization of greater Syria. Only a Moslem style temporary peace with Israel can assure him of any degree of success.

Dictatorships determine their policies according to the ambitions they harbor, not according to treaties they sign. Assad has no more respect for contracts than does Yasser Arafat. Besides violating every agreement it has ever made with Israel in the past, Syria also broke its word to the Saudis and the Reagan administration to respect the May 1983 Israel-Lebanon agreement.[151] It discarded the inter-Arab Taif agreement which stipulated the departure of Syrian troops from Lebanon by September of 1993,[152] and has broken every promise to grant independence to the Beirut government.[153] Assad has also **violated 18 agreements signed with Turkey** in 1993 and 1994."[154] Some may well argue that the Syrian-Israeli border on the Golan Heights has been the quietest of all of Israel's borders. But those that would argue along that line forget that Israeli tanks and planes are stationed on the Golan—less than 30 miles from Damascus—expressly for the purpose of keeping the border quiet.

The late Egyptian president Anwar Sadat—certainly an expert

on his Arab brothers—"heaped scorn and mockery on United States President Jimmy Carter for believing Assad's word could be trusted."[155] In his posthumous book, *Those I Have Known*, Sadat wrote: "He [Carter] imagined they would be as good as their word and was taken aback when he found that the word of a Syrian was in fact 1,001 words, and that what they agreed to one day they rejected the next, returning to it the day after."[156] Former Lebanese Prime Minister Michel Aoun, another expert on his Arab brothers, also warned against believing the Syrians: "They don't respect their word. They scheme, they promise you one thing and do something else on the side. They promised in the past, but **they never lived up to any agreement.**"[157] Arab leaders place no trust in Assad's word, and neither does Israeli intelligence officers. In a November 1994 report to the Knesset Foreign Affairs and Defense Committee, a senior intelligence officer said: "**The description of Assad as a man who keeps his agreements is a myth. It has no basis in reality.**"[158]

Israel is under pressure to relinquish the Golan and the strategic defense that it offers against Syria. Israelis remember the trauma of living under Syrian guns, and suffering "20 years of shelling and shooting and bombing."[159] They remember how "Syria had used the high ground to fire indiscriminately on the Israeli communities below. Farmers were shot in their tractors, and children spent months in cramped bomb-shelters as the artillery thundered overhead."[160] But, as Charles Krauthammer, columnist for the *Washington Post*, stated: "Why should the Israelis worry? Assad promises to be a good neighbor. They have Bill Clinton's word for it."[161]

Iraq

"**Israel is surrounded by dictators who sign treaties for tactical purposes, and then violate those treaties whenever it is to their advantage to do so.**"[162] Saddam Hussein's regime, headquartered in Baghdad, made peace with and officially recognized Kuwait in 1962. In August 1990, Hussein had a change of mind and sent his tanks rumbling over the border, and Kuwait fell to him in just a few short hours. World leaders did what they are good at doing—they talked. But when the Iraqi armor began to move toward the Kuwaiti border with Saudi Arabia, a coalition of nations sent a massive number of men and a vast array of equipment to Saudi Arabia's desert sands to defend much of the West's oil supplies. More than 500,000 troops, thousands of warplanes, helicopters, tanks, armored personnel carriers, howitzers, and even warships and aircraft carriers came to the Middle Eastern kingdom—to defend the supply of oil, not to defend the opulent Arab kingdom. Had Kuwait and Saudi Arabia grown carrots instead of oil, Saddam would be exercising his rule over that whole area today.

The coalition was led by the United States, whose heaviest fighting support came from Britain and France. The Soviet Union and China sent "negotiators" to try to influence Hussein to withdraw from Kuwait. Each of the coalition partners mentioned, together with the two peace emissaries, were the very nations whose unconscionable greed for profits drove them to sell the huge array of armaments required to build Saddam's massive war machine. The billions earned from the sales of arms to Iraq were nothing in comparison to the billions that have been spent on their destruction. The arms manufacturers went laughing all the way to their banks—they benefited both ways. The thousands left dead in the cities and on the battlefields do not disturb their night's slumber, neither will they be factored into negotiations with the next client—be it Mubarak, Assad or Arafat.

Saddam Hussein believes himself to be "a neo-Nebuchadnezzar—destined to lead Iraq into the greatness that once belonged to ancient Babylon."[163] Nebuchadnezzar's kingdom encompassed the lands of Iraq, Kuwait, Syria, Jordan, Israel and some of Iran. Nebuchadnezzar's greatest claim to fame was the destruction of Israel in the 6th century B.C. Since the early 1970s Saddam Hussein has been spending millions on the rebuilding of the ancient city of Babylon, and Nebuchadnezzar's palace which has 700 rooms.[164] Saddam believes it is his destiny to destroy the modern state of Israel, and this would establish his fame for posterity.

In an endeavor to have the United Nations sanctions against Iraq lifted, Saddam Hussein has once again offered to formally recognize the sovereignty of Kuwait. But this does not presuppose a change of heart toward possessing her again. The Iraqi leader has stated: "Kuwait belongs to Iraq, and we will never give it up even if we have to fight over it for 1,000 years."[165] Despite Iraq's defeat in the Gulf War and the continuing United Nations search-and-destroy operations against its surviving missiles, chemical and nuclear facilities, this country remains a grave threat to the region. In addition to its current substantial standing army, the United Nations "believes that Iraq still has about 100 missiles, which were transported by mobile launchers to underground hiding places."[166] CIA estimates of existing Iraqi missiles are much higher, "putting the number of these missiles at 200."[167] And a report prepared by Russian intelligence states that "the Ukraine is supplying Iraq with tactical nuclear weapons. The weapons were offered for sale as 'nuclear fuel'...Iraq also bought from the Ukraine an old, small nuclear reactor."[168] Iraq is ignoring United Nations orders by continuing to arm itself with chemical weapons. Thirty-five tons of ammonium perchlorate (used in the manufacture of chemical weapons) was seized from a German ship, the *Asian Senator*, in early February 1994. The vessel was on its way to Beirut, Lebanon, from where the cargo was to be transported overland to Iraq.[169] Iraq finances its purchases by defying United Nations sanctions prohibiting the sale of oil from its vast reserves. Iraq is allowed to export 75,000 barrels a day to Jordan to cover the costs of food and medicine. The sanction is to remain in effect until Saddam Hussein complies with the terms of the Gulf War cease-fire.

According to the *New York Times* Iraq is selling oil at the rate of 200,000 barrels a day and selling it at discount prices—$8 a barrel instead of $14[170]—even the PLO is negotiating to purchase 25,000 barrels a day![171] Iraq's Minister of Petroleum, however, recently stated at an OPEC meeting in Indonesia that Iraq is producing over 2 million barrels of oil a day. Iraq's daily requirement is less than 450,000 per day which means it is exporting some 1.5 million barrels per day to the black market.[172] The oil is taken overland through Kurdish territory into Turkey and Iran by hundreds of trucks and out to sea by dozens of small tankers. The Kurds are not bothering the trucks because they are collecting tax.[173]

Just as Iraq continues to eye Kuwait, so it also nurtures its dream of Israel's destruction. Speaking during a reception for the heads of his military on January 5, 1995, Saddam said (alluding to the 39 Scuds it launched against Israel in 1991): "The Arab countries should be asking themselves, 'Who will fire the 40th missile against Israel?'"[174]

Iran

At different times during the 1980–88 Iran-Iraq war, both sides made the claim that they would march on down to Jerusalem after they had won the war. Neither side emerged as victor after eight years of bitter fighting, but the coffers of these two oil producing nations were emptied. Oil, however, is a profitable export, and both countries refilled depleted treasuries and rebuilt their war machines. Both sides cherish the hope of dealing a deadly blow to the Jewish state.

Iran's government is radically and fundamentally Islamic. It also aspires to being the preeminent power in the Middle East in order to spread its fundamental Islamic doctrine. Its hatred of Israel is purely religious—it considers the Jewish presence in the otherwise Islamic Middle East to be an affront to Allah. Iran wants Israel eradicated, and to this end, 140 members of the Iranian parliament signed a document in March 1994, calling for the destruction of Israel.[175] Syria might host terrorist groups, but Iran is the leading instigator and financier of international terrorism. Most of the terrorism it finances is directed at Israel or Jewish communities abroad, and it provides terrorists with "vital logistic, financial and tactical support."[176]

Iran sometimes participates directly in terrorism against Jewish targets overseas, as was the case in the July 18, 1994 bombing of Argentina's main Jewish community center. Four Iranians from the Iranian embassy in Buenos Aires were arrested in connection with the bombing which leveled a seven-story building, killing nearly 100 people, and injuring almost 250. The bombing was almost identical to the attack on the Israeli embassy in Buenos Aires two years previously. It was seen as a retaliation for IDF actions against the Iranian sponsored Hizbullah terrorists in Lebanon. A spokesman for the Hizbullah (Party of Allah) terrorists operating out of Lebanon, said they receive $60 million annually from Iran. He also said: "We will show no mercy to anyone. With the existence of Israel there will be no peace."[177] In a July 1994 newspaper interview, Subhi Al-Tufeyli, a past Secretary of the Hizbullah movement, said: "If the whole world makes peace with Israel, Hizbullah will continue to fight the Jews."[178]

According to the Iranian news agency, Syrian Foreign Minister Farouk Sha'ara flew to Iran in January 1995 to "coordinate strategy."[179] The fingers of both regimes are stained with international terrorism, and perhaps they were coordinating attacks. But they were far more likely to have been coordinating their aggressive pursuits for nuclear capabilities. Remember, it was mentioned earlier that Syria had signed a "strategic cooperation agreement with Iran for developing and producing nuclear weapons."

Herbert Krosney, an American expert on weapons sales and technology, says Iran "**has about 5,000 people working in its nuclear program.**"[180] Krosney believes Iran is only "a few years away from developing atomic weapons."[181] While Iran maintains its nuclear program is for the production of power only, Robert Gates, director of the CIA from 1991–93, says: "The Iranians have pursued reactors that are optimized for the production of plutonium rather than nuclear power."[182] Israeli officials agree with Gates's argument that Iran is pursuing nuclear weapons, not power, and they also agree with Krosney that it is only a few years away (perhaps five) from becoming a nuclear power.

Israeli political and military analysts have pointed out that Egypt's military threat has never been greater, and that Egypt is Israel's most dangerous potential enemy for the battlefield, but **senior Israeli officials "consider Iran's nuclear potential to be the most serious threat facing the country."**[183] The same officials say that if Iran's program is not halted, "they would be forced to consider attacking Iran's nuclear reactors."[184] This is no idle threat—Israel destroyed Iraq's Osiraq reactor with surgical precision on June 7, 1981. But with the advent of missing Russian nuclear warheads turning up in Iran,[185] Israel would also need to destroy the Iranian plants working to produce missiles for delivering them.

Libya

Like Egypt, Syria and the PLO, Libya totally rejects Jordan's peace treaty with Israel—because it is an actual, bona fide agreement. Libya's dictator, Mu'ammar Qaddafi, says: "The Arab nation did not sacrifice so many sons for Palestine in order to demarcate a frontier between **so-called Israel** and Jordan."[186] Libya, says Qaddafi, welcomes Western policies "that make the Arabs hate the West, for this hatred produces the bombs and the real terror that sows fear...**This hatred will turn into a bomb that will destroy so-called Israel**."[187] Libya, like its cousin Syria, both finances and plays host to international terror groups. Qaddafi says: "The fleets of the Americans cannot protect Israel from simple folk with explosives."[188] Ultimately, Libya's terrorist groups exist only for the destruction of Israel.

Peace Brokers?

A word needs to be included about the two "brokers" of the Arab-Israeli peace process—Russia and the United States. Neither of these nations have gotten involved for the good of Israel's health, but for the good of their own nation and its corresponding ideology. Both are concerned with enhancing their prestige and dominance among the nations of the world. Prior to September 1991, the Soviet Union was the most powerful influence in the Middle East. It sided with the anti-Western Arab states against Israel in order to gain their support and custom. The United States cosseted Israel to get a foothold in the region and to have an ally there against the Soviet Union. The Soviet Union remained faithful to the Arab cause, but the United States played ball in both courts. Israel is nothing more and nothing less than a pawn in a power game between the Kremlin and the White House. As Yossi Beilin, Israel's deputy Foreign Minister so aptly said on July 15, 1994: **"The Americans and the Russians will decide upon the future of the Middle East."**[189]

Russia

Russia is now flexing its muscles, and "the signs that Russia seeks to reassume the former Soviet Union's position as an influential power in the Middle East are unmistakable."[190] Not only has Russia sought to assume this role, but it has now "consented" to take over that role as is apparent by its involvement. Just as Assad is unable to change the nature of his skin, so are hard-line communists unable to stop agitating trouble in their effort to achieve preeminence. The Soviet Union, "promoting subversion and war all over the world, described itself and its oppressed satellites as the 'peace camp.'"[191] Now Russia has picked up the Soviet Union's ball and is running with it. Victor Posuvaliuk, head of the Middle East department in the Russian Foreign Ministry, arrived in Jerusalem in August 1994, and said: "Russia deserves **and demands** a say in the political status of Jerusalem's holy sites in the future."[192] He went on to say: "I'd like to stress that Russia possesses the largest Christian Orthodox community in the world."[193] He simply forgot to add that Communist Russia had persecuted, jailed and tortured that community for decades, along with demolishing its churches.

In addition to "demanding" a say on the status of Jerusalem, Posuvaliuk stated that Russia will continue to sell arms to Syria, and: "We intend to develop our relationship with Syria in the military sphere."[194] Russia is indeed developing its relationship with Syria in the military sphere—when North Korea sent a shipment of Scud-C missiles to Syria in August 1993, the missiles were obligingly delivered by Russia.[195] Russia is also "working alongside Syrians in Lebanon and Iraqis in Iraq in a military capacity."[196] Also, Russia has ignored United States and Israeli requests not to sell Iran nuclear reactors, and is currently negotiating a $1 billion sale of several reactors to Teheran.[197] In addition, Russia is now fully "master-minding Iran's nuclear development."[198] After a brief lull due to the collapse of the Soviet empire, the first salvos in the renewed battle for control of the oil-rich Arab sheikdoms and anti-Western Arab-dictatorships have been fired.

United States

It has often been said that politics is a dirty business. Exactly how dirty, few people realize. The desire for fame and power is often the all-consuming interest of the one that enters the political arena. With one short stroke of a politician's pen, hundreds,

Peace: The Road that Leads to War 257

thousands, hundreds of thousands, and even millions of people can be affected detrimentally or even perish. When it comes to superpower status, it is usually the millions that are affected.

The American drive to surpass the Soviet Union in might and power has today helped make the United States the most powerful nation on planet earth. The Soviet Union crumbled under the strain of American competition, and a prominent Russian physicist said in April 1992: "Our economy is in absolute disarray, our Army is in retreat, our union is crumbled. We've had everything except a military defeat in the classical sense."[199] The Soviet Union collapsed and is no more, but the United States cannot slow its weapons machine—it must continue to produce and sell arms to whomsoever has the billions to buy—the employment and lifestyle of hundreds of thousands of Americans depend upon it. Israel's neighbors fully understand the lesson of the Egyptian-Israeli treaty: Make a treaty with Israel, and the doors to the great American arsenal are opened. A signed but violated agreement still places "the most advanced offensive and defensive systems" in Arab hands.[200]

When everything is all boiled down—are the motives of the United States government any cleaner than those of the Russian government? Does not America want to maintain a New World Order dominated from Washington? Does it not desire preeminence in the world and to act as its policeman? Almost the whole world knows that American interests lie more with Arab oil and arms sales than with Israel. Under the guise of being an "honest broker" in the Arab-Israeli peace negotiations, former United States Secretary of State James Baker not only promised PLO leaders that they would get their state,[201] but according to several sources, he used an obscene four-letter expletive which was translated for more sensitive ears as, "the Jews can go to hell."[202] On the issue of the Golan, Baker's boss, President Bush, also "promised Assad he would deliver the Heights."[203] Not content with promising to deliver Israel's land to its enemies, Bush directly interfered with the Israeli elections by refusing to grant the $10 billion in loan guarantees to the Shamir government which it sorely needed in order to absorb the hundreds of thousands of Jewish immigrants pouring into the country. The

Bush administration's propaganda machine magnified and distorted the request for "guarantees," and turned it into "an alleged request for $10 billion in "**aid**."[204] Apart from the corrupt election campaign conducted by the Labor party with Rabin at its head, Bush's refusal to grant the loan guarantees to the Likud government was the singularly most influencing factor that brought about the downfall of the Shamir government in June 1992. George Bush's ambition was to be president of the world, and Shamir's refusal to bow before him incurred his personal hatred just as Mordecai had incurred Haman's before him (Esther 3:1-5). As the Israeli elections came near, the then United States Ambassador to Israel, William Harrop, even appeared on Israeli prime-time television programs in a blatant pro-Labor capacity to influence Israelis against Shamir. Bush, however, did not remain in office long to enjoy the success of seeing Yitzhak Shamir ousted. He himself was tossed aside by the American voters a few months later, as was James Baker.

President Clinton follows hard in Bush's footsteps—he is hungry for power and "dishonest" as a "broker." Edward Djerejian, a former United States envoy to Syria, was appointed United States Ambassador to Israel by Clinton in June 1993. Djerejian was transparently sent "to 'oversee' the transfer of the Golan back to Syria and his old associate, Hafez Assad.[205] Djerejian resigned in May 1994, but gave an interview prior to his departure in which he said, "quite blithly,"[206] that "the Golan would go back either 'very, very soon,' or in three years."[207] Asked for the reason for the strange timetable, he replied: "**It depends on whether Clinton thinks it will hurt his election chances or not.**"[208] Apparently, "if it's too dicey, he'll wait an appropriate period, until after the next election."[209]

What right has any American president to pressure Israel into putting its head into a noose for a few votes? American prestige and presidential power is uppermost, not the multitude of lives that will be lost by surrendering the Golan. Those lives are no more important that the more than 35,000 Americans lost annually to Syrian drug production—Clinton was "fascinated" to meet the "notorious character" who kills them.

Prior to his meeting with Assad, Clinton was asked by American

Peace: The Road that Leads to War

columnists about the issues between the United States and Syria. Clinton replied: "**Forget about all the issues between us and Syria. Let's just talk about the peace process now.**"[210] The columnists should have insisted on talking about the issues between the United States and Syria—about terrorism and drug production. Syrian drug production alone, in just one single year, **kills far more Americans than the combined total of Jewish lives lost to terrorism and war since the beginnings of Israel's reestablishement in the 1800s.** When Clinton visited Israel's Knesset in October 1994, he told the Israeli parliament that "without an end to terror there can be no peace.[211] Those words rang with hypocrisy. He was "fascinated" to meet with one of the world's major sponsors of terrorism without even broaching the subject. Worse, he is trying "to persuade Congress to remove Syria from the State Department's list of countries which sponsor terrorism"![212]

Some years ago, Clinton said he was called to the bedside of the dying pastor of his Southern Baptist congregation. The pastor believed that Clinton would one day become president, and said solemnly, "God will never forgive you if you let any harm come to Israel."[213] Clinton has made much of this scene with his "pastor," and it has gained him the support of many Christians as well as much of America's Jewish vote. But Clinton is a "political Christian," not a real one. What he says and does is for effect.

Clinton arrived in Israel to witness the signing of the Israeli-Jordanian peace treaty, and an Israeli journalist described the experience as "**more like visiting Disney World** than witnessing the ceremonial signing of a historic peace treaty."[214] The journalist also wrote that it was obvious the flags and marching bands were for the benefit of "**the voters in the US** watching the festivities with their morning coffee on the *Today* show or *Good Morning, America*."[215] At the signing ceremony, Clinton's political "Christianity" came to the fore when he misquoted Jesus' sermon on the mount—one of the best known of all New Testament passages. Clinton said: "Here in this region, which is the **home of not only both your faiths, but mine**, I say: 'Blessed are the peacemakers, for they will inherit the earth,'"[216] Jesus, of course, said, *"Blessed are the peacemakers for they will be called sons of God"* (Matthew 5:9).

The United States State Department also plays along with the grand deception. In a recent report on PLO compliance with the Oslo DOP, it contended that the terror organization "has proven over a six-month period its 'commitment to seek a peaceful negotiated settlement.'"[217] The report also found that "the PLO had not been involved in terror activity over that period."[218] It should be well noted, that during the six-month period covered by the report, the Oslo Accords were violated repeatedly:

a) At least 12 indisputable PLO terror attacks were carried out against Israelis, and at least 11 Arab "collaborators" were murdered.[219]
b) There was no disciplining of PLO members involved in incidents of terror.[220]
c) There was no pursuit of terrorists.[221]
d) There was no extradition of terror suspects to Israel.[222]
e) The PLO continued hiring wanted fugitives as policemen.[223]
f) The *Fatah* Hawks have been rearmed as Arafat's private militia.[224]
g) The PLO continued to use "State of Palestine" and "President of Palestine" symbols and titles.[225]
h) The PLO continued to ignore the required change in the PLO charter which calls for Israel's destruction.[226]

The above list is not a complete list of violations by any means, but someone should at least tell the United States State Department that not everyone is fooled by its politicking.

In all fairness to the United States government, it has offered to guarantee Israel's security. However, certain considerations need to be borne in mind: Its 1957 guarantee to Israel that it would keep the Tiran Straits open in the face of Arab agression[227] **"proved worthless in its first test, only ten years later."**[228] And President Johnson's "promise of decisive American action on a multinational flotilla was **soon revealed as equally hollow**."[229] It was Egypt's blockade of the Tiran Straits in 1967 that led to the

Peace: The Road that Leads to War 261

June Six Day War. Had America honored its commitment made a decade earlier and broken the blockade, the terrible war and with its thousands of dead would not have occurred. Neither would there have been the Palestinian problem that there is today, or the suffering that it has involved. Just as Britain was responsible for the bloody 1948 war, so the United States was responsible for the 1967 war.

In chapter 8 it was pointed out by an American that commitments made by one American administration are often rejected by a subsequent one, and American guarantees, therefore, resemble "**a laundry list of betrayals.**"[230]

According to the *London Sunday Times*,[231] after Clinton had met with Assad in Damascus, he gave a "commitment" to Rabin that the United States would "deploy troops in the evacuated areas"[232] after Israel had withdrawn from the Golan Heights. Relying upon United States troops to be a defensive buffer between an aggressive Syrian regime and an indefensible Jewish state, however, is folly at its worst. American guarantees to Israel have proven to be little short of worthless on numerous occasions, and its troops providing security have fared little better. United States troops were sent in to Lebanon in August 1992, as part of a multinational force that was to provide stability for the Gemayel government and security for Israel against terrorism. The American troops came under such intensive fire that President Reagan sent a naval force to the Lebanese coast, and soon the battleship *Missouri* was firing its huge guns into terrorist positions. In October 1983, a "suicide bomb attack killed 241 marines,"[233] and the terrorists achieved their objective—by the following February, all United States troops had been withdrawn from Lebanon. Turning tail and running in the face of actions that Israel contends with daily, was seen as another "major American diplomatic and military fiasco."[234]

Binyamin Netanyahu, leader of Israel's Likud Knesset opposition, said that it was necessary to do everything possible to prevent the Americans from taking their posts on the Golan Heights. Netanyahu, basing his arguments on past history, said that Israel would never be sure "the United States would provide real-time intelligence.[235] At first glance, that statement from one of Israel's most prominent leaders appears to be a heavy slap in the face of Israel's ally, but is it?

Bruce Brill, a Mideast intelligence analyst who served in the United States Army Security Agency at the United States National Security Agency (NSA) at Fort Meade, Maryland, from 1971-74, told Israel about the "deliberate withholding of vital information by America."[236] Brill cited the catastrophic *Yom Kippur* War as an example—the war that is described as "the greatest trauma ever to have hit Israel."[237] He said:

> "I learned of the planned October 6, 1973, invasion of Israel by Syria and Egypt – **30 hours before the U.S. notified Israel... Upper echelon Agency personnel knew of the planned attack hours, if not days, prior to that**. Not passing this vital information along in time resulted in the **unnecessary deaths and maiming of thousands of young Israelis.**"[238]

In 1986, an American Jew, Jonathan Pollard, was sentenced to life imprisonment for spying for Israel. **Pollard was not convicted of treason**, but of **spying *in* the United States**.[239] Casper Weinberger, himself pardoned of four felonies,[240] fought hard and successfully, as he put it, to "put Pollard away for life, so **he will never see the light of day**."[241] Influenced by Weinberger, "the judge passed an unprecedented life sentence. **No spy for a friendly power has ever been sentenced to life imprisonment in the US**."[242] Not even "**spies for the USSR who compromised American security, have received a punishment as harsh as Pollard's**."[243] Pollard was first "sent to a mental hospital, then to solitary confinement in a basement cell in Marion, Illinois, federal penitentiary—the toughest prison in the United States"[244] When other cases of similar espionage "typically ended with prison terms in the range of two to five years,"[245] why did Pollard get such a heinous sentence?

Jonathan Pollard's work as a civilian intelligence analyst for the Navy brought him face to face with the fact that America was violating "the 1983 Executive Agreement on sharing intelligence between the United States and Israel."[246] The United States was withholding vital intelligence from Israel. Consequently, Pollard felt that he had a moral obligation to the Israeli people, and:

> "...passed on to Israel classified information concerning the **weapons systems and war making capabilities of such Arab states as Iraq, Syria and Libya, including evidence of Iraqi efforts to produce chemical, biological and nuclear weapons and deliver those weapons of mass destruction to Israel's population centers.**" [247]

Pollard had **lost 75 members of his immediate family** in the Nazi Holocaust.[248] From his prison cell he wrote:

> "The same gas which the Nazis used to murder our European brethren could just as easily be used today by the Arabs to exterminate the Jewish population of Israel." [249]

He also wrote:

> "I'd rather be rotting in prison that sitting *shiva* [mourning] **for the hundreds of thousands of Israelis who could have died because of my cowardice.**" [250]

Pollard was sentenced to the most degrading and harsh sentence possible. He never compromised United States security—he exposed the violations of its agreement with Israel. That was his real crime, and for that Pollard must rot in prison for the rest of his natural life.

In addition to that which was mentioned under "Egypt" (the turning down of United States offers for joint exercises, because it does not want its methods relayed to the Egyptians), the *Jerusalem Institute For Western Defense* states:

> "...the U.S. has been supplying Egypt and Saudi Arabia with information about Israel's military dispositions and defenses on an ongoing basis for many years—information duly passed on to Syria, the PLO and probably Libya."[251]

America is feeding the enemies of Israel—its supposed "ally"—with classified information relating to its defense and armaments. Still playing its power game, it withholds strategic information from its "ally," and hands down an unmercifully harsh prison sentence to the man who discovered the double-cross and tried to rectify it. But other Brills will expose, and other Pollards will spy.

With America promising the PLO and Syria that they will obtain the land demanded from Israel; withholding vital Arab military information from Israel while supplying information on Israel's defense and armaments to the Arab nations; and requesting that Israel sign the Nuclear Non-Proliferation Treaty as a "goodwill gesture"[252] to Egypt (effectively stripping it of its nuclear deterrent), proves that the United States is only interested in dominating the Middle East, not in Israel's survival.

Summation

In this historic day when peace treaties are being fabricated between the world's most ancient enemies, we see only one Arab-Moslem ruler—Jordan's King Hussein—desiring peace with any degree of sincerity. He has not long to live. He will either die from cancer or from an assassin's bullet. In due time, his kingdom will fall to fundamental Islam which rejects both his peace and Israel's right to exist.

Egypt has provided a cold-peace—an actual cease-fire—for more that 15 years. It rejects the Israeli-Jordanian peace treaty, and the country's secret police state that "there is no peace between Israel and Egypt." It is building a huge military force aimed at confronting Israel, declares that war with Israel is inevitable, and that it is ready for war. And Israel itself deems Egypt to be its greatest military threat.

The PLO is supposedly making peace with Israel and has almost the whole world fooled, including the United States State Department and the Clinton administration. Arafat and the PLO also reject the Israeli-Jordanian peace treaty, and Arafat's repeated declaration that the peace agreement with Israel is a "despicable truce"[253] is, according to Western and left-wing Israeli politicians, merely "Arab rhetoric." His call for *jihad*—holy war—to liberate

Peace: The Road that Leads to War

Jerusalem is only a call for a "peaceful" *jihad* according to the same experts.

The brutal murders of Israelis are increasing in number almost daily—the 1994 toll being the worst since the founding of the state. The more concessions Israel makes, the more deaths it suffers.

Syria rejects both the Israeli-Jordanian treaty, and also the Israel-Egypt treaty. Following in the footsteps of Arafat, Syria is trying to establish Mohammed's peace also. If it succeeds, it will get the Golan Heights, reduce Israel's chance of survival in the coming Arab-Israeli war, and rake from the shelves of America's vast arsenal the weapons to wage that war. It is almost within reach of its goal. Israel's Foreign Minister envisions the Jewish state being "integrated into the Moslem Middle East.[254] Syria rejects outright the idea that Israel should exist within the Arab world at all and says: "Are we to leave a legacy of Israeli conquest to future generations?"[255]

Iran is seen as the most dangerous threat facing Israel today—not militarily, but by its nuclear potential.

Iraq is rebuilding its massive military machine and pursuing a nuclear weapons program under the very noses of the United Nations. Saddam is also asking, "who will fire the 40th missile into Israel's population centers?"

Libya says Arab hatred alone will turn into a bomb that will destroy Israel, and it welcomes Western policies that fuel this hatred.

Russia is trying to pick up where the former Soviet Union left off. It is masterminding Iran's nuclear program and supplying it with weapons. It is also arming Iraq, Syria and Libya.

The United States is seen as Israel's great ally, but in reality, it is only seeking further American prestige and power. It has often left countries in the lurch, not the least being Israel itself. American world influence is being gained at the expense of Israel, which is simply a pawn in games played by superpowers. Washington recycles petro-dollars by selling Arab states immense quantities of sophisticated military equipment, which they in turn use against Israel.

In this chapter, we have concentrated upon the attitudes of Moslem and Arab leaders toward the Israeli-Arab peace process, but we also seen that the average Arab living in the Israeli administered territories agrees with the average Jordanian. Almost without exception, the leaders and masses desire the destruction of Israel. Peace, even among those signing the agreements, is considered to be only a temporary state until a more opportune time presents itself—Mohammed taught his followers well.

In what was by far the most comprehensive, thorough, far-reaching survey taken among Arabs—Lebanese, Syrians and ex-patriot Palestinians—the associate professor of political science at the American University of Beirut provides us with further proof of the Arab concept of "peace" with Israel. To begin with, "**not one of the respondents** who favored the peace process gave positive justification for peace with Israel."[256] They saw peace as "the only available alternative **at present.**"[257] According to the respondents: "It is **a chance to recover territory** occupied by Israel since the Six Day War."[258] The great majority of those interviewed saw the peace "as an interim measure **for Arabs to reorganize and strike later.**"[259] And "**more than 90 percent of those who now support peace would support a war if Israel became weaker.**"[260]

Over three-quarters of all Moslem Arabs, be they leaders or followers, look forward to war with Israel in the future. No matter what Western and Israeli left-wing, pro-peace politicians say, the future for Israel does not include a lasting peace—only Isaiah's *Prince of Peace* (Isaiah 9:6) can bring that. With every concession made by Israel (usually at the demand of United States and European leaders), the Jewish nation becomes strategically weaker. The pathway to peace that Israel has chosen to take is, in cold reality, the old Moslem road that leads to war.

12

Judgment of Nations

Mark Twain once said: "All things are mortal, but the Jew; other forces pass but he remains. What is the secret of his immortality?"[1] There is no secret regarding the Jew's immortality. It is a well-known Biblical fact that he was singled out from the nations—specifically chosen by Almighty God and destined to fulfill a particular purpose. That destiny largely remains unfulfilled in these closing days of the 20th century.

No other people have been chosen, have been the target of as much hatred, suffered as much persecution, or seen as much bloodshed. It has already been mentioned[2] that the great distresses that befell Israel of the ancient world was because it chose to walk the way of the nations and not the way of their God—*"She did not consider her destiny; therefore her collapse was awesome"* (Lamentations 1:9).

Israel is locked into its destiny—locked into being a part of God's plan of world redemption. It is impossible for Israel to be "like all other nations," as the current Israeli government desires. Israel is also locked into Biblical prophecy, and the odds for prophecies concerning Israel not being fulfilled are the same as the odds for the sun not rising tomorrow. There is a fixed inevitability about Biblical prophecy and history; man cannot alter what God has determined by His will. God is able to do absolutely anything. But there are some things that He will not do, and one of them is that He will never contradict His word.

Man rebelled against God in the garden of Eden and died spiritually. The Jews were chosen as a people by God to be the instrument He would use to restore man back to Himself. It was through them that the Messiah came to make man spiritually alive again. The Jews' calling is very obviously spiritual. And just as the Satanic force in the garden of Eden brought about man's spiritual death, so it has attempted, and still attempts, to destroy the Jewish people to prevent it from fulfilling its destiny. Satan hates the Jews and this is clearly seen in his treatment of them, but God's purposes cannot be frustrated. God's purposes can be opposed, even delayed, but His ultimate purpose can never be frustrated.

God, being faithful to His word, has preserved the Jewish people for thousands of years and taken them through every storm and whirlwind that the forces of hell have raised against them—including the Nazi Holocaust which took six million Jewish lives. Not only has God preserved the Jewish people, but again according to His word, He has brought them back to their ancient land and recreated the Jewish state.

The Arab nations, together with all other Islamic countries, tell us that the unrest in the Middle East is because the Jews stole Arab land. The news media—the real spokesman of the world—portrays the long-running Arab-Israeli conflict as a conflict over land, also. And the leaders of the world's most powerful nations pressure Israel to concede land to its Arab neighbors, who for over a thousand years, have together inhabited around 10 percent of the entire earth's land surface—a larger geographical area than any comparable ethnic group. By pressuring Israel to concede land, the world's leaders are enforcing the idea of a territorial dispute. But the conflict and bloodshed in the Promised Land is not a dispute over territory, it is a spiritual conflict waged by a satanic force against the people and purposes of God. A Gazan terrorist states what all true Moslems believe:

> "Israel will be destroyed. This is a Koranic fact. **It is a religious conflict. It is not an Arab-Israeli conflict or a Palestinian-Israeli conflict. It is a religious conflict between Moslems who are the true owners of this land, and Jews** who are using Zionism and Judaism to build a secular state."[3]

The following question was put to the terrorist: "But what if Israel defeats Islam?" He replied: "If they defeat Islam, it will not be the last battle, but once the Moslems defeat Israel, it will be the last."[4]

I reiterate: This is a spiritual conflict. And the evil spirit that operates through Islam—through the Arabs, through Iran, and through the PLO, has been fighting in and for Israel's land since time immemorial:

> *"The **Nephilim** were on the earth in those days—and also afterward—when **the sons of God went to the daughters of men and had children** by them. They were the heroes of old, men of renown"* (Genesis 6:4 NIV).

Nephilim is often wrongly translated as "giants" in some English translations, probably because many of the *nephilim* were of immense stature. But the Hebrew word for "giant" is *anak*, and the plural is *anakim*. *Nephilim*, however, is the plural of the Hebrew word *nephil* meaning "bully," and this has its root in the Hebrew word *naphal* which means to "fall." The *Nephilim*, were literally "fallen bullies." They were, in fact, the offspring of the "fallen angels"—*"the sons of God*—who copulated with human females and produced "half-flesh–half-spirit" beings. These in turn became the *"heroes of old, the men of renown."* Is it really surprising that these "beings" obtained pre-eminence in battle?

We need to remember, however, that "flesh" dies, while the "spirit" remains. This evil spirit manifests itself in barbaric men like Hafez Assad, Saddam Hussein, Yasser Arafat, Abu Nidal, George Habash, Ahmed Jibril—to whom torture and violent murder is as natural as breathing. Men like these find their excitement in planning murderous outrages, like exploding a jumbo passenger jet in the skies, or destroying a high rise building and its occupants.

Also wrongly translated as "giants" in some English versions is the Hebrew word *rephaim*. Here the translators obviously misunderstood the Hebrew text:

> *"Then the* LORD *said to me, "Do not harass Moab, nor provoke them to war, for I will not give you any of their land as a possession, because I have given Ar to the sons of Lot as a possession. (The Emim lived there formerly, a people as great, numerous, and **tall as the Anakim**. Like the **Anakim**, they **were also regarded as Rephaim**, but the Moabites call them Emim)"* Deuteronomy 2:9-11 NASB.

Anakim means "giants," **Emim** means "terrors." And because the **Emim** were *as tall* as the giant **Anakim**, **they were also**

regarded as Rephaim. Rephaim, however, means, "**ghosts, phantoms, the dead, the spirits of the dead.**"[5] The *nephilim* were indeed the physical by-product of the union between flesh and spirit. And as proof that the spirits of these beings live on in the land, I would like to say that I, personally, know a local Moslem Arab who was born with six fingers on each hand. His son was also born with six fingers, as was his father, and his father's fathers before him. Now consider the following:

> "*Yet again there was war at Gath, where there was a man of great stature, who had six fingers on each hand and six toes on each foot, twenty-four in number; and he also was born to the giant*" (2 Samuel 21:20).

Yes, the conflict is spiritual, and the opposing spirits are powerful, and evil. And in just a few short years we shall begin to witness wars of unutterably catastrophic dimensions. We might well see a lessor war first, but it will pave the way for the great wars—and Armageddon.

It is evident to any serious student of the Bible that warfare occupies a large place in the consummation of the age with a resultant great loss of life. It is also evident to the student that **the kingdom of God comes by catastrophe, not by development**. Living here in Jerusalem as I do, and closely monitoring the English, Hebrew and Arabic news pertaining to Israel, it is apparent that we are irretrievably on the countdown for war—whether the "peace process" continues or not.

The whole purpose of the "peace process" for the PLO is to sufficiently weaken Israel in order to bring about its annihilation—war is an integral part of the overall plan. Israel goes to the polls in June 1996, and it is highly improbable that Rabin and the Labor party will get reelected. Not only did they deceive the people during the last campaign, which turned out to be corrupt, but they have alienated the public by suicidal policies of appeasement on all fronts. Binyamin Netanyahu, the leader of the Likud party, who is consistently ahead of Rabin in the opinion polls, says, that should it come to power, "the Likud will not honor the present government's deal with the PLO."[6]

Judgment of Nations

Aborting the peace process and reassuming control of the areas given over to the PLO will incur the wrath of the whole world, not just Islam. A war would seem to be the inevitable result of such an action by any Israeli government, and the former IDF head, Lieutenant-General Ehud Barak, even declared during his term of duty that "an impasse at the peace negotiations would lead to an armed conflict."[7]

Israel provides the battlefields for the great Biblical confrontations of the future. The beautiful city of Jerusalem will again see rivers of blood flowing through her streets as Satan attempts to dethrone God in His own city. Jerusalem is a stone—an unmovable stone. Satan will enlist a multitude of nations in his effort to move that stone, but Mount Zion abides forever. It cannot be moved (Psalms 125:1). Praying *"for the peace of Jerusalem"* (Psalms 122:6) will accomplish as little in the coming days as it has done in the past. No other city has been the recipient of more prayer, and no other city has seen more bloodshed! It has been said that if blood was indelible, Jerusalem would be red—all red.

Contrary to religious tradition, the original Hebrew Bible text never enjoins us to *"pray for the peace of Jerusalem"*—that is an English mistranslation. But this mistranslation has become one of the better known Scripture verses, and no one Bible manufacturer would now dare to change it. The Hebrew text enjoins travelers coming up to Jerusalem for the three great feasts of the LORD, to "Say 'Hello' to Jerusalem"—on behalf of those who had hosted them on their journey. The Hebrew word for "hello" is *shalom*, the same as that for peace. (For a full teaching on this and other mistranslated words, see my book *Saga: Israel and the Demise of Nations*).

Even thought the conflict is spiritual, Israel's army—rated "the fourth most powerful fighting force in the world (only behind America, Russia and China)"[8]—will have to fight as if the confrontations are on an earthly plane. But as we race toward the end of the End Times and the completion of God's purposes for man and his planet, we should remember one cold, stark fact—God never loses in any confrontation.

And let us not entertain, for even one moment, the thought that the God of Israel desires to destroy the Islamic nations. This is so very far from the truth. The Moslem people are also very precious to God, but He does use people and events to accomplish His greater purposes. To begin to understand the impartial interventions of God, we need at least to understand the following passage of Scripture:

> *"Now when Joshua was near Jericho, he looked up and saw a man standing in front of him with a drawn sword in his hand. Joshua went up to him and asked, 'Are you for us or for our enemies?' 'Neither,' he replied, 'but as commander of the army of the LORD I have now come.' Then Joshua fell face down to the ground in reverence, and asked him, 'What message does my Lord have for his servant?' The commander of the LORD's army replied, 'Take off your sandals, for the place where you are standing is holy.' And Joshua did so"* (Joshua 5:13-15 NIV).

There is only one other passage in Scripture where a person is told to take the sandals from his feet:

> *"When the LORD saw that he turned aside to look, God called to him from the midst of the bush and said, 'Moses, Moses!' And he said, 'Here I am.' Then He said, 'Do not draw near this place. **Take your sandals off your feet, for the place where you stand is holy ground***'" (Exodus 3:4-5).

As Moses had stood in the presence of Deity, so also did Joshua. But the Commander of God's army had nothing to say to Joshua, the commander of the Israelite army, except for him to take his sandals off! We know from Scripture that the LORD had promised to drive out the inhabitants of the land and to deliver them over to defeat by the children of Israel (Deuteronomy 7:2,20,22-24). Yet when Joshua, not knowing who He was, asked the Commander of God's army if He was on Israel's side or the enemy's side, He said "neither," (Hebrew *lo*, meaning, "no," but more idiomatically, "neither") even though He was there to ensure an Israelite victory! Here we see the complete impartiality of the LORD in situations like the conquest of Canaan and the Islamic-

Israeli conflict. God had every intention of helping the Israelites conquer Canaan and has every intention of helping Israel defeat its Moslem aggressors. But He was not then, and is not now, personally against the other side! God will certainly use Islam's hatred of Israel, the nations' inherent anti-Semitism, Western and Eastern greed for profits and power, and the spiritual bankruptcy of Israel's current leaders, to set the scene for the final acts in this age.

The coming Islamic-inspired confrontations with Israel will be of major proportions. The spirit of Islam is the most powerful evil force active in the world today. The God of Israel, however, is the greatest power active in our universe! The spirit of Islam is on a collision course with *"the Mighty God of Jacob"* (Psalms 132:2,5, etc.), and so are the spirits of Mammon and power. But God's power is awesome. In the 8th century B.C. He struck down 185,000 Assyrians in a moment of time (Isaiah 37:36). Compare this power with that of the atomic bomb dropped on Hiroshima in August 1945 by the Americans—it killed a little more than half that amount. It will be through the Islamic-inspired confrontation over Jerusalem that the Moslem and non-Moslem worlds will finally and fully enter into God's plan of redemption.

Understanding that the Islamic-Israeli conflict is spiritual, not territorial, allows us to put the following "coincidences" into perspective. These few examples should serve as a warning to leaders of nations not to get involved in the "peace process," nor to lean too hard on Israel for any other reason:

a) The "peace process" was begun under the umbrella of the Bush administration. Former United States president, George Bush, and his Secretary of State, James Baker, were openly anti-Israel during their term in office. They brought United Nations condemnations against Israel and pushed her to the wall on several occasions. The Bush administration has been written into history as the most hostile administration toward Israel since the Eisenhower-Dulles duo of the 1950s,[9] and Bush goes down as the most hostile United States president in history.[10] Both Bush and Baker professed to be Bible-believing Christians, but both scoffed at the Jew's claim that their right to the land was God-given. Where are these two men today? Their anti-Israel stance brought the United States into severe recession, and they themselves were thrown out of the Oval Office like waste paper.

b) On the same day that members of Rabin's coalition government met with PLO leaders for the very first time in Washington D.C. in August 1992, hurricane Andrew slammed into Florida causing $22 billion in damages.

c) Johan Joergen Holst, former Norwegian Foreign Minister, hosted 14 secret meetings in Oslo between left-wing Israelis and PLO terrorist leaders. Holst "died unexpectedly"[11]—four months to the day following the signing of the DOP which he brokered. He was eulogized as being "at the height of his career."[12]

d) Three days after Holst's death, President Clinton was "fascinated" to meet and shake hands with the "somewhat notorious character"[13]—terrorist protecting, drug producing, president Hafez Assad of Syria. Assad demanded—before the world—that Israel "withdraw from all occupied Arab lands." The following day a devastating earthquake struck California. Fifty-two people died, 5,000 were injured, 24,000 rendered homeless and damages exceeded $30 billion— making it "the most expensive disaster in United States history."[14] Three days after the meeting, a record-crunching cold with temperatures below 40 degrees killed another 100 Americans and affected a further 75 million.[15] Five days after the meeting—publicized as Assad's greatest triumph— Assad's eldest son, 31-year-old Basil, the man being groomed to succeed the ailing Syrian leader, was killed in a car accident. Assad "openly cried at his son's funeral."[16]

Aside from those directly involved in the "peace process," it should perhaps be mentioned that war-torn Yugoslavia and famine stricken, disease ridden Somalia are the same two nations that

Judgment of Nations

have "introduced more anti-Israel resolutions in the United Nations than any other nations.[17]

Who Owns The Land?

In the early part of the 19th century B.C.—in what must surely be the oldest and most universally published deed of possession in the world—God covenanted to give the land of Canaan to Abraham, and, through Abraham's son, Isaac, to his descendants *forever* (Genesis 13:15. Other pertinent Scriptures are: Genesis 12:1,7, 13:14,15,17, 15:7,18-21, 17:8 etc.). The Moslem world, together with many Gentile nations, are seeking to deprive Israel of its God-given inheritance, ignoring the fact that Almighty God has already determined the rights of Israel to possess it. He covenanted to give the Jewish people *all the land of Canaan as an everlasting possession* (Genesis 17:8).

Nearly 500 years later, the Israelite nation were camped along the Jordan River awaiting Joshua's order to cross over and take possession of their land. There, on the banks of the Jordan opposite Jericho, it was again declared that the land was being given to them *for all time* (Deuteronomy 4:40). God has also stated repeatedly that the land He gave to Abraham (and through the line of Isaac to all the Jewish people) is actually His land (Leviticus 25:23; 2 Chronicles 7:20; Isaiah 14:25; Jeremiah 2:7, 16:8; Ezekiel 36:5, 38:16; Joel 1:6, 3:2). God is still the owner of the land today, and the Jews still have the right of possession. It would do us well to remember that something is right or wrong because of divine decree, not because of mans' feelings or reasoning.

Ishmael, from whom the Arabs sprang, was also a son of Abraham. He was born to Hagar, Abraham's wife's Egyptian maid (early Egyptians were not Arabs[18]). But Ishmael was not to share in the inheritance of the land of Canaan. That land was specifically given to the Jews through Isaac. God blessed Ishmael and made a separate covenant with him (Genesis 17:19-21), and other lands were given to him. And I have already mentioned above that the Arab nation has inhabited a larger geographical area than any other comparable ethnic group in history.

Land for Peace?

On November 19, 1977, the former president of Egypt, Anwar Sadat, made an historic visit to Jerusalem in a quest for peace with the Israelis. Sadat had masterminded the treacherous 1973 invasion of Israel on the holiest day of the Jewish calendar, *Yom Kippur*—the Day of Atonement. But even having the advantage of surprise, the war had still cost Egypt dearly in men, machines and territory. The June 1967 war, which Sadat's predecessor, Gamal Abd al-Nasser, instigated, was far more disastrous—Egypt had lost the entire Sinai peninsular together with tens of thousands of men. Sadat came to Jerusalem wanting the whole of the Sinai peninsular back in return for peace.

Israel was willing to return the Sinai despite the billions it had poured into development. Israel was willing to return it for the simple reason that the Sinai did not constitute part of the land covenanted by God to the Jewish people 3,900 years earlier. And so Israel destroyed its towns, villages and oil installations in the Sinai and handed it back—again. Israel had captured the Sinai previously, in November 1956, and had returned it three months later under United States and United Nations pressure. Which proves that any peace evolving from Israel's surrender of captured territory to its Moslem invaders, only lasts until the next war. I have said it before and will say it again—lasting peace can only come through Isaiah's *Prince of Peace* (Isaiah 9:6).

Sadat genuinely sought peace. He said he was "tired of the 'wasteful confrontation' with Israel."[19] Sadat's peace, however, branded him as a traitor to Islam, and he was condemned to death by Islamic fundamentalists. Israel's current "peace partner," PLO terrorist leader Yasser Arafat, said in March 1979: "Sadat should understand that he will be struck down. It is his destiny."[20] And struck down he was. Sadat died in a hail of Moslem Brotherhood bullets on October 19, 1981, while watching a military parade commemorating the 1973 war. For the first time in thousands of years of Egyptian history, "the people of Egypt had murdered their pharaoh."[21] Arafat knew Sadat would be murdered. Sadat had tried to make a genuine peace. Arafat is in little danger of assassination because his peace is tactical, not actual. He works closely with the most extreme Moslem fundamentalist factions in

Judgment of Nations

the Gaza Strip and Jericho, and has also extended his protection to them.

The Sinai was not part of the Promised Land, but Jericho is, as is half of the Gaza Strip and Israel's heartland—Biblical Judea and Samaria—now called the "West Bank" in order to obliterate the Jewish connection. God did not interfere with the return of the Sinai peninsular to Egypt, but He certainly intends to set the record straight concerning the Israel-PLO, Israel-Jordanian, and any other future accords such as an Israeli-Syrian one. We need to clearly understand that God means what He says. The Bible is emphatic about God's word being His bond: *"God is not a man that He should lie"* (Numbers 23:19); *"God, who cannot lie"* (Titus 1:2); *"It is impossible for God to lie"* (Hebrews 6:18). It is not that God will not lie—He simply *cannot lie*. It is *impossible* for Him to speak anything but truth. Therefore, whatever He speaks comes to pass, and whatever He promises is as certain to be fulfilled as surely as tomorrow follows today.

In the Islamic-Israeli conflict God's reputation is at stake. He promised the land of Canaan—from just above the Sinai to the Euphrates River in modern-day Iraq—to Israel *forever, for all time*. Anything less than this would make Him a liar and not to be trusted in any situation. If *forever* and *for all time* only mean a limited period of time, then it follows that *eternal life* is only good for a limited period also. And if this were indeed the case, many would throw their Bibles into the sea, or use them for some practical purpose like propping up tables. But God is not a liar; *forever* means forever, and *for all time* means for all time. The Israeli-PLO peace accords place large areas of Israel's land under Arab sovereignty, but these accords will come to nought for the following reasons:

a) The land was given to Israel, and only to Israel, for an eternal possession.

b) Israel is the possessor, not the owner of the land. The title deed remains in the hands of Almighty God, and Israel simply cannot give away His land to another people. God placed an injunction on the land, and even Israelites could not sell their plots *permanently* to one another. Israel has an everlasting possession, but God has absolute ownership—*"the land is Mine"* (Leviticus 25:23).

Whatever areas of the Promised Land are given over to the sovereignty of Arab nations or the PLO will, in time, return full-circle back into the possession of the Jewish people. The price for its return will be paid in blood. Each Arab-Israeli war of the past has seen Israel retake more of its land from those who would wage war against the Jews. And thus it will be in the future also.

War!

There are three sets of prophecies in the Old Testament describing future horrific wars on Israel's land. These wars are found in the books of Ezekiel, Joel and Zechariah. There is also a prophecy in the New Testament Book of Revelation—often called the Apocalypse—that portrays another war, the great and final battle of this age—Armageddon. All these wars must take place prior to the commencement of the thousand-year Messianic Age. The coming wars are contained in five separate prophecies. The question that nobody can answer with any degree of certainty is this: Are the prophets speaking of five different wars, or four wars, or three or two, or even one lone, catastrophic war fought on three battlefields and featuring two main, terrible battles? There are a number of very good exegetical reasons (too many and too lengthy to discuss here) for ascribing the five prophecies to a maximum of only three wars. Prophetic Scripture almost always omits more than it contains, and nothing is certain until prophecies are fulfilled or well into the process of fulfillment. I will endeavor to point out some of the more obvious hints that appear to link one war with another, and then leave the reader to form his or her own conclusion.

• The future wars are certainly Islamic inspired, of great magnitude, and with incomprehensible death-tolls. The outcome is already known, and to realize the Biblical description of the horrors portrayed, Israel will likely use its nuclear last resort. Israel is known to possess hundreds of nuclear-tipped missiles—

one of the world's largest arsenals. Its enemies will drown in the full fury of the most terrible weapons known to man.

Long gone are the days when man respected righteousness, truth and justice. Now they respect wealth, power and military might. God will use the Islamic-inspired wars with Israel to bring salvation to the nations. He will ultimately draw the focus of world attention to bear upon Himself, as he brings Israel onto center stage in world events through the medium of unutterably catastrophic wars. God specifically chose Israel as a nation through whom He would make a name for Himself—through miracles, signs, wonders and military conquests in the Promised Land:

"And who is like Your people, like Israel, the one nation on the earth whom God went to redeem for Himself as a people, to make for Himself a name—and to do for Yourself great and awesome deeds for Your land" (2 Samuel 7:23).

"To make for Yourself a name...by driving out nations from before Your people" (1 Chronicles 17:21).

"You showed signs and wonders...You made a name for Yourself" (Nehemiah 9:10).

And as God did in the ancient world through Israel, so He has done in the modern world through the miraculous victories Israel has achieved on the battlefield. This will be accentuated in the coming cataclysmic confrontations. The nations of the world will stand in awe:

"Thus says the LORD of hosts: "In those days ten men from every language of the nations shall grasp the sleeve of a Jewish man, saying, 'Let us go with you, for we have heard that God is with you'" (Zechariah 8:23).

In the Scripture immediately above, God uses His name *LORD of hosts*. This name occurs 219 times in Scripture, and in Hebrew it literally means *Yahweh of armies*. It is rather sad that most popular English translations use the word *hosts* in place of *armies* as it does great violence to the meaning of the text. The NIV's use of "sovereign" or "Almighty" is no better. The Hebrew word that has been translated *hosts* is *tsava*. This word is used 458 times in the Old Testament, and only on nine occasions is it used outside of a military setting. Four times it refers to *the sun, the moon, and the stars*, and five times it refers to the thousands of Levites that serve in the temple. God is indeed the God of armies. He has immense forces of warrior angels that carry out His will, and these forces will oppose the nations that come against Israel. On more than 70 occasions it is clearly stated in Scripture that this God of armies is Israel's God. For example: *Thus says the LORD, the God of armies, the God of Israel...* (Jeremiah 38:17).

The Old Testament prophecies concerning the great wars came to three individuals with relatively few years in between. Placing dates on a prophet's period of ministry is sometimes difficult due to the lack of definite information, but Ezekiel definitely went into captivity to Babylon around 586 B.C., when he was about 25 years of age. Scholars are also in agreement that Zechariah began his ministry around the year 520 B.C. Joel, however, has presented scholars with a difficult task in pinning down the time of his prophetic ministry. Widely differentiating dates have been proposed—from 800 – 400 B.C., from pre-exilic to post-exilic. But there has, however, been a near uniformity in dates given by eminent scholars such as Jacob M. Myers, Gösta W. Ahlström, Leslie C. Allen, etc., for Joel having begun his period of activity between 520 – 500 B.C., making him a contemporary of Zechariah. And Ezekiel would still have been alive during the ministries of Joel and Zechariah. Thus, the gap is quite narrow between the times of the individual receipt of God's word concerning the great wars prophesied by these prophets. The Apostle John's vision of Armageddon that came some 600 years later has a distinct possibility of being the final battle in a terrible war foretold by all three Old Testament prophets—Ezekiel, Joel and Zechariah.

With the current situation in the Middle East, we should not rule out the very real possibility of the head-on clash between

Israel and Islam taking place quite soon. At the same time, a fairly limited Arab-Israeli war could also take place at any time. If a limited clash involving missiles occurs, it would simply be a forerunner of what is yet to come. But we should be aware of the fact that the countdown to Armageddon has already begun.

On September 13, 1993, Israel signed the DOP (Declaration of Principles) along with Yasser Arafat of the PLO. Arafat is a Moslem who has sworn, along with other Moslem leaders, to liquidate Israel for Allah's sake. Arafat's mentor is Mohammed, the founder of Islam, and Arafat is emulating his mentor's use of deceit in the war to destroy Israel. The DOP and the peace agreement signed by Arafat in Cairo is a tactical military maneuver known in Arabic as the Truce of *Hudaybiyyah*. Mohammed first used the Truce against the inhabitants of Mecca in the 7th century—two years before he destroyed them. Saladin, the famous 12th century Moslem Prince, also used the Truce and made "peace" with the Crusaders in the Holy Land before attacking and defeating them. The Truce has become a model for all agreements with non-Moslems (infidels). It is never permanent: never lasting more than 10 years (with the possibility of another 10 years extension, no more). Islam is not permitted to stop its war against non-Moslems for more than this period. The countdown to Armageddon, therefore, began in September 1993, and the war ought to be launched before September 2003, but must begin, at the very latest, in September 2013. The actual timing for the war will entirely depend upon Islam's perception of its own strength, and that of Israel's weakness brought about by the Truce.

The actual timing of the cataclysmic wars, of which Armageddon is the last battle, is crucial only insofar as our own personal relationship to God is concerned. The battle is the cut-off point—it ushers in the Messianic Age, and there is nothing further to speak of with regard to cultivating a relationship with the *Prince of Peace*. We should all seek Him while He is yet to be found, and heed well the words of the psalmist: *"Today, if you will hear His voice: do not harden your hearts..."* (Psalms 95:7,8). It will not always be *today*—Armageddon ushers in tomorrow.

Make peace with God now. Putting it off until a more convenient time means you have already hardened your heart.

The Prophets

We have three prophecies in the Old Testament concerning this terrible confrontation and one in the New Testament. As is to be expected, Scripture is silent on many details, but there are sufficient pointers for us to ascertain When?, Where?, Why? and Who? (When the battles take place, where they take place, why they take place, and who is involved).

Ezekiel's prophecy:
"Son of man, set your face against **Gog, of the land of Magog**, *the prince of Rosh, Meshech, and Tubal, and prophesy against him, and say, 'Thus says the Lord GOD: Behold, I am against you, O Gog, the prince of Rosh, Meshech, and Tubal. I will turn you around, put hooks into your jaws, and lead you out, with all your army, horses, and horsemen, all splendidly clothed, a great company with bucklers and shields, all of them handling swords.* **Persia, Ethiopia,** *and* **Libya** *are with them, all of them with shield and helmet;* **Gomer** *and all its troops; the house of* **Togarmah from the far north** *and all its troops...***In the latter years you will come** *into the land of those brought back from the sword and gathered from many people on* **the mountains of Israel,** *which had long been desolate; they were* **brought out of the nations**...*You will ascend, coming like a storm, covering the land like a cloud, you and all your troops and* **many peoples with you**...*Then you will come from your place* **out of the far north, you and many peoples with you,** *all of them riding on horses, a great company and a mighty army.* **You will come up against My people Israel like a cloud, to cover the land. It will be in the latter days that I will bring you against My land, so that the nations may know Me'**...*And it will come to pass at the same time, when Gog comes against the land of Israel,' says the Lord GOD, 'that My fury will show in My face...I will call for a sword against Gog throughout*

Judgment of Nations

all My mountains,' says the Lord GOD. 'Every man's sword will be against his brother. And I will bring him to judgment with pestilence and bloodshed; I will rain down on him, on his troops, and on the many peoples who are with him, flooding rain, great hailstones, fire, and brimstone. Thus I will magnify Myself and sanctify Myself, and I will be known in the eyes of many nations. Then they shall know that I am the LORD.' And you, son of man, prophesy against Gog, and say, 'Thus says the Lord GOD: Behold, I am against you...You shall fall upon the mountains of Israel, you and all your troops and the peoples who are with you...'" (Ezekiel 38:1-6,8,9,15-16,18,21-39:1,4).

Some Bible commentators believe that the above prophecy (and also that from Zechariah 14, below) will be fulfilled in the Messianic age. Many others, including myself, disagree for a number of reasons, not the least being that these prophecies are completely out of character with the Biblical portrayal of the Messianic reign—*"the wolf shall dwell with the lamb; the calf, the lion, and the fatling together; **they shall not hurt nor destroy in all My holy mountain,**"* etc. (See Isaiah 11:6-9). The war is a precursor to the Messianic reign; it can not take place within a reign of peace.

In the above prophecy we should note the following:

a) Israel's invaders. In evangelical circles the general belief for years has been that the prophecy spoke of a massive invasion of Israel by Russia. This came about from the mistaken assumption that *"Gog, of the land of Magog,"* was actually Russia itself. This is not so. There is little indication of who *Gog* really is, but some commentators do link him to the Scythians who inhabited a region "north of the Black and Caspian seas."[22] The use of *"Gog, of the land of Magog,"* most probably represents "the demonic and sinister leader of ungodly peoples far distant from Israel."[23] We are, however, better informed about the nations that are actually named in the assault upon Israel.

Persia is the radically Islamic nation of Iran.

Ethiopia (*Cush*, in some translations) is south of Israel, currently communist, but bordered on its east by radically Islamic Sudan, and on its west by radically Islamic Somalia. Ethiopia may fall to Islam, either by war or conversion.

Libya (*Put*, in some translations) is an avowed Islamic enemy of Israel.

Gomer is a "barbaric horde" that left its abode in Southern Russia in the 7th century B.C. and "poured through the Caucasus into Western Asia causing serious trouble to the Assyrians and other nations."[24] *Gomer* appears to have been were better known as the Cimmerians, and their migration ended in what is now Islamic East Turkey.[25]

Togarmah is generally accepted as having been "Southeastern Armenia."[26] Sizable portions of Armenia, such as the Northeastern sector, are fully Islamic today, and Armenia's southern neighbor is radical Iran. Since the collapse of the Soviet Union Armenians have been engaged in an armed conflict with their eastern neighbor—radically Islamic Azerbaijan.

It is not just the six named nations that are involved in the invasion of Israel, twice the prophecy says *"many peoples"*—many different ethnic groups or nations. All of *Gog's* troops, and all of the *peoples* will fall on *"the mountains of Israel,"* and here we should particularly note that they are *"the mountains of Israel"* not the "mountains of Palestine."

It might surprise some readers to learn that Moslems in the C.I.S. are estimated to constitute "an absolute majority"[27] by the year 2020. And it might surprise some readers even more to know that 50 percent of China is inhabited by non-Chinese, and China today actually has more Moslems than Saudi Arabia, Kuwait and United Arab Republic combined![28]

- b) The 5th century B.C. prophecy states that the horrendous battle will take place *"in the latter years,"* meaning, the End Times—these are the days in which we are now living.

- c) The war is fought on *"the mountains of Israel"*—Judea and

Judgment of Nations 285

Samaria, the so-called West Bank—a large, elongated geographical area extending from below Beersheva in the South, dividing into a fork at the southern end of the Valley of Jezreel in the North, and enclosing much of the Valley. A huge part of this area is slated to be handed over to the sovereignty of Yasser Arafat and the PLO in the very near future. God reiterates that he is the owner: *"My land"* (verse 16), *"My mountains"* (verse 21).

d) *"Pestilence (disease), fire, and brimstone,"* is rained upon the enemy—casualties are colossal—it takes Israel seven months to bury the corpses (Ezekiel 39:12). The description given in Ezekiel 39:15 would seem to indicate that the bones are either radioactive from nuclear fission, or contaminated from biological weapons. Contact with anthrax, for example, is known to remain lethal for several decades after an explosion.

e) God directly intervenes on Israel's behalf—*"I will rain down on him, on his troops, and on the many peoples."*

f) The overriding objective is salvation—*"I will bring you against My land, so that the nations will know Me,"* etc.

Joel's prophecy:
*"For behold, in those days and at that time, **when I bring back the captives of Judah and Jerusalem**, I will also gather **all nations**, and bring them down to the Valley of Jehoshaphat; and **I will enter into judgment with them** there on account of My people, My heritage Israel, whom they have scattered among the nations; **they have also divided up My land**...Proclaim this among the nations: 'Prepare for war!' Wake up the mighty men, let all the men of war draw near, let them come up. Beat your plowshares into swords and your pruning hooks into spears; let the weak say, 'I am strong.' Assemble and come, all you nations, and gather together all around. **Cause Your mighty ones to go down there, O LORD**. Let the nations be wakened,*

*and come up to the Valley of Jehoshaphat; for **there I will sit to judge all the surrounding nations**. Put in the sickle, for the harvest is ripe. Come, go down; for the winepress is full, the vats overflow—for their wickedness is great. **Multitudes, multitudes in the valley of decision! For the day of the LORD is near in the valley of decision**. The LORD also will roar from Zion, and utter His voice from Jerusalem; **the heavens and earth will shake**; but the LORD will be a shelter for His people, and the strength of the children of Israel"* (Joel 3:1-2,9-12,14-16).

We should note the following:

a) The time frame is current—*"when I bring back the captives."* Jews from nearly 150 nations have returned to a recreated Israel since 1948. Ten of thousands—even hundreds of thousands—of returning Jews are still pouring in annually. The ingathering could as yet continue for another decade or two, but anti-Semitism is on a rapid rise throughout the world and this will accelerate the return.

b) The battlefield is the *"Valley of Jehoshaphat."* This large, often deep, valley (now known as the Kidron Valley), begins in *"the mountains of Israel"* and runs alongside the walls of the Old City of Jerusalem, continuing down to the Dead Sea.

c) The aggressors might not be restricted to the Islamic peoples. It involves *"all nations"* involved in the persecution of Jews during Israel's exile from their land (Arab nations were leaders in their hatred of Jews, but so was Germany, etc.), and *all nations* involved in the division of God's land. This could even mean that the "broker" powers, some European and Scandinavian countries, and possibly a number of countries in the United Nations will be a part of the conflict. The PLO, and the surrounding Arab states are God's actual neighbors—*"**My evil neighbors who touch the inheritance which I have caused My people Israel to inherit....**"*

Judgment of Nations

d) There is direct intervention by angelic warriors. *"Cause Your mighty ones to go down there, O LORD,"* literally means in Hebrew— "Send down the heroes!"

e) The overriding objective is salvation—*"Multitudes, multitudes in the valley of decision! For the day of the LORD is near in the valley of decision."* Hundreds of thousands of troops— possibly millions—feeling the full fury of God's wrath. They are in the valley of decision—will they continue on their stubborn, evil path, or will they repent and worship the King on His holy hill?

First prophecy from Zechariah:
*"Behold, **I will make Jerusalem a cup of drunkenness** to all the surrounding peoples, when they **lay siege against Judah and Jerusalem**. And it shall happen in that day that I will make Jerusalem a very heavy stone for all peoples; all who would heave it away will surely be cut in pieces, **though all nations of the earth are gathered against it**...In that day I will make the governors of Judah like a firepan in the woodpile, and like a fiery torch in the sheaves; they shall **devour all the surrounding peoples** on the right hand and on the left...In that day **the LORD will defend the inhabitants of Jerusalem; the one who is feeble among them in that day shall be like David, and the house of David shall be like God, like the Angel of the LORD before them. It shall be in that day that I will seek to destroy all the nations that come against Jerusalem**. And I will pour on the house of David and on the inhabitants of Jerusalem the Spirit of grace and supplication; then **they will look on Me whom they have pierced**; they will **mourn for Him** as one mourns for his only son, and grieve for Him as one grieves for a firstborn"* (Zechariah 12:2-5,6,8-10).

We note the following:

a) The cause of the war is Jerusalem itself—*"I will make Jerusalem an immovable rock for all the nations. All who try to move it will injure themselves"* (NIV). The PLO declare that Jerusalem is the capital of their "state," and Arafat has called for *jihad* (Moslem holy war) to liberate it from the Jews. The city of Jerusalem became the Jewish capital 3,000 years ago, and has never been an Islamic capital of anything—it is not mentioned in the Koran.

b) There is a very large number of countries involved in the siege of Jerusalem and Judea—*"though **all nations of the earth are gathered against it.**"* This does not mean that every nation is being brought to do battle against Israel, but rather that it appears to be so due to the great number embroiled in the conflict. It is not just the city of Jerusalem that is besieged, but also the wide, surrounding area known as "greater," or "metropolitan" Jerusalem—also in *"the mountains of Israel."*

c) There is direct intervention by the God's mighty warrior angels—*"**the house of David shall be like God, like the Angel of the** Lord **before them.**"*

d) The Israeli army will devour the aggressors—*"**like a firepan in the woodpile, and like a fiery torch in the sheaves.**"* Israel has developed a number of dreadful weapons due to being surrounded by aggressive nations seeking its destruction. Israel develops weapons for survival not to wage war, but will not hesitate to use its arsenal when attacked.

e) The overriding objective is the salvation of the Jewish nation— *"I will pour **on the house of David** and on the inhabitants of Jerusalem the Spirit of grace and supplication; then **they will look on Me whom they have pierced**; they will **mourn for Him**."* The Hebrew, *eli*, translated, *"on Me,"* is not correct. *Eli* means, *to Me*—*ali* means, *on Me*. Therefore, the Jewish people will look "to Him" *"whom they have pierced."* God has been pierced many a time by Israel's repeated unfaithfulness. The Jews will *"mourn for Him,"* that is, their messiah—Isaiah's *"Prince of Peace"* (Isaiah 9:6). They will mourn in deep, acute, soul saving repentance.

Judgment of Nations

Second prophecy from Zechariah:

*"For **I will gather all the nations to battle against Jerusalem**; the city shall be taken, the houses rifled, and the women ravished. Half of the city shall go into captivity, but the remnant of the people shall not be cut off from the city. Then **the LORD will go forth and fight against those nations, as He fights in the day of battle**. And in that day **His feet will stand on the Mount of Olives, which faces Jerusalem on the east. And the Mount of Olives shall be split in two, from east to west, making a very large valley;** half of the mountain shall move toward the north and half of it toward the south...And this shall be the plague with which the LORD will strike all the people who fought against Jerusalem: **their flesh shall dissolve while they stand on their feet, their eyes shall dissolve in their sockets, and their tongues shall dissolve in their mouths**...And it shall come to pass that **everyone who is left of all the nations which came against Jerusalem shall go up from year to year to worship the King, the LORD of hosts...**"* (Zechariah 14:2-4,12,16).

Here we can note the following:

a) This battle also, is over Jerusalem—the most hotly disputed city in the world.

b) There are also many countries involved in this battle for Jerusalem—*"all the nations"*—probably not just Islamic nations.

c) Israel is vastly outnumbered and the battle appears to be lost—*"the city shall be taken, the houses rifled, and the women ravished. Half of the city shall go into captivity."* God must bring Israel to its knees to break its idolatry in worshipping its armed forces. He will get them to acknowledge that it is He who wins battles, not IDF strength. Thus Israel must *"look to Me whom they have pierced"* before divine help (d) is forthcoming. This also seems to indicate that both of Zechariah's prophecies are speaking of a single war.

d) There is direct intervention by the mighty warrior angels—*"the LORD will go forth and fight against those nations, as He fights in the day of battle."*

e) Israel will likely use either its nuclear option (known as the "Samson Option," when as a last resort it brings the roof down upon itself and its enemies), or some other terrible weapon that it has developed—*"their flesh shall dissolve while they stand on their feet, their eyes shall dissolve in their sockets, and their tongues shall dissolve in their mouths."*

f) The casualties are incalculable—*"everyone who is left of all the nations."*

g) An earth-rending earthquake takes place with the presence of God—*"the LORD will go forth and fight...in that day **His feet will stand on the Mount of Olives, which faces Jerusalem on the east. And the Mount of Olives shall be split in two.**"* At this point, we enter the Messianic Age.

h) The overriding objective is salvation—*"everyone who is left of all the nations...shall go up from year to year to worship the King, the LORD of hosts."*

John's vision in Revelation—the Apocalypse:
*"Then the sixth angel poured out his bowl on **the great river Euphrates**, and its water was dried up, so that **the way of the kings from the east** might be prepared. And I saw three unclean spirits like frogs coming out of the mouth of the dragon, out of the mouth of the beast, and out of the mouth of the false prophet. For they are **spirits of demons**, performing signs, which go out to the kings of the earth and of the whole world, to gather them to **the battle of that great day of God Almighty**. 'Behold, **I am coming as a thief. Blessed is he who watches**, and keeps his garments, lest he walk naked and they see his shame.' And **they gathered them together to the place called in Hebrew, Armageddon**. Then the seventh angel poured out his bowl*

*into the air, and a loud voice came out of the temple of heaven, from the throne, saying, 'It is done!' And there were noises and thunderings and lightnings; and there was **a great earthquake, such a mighty and great earthquake as had not occurred since men were on the earth"*
(Revelation 16:12-18)

We note the following:

a) The Euphrates river rises in Turkey and flows through Syria into Iraq, where it meets with the Tigris. The river is crossed by the *"kings of the east,"* most probably *Gog* with the *"many peoples"* spoken of by Ezekiel.

b) The *"spirits of demons"* is Islam.

c) The final, cataclysmic battle is fought at a place called Armageddon. The word Armageddon comes from the two Hebrew words, *Har Megiddo*, which mean Mount Megiddo. Mount Megiddo stands on the Southwestern edge of the Valley of Jezreel (Hebrew: *yizrael*, meaning, "God Scatters"), and this valley in Biblical times was literally the graveyard of kingdoms due to the many great military battles fought there. The valley is also known as the Valley of Megiddo, and when Napoleon cast his eyes upon it, he called it "the world's greatest battlefield."[29] The Valley of Jezreel lies in Samaria—at the northern end of *"the mountains of Israel."*

d) God calls out: *"It is done!"* An earth-rending earthquake takes place and this must surely be the same earthquake depicted by Zechariah. The Messianic Age is ushered in. The battle of Armageddon is most likely the same battle as that described by Zechariah.

Are there five wars, or is there only one? The reader can draw his or her own conclusion to the number, but we do know that there will be at least one terrible, gruesome war, such as the world has never before witnessed.

We might, however, ask ourselves some questions concerning the above wars: Why, in a technological age of missiles, nuclear, chemical and biological warheads, do the nations come down to *the mountains of Israel* to fight? Is it not true, as the military experts are claiming, that the wars of the future will be fought from long distances?

I believe the questions are relatively easy to answer: The Arab nations are known to possess more than 1,200 missiles at the time of writing. Since the Missile Technology Control Regime (MTCR) was signed in 1987, over 1,000 ballistic missiles were fired in less than five years by Moslem nations—Iran, Iraq and Afghanistan.[30] Israeli military sources acknowledge that eventually some 2,000 enemy missiles will be aimed at the Jewish state.[31] And it is reported from a reliable source that the Arabs plan to simultaneously launch half of these missiles at Israel at one time. To this end, Israel has not only been developing far more advanced missile systems, but it has also been developing anti-missile missile systems. The American Patriot system that was so widely lauded during the Gulf War was, in fact, a dismal failure. Of the 39 Soviet Scud-B missiles launched against Israel's civilian population centers by Iraq in 1991, 31 missiles hit their target. The Patriots were unsuccessful, because they were too slow. They could not catch the Scuds, and thereby had almost no chance of intercepting and destroying them.

Israel's Barak missile, however, locks on to enemy missiles, chases, intercepts, and destroys them.[32] But Israel's Arrow system—designed to be fully operational by the end of 1995—is the most sophisticated anti-missile missile system being developed anywhere in the world. In June 1994, Dr. Michael Holtcamp from the United States Ballistic Missile Development Organization, told Israeli engineers working on the Arrow, that the Arrow missile's successful interception and destruction of an incoming missile "has placed Israel at the cutting edge of international technology."[33] The June intercept was the last test in the initial stage of developing a prototype, and Israel is now racing toward full production.

Israeli sources have consistently refused to reveal technical details about the Arrow, but reports in the foreign press including

Jane's Defense Weekly, suggest that it will be able to destroy hostile short range missiles at a distance of ninety kilometers (fifty-six miles) from the defended position. To that end, it will be able to develop a velocity of Mach-9—nine times the speed of sound and to climb to an altitude of up to 30,000 meters (almost twenty miles). In order to remain operational under those conditions, the Arrow's component systems are said to be capable of withstanding accelerations of up to two hundred gravities (6,600 kph per sec.—4,100 mph per sec.).[34]

The Arrow's June 1994 intercept of an actual missile was not only seen by all of Israel, but by all the policy makers of its neighbors, too. The Arrow is not just a defense missile, it is also a deterrent against missile attacks. The Arrow will effectively explode a missile's warhead— nuclear, chemical or biological— over the attackers own territory within seconds of the missile's launch, spewing the payload onto the aggressor's own civilian population. And this is the most likely reason that the nations will come up to *the mountains of Israel* to wage their wars.

Israel has also pursued a limited space program designed to furnish her with intelligence on military equipment and troop movements. Since 1988, three satellite launch and retrievals have taken place amid great secrecy. In 1992, Israeli officials were outraged over the possible sale of an American super-secret spy satellite to the United Arab Emirates. An Israeli Defense Ministry official in Tel Aviv said:

> "For years we have been begging the Americans for more detailed pictures from their satellites and **often got refusals—even when Iraqi Scud missiles were falling on Tel Aviv.** The Americans have also **done their best to deny us all help** in building our own reconnaissance satellite. Now, they are going to supply the Arab countries with binoculars that will enable them to see every military movement here."[35]

On November 18, 1992, the State Department confirmed that the United States was "weighing the unprecedented sale of a super-secret spy satellite to the UAE."[36] Israel pushed ahead with accelerated efforts with its own spy-satellite program, and according to an anonymous Israel Aircraft Industries (IAI) official, the Ofek-3 satellite launched in April 1995, could read "the license plates on cars in Baghdad."[37]

Conclusion

Any world view that does not rise above man's horizon is meaningless and frustrating, and when based upon earthly ambitions, life is the ultimate in futility. The world view of today's modern nations does not rise above the horizon of man, and its ambitions are to obtain wealth, power and prestige. The Islamic world view rises above the horizon of man, but its ambition is also earthly—it seeks to subjugate the whole world to itself by force. Both the Islamic and non-Islamic worlds are chasing a rainbow in their exercises in futility. The God of Creation—Israel's God—is about to lower the curtain upon this age, and the future will then prove to be the solution to the mysteries and frustrations of the present.

The ambitions of the modern nations—Western and Eastern—play into the hands of the Islamic world and furthers its cause. The cynical rewriting of history dealt with in chapter 7 is undertaken through a harmony of Arabs, the news media and the academe—manipulated facts generated in the interests of Islam, oil and anti-Semitism. And untold millions of people—white collar, blue collar, students, even American Jews—have been persuaded by CNN and other news services that Israel is the place where helmeted stormtroopers shoot Arab children on the dirty streets stolen earlier from them. Jew-hating forces are unwittingly setting the stage for the great Biblical wars of the future, where the armies of many nations will be sucked into the vortex of a nuclear inferno that will consume them.

The Islamic world seeks to fully and finally annihilate the Jewish state from the Middle East—from what they consider to be Allah's land. There will be no peace, and can be no peace, between Islam and Israel, because the Koran forbids it. Moslems reverence both the Koran and Mohammed, Allah's prophet, and the Koran states that the Jews are: **"enemies of Allah, the Prophet and the angels."**[38]

The Koran is the real root of the Islamic-Israel conflict, and this conflict must continue, until either Islam or Israel ceases to exist. Mohammed became filled with hatred for the Jews because they would not forsake their beliefs and follow him 1,300 years ago. Mohammed pieced together the Koran from various snippets of Judaism, Christianity, Arab folklore and "revelations," and liberally mixed the contents with a hatred of Jews. All the while the Koran is read and reverenced by Mohammed's followers, fundamental Moslems will continue to be (in Rabin's own words) "bloody murders filled with hate."[39]

Moslems believe the 21st century to be the "century of Islam," when all the world must be subjugated to Islam, and they also believe that the annihilation of Israel is their precursor to the conquest of the West. Western politicians (even some Israeli politicians) claim that Arabs get carried away with rhetoric—threatening, shouting, shaking fists, pounding tables—and never do anything. But, we have shown in earlier chapters that the one great exception to this rule is war against the Jewish state, and the wars of 1948, 1956, 1967, 1968–71, 1973 and 1982, are evidence enough that Arab hatred of Jews always overcomes Arab rhetoric. Western leaders also considered Saddam Hussein's historic 1990 threat to "incinerate half of Israel"[40] to be nothing more than "flowery Arab rhetoric."[41] Saddam duly launched 39 Soviet-made Scud-B missiles at Israel's civilian population centers, destroying or damaging some 5,000 Israel homes. Four years later, the same leaders still consider Arab threats against Israel to be rhetoric, and continue to bully Israel into complying with their wishes.

The nations' interest in the "peace process" lies not with a genuine desire to bring peace between old enemies, for that would severely affect their weapons industries. The interest lies in what wealth can be extracted from the resultant "Palestinian state." In February 1995, the British representative from the European Union (known as the 'troika') delegation visiting Israel said, "It was in the interest of Europe to assist the peace process—**the loss of business is much more than the millions we throw to the Palestinians**."[42] And we have already seen why America and Russia have gotten involved.

But Islam's hatred of the Jewish state, the nations' greed for profits, power and preeminence, could not find a place to rest in the "peace process" without the willing cooperation of the Israeli government. The current coalition includes the godless, the deceitful, the unscrupulous and the corrupt, and they have linked hands with those who openly seek to destroy the Jewish state. The prophet speaks in the open that which is spoken in secret:

"We have made a covenant with death, and with Sheol we are in agreement...we have made lies our refuge, and under falsehood we have hidden ourselves" (Isaiah 28:14,15).

The Israel-PLO accords are, indeed, a covenant with death. And Israel's current leaders have made lies their refuge, and they have hidden themselves under falsehood. God is using those who deny His existence, presence and involvement in world affairs to position the nation for future distress. The Jewish state is running full steam into the arms of Armageddon, history's final battle.

Redemption stands at the threshold, ready to enter the world scene. Whether you are Gentile, Jew or Moslem, call now upon the *"Coming One in whom is salvation"* (Zechariah 9:9). Everlasting life is the gift of God—He promises to give us *"a new heart"* and *"put His Spirit within"* us (Ezekiel 36:26-27). Now, could be the *"acceptable time,"* today, could be your *"day of salvation"* (Isaiah 49:8). Look up! Rejoice! Redemption draws near!

FOR YOUR INFORMATION

Letters sent to the author via the publisher will be duly passed on. Address your correspondence to:

> Ramon Bennett, C/- ARM OF SALVATION,
> P.O. Box 32381, Jerusalem 91322, ISRAEL.

Ramon Bennett also writes for the *Ministry & Prayer Update*, the periodic newsletter of the *Arm of Salvation Ministries*. The *Update* keeps readers informed on current events in Israel and, also, on the ministry and movement of the Bennetts. An annual donation of US$15.00 (or foreign currency equivalent) is requested toward production and postage costs.

If you would like to be advised of forthcoming books by the same author, please inform *Arm of Salvation*, and you will be notified immediately as they are released. Details of other available works by Ramon Bennett are shown on the following page.

Signed copies of *Philistine* are available by mail from Jerusalem and can be purchased by sending US$10.95 (or foreign currency equivalent) plus $3.00 ($6.00 Airmail) shipping and handling to: **Ramon Bennett**, P.O. Box 32381, Jerusalem 91322, ISRAEL.

Arm of Salvation is an Israeli ministry dependent upon gifts and proceeds from their books and tapes to sustain work in and for Israel and the Jewish people. Your support is warmly appreciated.

Books by Ramon Bennett are generally not available in bookstores. We encourage readers to purchase 10 or more books at 40% discount for gifts, or to sell to members of their prayer and church groups. Send US$6.57 for each book in an order of 10 or more, and add 18% for shipping and handling charges. Mail your check or Money Order to:

> SHEKINAH BOOKS,
> 4118 Rustle Cove, Georgetown, Texas 78628, U.S.A.
> Telephone and Fax: (512) 869-4848.

CHAPTER NOTES

Chapter 1

1. During the "Blitz" the Author's father was in charge of London's "bomb damage" and commanded a virtual army of construction workers that quickly cleared streets of rubble, restored vital services and repaired damaged buildings wherever possible. Out of respect for the "guv'ner," as the Author's father was called, his house was usually repaired first. During the prolonged aerial bombardment the Author's home was often the only one in the street with glass windows, and sometimes the only one with a proper roof.
2. John Laffin, *The Arab Mind* (London: Cassell, 1975), p.143.
3. Ibid., p.104.
4. "Hussein Doesn't Deny 'Butcher of Baghdad' Nickname," *Chicago Tribune*, Aug. 3, 1990.
5. Quoted from "Saddam and the Smokers," *Jerusalem Post*, May 20, 1994.
6. From the 1983 *Amnesty International* Report.
7. Arie Stav of the Nativ Center for Policy Research, writing in "On the threshold of Critical Mass. Part II," *Middle East Intelligence Digest*, June 1993.
8. Ibid.
9. Quoted from "The Line in the Sand," *Los Angeles Times*, Nov. 25, 1990.
10. *Associated Press* report, "Study tracks $163 billion in arms to Mideast," *Cedar Rapids Gazette*, May 6, 1991.
11. Arie Stav of the Nativ Center for Policy Research, writing in "On the threshold of Critical Mass. Part II," *Middle East Intelligence Digest*, June 1993.
12. Benjamin Netanyahu, *A Place Among The Nations: Israel and the World* (New York: Bantam, 1993), p.102.

Chapter 2

1. Raphael Patai, *The Arab Mind* (New York: Macmillan, 1983), p.81.
2. Ibid., p.101.
3. Ibid., p.105.
4. al-Ghazali, quoted in Laffin, *The Arab Mind*, p.79.
5. Ibid.
6. Ibid.
7. Abu l'Ala 973—1057, quoted in Ibid., p.50.
8. Quoted in *Dispatch From Jerusalem*, Jan./Feb. 1994.
9. Laffin, *The Arab Mind*, p.70.
10. From "A Palestinian version of the New Testament," *Jerusalem Post*, International Edition, Jan. 18, 1992.
11. Patai, *The Arab Mind*, p.102.
12. King Hussein, *My War with Israel* (New York: Morrow, 1969), p.66., quoted in Ibid., p.103.
13. Laffin, *The Arab Mind*, p.50.
14. The editor of *Al-Ahram*. Quoted in John Laffin, *Fedayeen: The Arab-Israeli*

Dilemma (London: Cassell, 1973), p.105.
15. Laffin, *The Arab Mind*, p.50.
16. "A Shameful Statistic," Christian Friends of Israel *Watchman's Prayer Letter*, Feb. 1995.
17. Cited in Patai, *The Arab Mind*, p.42.
18. Ameen Faris Rihani, quoted in Ibid., p.219.
19. Cited in Ibid., p.212.
20. Laffin, *The Arab Mind*, p.38.
21. Ibid.
22. Ibid., p.39.
23. Quoted in "Poised to Strike," *Jerusalem Post Magazine*, Nov. 12, 1993.
24. Laffin, *Fedayeen*, p.100.
25. Netanyahu, *A Place Among The Nations*, pp.102.
26. Winifred Blackman cited in Patai, *The Arab Mind*, p.158.
27. Cited in Ibid., p.161.
28. Quoted from "The Old Villain," *New Leader*, Oct. 29, 1990.
29. In the Spring issue of *Foreign Affairs*. Cited in Patai, *The Arab Mind*, p.337.
30. Laffin, *The Arab Mind*, pp.97–98.
31. Ibid., p.98.
32. Ibid., p.99.
33. Ibid.
34. Ibn Khaldun (1332–1406), *The Muqaddimah—An Introduction to History*, quoted in Laffin, *The Arab Mind*, p.97.
35. Ibid., p.95.
36. Ibid.
37. Ibid., p.108.
38. Ibid., pp.101–102.
39. Reported on *Voice of Israel Radio*, Dec. 12, 1992.
40. Laffin, *The Arab Mind*, p.116.
41. Ibid., p.111.
42. Ibid., p.121.
43. Ibid., p.120.
44. Ibid., p.119.
45. Philip K. Hitti, *History of the Arabs*, quoted in Patai, *The Arab Mind*, p.81.
46. Wilfred C. Smith, *Islam in Modern History*. Cited in Ibid., p.296.
47. Suleiman Al-Khash in *Al-Thaura*, the Ba'ath party newspaper, May 3, 1968.
48. *Glances at Arab Society*, p117, an exercise for Jordanian first-year high school students. Cited in Joan Peters, *From Time Immemorial: The Origins of The Arab-Jewish Conflict Over Palestine* (London: Michael Joseph, 1984), p.79.
49. *Basic Syntax and Spelling*, an exercise for Syrian fifth-year elementary students. Cited in Ibid., p.79.
50. *Grammar*, p.244, an exercise for Egyptian first-year junior high school students. Cited in Ibid., p.79.
51. *Zionist Imperialism*, p.249, for Egyptian ninth-grade secondary schools. Cited in Ibid., p.79.

Chapter Notes

52. Laffin, *Fedayeen*, p.88.
53. Cited in Peters, *From Time Immemorial*, p.113.
54. David Bar-Illan, *Eye on the Media* (Jerusalem: *The Jerusalem Post*, 1993), p.211.
55. Laffin, *The Arab Mind*, p.109.
56. "Two Gazans stab nursing mother, 23, in Gush Katif," *Jerusalem Post International Edition*, April 30, 1994.
57. "Hamas car bomb kills 7, wounds 52 in Afula." Ibid., April 16, 1994.
58. Laffin, *The Arab Mind*, p.167.
59. Ibid.
60. Ibid.
61. Ibid., p.168.
62. "To Our People of Israel," *Jerusalem Post International Edition*, March 19, 1994.
63. "78.8% of Israelis condemn massacre." Ibid., March 12, 1994.
64. Patai, *The Arab Mind*, p.124.
65. Ibid., p.123.
66. Ibid.
67. "Problem of female circumcisions in Holland, *Jerusalem Post*, May 10, 1992.
68. Patai, *The Arab Mind*, p.134.
69. Ibid., p.135.
70. Ibid., p.118.
71. Nazar Qabbani, *On Poetry, Sex and Revolution*, quoted in Laffin, *The Arab Mind*, p.2.
72. Ibid., p.86, 90.
73. Ibid., p.90.
74. Sigmund Freud, *Beyond the Pleasure Principle* (London: Hogarth Press, 1922), p.69.
75. Laffin, *The Arab Mind*, p.93.
76. Ibid.
77. Cited in Patai, *The Arab Mind*, p.60.
78. "A misplacing of confidence," *Jerusalem Post*, May 10, 1994.
79. Ramon Bennett, *When Day and Night Cease* (2nd ed., Jerusalem: Arm of Salvation, 1993), pp.176–177.
80. Ibid.
81. *Associated Press* report published in *Bangkok Post*, Dec. 28, 1990.
82. Laffin, *The Arab Mind*, p.162.
83. *Al-Ahram* editorial, May 15, 1964. Cited in Ibid., p.82.
84. Speech by President Nasser on Aug. 11, 1963, quoted in Ibid., p.82.
85. *Al-Ahram* editorial, Feb. 25, 1971. Cited in Ibid., p.163.
86. Patai, *The Arab Mind*, p.43.

Chapter 3

1. Sura 5:33. Note: Verses in the Koran may differ in the English translations by as much as 10 verses; look within this range beginning with one verse up or down if given references do not correspond.

or down if given references do not correspond.
2. "Sound The Alarm!" *Jerusalem Courier & Prophecy Digest,* Volume 11, 1993.
3. Laffin, *The Arab Mind,* p.121.
4. Sura 4:34. Some English translations use the word "beat." The Arabic, however, is "scourge."
5. "Have we all beaten our wives today?" *Jerusalem Post,* Aug. 30, 1991.
6. Ray A. Pritz, *Nazarene Jewish Christianity* (Jerusalem: Magnus, 1988), p.17.
7. *Associated Press* report, "Women flogged by clerics in outlaw justice, *New Zealand Herald,* Dec. 27, 1994.
8. Ibid.
9. Ali Dashti, *23Years: A Study of the Prophetic Career of Mohammad* (London: George Allen & Unwin, 1985), p.56. Cited in Robert Morey, *The Islamic Invasion: Confronting the World's Fastest Growing Religion* (Eugene: Harvest House, 1992), p.32.
10. *Israel Vistas,* Spring/Summer 1994, p.7.
11. Ibid., p.9.
12. International Institute for the Study of Islam and Christianity, *Press Release,* Jan. 1994.
13. Anis A. Shorrosh, *Islam Revealed: A Christian Arab's View of Islam* (Nashville: Thomas Nelson, 1988), p.198.
14. Morey, *The Islamic Invasion,* p.119.
15. Ali Dashti. Ibid.
16. Ibid.
17. Arthur Jeffery. Ibid.
18. Ibid., p.123.
19. Sura 3:35ff.
20. Sura 19:28.
21. Suras 27:4-6; 28:6,38; 29:39; 40:23,24,36,37.
22. Suras 21:68,69; 9:69.
23. Shorrosh, *Islam Revealed,* p.48.
24. Morey, *The Islamic Invasion,* p.71.
25. Ibid.
26. Sura 4:3.
27. Ali Dashti, *23 Years,* pp.120-138. Cited in Morey, *The Islamic Invasion,* p.85.
28. Shorrosh, *Islam Revealed,* p.56.
29. Ibid., p.58.
30. Ibid., p.62.
31. Ibid.
32. Sura 33:50.
33. Sura 4:24.
34. "Evil anniversary, *Jerusalem Post,* Feb. 17, 1995.
35. Morey, *The Islamic Invasion,* p.78.
36. Sura 2:106.
37. Morey, *The Islamic Invasion,* p.79.
38. Ibid.

Chapter Notes 305

40. Laffin, *The Arab Mind*, footnote p.35.
41. Morey, *The Islamic Invasion*, p.82.
42. Ibid., p.42.
43. Ibid., p.27.
44. Jordanian text book for second-year high school Art Students: *General History, Ancient and Medieval Civilizations*, p.160.
45. Morey, *The Islamic Invasion*, p.52.
46. Ibid., pp.47–48.
47. Ibid., p.48.
48. Hastings *Encyclopedia of Religion and Ethics*, Ibid.
49. Ibid., p.49.
50. *Encyclopedia of Religion*, Ibid., p.48
51. *Encyclopedia of Islam*, Ibid.
52. E.M. Wherry, *A Comprehensive Commentary on the Quran* (Osnbruck: Otto Zeller Verlag, 1973), p.36, Ibid., p.50.
53. Ibid.
54. Ibid.
55. Dr. Anis Shorrosh quoted in *Jerusalem Post International Edition*, May 1, 1993.
56. Chuck Missler, *Personal Update*, Vol. 4, No. 2, Feb. 1994, p.8.
57. Morey, *The Islamic Invasion*, p.52.
58. N.J. Dawood, *The Koran* (London: Penguin 1993), p.2.
59. Dr. Anis Shorrosh quoted in *Jerusalem Post International Edition*, May 1, 1993.
60. Bernard Lewis, *The Political Language of Islam* (Chicago: University of Chicago, 1988), p.3.
61. Hadith, para. 7.
62. Recorded in the *Sahih Moslem* annals. Cited in George Grant, *The Blood of the Moon* (Brentwood: Wolgemuth & Hyatt, 1991), p.49.
63. Netanyahu, *A Place Among the Nations*, p.41.
64. *The World Almanac and Book of Facts* (New York: Pharos, 1993), p.766.
65. *Al-Ahram* editorial, May 15, 1964. Cited in Laffin, *The Arab Mind*, p.82.
66. Published in *Al-*Ahram, Nov. 26, 1955. Cited in Ibid., p.157.
67. Anwar Sadat, April 25, 1972, quoted in David Berger, *History and Hate: The Dimensions of Anti-Semitism* (New York: Jewish Publication Society, 1986), p.89.
68. Yasser Arafat quoted in Grant, *The Blood of the Moon*, p.47.
69. Imam Hassan al-Bana, former leader of Egyptian Muslim Brotherhood, quoted in David Dolan, *Holy War for the Promised Land* (Nashville: Thomas Nelson, 1991), p.248.
70. King Abdul Aziz Ibn Saud, quoted in Grant, *The Blood of the Moon*, p.59.
71. King Farouk of Egypt, Ibid., p.54.
72. King Idris of Libya, Ibid.
73. Haj Amin el Husseini, Grand Muslim Mufti 1946, Ibid., p.53.
74. Dr. Abdul Halim Mahmoud, Grand Sheik of Al-Azhar, Oct. 8, 1973.
75. Document signed by Ibrahim Ghousha, a senior Hamas leader, Jan.2, 1993.

76. Hashemi Rafsanjani, President of Iran, 1991, quoted in Grant, *The Blood of the Moon*, p.56.
77. Professor Augustus H. Strong, quoted in Morey, *The Islamic Invasion*, p.43.
78. Yasser Arafat speaking in a Johannesburg mosque, May 10, 1994.
79. Hamas leader in an interview with the BBC, early January, 1994.
80. Quoted by Sheik Abd Allah Al Meshad in D.F. Green, *Arab Theologians on Jews and Israel* (Genève: Editions de l'Avenir, 1974), p.22.
81. Moslem spokesman quoted in *Signs Following*, official Newsletter of Mahesh Chavda Ministries International, Spring, 1988.
82. Lewis, *The Political Language of Islam*, p.78.
83. Sheik Mohammed Abu Zahra, quoted in Green, *Arab Theologians on Jews and Israel*, p.55.
84. Sheik Abdullah Ghoshah, Ibid., p.61.
85. *Islam at a Glance*, a brochure distributed in Birmingham, England, in July 1985.
86. Shorrosh, *Islam Revealed*, p.35.
87. "Basic Tenets of Islam," *Bridges For Peace*, Tenets 2nd Qtr. 1990, p.1.
88. Lameh Chrysostine, quoted in Grant, *The Blood of the Moon*, p.64.
89. Patai, *The Arab Mind*, p.146.
90. Laffin, *The Arab Mind*, p.93.
91. "Living bomb," *Eton Yerushaliyim*, April 20, 1995.
92. Ibid.
93. Ibid.
94. Quoted in Amir Taheri, *Holy Terror: The inside story of Islamic terrorism* (London: Sphere Books, 1987). Cited in *Middle East Intelligence Digest*, Aug. 1994, p.6.
95. Quoted in "Behind the PLO boss's words," *Jerusalem Post*, May 27, 1994.
96. Ibid.
97. Lewis, *The Political Language of Islam*, p.77.
98. King Abdullah of Jordon, Sept. 1947.
99. Ayatollah Khomeini, quoted in Grant, *The Blood of the Moon*, p.72.
100. Ibid.
101. Ibid.
102. Shorrosh, *Islam Revealed*, p.56.
103. "Holy Axe," *In Jerusalem*, March 18, 1994.
104. Quoted from "On the Threshold of Critical Mass Part I," *Middle East Intelligence Digest*, Vol. 3, No.7, May 1993. p.6.
105. "Sound The Alarm!" *Jerusalem Courier & Prophecy Digest*, Volume 11, 1993.
106. Elwood McQuaid, published in *Jerusalem Post International Edition*, Dec. 26, 1992.
107. "Missing feminist writer mystifies Bangladesh police," *Jerusalem Post*, June 15, 1994.
108. Ibid.
109. Ibid.
110. Quoted from " Islam and democracy — squaring the ancient circle." Ibid., Jan. 18, 1992.

Chapter Notes

111. "The West—Digging its Own Grave," *Middle East Intelligence Digest*, May 1993. p.4.
112. International Institute for the Study of Islam and Christianity, *Press Release*, Jan. 1994.
113. "Fanatics on the warpath," *Middle East Intelligence Digest*, May 1993. p.2.
114. Christian Institute for Middle East Studies, reported in *Israel Vistas*, Spring/Summer 1994, p.9.
115. "Sudan: A brutal preview," *Jerusalem Post International Edition*, April 9, 1994.
116. Reported in "The Sudanese Connection." Ibid., Jan. 23, 1993.
117. "Sudan," *Middle East Intelligence Digest*, May, 1993. p.4.
118. Quoted from "Promises," *Jerusalem Post International Edition*, Feb. 12, 1994.
119. Reported in "The Sudanese Connection." Ibid., Jan. 23, 1993.
120. "Massacre in Egypt," Ibid., April 16, 1994.
121. "Islamic guerrillas kill four priests," *New Zealand Herald*, Dec. 29, 1994.
122. *Agence France Presse*, quoted in *The Jerusalem Institute for Western Defence*, Digest 6, June 1994, p.2.
123. "Algeria's week of killing spree continues as pop singer is slain," *Jerusalem Post*, Feb. 17, 1995.
124. "Church Bomb," *Jerusalem Post International Edition*, March 26, 1994.
125. "Moslem exclusivism blamed for emigration of Christians." Ibid., Dec. 5, 1992.
126. "Christian minorities in the Middle East," *Middle East Intelligence Digest*, June 1994. p.7.
127. "Oh, little town of Bethlehem." Ibid., Feb. 1995, p.6.
128. "Christian minorities in the Middle East." Ibid., June 1994. p.7.
129. "Oh, little town of Bethlehem." Ibid., Feb. 1995, p.6.
130. "Moslem exclusivism blamed for emigration of Christians," *Jerusalem Post International Edition*, Dec. 5, 1992.
131. Reported on *Voice of Israel Radio*, March 2, 1994.
132. "Eye on the Media," *Jerusalem Post International Edition*, March 12, 1994.
133. "Palestinian Baptist slams Islam, *Jerusalem Post*, Sept. 23, 1994.

Chapter 4

1. "The Resurgent Threat," *Middle East Intelligence Digest*, Feb. 1993. p.10.
2. Sheik Abdul-Hamid 'Attiyah al-Dibani, quoted in Green, *Arab Theologians on Jews and Israel*, p.35.
3. Shorrosh, *Islam Revealed*, p.185.
4. Ibid.
5. "The Terror Within," *Time*, July 5, 1993, p.24.
6. Shorrosh, *Islam Revealed*, p.184.
7. Ibid.
8. "Watching Islamic policy in action," *Jerusalem Post International Edition*, Feb. 27, 1993.
9. "The Iranian threat." Ibid., Jan. 16, 1993.
10. Gamal Abdel Nasser, September 1955.

11. Patai, *The Arab Mind*, p.269.
12. Ramon Bennett, *Saga: Israel and the Demise of Nations* (Jerusalem: Arm of Salvation, 1993), pp.129–137.
13. Les Krantz, *Facts that matter: Everything you need to know about everything* (Los Angeles: Price Stern Sloan, 1993), p.20.
14. Ibid. p.51.
15. "Two Arab Americans remanded on suspicion of being Hamas agents,"*Jerusalem Post International Edition*, Feb. 13, 1993.
16. Ibid.
17. "American charged with being world commander of Hamas military wing," *Jerusalem Post*, Oct. 22, 1993.
18. "Two Arab Americans remanded on suspicion of being Hamas agents," *Jerusalem Post International Edition*, Feb. 13, 1993.
19. "The FBI wakes up." Ibid., March 8, 1993.
20. "The Terror Within," *Time*, July 5, 1993, p.22.
21. "Another Palestinian held in WTC bombing," *Jerusalem Post International Edition*, March 20, 1993.
22. "Moslem terror plot foiled in New York," *Jerusalem Post*, June 25, 1993.
23. "The Terror Within," *Time*, July 5, 1993, p.25.
24. Ibid.
25. Ibid., p.22.
26. To obtain a copy of *Jihad in America* write to: PBS, 1320 Braddock Place, Alexandria, VA, 22314, U.S.A.
27. "Farid Kassim, spokesman for *Hizb Ut-Tahrir*. Quoted in "A new trend in UK Moslem extremism," *Jerusalem Post*, Aug. 12, 1994.
28. *The World Almanac and Book of Facts*, p.178.
29. Morey, *The Islamic Invasion*, p.9.
30. Ibid.
31. Richard Booker, at the I.C.E.J. *Feast of Tabernacles Celebration*, Oct. 1992.
32. Netanyahu, *A Place Among the Nations*, p.153.
33. "The hidden sword of Islam," *Jerusalem Post International Edition*, Dec. 26, 1992.
34. Sir Alfred Sherman, writing in "Islam's new drive into Europe," *Bulletin of the Jerusalem Institute for Western Defence*, Bulletin 3, Oct. 1993, p.4.
35. "History of Islam," *Bridges For Peace*, Islam, 2nd Qtr. 1990, p.1.
36. Ibid.
37. *Associated Press* report, "Conference calls for global Islamic state," *New Zealand Herald*, Aug. 9, 1994.
38. Ibid.
39. Ibid.
40. "Muslims worship in Auckland University chapel," *Crosslink*, June 1994.
41. Morey, *The Islamic Invasion*, p.62.
42. "Hebron: A Tale of Two Kingdoms," CFI's *Zion Quarterly*, 2nd Quarter, 1994, p.1.
43. "Abraham was a Moslem: Arab professor," *Jerusalem Post International Edition*, April 3, 1993.
44. "One-way thinking." Ibid., Feb. 20, 1993.

45. Lewis, *The Political Language of Islam*, p.94.
46. Yasser Arafat quoted in "One-way thinking," *Jerusalem Post International Edition*, Feb. 20, 1993.
47. Morey, *The Islamic Invasion*, p.63.
48. "Muslims worship in Auckland University chapel," *Crosslink*, June 1994.
49. Patai, *The Arab Mind*, p.286.
50. Quoted from "The Key to Success," Editorial in *Signs Following*, Fall, 1988.
51. "At the Crossroads," *Bulletin of the Jerusalem Institute for Western Defence*, Bulletin 3, Oct. 1993, p.6.
52. Mike Evans, *Israel—America's Key to Survival* (Plainfield: Logos International, 1981), p.72.
53. Ibid.

Chapter 5

1. "Rabin, Arafat sign Gaza/Jericho pact," *Jerusalem Post*, May 5, 1994.
2. Ibid.
3. Shimon Peres in Cairo after the signing ceremony and broadcast over *Voice of Israel Radio*, May 4, 1994.
4. Source: *Realities, A Journal of Timely Analysis*, reprinted in *Dispatch From Jerusalem*, Jan.-Feb. 1994, p.2.
5. Ibid.
6. Netanyahu, *A Place Among the Nations*, p.188.
7. Ibid.
8. Source: *Realities, A Journal of Timely Analysis*, reprinted in *Dispatch From Jerusalem*, Jan.-Feb. 1994, p.2.
9. Thomas Kierman, *Yasir Arafat* (London: Sphere Books, 1976), p.138.
10. Ibid.
11. Ibid.
12. Ibid., pp.153-154.
13. *Realities, A Journal of Timely Analysis*, reprinted in *Dispatch From Jerusalem*, Jan.-Feb. 1994, p.2.
14. Ibid.
15. Ibid.
16. Ibid.
17. Ibid.
18. John Laffin, *The PLO Connections* (London: Transworld, 1982), p.18.
19. Ibid.
20. Ibid.
21. Ibid.
22. *Realities, A Journal of Timely Analysis*, reprinted in *Dispatch From Jerusalem*, Jan.-Feb. 1994, p.2.
23. "Blood on their hands," *Jerusalem Post International Edition*, May 14, 1994.
24. "Terrorism Pays," *Middle East Intelligence Digest*, Nov. 1993, p.8.
25. "Arafat's 'Mein Kampf,'" *Jerusalem Post*, May 27, 1994.
26. "Media pour in to cover Arafat's arrival." Ibid., July 1, 1994.
27. "Arafat's plan for democracy: Freedom from the press." Ibid., Dec. 3, 1993.

28. "Yasser, Yasser, Mr. Arafat!" *Jerusalem Post International Edition,* June 18, 1994.
29. "Arafat's plan for democracy: Freedom from the press," *Jerusalem Post,* Dec. 3, 1993.
30. "Yasser, Yasser, Mr. Arafat!" *Jerusalem Post International Edition,* June 18, 1994.
31. Ibid.
32. "Arafat's plan for democracy: Freedom from the press," *Jerusalem Post,* Dec. 3, 1993.
33. Ibid.
34. "Terrorists and policemen." Ibid., Oct. 3, 1993.
35. Jill Becker, *The PLO: The Rise and Fall of the Palestine Liberation Organization* (New York: St. Martin's, 1984), p.13.
36. Howard M. Sachar, *A History of Israel: From the Rise of Zionism to Our Time* (New York: Alfred A. Knoff, 1991), p.619.
37. Ibid., p.633.
38. Ibid., pp.633–634.
39. Ibid., p.631.
40. Ibid., p.639.
41. Ibid., p.642.
42. Mitchell G. Bard and Joel Himelfarb, *Myths and Facts: A concise record of the Arab-Israeli Conflict,* (Washington: Near East Report, 1992), p.59.
43. Laffin, *Fedayeen,* p.30.
44. Samuel M. Katz, *Israel Versus Jibril: The Thirty-Year War Against a Master Terrorist,* (New York: Paragon House, 1993), p.18.
45. Ibid.
46. Laffin, *Fedayeen,* p.58.
47. Samuel M. Katz, *Israel Versus Jibril,* p.34.
48. Ibid., p.37.
49. Ibid.
50. Ibid.
51. Ibid.
52. Ibid., p.89.
53. Frank Gevasi, *The War in Lebanon.* Cited in Frank Keretzky, *The Media's Propaganda War Against Israel* (New York: Weidenfeld & Nicolson, 1984), pp.244–250, reprinted in "Come, let us reason together," *Middle East Intelligence Digest — Document,* Feb. 1993, p.A2.
54. Cited in Bard and Himelfarb, *Myths and Facts,* p.98.
55. *New York Times,* June 21, 1982. Ibid.
56. Bar-Illan, *Eye on the Media,* p.250.
57. Cited in Bard and Himelfarb, *Myths and Facts,* p.97.
58. Ibid.
59. Peter Grace, *The Rape of Lebanon* (Beirut: Evangelical Press, 1983), pp.76–79.
60. Ibid.
61. Ibid.
62. Ibid.

Chapter Notes 311

63. Ibid.
64. Ibid.
65. Frank Gervasi cited in Keretzky, *The Media's Propaganda War Against Israel*, p.242, reprinted in "Come, let us reason together," *Middle East Intelligence Digest — Document*, Feb. 1993, p.A2.
66. Grace, *The Rape of Lebanon*, p.16.
67. Ibid., p17.
68. *Los Angeles Herald-Examiner*, July 13, 1982. Cited in Bard and Himelfarb, *Myths and Facts*, p.98.
69. Frank Gervasi cited in Keretzky, *The Media's Propaganda War Against Israel*, p.242, reprinted in "Come, let us reason together," *Middle East Intelligence Digest — Document*, Feb. 1993, p.A2.
70. *Ma'ariv*, July 16, 1982. *Ha'aretz*, July 26, 1982.
71. Grace, *The Rape of Lebanon*, p.153.
72. Ibid.
73. Ibid.
74. Salah Shafro, Mukhtar of Burj-Bachel, *Ma'ariv*, July 16, 1982. Also described in Grace, *The Rape of Lebanon*, p.177.
75. Grace, *The Rape of Lebanon*, p.175–176.
76. Ibid.
77. Gillian Becker, *The Rise and Fall of the PLO*. Cited in "The face of terror...," *Middle East Intelligence Digest*, Aug. 1992, p.5.
78. Bard and Himelfarb, *Myths and Facts*, p.98.
79. Interview with Israel Television, July 23, 1982. Cited in Bard and Himelfarb, *Myths and Facts*, p.98.
80. "Come, let us reason together," *Middle East Intelligence Digest — Document*, Feb. 1993, p.A1.
81. Frank Gervasi cited in Keretzky, *The Media's Propaganda War Against Israel*, pp.244–250, reprinted in Ibid., p.A2.
82. Ibid., p.A1.
83. Ibid., p.A2.
84. Ibid.
85. Ibid.
86. Ibid.
87. Ibid.
88. Ibid., p.A1.
89. Netanyahu, *A Place Among the Nations*, p.384.
90. Bar-Illan, *Eye on the Media*, p.409.
91. "UPI Objectivity," *Jerusalem Post*, Nov. 4, 1992.
92. Netanyahu, *A Place Among the Nations*, p.385.
93. Michael L. Brown, *Our Hands Are Stained With Blood: The tragic story of the "Church" and the Jewish people* (Shippensburg: Destiny Image, 1992), p.44.
94. Ibid.
95. Ibid.
96. Netanyahu, *A Place Among the Nations*, pp.385–386.
97. Katz, *Israel Versus Jibril*, p.88.

98. Ibid.
99. Ibid.
100. Neil Livingstone and David Halevy, *Inside the PLO: Cover Units, Secret Funds, and the War Against Israel and the United States* (New York: William Morrow, 1990), p.64. Cited in Netanyahu, *A Place Among the Nations,* p.204.
101. Isser Harel quoted in Evans, *Israel—America's Key to Survival,* p.72.
102. "The Sudan Connection," *Middle East Intelligence Digest,* Feb. 1993, p.1.
103. *Los Angeles Times,* Jan. 21, 1976. Cited in Evans, *Israel—America's Key to Survival,* p.56.
104. *Middle East Intelligence Digest,* March 1994, p.4.
105. "Syrian drug connection," *Jerusalem Post,* April 4, 1994.
106. Ibid.
107. "The B'tselem report." Ibid., Jan. 10, 1994.
108. Ibid.
109. Ibid.
110. Netanyahu, *A Place Among the Nations,* p.166.
111. "The B'tselem report," *Jerusalem Post,* Jan. 10, 1994.
112. Eliakim Haetzni, *Voice of Israel Radio,* July 9, 1994.
113. "Come, let us reason together," *Middle East Intelligence Digest — Document,* Feb. 1993, p.A4.
114. Bennett, *Saga,* p.169.
115. "Recruits for Palestinian police may come from up the river," *Jerusalem Post,* Oct. 3, 1993.
116. "Justice never done." Ibid., July 1, 1994.
117. Dorit Rosenfeld, "Letters to the Editor." Ibid., July 1, 1994.
118. "Arafat's remarkable consistency." Ibid., Nov. 18, 1994.
119. Ibid.
120. Ibid.
121. Ibid.
122. "Words, and more words." Ibid., Aug. 26, 1994.
123. Ibid.
124. "Likud MKs ask to deny PA officials entry permits." Ibid., Jan. 13, 1995.
125. Ibid.
126. "Palestinian policewomen get boss," Ibid., July 27, 1994.
127. "Heil Arafat," Ibid., Jan. 24, 1995.
128. An Arab detained on suspicion of collaborating with Israel died in custody. Following an outcry by Palestinian human rights groups, PLO officials admitted that he was tortured to death. Reported in CFI's *Israel New Digest,* Aug. 1994, p.3.
129. Ibid.
130. "Palestinian Police arrest suspected car thieves," *Jerusalem Post,* May 20, 1994.
131. *Voice of Israel Radio,* Sept. 20, 1994.
132. *Reuter* report. "PLO will license stolen cars in Gaza," *Jerusalem Post,* April 4, 1995.
133. Ibid.

134. Laffin, *Fedayeen*, p.129.
135. *Voice of Israel Radio*, Jan. 3, 1995.
136. Ibid.
137. "Jihad Martyrs," CFI's *Israel New Digest*, Feb. 1995, p.3.
138. Ibid.
139. A PLO official's statement made on Aug. 31, 1993. Quoted in "On Destroying Israel," *Yesha Report*, Sept.-Oct. 1993, p.4.
140. "Giants in the Land," CFI's *Zion Quarterly*, 2nd Quarter, 1994, p3.
141. Rabin's scapegoat," *Jerusalem Post*, Jan. 27, 1995.
142. Reported in the pro-PLO *Jerusalem Times*, Oct. 7, 1994. Published in "The seeds of civil war," *Middle East Intelligence Digest*, Nov. 1994. p.5.
143. "The Cairo summit," CFI's *Israel New Digest*, March, 1995, p.3.
144. "Public police or Arafat's private army?" *Jerusalem Post*, April 8, 1994.
145. "Dehaishe will greet Palestinians as an occupying army," Ibid., Feb. 10, 1995.
146. "Public police or Arafat's private army?" Ibid., April 8, 1994.
147. Ibid.
148. "Rabin's scapegoat," Ibid., Jan. 27, 1995.
149. "Terrorism and the PLO: September 13 plus seven months," *Bulletin of the Jerusalem Institute for Western Defence*, Bulletin 2, June 1994, pp.3–7.
150. Ibid.
151. "GSS kills two Hamas fugitives in A-Ram village," *Jerusalem Post International Edition*, June 11, 1994.
152. "Terrorism and the PLO: September 13 plus seven months," *Bulletin of the Jerusalem Institute for Western Defence*, Bulletin 2, June 1994, p.5.
153. Ibid., p.4.
154. "Even as they speak peace," *Middle East Intelligence Digest*, Nov. 1994, p.1.
155. *Voice of Israel Radio*, July 9, 1994.
156. Senior PLO official quoted on Ibid, June 17, 1994.
157. Arafat's official text, Geneva, Dec. 13, 1988, quoted in Netanyahu, *A Place Among the Nations*, pp.212–213.
158. Ibid.
159. Abu Iyad quoted in *Al-Rayah*, Jan.13, 1990. Cited in Netanyahu, *A Place Among the Nations*, p.216.
160. Abu Iyad on Radio Monte Carlo, March 4, 1989, Ibid., p.215.
161. Cited in "Terrorism and the PLO: September 13 plus seven months," *Bulletin of the Jerusalem Institute for Western Defence*, Bulletin 2, June 1994, p.2.
162. Ibid., p.11.
163. Arafat in Riyadh, Jan.1, 1989, quoted in Netanyahu, *A Place Among the Nations*, p.164.
164. "Support for peace talks drops," *Jerusalem Post*, June 4, 1994.
165. "Majority of Israelis want PLO officials tried," *Jerusalem Post International Edition*, July 2, 1994.
166. "Seeing Hamas for what it is." Ibid., March 13, 1993.
167. "The Intifada: Coming soon to a town near you!" Ibid., June 18, 1994.
168. "Intifada violence up 30% in capital – police chief." Ibid., June 4, 1994.
169. "Blood brothers," CFI's *Israel News Digest*, May, 1994, p.2.

170. "Eyeless in Gaza," Ibid, June, 1994, p.3.
171. "Hamas, Fatah near second agreement," *Jerusalem Post*, April 22, 1994.
172. "Hamas men apply to join Gaza police." Ibid., Nov. 18, 1994.
173. "Palestinians bar Israelis with guns from Jericho synagogue." Ibid, May 20, 1994.
174. "A new Palestinian dream." Ibid., April 4, 1995.
175. "Yasser, Puppet-master." Ibid., June 30, 1994.
176. "Tel Aviv bus bombing kills at least 20." Ibid., Oct.20, 1994.
177. "Bus Number 5," Arm of Salvation *Ministry & Prayer Update*, Dec. 1994, pp.4,5.
178. "Slaughter in Tel Aviv," *Jerusalem Post*, Oct. 20, 1994.
179. "The Beit Lid Massacre," CFI's *Israel News Digest*, March, 1995, p.1.
180. Ibid.
181. *Reuter* report. "Israel, PLO vow to punish Islamic militants," *New Zealand Herald*, Jan. 25, 1995.
182. "Clinton sends his condolences," *Jerusalem Post*, Jan. 25, 1995.
183. "Wachsmans make ransom offer to Hamas." Ibid., Oct. 14, 1994.
184. "Palestinian force has day of reckoning." Ibid.
185. *Voice of Israel Radio*, Feb. 26, 1995.
186. "Closure to continue until further notice," *Jerusalem Post*, Oct. 21, 1994.
187. "Quotable quotes," *Dispatch From Jerusalem*, Jan.-Feb., 1994.
188. "Beware the prophets of peace," *Jerusalem Post International Edition*, Jan. 8, 1994.
189. Yasser Arafat on Jordan Television, Sept. 13, 1993.
190. "Arafat letter to rejectionists," *Jerusalem Post*, Nov. 18, 1994.
191. Reported in *US News and World Report*, Sept. 1993.
192. A *Fatah* pronouncement quoted in Laffin, *Fedayeen*, p.89.
193. Benjamin Netanyahu, "Jihad For Jerusalem," CFI's *Israel News Digest*, July 1994, p.1.
194. "Arafat's promises," *Jerusalem Post*, April 19, 1994.
195. Arafat quoted on CBS, *48 Hours*, Feb. 9, 1988.
196. "Arafat's 'Mein Kampf,'" *Jerusalem Post*, May 27, 1994.
197. Broadcast on *Saut Falastin Radio*, Egypt, reproduced in full in Appendix I, Netanyahu, *A Place Among the Nations*, p.433.
198. Abu Iyad, Arafat's deputy, *Al-Sachrah*, Kuwait, Jan. 6, 1987.
199. George Habash, head of the PFLP faction of the PLO, *Voice of the Mountain Radio*, Lebanon, June 9, 1989.
200. Nabil Sha'ath, head of the PLO delegation currently negotiating the "Peace Accord," *Al-Siyassa*, January 1989, quoted in *Middle East Intelligence Digest*, May 1993. p.6.
201. Yasser Arafat, *Newsweek*, March 1977, Ibid.
202. Farouk Kadoumi, PLO "Foreign Minister," Ibid.
203. Yasser Arafat, Jan. 1, 1994, quoted in CFI's *Israel News Digest*, Feb. 1994, p.1.
204. Leila Khaled, Sec. General of the PLO's GUPW, *Al-Sakra*, October 1988, quoted in *Middle East Intelligence Digest*, May 1993. p.7.

Chapter Notes 315

205. George Habash, head of the PFLP faction of the PLO, *Al-Hadaf,* April 1989, Ibid.
206. Basam Abu Sharif, PLO spokesman and Arafat's Aide, *Kuwait News Agency,* May 1986, Ibid.
207. Feisal al-Husseini, member of the PLO negotiating team, Nov. 1994, quoted in "Terrorism and the PLO: September 13 plus seven months," *Bulletin of the Jerusalem Institute for Western Defence,* Bulletin 2, June 1994, p.11.
208. Abbas Zaki, member of the PLO Executive, Ibid.
209. Brown, *Our Hands Are Stained With Blood,* p.71.
210. Abdul Halim Haddam, Vice-President of Syria, *Al Hayat,* Jan. 5, 1994, quoted in "Munich in the making?" *Bulletin of the Jerusalem Institute for Western Defence,* Digest 2, Feb. June 1994, p.5.
211. Ibid.
212. Laffin, *The Arab Mind,* p.45.
213. Yasser Arafat, *El Mundo,* Venezuela, Feb. 11, 1980.
214. Arafat quoted in Saudi News Agency, Jan. 2, 1989. Cited in Netanyahu, *A Place Among the Nations,* p.123.
215. Moshe Sharon, professor of Islamic history at the Jerusalem's Bar-Ilan and Hebrew Universities, writing in "Behind the PLO boss's words," *Jerusalem Post,* May 27, 1994.
216. Valerie Luke Waller, *A Stranger in the Land,* (Houston: Daughters of Truth, 1984), p.22.
217. Lewis, *The Political Language of Islam,* p.73.
218. Laffin, *The Arab Mind,* p.73.
219. "Promises," *Jerusalem Post International Edition,* Feb. 12, 1994.
220. Yasser Arafat's recorded speech in a Johannesburg mosque, May 10, 1994.
221. Sura 17:9.
222. "Arafat tells Palestinians: We must honor bad accord," *Jerusalem Post,* July 3, 1994.
223. "Arafat pledges: 'We will build this homeland.'" Culled from news agency reports and printed in Ibid.
224. Ibid.
225. "Jabalya meets Yasser face-to-face," Ibid.
226. "The Israeli suicide drive," *Jerusalem Post International Edition,* July 2, 1994.
227. Abu Iyad, Arafat's deputy. Interviewed on *Voice of Israel Radio,* July 26, 1995.
228. "The Israeli suicide drive," *Jerusalem Post International Edition,* July 2, 1994.
229. Ibid.
230. From 1901 – 1990 the Jews, although comprising less than half of one percent of the world's population, have been awarded 21% of the total number of Nobel Prizes in Science. Jews receive 30 prizes for every 1 awarded to a Gentile. Source: John Hulley, a former senior economist at World Bank Headquarters in Washington, D.C. His figures are taken from the *Nobel Foundation Directory* 1991–92.

Chapter 6

1. Peters, *From Time Immemorial*, p.10.
2. A popular misbelief is five attacking nations: See Bennett, *When Day and Night Cease*, p.212; Sacher, *A History of Israel*, p.315; William L. Hull, *The Fall and Rise of Israel: The Story of the Jewish People During the time of their Dispersal and Regathering* (Grand Rapids: Zondervan, 1954), p.328; etc.
3. *Falastin*, Jordan, Feb. 19, 1949. Cited in Bennett, *When Day and Night Cease*, p.217.
4. Peter Dodd and Halim Barakat, *River Without Bridges: A Study of the Exodus of the 1967 Arab Palestinian Refugees* (Beirut: Institute for Palestine Studies, 1969). Cited in Peters, *From Time Immemorial*, p.13.
5. *Ad Difaa*, Jordan, Sep. 6, 1954. Cited in Samuel Katz, *Battleground: Facts and Fantasy in Palestine* (New York: Bantam, 1973), p.18.
6. *Al-Urdun*, Jordan, April 9, 1953. Cited in Bennett, *When Day and Night Cease*, p.217.
7. Hull, *The Fall and Rise of Israel*, p.329.
8. Peters, *From Time Immemorial*, p.79.
9. Ibid.
10. Ibid., p.80.
11. Cited in Peters, *From Time Immemorial*, p.29.
12. "Jewish refugees from Arab lands: time to present a bill," *Jerusalem Post International Edition*, Jan. 11, 1992.
13. Howard Kennedy, May 1950, quoted in Peters, *From Time Immemorial*, footnote p.18.
14. John Davis, quoted in Ibid., p.19.
15. Ibid., chapter note p.447.
16. Senators Gale McGee and Albert Gore in a cable to President Eisenhower and Secretary of State Christian Herter, quoted in Ibid., p.18.
17. Cited in Ibid., footnote p.19.
18. "'Inflated Palestinian population figures incorrect,'" *Jerusalem Post*, Dec. 9, 1994.
19. Bar-Illan, *Eye on the Media*, p.205.
20. Peters, *From Time Immemorial*, p.262.
21. Ibid.
22. Ibid.
23. Ibid., p.262.
24. Ibid., p.262,263.
25. Ibid., p.5.
26. Marguerite Cartwright, "Plain Speech on the Arab Refugee Problem," Ibid., p17.
27. Peters, *From Time Immemorial*, p.17.
28. Netanyahu, *A Place Among The Nations*, p.143.
29. Bard and Himelfarb, *Myths and Facts*, p.121.
30. Peters, *From Time Immemorial*, p.33.

Chapter Notes 317

31. "Jewish refugees from Arab lands: time to present a bill," *Jerusalem Post International Edition*, Jan. 11, 1992.
32. Bard and Himelfarb, *Myths and Facts*, p.121.
33. Sacher, *A History of Israel*, p.669.
34. Ibid., p.670.
35. *The World Almanac and Book of Facts* (New York: Pharos, 1993), p.820.
36. "Jewish refugees from Arab lands: time to present a bill," *Jerusalem Post International Edition*, Jan. 11, 1992.
37. Cited in Netanyahu, *A Place Among The Nations*, p.32.
38. Kamal Ahmad Own, quoted in Green, *Arab Theologians on Jews and Israel*, p.13.
39. Ibid.
40. "The Ramban's New Neighbor," *In Jerusalem*, April 22, 1994.
41. Peters, *From Time Immemorial*, p.69.
42. M.M. Raysher, *Sha'arei Yerushalayim* (Lemberg, 1866), p.29. Cited in Ibid., p.62.
43. Ibid., p.176.
44. Ibid.
45. Ibid. p.34.
46. *New York Times*, Nov. 7, 1945. Ibid.
47. *New York Times*, Nov. 14, 1945. Ibid., p.70.
48. Peters, *From Time Immemorial*, p.75.
49. Ibid. p.175
50. Ibid., p.70.
51. J.R. Chancellor quoted in Ibid., p.172.
52. Moslem Mufti Haj Amin al-Husseini, 1937. Quoted in Ibid.
53. Moh. Taha Yahia, quoted in Green, *Arab Theologians on Jews and Israel*, p.19.
54. Dr. Abdel Aziz Kamil, quoted in Ibid., p.20.
55. Shaul, on life in Iraq, quoted in Peters, *From Time Immemorial*, p.102.
56. Shimon, on life in Iraq, Ibid., p.103.
57. Yaacov, on life in Egypt, Ibid., p.104.
58. Shlomo, on life in Egypt, Ibid., p.105.
59. Shoshana, on life in Syria, Ibid., p.111–112.
60. "The Gaza Dilemma," *Dispatch From Jerusalem*, July/Aug. 1993, p.13.
61. Ibid.
62. "Jewish refugees from Arab lands: time to present a bill," *Jerusalem Post International Edition*, Jan. 11, 1992.
63. Netanyahu, *A Place Among The Nations*, p.355.
64. Official information release in January, 1988, by the Israeli Embassy in Wellington, New Zealand. Reprinted in full in Bennett, *When Day and Night Cease*, pp.215 – 216.
65. Ibid.
66. Ibid.
67. Ibid.
68. Ibid.
69. Ralph Galloway quoted in Peters, *From Time Immemorial*, p.23.

70. Laffin, *Fedayeen*, p.86.
71. John McCarthy, the United States Catholic Conference's expert, in an interview with Joan Peters in Peters, *From Time Immemorial*, p.28.
72. Patai, *The Arab Mind*, p.24.
73. Khaled al-Azzem, former Syrian Prime Minister, in his memoirs 1973. Cited in Bennett, *When Day and Night Cease*, p.217.
74. The Memoirs of Haled al Azm, Beirut, 1973, Part 1, pp. 386 – 387. Cited in *Middle East Intelligence Digest*, June 12, 1992.
75. King Hussein of Jordan, 1960. Quoted in Peters, *From Time Immemorial*, p.11.
76. *Falastin*, Jordan, May 30, 1955. Cited in Bennett, *When Day and Night Cease*, p.217.
77. Full page advertisement by the Sephardi Federation in *New York Times*, Jan. 11, 1976. Cited in Peters, *From Time Immemorial*, footnote p.31.
78. Yasser Arafat, quoted on *Voice of Israel Radio*, June 23, 1994.
79. *Al-Ziyyad*, Lebanon, April 6, 1950. Cited in Peters, *From Time Immemorial*, p.22.
80. Ibid.
81. President Nasser, 1961, quoted in Isi Liebler, *The Case For Israel* (Australia: The Globe Press, 1972), p.45. Cited in Bard and Himelfarb, *Myths and Facts*, p.144.
82. *Beirut al Massa*, Lebanon, July 15, 1957. Cited in Bard and Himelfarb, *Myths and Facts*, p.138.
83. *Al-Misri*, Oct. 11, 1949. Cited in Ibid.
84. Ratskoy, quoted in "Conditions of Arabs in Jerusalem," *Jerusalem Post*, Aug. 12, 1994.
85. "Wolves in Sheep's Clothing: Part IV," *Middle East Intelligence Digest*, May 11, 1993, p.7.
86. "83 Bosnian Moslem refugees arrive despite Arab refusal to accept them," *Jerusalem Post International Edition*, Feb. 27, 1993.
87. Ibid.
88. Ibid.
89. Ibid.
90. "Pull this racist show out of the Knesset." Ibid., Nov. 28, 1992. Cited in Bennett, *When Day and Night Cease*, p.218.

Chapter 7

1. Peters, *From Time Immemorial*, footnote p.173.
2. Aharon Megged, "The Israeli suicide drive," *Jerusalem Post International Edition*, July 2, 1994.
3. Ibid.
4. *NIV Study Bible*, (Grand Rapids: Zondervan, 1985). Notes on Genesis 15:17.
5. See for example, *A Commentary: Critical, Experimental, and Practical on the Old and New Testaments* (Robert Jamieson, A.R. Faucet, and David Brown, Eerdmans, 1990), Vol.I, p.317.
6. *Complete Works of Flavius Josephus*, (Grand Rapids: Kregel,1980), p.587.

Chapter Notes 319

      Cited in Bennett, *When Day and Night Cease*, p.99.
7. Ibid.
8. *Encylopædia Judaica*, (Jerusalem: Keter, 1971), Vol.2, p.319.
9. Cited in Peters, *From Time Immemorial*, p.82.
10. *Palestine Royal Commision Report* (London, 1937), pp.2–5,7,9, particularly p.11, para. 23. Cited in Ibid., p.82.
11. "Reference books are promoting a bogus Middle East history," *Jerusalem Post*, Oct. 16, 1992.
12. Cited in Bennett, *When Day and Night Cease*, p.99.
13. Ian V. Hogg, *Israeli War Machine: The Men; The Machines; The Tactics*, (London: Hamlyn, 1983), p.20. Cited in Bennett, *When Day and Night Cease*, p.174.
14. Ibid.
15. Bennett, *When Day and Night Cease*, pp.176–177.
16. Ibid. p.131.
17. Bennett, *Saga*, p.192.
18. Hull, *The Fall and Rise of Israel*, p.349.
19. Netanyahu, *A Place Among The Nations*, footnote p.27.
20. Prof. Bernard Lewis quoted in Ibid, p.4.
21. Musa Alami, "The Lesson of Palestine," *The Middle East Journal*, Oct. 1949. Cited in Peters, *From Time Immemorial*, p.13.
22. Ibid.
23. Bernard Lewis quoted in "The Mythtory of Palestine,"*A letter from Jerusalem*, Christian Friends of Israel, 1994.
24. "Reference books are promoting a bogus Middle East history," *Jerusalem Post*, Oct. 16, 1992.
25. Zuheir Muhsin quoted in the Dutch daily *Trouw*, March 1977. Cited in Peters, *From Time Immemorial*, p.137.
26. Zuheir Muhsin quoted in the Dutch daily *Trouw*, March 1977. Cited in *Dispatch From Jerusalem*, 3rd Quarter, 1991.
27. Philip K. Hitti speaking to the Anglo-American Committee of Inquiry in 1946. Quoted in Bar-Illan, *Eye on the Media*, p.166.
28. Ibid.
29. Anwar Sadat quoted in *Ha Ubal Or*, Jerusalem edition, Jan. 3, 1991. Cited in Grant, *The Blood of the Moon*, p.47.
30. *Websters Unabridged Dictionary* 2nd ed. (New York: Simon and Schuster, 1983).
31. "Philistines," Vol. VII *Encyclopædia Britannica* 15th ed. (Chigago: Helen Hemingway Benton, 1977), p.948.
32. "Peoples of the World: Philistines," *Random House Encyclopedia: Electronic Edition*, (New York: Microlytics, 1990).
33. "Coptic chant," Vol. VII *Encyclopædia Britannica*, p.137.
34. Ibid.
35. Arafat in an interview with Oriana Fallaci, 1974. Quoted in Bar-Illan, *Eye on the Media*, p.408.
36. Eban, *Personal Witness*, p.66.
37. Netanyahu, *A Place Among The Nations*, p.148.

38. King Hussein in *Al-Nahar Al-Arabi*, Dec.26, 1981. Cited in Ibid., p.147.
39. Ibid.
40. Crown Prince Hassan to the Jordaninan National Assembly and reported in *Al-Destour*, Feb. 5, 1970. Cited in Ibid.
41. Yasser Arafat in *New Republic*, 1974. Cited in Bennett, *When Day and Night Cease*, p.211.
42. Chafiq el Hout, PLO official on *Radio Cairo*, May 30, 1967. Cited in Netanyahu, *A Place Among The Nations*, p.147.
43. Abu Iyad, Arafat's deputy in *Al-Majallah*, Nov. 8, 1988. Cited in Ibid.
44. Arafat quoted in "The Mythtory of Palestine,"*A letter from Jerusalem*, Christian Friends of Israel, 1994.
45. Green, *Arab Theologians on Jews and Israel*, p.16.
46. "City of Peace, hornet's nest," *U.S. News & World Report*, March 26, 1990. Cited in Bennett, *When Day and Night Cease*, p.188.
47. Teddy Kollek, Mayor of Jerusalem, in a letter to the editor of *Commentary*, April, 1991. Cited in Ibid.
48. "What connection?," *Jerusalem Post*, Aug. 26, 1994.
49. Mohammed Azzah Darwaza in a paper given at the Academy of Islamic Research, quoted in Green, *Arab Theologians on Jews and Israel*, p.30.
50. See Chap. 6, p.114.
51. Martin Kabtanik quoted in Peters, *From Time Immemorial*, p.176.
52. Philip K. Hitti, *The Arabs, A Short History* (Princeton, 1943), p.83. Cited in Ibid., p.148.
53. Quoted in Charles Gulston, *Jerusalem: The Tragedy and the Triumph* (Grand Rapids: Zondervan, 1979), p.23.
54. "Kurds," Editor-In-Chief Amiram Gonen, *The Encyclopedia of the peoples of the world* (New York: Henry Holt, 1993), p.342.
55. Ibid.
56. James William Parkes, *Whose Land? History of the Peoples of Palestine* (Great Britain, Harmondsworth, 1970), p.74. Cited in Peters, *From Time Immemorial*, p.148.
57. Cited in Ibid.
58. David George Hogarth, "Arabs and Turks," *The Arab Bulletin*, April 21, 1917, No.48. Cited in Ibid.
59. The Moslem chairman of the Syrian Delegation to the Paris Peace Conference in Feb. 1919, recorded in the Minutes of the Supreme Council and cited by D.H. Miller in *My Diary at the Conference of Paris*, 22 vols. (New York, 1924), vol.14, p.405. Cited in Ibid., p.138.
60. Peters, *From Time Immemorial*, p.151.
61. Ibid.
62. Parkes, *Whose Land?*, p.66. Cited in Ibid.
63. Peters, *From Time Immemorial*, p.152.
64. Jacob De Haas, *History of Palestine, the Last Two Thousand Years* (New York, 1934), p.300, citing Gaudefroy-Demombynes, *La Syrie au debut du Quinzième Siècle d'après Qal Qachandi* (Paris, 1923), p.xxxii. Also Ernest Frankenstein, *Justice for My People* (New York, 1944), p.121. Cited in Ibid.
65. Peters, *From Time Immemorial*, pp.155,156.

Chapter Notes

66. De Haas, *History of Palestine*, p.258. John of Wurzburg list from Reinhold Rohricht edition, pp.41,69. Cited in Ibid., p.156.
67. Cited in Ibid.
68. Ibid., p.152.
69. Bar-Illan, *Eye on the Media*, p.278.
70. Ibid.
71. Ibid., p.295.
72. Eban, *Personal Witness*, p.641.
73. "Judea and Samaria," Letters to the Editor *Jerusalem Post Internationa Edition*, Jan. 18, 1992.
74. Yasser Arafat quoted in "The anti-Israel crusade," *Jerusalem Post*, Oct. 4, 1992.
75. A Jordanian TV production, Ibid.
76. Reported in *Middle East Intelligence Digest*, Oct. 1992.
77. "Neo-Philistine nature laid bare," *Jerusalem Post International Edition*, Oct. 17, 1992.
78. Reported in *Middle East Intelligence Digest*, Oct. 1992
79. Ibid.
80. "Christmas Cards," Letters to the Editor, *Jerusalem Post International Edition*, Dec. 12, 1994.
81. Peters, *From Time Immemorial*, p.4.
82. Ibid.
83. Carl Hermann Voss, *The Palestine Problem: Today, Israel and Its Neighbors* (Boston, 1953), p.13. Cited in Ibid., p.157.
84. Gunner Edward Webbe, *Palestine Exploration Fund, Quarterly Statement,* p.86, cited in de Hass, *History of Palestine*, p.338. Cited in Ibid., p.158.
85. de Hass, *History of Palestine*, p.337. Cited in Ibid.
86. Count Constantine François Volney, *Travels Through Syria and Egypt in the Years 1783, 1784, 1785* (London, 1788), vol. 2, p.147. Cited in Ibid.
87. Thomas Shaw, *Travels and observations Relating to Several Parts of Barbary and the Levant* (London, 1767), p.331ff. Cited in Ibid.
88. Brockhaus, *Allg. deutsch Real-Encyklopaedie*, 7th ed. (Leipzig, 1827), vol.VIII, p.2, pp.438–439. Cited in Ibid, pp.158,159.
89. Alphonse de Lamartine, *Recollections of the East* Vol. I (London, 1846), pp.268,308. Cited in Netanyahu, *A Place Among The Nations*, pp.38,39.
90. James Finn to the Earl of Clarendon, Sep. 15, 1857. Cited in Ibid., p.39.
91. Mark Twain, *The Innocents Abroad* (London, 1881), pp.349,441–442. Cited in Peters, *From Time Immemorial*, p.159,160.
92. W.M. Thompson, *The Land and the Book* (1866). Cited in Norma Archbold, *The Mountains of Israel: The Bible & The West Bank* (Jerusalem: Phoebe's Song Publication, 1993), p.28.
93. Gulston, *Jerusalem*, p.206.
94. Pierre Loti, *La Galilee* (Paris, 1895). Cited in Peters, *From Time Immemorial*, p.161.
95. Cited in Netanyahu, *A Place Among The Nations*, p.37.
96. H.B. Tristam, *The Land of Israel: A Journal of Travels in Palestine* (London, 1865), p.490. Cited in Peters, *From Time Immemorial*, p.167.

97. Charles Issawi, ed. *The Economic History of the Middle East, 1800–1914* Chicago and London, 1966), p.258. Cited in Ibid., p.166.
98. "Jerusalem History," Letters to the Editor, *Jerusalem Post International Edition*, Jan. 18, 1992.
99. Peters, *From Time Immemorial*, p.251.
100. Ibid.
101. Ibid.
102. *When Day and Night Cease*, p.222.
103. Cited in Netanyahu, *A Place Among The Nations*, p.36.
104. Peters, *From Time Immemorial*, p.254.
105. A. Druyanow, *Ketavim letoldot hibbat ziyyon ve-yishshuv erez yisra'el* (Tel Aviv, Odessa, 1919, 1925, 1932) vol.3, pp.66–67. Cited in Ibid., p.252.
106. Peters, *From Time Immemorial*, p.253.
107. Michael Comay, *Zionism, Israel, and the Palestinian Arabs. Questions and Answers* (Jerusalem: Keter, 1983), p.40. Cited in Brown, *Our Hands Are Stained With Blood*, p.70.
108. "Palestine," *The Zondervan Pictorial Encyclopedia of the Bible* (Grand Rapids: Zondervan, 1976), vol 4, p.584.. Cited in Bennett, *When Day and Night Cease*, p.290.
109. Arieh Avneri, *The Claim of Dispossession: Jewish Land Settlement and the Arabs, 1878–1948* (New York: Herzl Press, 1982), p.262. Cited in Netanyahu, *A Place Among The Nations*, p.36.
110. "Palestinian police deliberately shot at us," *Jerusalem Post*, July 18, 1994.
111. "Redrawing the Borders," CFI's *Israel News Digest*, July 1993., p.2.
112. Bernard Lewis, *The Arabs in History*, 4th rev. ed. (New York: Harper-Colophon Books, 1966), p.40.
113. Peters, *From Time Immemorial*, p.146.
114. *Encyclopædia Judaica*, vol. 11, p.670.
115. "Neo-Philistine nature laid bare," *Jerusalem Post International Edition*, Oct. 17, 1992.
116. Novelist Mary McCarthy used to say this about her colleague Lillian Hellman.
117. "Battle for the holy city," *Jerusalem Post International Edition*, May 29, 1993.
118. Lortet, *La Syrie d'aujourd'hui: Voyages dands la Phénicie, le Leban et la Judée, 1875–80* (Paris, 1881, p.137. Cited in Peters, *From Time Immemorial*, p.167.
119. Peters, *From Time Immemorial*, p.168.
120. "The gospel according to Husseini," *Jerusalem Post International Edition*, Dec. 12, 1992.
121. "Israel: History," Random House Encyclopedia Electronic Edition, (New York: Microlytics, 1990).
122. "Palestine," Ibid.
123. "Principal events 1200–700 BC : 1100–1050 BC. Ibid.
124. "Gaza," Ibid.
125. "Sennacherib," Ibid.

Chapter Notes 323

126. "Philistines," *The Software Toolworks Illustrated Encyclopedia* (Novato CA: Grolier Electronic Publishing, 1990).
127. "Palestine," Ibid.
128. "Peoples of the World: Philistines," *Random House Encyclopedia: Electronic Edition.*
129. *Websters Unabridged Dictionary.*
130. "Philistines," *Encyclopædia Britannica*, Vol. VII, p.948.
131. "Palestine," Ibid., p.694.
132. "Britannica redefines history," *Jerusalem Post International Edition*, March 27, 1993.
133. Ibid.
134. Quoted in "Reference books are promoting a bogus Middle East history," *Jerusalem Post*, Oct. 16, 1992.
135. Ibid.
136. Quoted from *Dispatch From Jerusalem*, March/April 1994.
137. Ibid.
138. Quoted by David Bar-Illan in "A terrorist attack becomes a military clash," *Jerusalem Post*, July 9, 1993.
139. Ibid.
140. "Authenticating the Big Lie," *Middle East Intelligence Digest*, Oct. 1992, p.7.
141. NKJV marginal explanation of SHULAMITE, Song of Solomon 1:1.

Chapter 8

1. David Bar-Illan writing in "Expulsion backlash is typical," *Jerusalem Post International Edition*, Dec. 26, 1992.
2. Netanyahu, *A Place Among The Nations*, p.86.
3. Bar-Illan, *Eye on the Media*, p.205.
4. *The Oxford English Dictionary* 2nd ed., (Oxford: Clarendon Press, 1991).
5. *Collins Dictionary of the English Language*, (Sydney: William Collins Sons & Co., 1979).
6. *Webster's Unabridged Dictionary.*
7. "The UN antisemitism resolution," *Jerusalem Post*, March 13, 1994.
8. Ibid.
9. "UN Official ignored Rafiah mob killing; IDF investigating." Ibid., March 7, 1993.
10. UNRWA Gaza Strip refugee affairs officer. Ibid.
11. "The UN Rafiah incident." Ibid.
12. "The Myth of UN Fairness to Israel," *Dispatch From Jerusalem*, 3rd Quarter 1991, p.2.
13. Bar-Illan, *Eye on the Media*, p.ix.
14. Ibid.
15. "The Myth of UN Fairness to Israel," *Dispatch From Jerusalem*, 3rd Quarter 1991, p.2.
16. Amnesty International 1983 Report. Cited in Bennett, *Saga*, pp.222–223.
17. *Dispatch From Jerusalem*, Vol.16, No.3, 3rd Quarter 1991. Cited in Bennett, *When Day and Night Cease*, p.130.

18. "The Myth of UN Fairness to Israel," *Dispatch From Jerusalem*, 3rd Quarter 1991, p.2.
19. Bennett, *Saga*, p.78.
20. Ibid.
21. Ibid.
22. The horrific results from the German use of chemical weapons (various types of poison gas) during World War I resulted in the League of Nations—forerunner of the United Nations—banning them from further use. In 1982 the United Nations issued a second ban against the use of poison gas in warfare.
23. Bennett, *Saga*, p.222.
24. "What Aridor should have said," *Jerusalem Post International Edition*, Jan. 18, 1992.
25. Douglas Bloomfield quoted in *Middle East Intelligence Digest*, No. 10, 1992, p.5
26. "Makes You Think—Doesn't It? Ibid., p.5.
27. "Expulsion backlash is typical," *Jerusalem Post International Edition*, Dec. 26, 1992.
28. *Voice of Israel Radio*, Jan. 26, 1993.
29. "Collision Course," CFI's *Israel News Digest*, Feb. 1993, p.2.
30. "The Double Standard," Ibid., March 1993, p.2.
31. "Lebanese newspaper satirizes deportees," *Jerusalem Post International Edition*, March 20, 1993.
32. Ibid.
33. Shmuel Katz writing in "Sheer distortion," Ibid., Jan. 30, 1993.
34. "Expulsion backlash is typical," Ibid., Dec. 26, 1992.
35. Ibid.
36. "The Double Standard," CFI's *Israel News Digest*, March 1993, p.2.
37. Katz, *Israel Versus Jibril*, p.54.
38. Ibid., pp.54–55.
39. Ibid., p.56.
40. Ibid., p.55.
41. Ibid., p.56.
42. Ibid.
43. Ibid., p.57 footnote.
44. Ibid.
45. Ibid., p.56 footnote.
46. Ibid.
47. See Chap. 3, pp.42–43.
48. "Security Council condemns massacre, wants 'foreign presence' in territories," *Jerusalem Post International Edition*, March 26, 1994.
49. "International observers in Hebron," *Middle East Intelligence Digest*, June 1994, p.2.
50. Ibid.
51. Sacher, *A History of Israel*, p.811.
52. Bard and Himelfarb, *Myths and Facts*, p.115.
53. Quoted from "An ill wind blowing," *Middle East Intelligence Digest*, March/

Chapter Notes

April 1995, p.8.
54. Ibid.
55. Cited by Gary H. Kah, *En Route to Global Occupation* (Lafayette, LA: Huntington House, 1992), p.37.
56. "US report on Waldheim gives 'devastating' picture of World War II activities," *Jerusalem Post International Edition*, March 26, 1994.
57. Ibid.
58. Sacher, *A History of Israel*, p.811.
59. Evans, *Israel—America's Key to Survival*, p.67.
60. Sacher, *A History of Israel*, p.812.
61. Laffin, *The PLO Connection*, p.19.
62. Ibid.
63. "Middle East : Arafat, Yasir," *Random House Encyclopedia*.
64. Farouk Kadoumi, PLO "Foreign Minister," *Quotidien de Paris*, Nov. 11, 1985.
65. "Israel to ignore human rights investigator," *Jerusalem Post International Edition*, Feb. 27, 1993.
66. Maj. Haddad quoted in Evans, *Israel—America's Key to Survival*, p.58.
67. *Jerusalem Post*, June 13, 1978. Cited in Dr. Irving Moskowitz, *Should America Guarantee Israel's Safety?*, (New York: Americans For A Safe Israel, 1993), p.24.
68. *Jerusalem Post*, Dec.25, 1978. Cited in Ibid., p.26.
69. Ibid., p.24.
70. *Jerusalem Post*, June 14, June 15, 1978. Cited in Ibid., p.24.
71. Katz, *Israel Versus Jibril*, p.83.
72. Ibid.
73. Ibid.
74. Moskowitz, *Should America Guarantee Israel's Safety?*, p.25.
75. *Jerusalem Post*, Aug. 20, 1979. Cited in Ibid.
76. *Jerusalem Post*, Feb. 20, 1979. Cited in Ibid.
77. *Jerusalem Post*, Feb. 24, 1992. Cited in Ibid.
78. *Maariv*, Aug. 19, 1987, *Jerusalem Post*, March 22, 1989. Cited in Ibid., p.26.
79. *Jerusalem Post*, April 27, 1979. Cited in Ibid.
80. *Jerusalem Post*, April 30, 1979. Cited in Ibid.
81. Ibid.
82. See Chap. 5, p.79.
83. *Jerusalem Post*, June 16, 1982. Cited in Moskowitz, *Should America Guarantee Israel's Safety?*, p.28.
84. "The Myth of UN Fairness to Israel," *Dispatch From Jerusalem*, 3rd Quarter 1991, p.2.
85. Ibid.
86. Laffin, *Fedayeen*, p.141.
87. Ibid., p.142.
88. *Jerusalem Post*, July 9, 1982. Cited in Moskowitz, *Should America Guarantee Israel's Safety?*, p.24.
89. Ibid., pp.24,25.

90. Bennett, *When Day and Night Cease*, p.179.
91. Ibid., pp.179,180.
92. Eban, *Personal Witness*, p.357.
93. Ibid.
94. Ibid.
95. Ibid., p.358.
96. Ibid.
97. Ibid.
98. Moskowitz, *Should America Guarantee Israel's Safety?*, p.7.
99. Eisenhower confirmed: "We should not assume...Egypt will prevent Israeli shipping from using the Suez Canal of the Gulf of Aqaba. If, unhappily, Egypt does hereafter violate the Armistice Agreement or other international obligations, then this should be dealt with firmly by the family of nations." Netanyahu, *A Place Among The Nations*, note p.445,446.
100. Ibid., p.134.
101. Eban, *Personal Witness*, p.360.
102. Ibid., p.414.
103. Peters, *From Time Immemorial*, p.403.
104. Maj. Saad Haddad quoted in Evans, *Israel—America's Key to Survival*, p.58.

Chapter 9

1. Jim Lederman, *Battle Lines: The American Media and the Intifada* (New York: Henry Holt, 1992), p.281.
2. Ibid., p.280.
3. Ibid.
4. ABC's Tel Aviv bureau chief Bill Seamans, quoted in Ibid., p.138.
5. Ibid.
6. Bar-Illan, *Eye on the Media*, p.x.
7. Lederman, *Battle Lines*, p.99.
8. Ibid.
9. Ibid., p.280.
10. Cited in Bennett, *Saga*, p.132.
11. Bar-Illan, *Eye on the Media*, p. 344.
12. Ibid., p.325.
13. Lederman, *Battle Lines*, p.145.
14. Ibid., p.131.
15. Ibid., pp.131-134.
16. "Murder photographs raise ethics charge," *Jerusalem Post International Edition*, Dec. 12, 1992.
17. Lederman, *Battle Lines*, p.141.
18. "Senseless, mind-blowing journalistic punditry," *Jerusalem Post*, Sept. 11, 1992.
19. See Chap. 5, p.81.
20. "Senseless, mind-blowing journalistic punditry," *Jerusalem Post*, Sept. 11, 1992.
21. See Chap. 5, p.81,82.
22. "Prime time and prejudice," *Jerusalem Post*, Feb. 8, 1991.

23. Bar-Illan, *Eye on the Media*, p.191.
24. Ibid.
25. Ibid., p.190.
26. *The Jerusalem Institute For Western Defense: Periodic New Digest from the Arab World and Iran*, Digest 11, Nov.1994, pp.1,6.
27. Ibid., p.6.
28. Ibid.
29. "Special Editions: Ex-Israel Extras at Time an Newsweek," *New Republic*, Oct. 8, 1990.
30. Ibid.
31. Ibid.
32. Ibid.
33. Ibid.
34. Ibid.
35. Ibid.
36. "Faking it with pictures," *Jerusalem Post*, Aug. 21, 1992.
37. Lederman, *Battle Lines*, p.241.
38. "Ya'ari-Shara interview: An excercise in manipulation," *Jerusalem Post*, Oct. 14, 1994.
39. Lederman, *Battle Lines*, p.314.
40. Bar-Illan, *Eye on the Media*, p.129.
41. "TV news fabrication," *Jerusalem Post*, Oct. 12, 1990.
42. Quoted from a letter by Teddy Kollek to the editor of *Commentary*, April 1991.
43. "'60 Minutes' & the Temple Mount," *Commentary*, Feb.1991.
44. Ibid.
45. Published in a 1983 book entitled *Split Vision—the Portrayal of Arabs in the American Media*. Cited in "Prime time and prejudice," *Jerusalem Post*, Feb. 8, 1991.
46. Bar-Illan, *Eye on the Media*, p.291.
47. Ibid.
48. Ibid.
49. Ibid.
50. Ibid.
51. Ibid., 291.
52. "Prime time and prejudice," *Jerusalem Post*, Feb. 8, 1991.
53. Ibid.
54. Bar-Illan, *Eye on the Media*, p.216.
55. Ibid., p.102.
56. Ibid., p.143.
57. Ibid.
58. Ibid., pp.143,144.
59. "Murderer loses 'dispute' over an Israeli's life," *Jerusalem Post*, Nov. 5, 1993.
60. "All the news that's fit to slant," *Jerusalem Post International Edition*, April 3, 1993.
61. "Blimey! BBC surpasses even itself," Ibid., May 21, 1994.

62. Bar-Illan, *Eye on the Media*, p.93.
63. Ibid.
64. Ibid., p94.
65. "The body count as an effective bash-Israel device," *Jerusalem Post*, Jan. 7, 1993.
66. "How the world media turn news into a nonevent." Ibid., Sept. 30, 1994.
67. "Terminology—the ultimate weapon," *Jerusalem Post International Edition*, Feb. 27, 1993.
68. "PLO moderating its love of peace," *Jerusalem Post*, Dec. 3, 1993.
69. Ibid.
70. "Cheaters, liars and videotape," *Jerusalem Post International Edition*, March 13, 1993.
71. Ibid.
72. Bar-Illan, *Eye on the Media*, p.423.
73. Ibid.
74. "Trashing Israel—again," *Guardian Weekly*, March 11, 1994, reported in *Middle East Intelligence Digest*, Vol. 5, No. 4, April. 1994, p.7.
75. Ibid.
76. Ibid.
77. Ibid.
78. "Anything but the facts, ma'am," *Jerusalem Post International Edition*, May 22, 1993.
79. Ibid.
80. Ibid.
81. Ibid.
82. Alan Ray, "That Mideast Peace," *New Leader*, Oct. 29,1990.
83. Ibid.
84. Lederman, *Battle Lines*, p.314.
85. "Foreign media dance to piper-payer's tune," *Jerusalem Post*, Sept. 4, 1992.
86. Kah, *En Route to Global Occupation*, p.62.
87. Ibid., p.56.
88. Ibid., p.55.
89. Ibid., pp. 33,34.
90. "Foreign media dance to piper-payer's tune," *Jerusalem Post*, Sept. 4, 1992.
91. Ibid.
92. Kah, *En Route to Global Occupation*, p.16.
93. Ibid.
94. "Foreign media dance to piper-payer's tune," *Jerusalem Post*, Sept. 4, 1992.
95. David Bar-Illan replying to a letter from Jonathan Ferziger, UPI Bureau Chief. Ibid., Oct. 23, 1992.
96. "Yasser, Yasser, Mr. Arafat!" *Jerusalem Post International Edition*, June 18, 1994.
97. "'Color' columnists distort black-and-white facts," *Jerusalem Post*, Oct. 28, 1994.
98. Bar-Illan, *Eye on the Media*, p.243.
99. Ibid., p.350.
100. "'Color' columnists distort black-and-white facts," *Jerusalem Post*, Oct. 28,

1994.
101. Broadcast on *Voice of Israel Radio*, Nov. 5, 1994.
102. "Police detain journalists," *Jerusalem Post*, Oct. 14, 1994.
103. *Maoz* newsletter, Dec. 1994, p.1.
104. "Gaza journalist, brother arrested," *Jerusalem Post*, Oct. 28, 1994.
105. Ibid.
106. "Terminology—the ultimate weapon," *Jerusalem Post International Edition*, Feb. 27, 1993.
107. "Symbol of struggle never lost faith," *New Zealand Herald*, Oct. 17, 1994.
108. Ibid.
109. "Five die as Gaza mob turns against troops." Ibid., July 16, 1994.
110. "Palestinian Police deliberately shot at us," *Jerusalem Post*, July 18, 1994.

Chapter 10

1. "A nation unlike any other," *Jerusalem Post*, May 15, 1994.
2. Spoken to world renowned *Dry Bones* cartoonist Ya'akov Kirschen by a supporter of the peace process. Printed in *Middle East Intelligence Digest*, Oct. 1994, p.2.).
3. Shulamit Aloni speaking in defense of Shimon Peres who had angered religious MKs by criticizing King David. *Voice of Israel Radio*, Dec. 18, 1994.
4. "Statements by Aloni that have angered Shas," *Jerusalem Post*, May 10, 1993.
5. Ibid.
6. "Stock Market bulls run wild." Ibid., June 25, 1992.
7. "Figuring out the elections. Who voted for whom – and why." Ibid., July 10, 1992.
8. Eban, *Personal Witness*, p.648.
9. "Figuring out the elections. Who voted for whom – and why," *Jerusalem Post*, July 10, 1992.
10. "Likud urges no-confidence,"Ibid., Jan. 12, 1993.
11. Ibid.
12. Ibid.
13. "Ben-Porat blasts election financing. Heaviest fines to Labor and Shas." Ibid., Jan. 12, 1993.
14. Ibid.
15. Ibid.
16. Ibid.
17. "Likud urges no-confidence." Ibid.
18. Ibid.
19. Ibid.
20. Ibid.
21. "Undermined by Scandal, Israel's Labor Party Shows Signs of Falling Apart," *International Herald Tribune*, March 13, 1995.
22. Alan E. Shapiro writing in "The right to back off," *Jerusalem Post*, Jan. 15, 1993.
23. "Arab vote helped Labor to victory." Ibid., June 26, 1992.

Chapter Notes

24. *The Jerusalem Institute For Western Defense: Periodic New Digest from the Arab World and Iran,* Digest 5, May 1994, p.1.
25. "It's the last time I vote for Darawshe," *Jerusalem Post,* Nov. 29, 1992.
26. "The settlers are our calamity ...". Ibid., Aug. 26, 1992
27. "Harish orders probe of Mahameed." Ibid., Dec. 29, 1992.
28. "Knesset votes to suspend Mahameed's travel privileges." Ibid., Jan. 7, 1993.
29. "Israeli Arab loyalties." Ibid., Dec. 29, 1992.
30. "Gov't decisions invalid — Goren," *Jerusalem Post International Edition,* Jan. 22, 1994.
31. "'Spectacular' Court Trial," Arm of Salvation *Ministry & Prayer Update,* Sept. 1994, p.4.
32. Ibid.
33. Ibid., p.6.
34. Rabin addressing the Knesset on Oct. 3, 1994.
35. Rabin quoted in "Rabin's giving away of the Golan," *Jerusalem Post,* Dec. 3, 1993.
36. "Fighting back," *Middle East Intelligence Digest,* Oct. 1994, p.4.).
37. Rabin quoted in "Rabin's giving away of the Golan," *Jerusalem Post,* Dec. 3, 1993.
38. Ibid.
39. Ibid.
40. Ibid.
41. "Fighting back," *Middle East Intelligence Digest,* Oct. 1994, p.4.).
42. Rabin to Egypt's President Hosni Mubarak on May 30, 1994. Reported in "Grandma's tales as told by Rabin," *Jerusalem Post International Edition,* June 18, 1994.
43. Rabin to Egypt's President Hosni Mubarak on May 30, 1994. Reported in "A question of credibility." Ibid., June 18, 1994.
44. Yesha Report. Reprinted in "I changed my mind," *First Fruits of Zion,* Jan. 1995, p.7.
45. "Rabin: Golan settlers can 'spin like propellers," *Jerusalem Post,* June 8, 1993.
46. "Labor MKs given rough reception by Golan activists." Ibid., Sept. 23, 1994.
47. Ibid.
48. Ibid.
49. "A luxury we can't afford." Ibid., Nov. 23, 1993.
50. According to the latest government survey broadcast on *Voice of Israel Radio,* Jan. 14, 1995, there are more than 140,000 Jews living in Gaza, Judea and Samaria.
51. Ibid.
52. "Moral equivalence," *Jerusalem Post,* Nov. 1, 1993.
53. "Rabin's unwanted child." Ibid.
54. Ibid.
55. Ibid.
56. "'Let the People Decide:' Israelis Protest Accord with PLO," *The Yesha Report,* Sept.–Oct. 1993, p2.

Chapter Notes

57. "What 'Peace Process'?," *Jerusalem Post*, Dec. 24, 1993.
58. "The polarization danger." Ibid., Dec. 9, 1993.
59. "'Let the People Decide:' Israelis Protest Accord with PLO," *The Yesha Report*, Sept.–Oct. 1993, p2.
60. Ibid.
61. Ibid.
62. "Wombs and weapons," *Jerusalem Post*, Oct. 14, 1994.
63. Ibid.
64. Ibid.
65. A spokesman commenting on the force used against Anat Cohen. Ibid.
66. Ibid.
67. Ibid.
68. "Shahal versus Ida Nudel," *Jerusalem Post*, Jan. 24, 1995.
69. Ibid.
70. Ibid.
71. Ibid.
72. Ibid.
73. Ibid.
74. "Amending a prayer to today's headlines." Ibid., Oct. 1, 1993.
75. Ibid.
76. Ibid.
77. Ibid.
78. "A luxury we can't afford." Ibid., Nov. 23, 1993.
79. Eve Harrow interviewed by *Jerusalem Post International Edition*, Feb. 12, 1994.
80. *Voice of Israel Radio*, July 25, 1994.
81. "Rabin's unwanted child," *Jerusalem Post*, Nov. 1, 1993.
82. "Talks show Shas in Gov't, UTJ close, NRP still talking." Ibid., July 6, 1992.
83. "Left and right parties oppose referendum idea," *Jerusalem Post International Edition*, Jan. 29, 1994.
84. "Bills on Golan concessions defeated," *Jerusalem Post*, April 28, 1994.
85. "Rabin caves in." Ibid., Aug. 30, 1993.
86. In "Going All The Way?" *Jerusalem Post Magazine*, Dec. 10, 1993, Steve Rodan interviewed senior Labor Party officials who confirmed that Rabin and Peres plan a full withdrawal to the 1967 borders and beyond. "They don't admit it publicly" said a senior official close to Peres, "They don't think the Israeli public is ready yet." And on October 19, 1993 says Rodan, Likud Knesset member Eliahu Ben-Elissar looked Rabin 'straight in the eye' and said: 'The policy of your government will lead to the establishment of a Palestinian state along the 1949 armistice lines. And in the end, along the Golan Heights, the border will be set along the lines of the French and British Mandates.' Rabin did not reply." And it was reported in "Zvilli: There will be a Palestinian state by the year 2000," *Jerusalem Post International Edition*, Feb. 19, 1994, that the Labor Party secretary-general Nissim Zvilli "predicted that, by the year 2000, a Palestinian state will be established in the [Israeli administered] territories."

87. "Jerusalem not open to negotiation," *In Jerusalem,* July 17, 1992.
88. "Rabin affirms Jerusalem stand," *Jerusalem Post,* June 27, 1994.
89. "Kahanism and pragmatism." Ibid., Oct. 21, 1994.
90. "Labor MKs, PLO leaders to discuss dividing Jerusalem." Ibid., June 25, 1994.
91. *Voice of Israel Radio,* Dec. 19, 1994.
92. Ibid.
93. "Rabin praises US role in peace process," *Jerusalem Post,* Aug. 10, 1993.
94. "Jerusalem not open to negotiation," *In Jerusalem,* July 17, 1992.
95. "With the clear eyes of youth," *Jerusalem Post,* July 2, 1994.
96. "Peres letter in October 93 encouraged Palestinian institutions in capital." Ibid., June 7, 1994.
97. "Rabin's pretend world." Ibid., June 8, 1994.
98. "Government—Israeli Style," Arm of Salvation *Ministry & Prayer Update,* Sept. 1994, p.7.
99. Ibid.
100. "Opposition furor over 'Gaza First' plan," *Jerusalem Post,* Aug. 30, 1993.
101. "Shimon Peres: We are not on Assad's agenda." Ibid., Dec. 23, 1994.
102. "The Vultures Gather," Arm of Salvation *Ministry & Prayer Update,* Jan. 1994, p.2.
103. Adam Shindron quoted in "Dancing in the park," *Jerusalem Post,* Sept. 14, 1993.
104. Ibid.
105. Ellen and Nir Shmueloff, "Israel's Rallying Cry 'Jerusalem Must Stay United' Loses Steam," *Wall Street Journal,* Nov. 3, 1993.
106. "78% of Capitol Youth Oppose Golan Withdrawal," *In Jerusalem,* Oct.14, 1994.
107. Ibid.
108. "Majority of Israelis want PLO officials tried," *Jerusalem Post International Edition,* July 2, 1994.
109. "Support for peace talks drops," *Jerusalem Post,* June 4, 1994.
110. Ibid.
111. "Poll shows majority of Israelis oppose full Golan withdrawal." Ibid., Oct. 7, 1994.
112. "A startling poll," *Jerusalem Post International Edition,* May 9, 1993.
113. Ibid.
114. "TA election a referendum on peace, Rabin says," *Jerusalem Post,* Oct. 27, 1993.
115. "Rabin throws his weight behind Kollek." Ibid., Oct. 25, 1993.
116. "North Tel Aviv's betrayal, Jerusalem's haredi revenge." Ibid., Nov. 5, 1993.
117. "Olmert Takes the Town," *In Jerusalem,* Nov. 5, 1993.
118. Ibid.
119. "North Tel Aviv's betrayal, Jerusalem's haredi revenge," *Jerusalem Post,* Nov. 5, 1993.
120. "PM: Labor must change to survive." Ibid., Jan. 6, 1995.
121. Ibid.
122. "Israel TV's surrender to diktat," *Jerusalem Post International Edition,*

Chapter Notes 333

      April 9, 1994.
123. Ibid.
124. Ibid.
125. Ibid.
126. Ibid.
127. "Foreign Ministry declares war on 'Post.'" Ibid., Feb. 5, 1994.
128. Ibid.
129. "'Post': Ministry lied over subscriptions." Ibid., Jan. 29, 1994.
130. "Foreign Ministry declares war on 'Post.'" Ibid., Feb. 5, 1994.
131. Ibid.
132. Ibid.
133. "Israel Radio suspends editor for quoting from 'Post' story," *Jerusalem Post*, Dec. 13, 1994.
134. "Let's watch our words." Ibid., Nov. 19, 1993.
135. Ibid.
136. "Government—Israeli Style," Arm of Salvation *Ministry & Prayer Update*, Sept. 1994, p.6.
137. Ibid.
138. Ibid.
139. "Likud blasts Labor's alleged 'hiring of demonstrators,'" *Jerusalem Post*, May 6, 1994.
140. Ibid.
141. Ibid.
142. "Abu Mazen's book: Dog-eared revelations with little bite despite the barking." Ibid., Jan. 13, 1995.
143. "Peres-Rabin clash 'not like old days,' says Zadok." Ibid., Dec. 6, 1988.
144. "Going all the way?" Ibid., Dec. 10, 1993
145. Ibid.
146. Ibid.
147. Ibid.
148. *Voice of Israel Radio*, Jan. 7, 1995.
149. "Labor reaction may do more damage than book itself," *Jerusalem Post*, Jan. 13, 1995.
150. Ibid.
151. "The Arafat bombshell," *Jerusalem Post International Edition*, May 18, 1994.
152. Ibid.
153. "Premier again denies secret deal with Syria." Ibid., Jan. 16. 1993.
154. "Behind closed doors," *Jerusalem Post Magazine*, Dec. 2, 1994.
155. Ibid.
156. "Aloni: Say farewell to Golan," *Jerusalem Post International Edition*, April 9, 1994.
157. Reported in *Dispatch From Jerusalem*, Sept.–Oct., 1994, p.10.
158. "Beilin: Pursue peace process as if Labor won't win next election," *Jerusalem Post*, Jan. 13, 1995.
159. Lt.-Gen. Ehud Barak quoted in "In their own words," *Middle East Intelligence Digest*, Oct. 1994, p.5.

160. Ibid.
161. Ibid.
162. "Shahak to be appointed next chief of general staff," *Jerusalem Post*, Oct. 7, 1994.
163. *The Jerusalem Institute For Western Defense: Periodic New Digest from the Arab World and Iran*, Digest 11, Nov.1994, p.1.
164. "Stark realities against a barren hilltop," *Jerusalem Post*, Jan. 6, 1995.
165. *The Jerusalem Institute For Western Defense: Periodic New Digest from the Arab World and Iran*, Digest 11, Nov.1994, p.1.
166. "A Zionist Tragedy," CFI's *Zion Quarterly*, 4th Quarter 1994, p.3.
167. "Behind Rabin's Beilin barb," *Jerusalem Post*, Dec. 9, 1988.
168. "Good riddance to Gaza," *Jerusalem Post International Edition*, May 14, 1994.
169. Mark Halter quoted in "Peres Sell Jerusalem To The Vatican," *Inside Israel*, September 1994.
170. "Israel, Vatican establish full diplomatic ties," *Jerusalem Post*, June 16, 1994.
171. Henry Kissinger in *A World Restored*, cited in *Jerusalem Post International Edition*, Feb. 19, 1994.
172. "Netanyahu: Gov't planning redivision of Jerusalem," *Jerusalem Post*, May 18, 1994.
173. Kett quoted by Ariel Sharon in "Dangerous government." Ibid., Jan. 20, 1993.
174. "The army's intervention." Ibid., Feb. 7, 1994.
175. Ibid.
176. Netanyahu, *A Place Among The Nations*, p.286.
177. Ibid., p.287.
178. "Israel's water," *Jerusalem Post*, Dec. 23, 1994.
179. "IDF brass ignored Agranat findings, repeated mistakes." Ibid., Jan. 6, 1995.
180. "Aloni: Machpela cave not sacred to Jews." Ibid., March 25, 1994.
181. "Rabin's realistic vision." Ibid.,Aug. 14, 1992.
182. Ibid.
183. "Peres: Scud tests show Syrian power and intent. Gur warns Damascus of Israel response if attacked." Ibid., Aug. 14, 1992.
184. "Rabin calls for direct negotiations with Syrians," *Jerusalem Post International Edition*, July 2, 1994.
185. i.e. "Defense in depth," *Jerusalem Post*, June 7, 1994.
186. Taken from the jacket: Robert Slater, *Rabin of Israel* (London: Robson, 1993).
187. Yaacov Shimoni, *Biographical Dictionary of the Middle East* (New York: Facts On File, 1991), p.190.
188. Ibid.
189. i.e. Ibid., p.189. Susan Hattis Rolef Ed., *Political Dictionary of the State of Israel*, (Jerusalem: Jerusalem Publishing House, 1993), p.257.
190. "Is he a man of straw or a man of iron," Advertisement inserted by the Women in Green, *Jerusalem Post International Edition*, June 25, 1994.
191. Slater, *Rabin of Israel*, pp.70,71.

Chapter Notes 335

192. Sacher, *A History of Israel*, p.631.
193. Eban, *Personal Witness*, p.382.
194. Ezer Weizman, *On Eagles' Wings* (Jerusalem: Steimatzky's, 1976). Cited in "Is he a man of straw or a man of iron," Advertisement inserted by the Women in Green, *Jerusalem Post International Edition*, June 25, 1994.
195. Weizman, *On Eagles' Wings*, p.211. Cited in Slater, *Rabin of Israel*, p.130.
196. Eban, *Personal Witness*, p.462.
197. "Agranat report's crucial, unheeded lesson," *Jerusalem Post*, Jan. 6, 1995.
198. "IDF brass ignored Agranat findings, repeated mistakes." Ibid., Jan. 6, 1995.
199. Ibid.
200. "A misplacing of confidence." Ibid., May 10, 1994.
201. Ibid.
202. *The Jerusalem Institute For Western Defense: Periodic New Digest from the Arab World and Iran*, Digest 6, June 1994, p.3.
203. Slater, *Rabin of Israel*, p.365.
204. Yaacov Shimoni, *Biographical Dictionary of the Middle East*, p.183.
205. "Behind Rabin's Beilin barb," *Jerusalem Post*, Dec. 9, 1988.
206. Moshe Sharett's Personal Diary, 1957. Vol. 8, p.2301.
207. "Kissinger: Peres is on an emotional binge," *Jerusalem Post*, Sept. 15, 1993.
208. *Voice of Israel Radio*, Sept. 4?, 1994.
209. *Middle East Intelligence Digest*, Nov. 1994, p.1.
210. *Voice of Israel Radio*, May 4, 1994.
211. *Webster's Unabridged Dictionary*.
212. Ibid.
213. "Peres: Palestinian Police has prevented terror attacks," *Jerusalem Post*, Jan. 24, 1995.
214. Ibid.
215. "Yasser, puppet-master." Ibid., June 30, 1994.
216. Ibid.
217. "Israel, PLO to sign agreements today. Rejectionist groups step up terror campaign in protest. Signing at 5 p.m. Israel time." Ibid., Sept. 13, 1993.
218. "Rabin and Peres expected to hold reconciliation meeting early next week." Ibid., July 29, 94.
219. Ibid.
220. Ibid.
221. "Norway's No-Show," *In Jerusalem*, Dec. 9, 1994.
222. David Bar-Illan, Chairman of the meeting and Executive Editor of *Jerusalem Post*, speaking with the author the following day.
223. "On toeing the line," *Jerusalem Post*, Dec. 23, 1994.
224. Moshe Kohn writing in "Of peace and redemption." Ibid., Oct. 21, 1994.
225. "Security at highest level in Oslo." Ibid., Dec. 9, 1994.
226. Kaare Kristiansen speaking at the Renaissance Hotel, Jerusalem, Dec. 10, 1994.
227. Ibid.
228. Ibid.
229. Ibid.

230. Ibid.
231. Ibid.
232. "Give That Man A Hand," *In Jerusalem*, Dec. 23, 1994.
233. Shimon Peres, in an interview with *Voice of Israel Radio*, Jan. 21, 1995.
234. In the March 6, cabinet meeting and reported in "Hebron's Jews," *Jerusalem Post*, March 7, 1994.
235. "PM: Goal of peace is to separate Israelis, Palestinians." Ibid., 1995.
236. Ibid.
237. *The Jerusalem Institute For Western Defense: Periodic New Digest from the Arab World and Iran*, Digest 6, Dec. 1994, p.1.
238. "Rabin to military: Make plowshares," *Jerusalem Post International Edition*, June 25, 1994.
239. "Large cuts proposed in army service." Ibid., Jan. 15, 1994.
240. "Police uncertain whether 2 terrorists involved in atrocity," *Jerusalem Post*, Jan. 24, 1995.
241. "A game of make-believe," Ibid.
242. Ibid.
243. "PM: Goal of peace is to separate Israelis, Palestinians," Ibid.

Chapter 11

1. This *hadith* appears in several canonical Moslem collections. Cited in Peters, *From Time Immemorial*, p.144.
2. Lafin, *Fedayeen*, p.91.
3. *Pravda*, Sept. 2, 1964. Referring specifically to the Soviet Union's occupation of Eastern Europe during and after WW II when it had defeated Nazi invading forces. Quoted in "Strong Stand," *Jerusalem Post International Edition*, Jan. 16, 1993.
4. Quoted in "Egypt's strange game," *Jerusalem Post*, Sept. 30, 1994.
5. *The Jerusalem Institute For Western Defense: Periodic New Digest from the Arab World and Iran*, Digest 10, Oct.1994, p.7.
6. "Manifest stupidity," *Jerusalem Post International Edition*, Jan. 22, 1994.
7. *Voice of Israel Radio*, Nov. 29, 1994.
8. "A vain search for signs," *Jerusalem Post*, Nov. 7, 1993.
9. Reuter report. "Sudan offers armed Islamists a rare chance to meet." Ibid., April 4, 1995.
10. Brig. Gen. Ya'akov Ami Dror in an interview with *Jerusalem Post*, Sept. 1994. Quoted in "They Said ...," *First Fruits of Zion*, Jan. 1995, p.7.
11. Brig. Gen. Ya'akov Ami Dror in an interview with *Jerusalem Post*, Sept. 1994. Quoted in "No Arab leader has accepted peace—top intelligence man, *Middle East Intelligence Digest*, Oct. 1994, p.7.
12. Ibid.
13. "Manifest stupidity," *Jerusalem Post International Edition*, Jan. 22, 1994.
14. Ibid.
15. Quoted in "Gaza—soft underbelly of the Jewish state," *Middle East Intelligence Digest*, Feb. 1993, p.4.
16. Ibid., June 12, 1992.
17. "Egyptians feel left out of the celebration," *Jerusalem Post*, Oct. 28, 1994.

Chapter Notes

18. *Voice of Israel Radio*, Dec. 20, 1994.
19. Quoted in "Repeated violations," *Jerusalem Post International Edition*, Jan. 22, 1994.
20. Ibid.
21. "Peace in the Middle East (2)." Ibid., May 7, 1994.
22. Faika Musrati describing her treatment by Egyptian police in "Egypt frees four Israelis held for espionage." Ibid., May 16, 1992.
23. "Peace in the Middle East (2)." Ibid., May 7, 1994.
24. "Cairo conference closed to Israeli scientists." Ibid., Jan. 8, 1994.
25. *Voice of Israel Radio*, Nov. 24, 1994.
26. *Ma'ariv*, Nov. 18, 1994.
27. *Voice of Israel Radio*, March 27, 1995.
28. Ibid., Dec. 1st, 1994.
29. Ibid.
30. "Warm ties compete with chill factor," *Jerusalem Post*, Nov. 25, 1994.
31. *Voice of Israel Radio*, Nov. 24, 1994.
32. *The Jerusalem Institute For Western Defense: Periodic New Digest from the Arab World and Iran*, Digest 1, Jan. 1995, p.3.
33. "Peace in the Middle East (2)," *Jerusalem Post International Edition*, May 7, 1994.
34. Bar-Illan, *Eye on the Media*, p.177.
35. Ibid.
36. Ibid.
37. Ibid.
38. "Peace in the Middle East (2)," *Jerusalem Post International Edition*, May 7, 1994.
39. Hassan Fouad, deputy editor-in-chief of *Al-Ahram*, quoted in "Boycott keeps Egyptians away." Ibid., Dec. 26, 1992.
40. "'Al-Ahram' poll: Most Egyptians shun Israel despite 15 years of peace," *Jerusalem Post*, Dec. 30, 1994.
41. "Survey: Most Egyptians favor cold peace." Ibid., May 3, 1995.
42. Ibid.
43. Ibid.
44. "The battle for parity," *Jerusalem Post Magazine*, March 11, 1994.
45. "Egyptians improve army 'impressively,'" *Jerusalem Post International Edition*, June 25, 1994.
46. "The battle for parity," *Jerusalem Post Magazine*, March 11, 1994.
47. *The Jerusalem Institute For Western Defense: Periodic New Digest from the Arab World and Iran*, Digest 7, July 1994, p.3.
48. "The battle for parity," *Jerusalem Post Magazine*, March 11, 1994.
49. *The Jerusalem Institute For Western Defense: Periodic New Digest from the Arab World and Iran*, Digest 7, July 1994, p.3.
50. "The battle for parity," *Jerusalem Post Magazine*, March 11, 1994
51. Ibid.
52. Ibid.
53. "The Samson Option," *Middle East Intelligence Digest*, March/April 1995, p.5.

Chapter Notes

54. "Egypt's agenda - and Israel's nuclear shield," *The Source*, a Supplement of Ibid., Jan. 1995.
55. "Egypt's strange game," *Jerusalem Post*, Sept. 30, 1994.
56. *The Jerusalem Institute For Western Defense: Periodic New Digest from the Arab World and Iran*, Digest 7, July 1994, p.3.
57. Ibid., Digest 1, Jan. 1995, p.1.
58. Ibid., p.3.
59. Labor MK Ra'anan Cohen quoted in "Egypt sheds neutrality," *Middle East Intelligence Digest*, Feb. 1995, p.1.
60. Dov Shilansky quoted in Ibid.
61. "The battle for parity," *Jerusalem Post Magazine*, March 11, 1994.
62. "Whirlwind on the rise?," *Middle East Intelligence Digest*, March/April 1995, p.1.
63. Ibid.
64. "The next war has begun," *Jerusalem Post*, Jan. 27, 1995.
65. See Chap. 5, p.100,101.
66. Ibid., p.100.
67. Ibid., p.100,101.
68. Farouk Khadoumi quoted on the BBC Arabic service, April 5, 1989
69. Farouk Khadoumi speaking in Algeria and quoted by Robert Franklin in "The armed struggle continues," CFI's *Zion Quarterly*, 1st Quarter 1995.
70. "Poll: Many Palestinians back attacks against Israelis," *Jerusalem Post*, Jan. 27, 1995.
71. *Voice of Israel Radio*, Jan. 31, 1995.
72. "Urge to kill," CFI's *Israel News Digest*, Jan. 1995, p.4.
73. Ibid.
74. "Pact with the Devil," CFI's *Zion Quarterly*, 1st Quarter 1995, p.1.
75. A Gazan Arab interviewed by Robert Franklin. Ibid.
76. "Arafat retracts statement on meetings with Israeli officials, *Jerusalem Post*, July 14, 1993.
77. "King Hussein twice hosted Shabbat meals for Shamir," *Jerusalem Post International Edition*, Feb. 12, 1994.
78. Ibid.
79. Ibid.
80. Ibid.
81. See Chap. 5, p.75.
82. "Hussein and Arafat in conflict," *Jerusalem Post*, Oct. 28, 1994.
83. *The Jerusalem Institute For Western Defense: Periodic New Digest from the Arab World and Iran*, Digest 10, Oct.1994, p.6.
84. "Treaty with Jordan," CFI's *Israel News Digest*, Nov. 1994, p.1.
85. *The World Almanac and Book of Facts*, p.820.
86. See Chap. 7, p.132.
87. "Hussein: between a rock and a hard place," *Middle East Intelligence Digest*, Aug. 1994, p.5.
88. "Across the Jordan," CFI's *Israel News Digest*, Dec. 1994, p.4.
89. *Voice of Israel Radio*, Aug. 8, 1994.
90. *Reuter* report published in "Historic treaty centrepiece of Clinton's trip,"

Chapter Notes

      New Zealand Herald, Oct. 27, 1994.
91. *Middle East Intelligence Digest*, Dec. 1994, p.3.
92. *Voice of Israel Radio*, Aug. 8, 1994.
93. *Israel News Digest*, Dec. 1994, p.4.
94. Ibid.
95. *Voice of Israel Radio*, Dec. 21, 1994.
96. Ibid., Dec. 27, 1994.
97. "MKs do Amman — royally," *Jerusalem Post*, Feb. 10, 1995.
98. "'Very senior' source forewarns: 'Hussein's days are numbered.'" Ibid., Sept. 9, 1990.
99. Ibid.
100. *Associated Press* report, March 6, 1995, Quoted in "True colors," *Middle East Intelligence Digest*, March/April 1995, p.11.
101. "Mufti wants jihad," *Jerusalem Post*, May 3, 1995
102. "Syrian signs of change." Ibid., July 22, 1993.
103. "Mubarak: Syria understands peace means full normalization." Ibid., Nov. 25, 1993.
104. "Assad ready for normalization after withdrawal." Ibid., May 3, 1994.
105. "Assad smiling." Ibid., Jan. 17, 1994.
106. "Clinton to meet Assad in January." Ibid., Dec. 10, 1993.
107. "'Syria won't promise peace for Golan.'" Ibid., Feb. 11, 1993.
108. "Out of Damascus," CFI's *Israel News Digest*, Nov. 1994.
109. "Assad refuses to clarify 'full peace' for Clinton," *Jerusalem Post*, June 10, 1993.
110. "Peace of the brave." Ibid., Jan. 31, 1994.
111. "Assad smiling." Ibid., Jan. 17, 1994.
112. Ibid.
113. Ibid.
114. *Voice of Israel Radio*, March 28, 1995, quoting a leading government controlled Syrian newspaper.
115. "The Golan under Syria — Israelis remember," *Middle East Intelligence Digest*, Dec. 1992, p.6.
116. "'Moments of tension' in Clinton-Assad talks. 'U.S. leader fascinated to meet notorious character,'" *Reuter* report published in *Jerusalem Post*, Jan. 17, 1994.
117. "Day out in Damascus." Ibid., Oct. 28, 1994.
118. Ibid.
119. "Don't mention that Assad is from a minority," *Maoz Newsletter*, Oct. 1994, p.3.
120. Ibid.
121. Ibid.
122. See Chap. 1, p.18.
123. See Chap. 8, p.167.
124. From the jacket of Katz, *Israel Versus Jibril*.
125. Ibid., p.3.
126. "Day out in Damascus," *Jerusalem Post*, Oct. 28, 1994.
127. Expel Islamic Jihad, US urges Syria." Ibid., Jan. 21, 1995.

128. Zalman Shoval, a former ambassador to the U.S. quoted in "Continuing violence in Lebanon shows up mistaken assumptions about Syria," *Jerusalem Post International Edition*, April 2, 1994.
129. "International network," CFI's *Israel News Digest*, Jan. 1995, p.4.
130. *Voice of Israel Radio*, Jan. 25, 1995.
131. Shimoni, *Biographical Dictionary of the Middle East*, p.38.
132. Ibid.
133. "Syrian drug connection," *Jerusalem Post*, April 4, 1994.
134. Ibid.
135. Ibid.
136. Ibid.
137. Ibid.
138. Ibid.
139. *Middle East Intelligence Digest*, Feb. 1994, p.3.
140. "'We want peace, says Syria," *Middle East Intelligence Digest*, Dec. 1992, p.5.
141. Ibid.
142. Ibid.
143. Ibid.
144. "German defense minister visits," *Jerusalem Post International Edition*, May 8, 1993.
145. "Military Views," CFI's *Israel News Digest*, Oct. 1994.
146. Ibid.
147. Quoted in "Dynamic Duo," *Jerusalem Post Magazine*, Oct. 14, 1994.
148. Ibid.
149. *Associated Press* report published in "Syria: War against Israel to last for ever," *The Bangkok Post*, March 10, 1990.
150. *Reuter* report published in "Syria urges withdrawal," *New Zealand Herald*, Dec. 28, 1994.
151. "Reality and Assad's Image," *Jerusalem Post*, May 29, 1994.
152. Ibid.
153. Ibid.
154. *The Jerusalem Institute For Western Defense: Periodic New Digest from the Arab World and Iran*, Digest 12, Dec.1994, p.1.
155. "Sadat's opinion of Syria," *Jerusalem Post*, Oct. 7, 1994.
156. Quoted in Ibid.
157. Quoted in "Exiled Michel Aoun's mantra: Next year in Beirut." Ibid., Dec. 2, 1994.
158. Reported in "Quotes," *Dispatch From Jerusalem*, Jan. – Feb. 1995, p.10.
159. *Middle East Intelligence Digest*, Dec. 1992, p.6.
160. Ibid.
161. *Jerusalem Post*, Jan. 25, 1994. Cited in "Don't worry, be happy," *Maoz Newsletter*, Oct. 1994.
162. "Repeated violations," *Jerusalem Post International Edition*, Jan. 22, 1994.
163. Bennett, *Saga*, p.199.
164. Ibid., p.200.
165. *Time magazine*, Oct. 8, 1990, cited in Ibid., p.199.

Chapter Notes

166. *The Jerusalem Institute For Western Defense: Periodic New Digest from the Arab World and Iran*, Digest 12, Dec.1994, p.4.
167. Ibid.
168. *Al-Watan Al-Arabi* (published in Paris). Translated and printed in Ibid., Digest 8, Aug. 1994, p.7.
169. "Iraq still making chemical weapons, *Jerusalem Post International Edition*, Feb. 19, 1994.
170. Reported by the *New York Times* and broadcast on *Voice of Israel Radio*, Feb. 16, 1995.
171. "Palestinians to Buy Oil From Iraq," *Dispatch From Jerusalem*, Jan. – Feb. 1995, p.10.
172. *The Jerusalem Institute For Western Defense: Periodic News Digest from the Arab World and Iran*, Digest 2, Feb. 1995, p.7.
173. Reported by the *New York Times* and broadcast on *Voice of Israel Radio*, Feb. 16, 1995.
174. Broadcast on Iraqi Radio, Jan. 5, 1995; reported on *Voice of Israel Radio*, and quoted in "Saddam: Arabs should rocket Israel, *Jerusalem Post*, Jan. 6, 1995.
175. See Chap. 3, p.58.
176. "Buenos Aires again," *Jerusalem Post*, July 19, 1994.
177. Broadcast on *Voice of Israel Radio*, May 12, 1994.
178. Extract from an interview with Subhi Al-Tufeyli published in *L'Orient du Jour*, July 30, 1994.
179. "War games," CFI's *Israel News Digest*, Feb. 1995, p.4.
180. "Watchdog reporter," *Jerusalem Post Magazine*, April 22, 1994.
181. Ibid.
182. "Iran: Going for it," Ibid.
183. "Local experts: Unclear when Iran will become nuclear power," *Jerusalem Post*, Jan. 6. 1995.
184. Ibid.
185. See Chap. 4, p.60.
186. Mu'ammar Qaddafi's speech on June 21, 1994 and reported by the *Libyan News Agency*, June 23, 1994. Quoted in *The Jerusalem Institute For Western Defense: Periodic New Digest from the Arab World and Iran*, Digest 10, Oct.1994, p.2.
187. Ibid.
188. Ibid.
189. Yossi Beilin interviewed on *Voice of Israel Radio*, July, 15, 1994.
190. *The Jerusalem Institute For Western Defense: Periodic New Digest from the Arab World and Iran*, Digest 10, Oct.1994, p.7.
191. Shmuel Katz writing in "Beware the prophets of peace," *Jerusalem Post International Edition*, Jan. 8, 1994.
192. Quoted in "Russia demands say on status of Jerusalem," *Jerusalem Post*, Aug. 26, 1994.
193. Ibid.
194. Ibid.
195. "Future Intentions," CFI's *Israel News Digest*, Sept. 1993, p.3.

196. *Voice of Israel Radio*, Oct. 22, 1994.
197. "Russia rejects US appeal on Iran nuclear deal," *Jerusalem Post*, April 4, 1995.
198. *The Jerusalem Institute For Western Defense: Periodic New Digest from the Arab World and Iran,* Digest 8, Aug.1994, p.10.
199. Sergei Kapitza, interviewed by *U.S. News & World Report*, April 1992. Cited by Bennett, *Saga*, p.126,127.
200. "Syrian grand strategy," *Jerusalem Post International Edition*, Feb. 19, 1994.
201. "Palestinian leaders: Baker promised us a state," *Jerusalem Post*, Feb. 7, 1993.
202. "The hazards of diaspora living." Ibid., March 10, 1992.
203. "Golan: more than geography." Ibid., March 5, 1993.
204. "Who needs a crisis with the US?," *Jerusalem Post International Edition*, March 21, 1992.
205. "Garbage truck at Israel's door," *Jerusalem Post*, May 27, 1994.
206. Ibid.
207. Ibid.
208. Ibid.
209. Ibid.
210. *Middle East Intelligence Digest*, Feb. 1994, p.3.
211. "The American connection," CFI's Zion Quarterly, 4th Quarter 1994, p.4.
212. "Pact with Syria before 1995, *Middle East Intelligence Digest*, Dec. 1994, p.7.
213. "Clinton: Bush will ok guarantees to win votes," *Jerusalem Post*, June 4, 1992.
214. "Disney world comes to the desert for a day." Ibid., Oct. 28, 1994.
215. Ibid.
216. "Israel, Jordan sign treaty. Peace sealed in gala Arava ceremony." Ibid., Oct. 27, 1994.
217. "Well, you could have fooled us," *Middle East Intelligence Digest*, Feb. 1995, p.8.
218. Ibid.
219. Ibid.
220. Ibid.
221. Ibid.
222. Ibid.
223. Ibid.
224. Ibid.
225. Ibid.
226. Ibid.
227. See Chap. 5, p.74; Chap. 6, p.111.
228. Sacher, *A History of Israel,* p.631.
229. Ibid., pp.630,631.
230. See Chap. 8, p.178.
231. Reported in "Pact with Syria before 1995, *Middle East Intelligence Digest*, Dec. 1994, p.7.

232. Ibid.
233. Sacher, *A History of Israel*, Vol. II, p.206.
234. Ibid.
235. "Netanyahu: 'I have details of Golan plan,'" *Jerusalem Post International Edition*, Feb. 27, 1993.
236. Bruce Brill in "One man's agony after the fact," *Jerusalem Post*, Oct. 23, 1992. Cited in Bennett, *Saga*, p.142.
237. See Chap. 10, p.223.
238. Ibid., cited in Bennett, *Saga*, p.143.
239. "Pardon Pollard," Dec. 19, 1993.
240. "Pollard pardon due," *Jerusalem Post*, Dec. 28, 1992.
241. Ibid.
242. "Pardon Pollard." Ibid., Dec. 19, 1993.
243. "Pollard pardon due." Ibid., Dec. 28, 1992.
244. Ibid.
245. "Justice, not vengeance." Ibid., Aug. 20, 1993.
246. Ibid.
247. Ibid.
248. Ibid.
249. Ibid.
250. Ibid.
251. *The Jerusalem Institute For Western Defense: Periodic News Digest from the Arab World and Iran*, Digest 2, Feb. 1995, p.2.
252. "How to destroy friends and help enemies," *The Jerusalem Institute For Western Defense: Periodic News Digest from the Arab World and Iran*, Bulletin No. 1, March 1995, p.7.
253. See Chap. 5, p.102.
254. See Chap. 10, p.229,230.
255. See Chap. 5, p.98.
256. "Arab Poll on Peace," *Messianic Times*, Summer 1994, p.11.
257. Ibid.
258. Ibid.
259. Ibid.
260. Ibid.

Chapter 12

1 Mark Twain, *The Complete Essays of Mark Twain*, Charles Neider, ed. (New York: Doubleday, 1963), p.49.
2 See Chap. 10, p.191.
3 Mahmoud Zahar interviewed by Robert Franklin and published in "An Islamic-Israeli Conflict," *Zion Quarterly*, 4th Quarter 1994, p.4.
4 Ibid.
5 Reuben Alcalay, *The Complete Hebrew-English Dictionary* (Jerusalem: Masada, 1963).
6 "Netanyahu: Likud won't honor Gaza/Jericho deal,*Jerusalem Post International Edition*, Jan. 15, 1995.
7 Cited in "The march of folly." Ibid., May 22, 1993.

8   Quoted by David Pawson in "Gods Eternal Covenant With Israel," *Tishrei*, Autumn 1992, p.24.
9   "Let's sit this administration out," *Jerusalem Post*, Sept. 17, 1991.
10 "It's time to start fighting back." Ibid., April 3, 1992.
11 "Norwegian FM Holst dies at 56," *Jerusalem Post International Edition*, Jan. 22, 1994.
12 Ibid.
13 See Chap. 11, pp. 246,248,258.
14 "From the Editor," *Middle East Intelligence Digest*, Feb. 1994, p.2.
15 Ibid.
16 "Assad lines up his options, *Jerusalem Post*, Jan. 28, 1994.
17 Freida Keets speaking in the First Assembly of God Church, Fort Meyers, Florida. Quoted in "Terror in New York at Twin Trade Towers," *Jerusalem Courier & Prophecy Digest*, Vol. 11, No. 1, p.2.
18 See Chap. 7, p.138.
19 Anwar Sadat quoted in Bennett, *When Day and Night Cease*, p.206.
20 *Associated Press* report, March 12, 1979. Quoted in Bard and Himelfarb, *Myths and Facts*, p.297.
21 Sacher, *A History of Israel*, Vol. II, p.135.
22 *The International Standard Bible Encyclopedia* (Peabody: Hendrikson, 1994), Vol. 4, p.2706.
23 *The Zondervan Encyclopedia of the Bible*, Merrill C. Tenney, Ed. (Grand Rapids: Zondervan, 1975), Vol. 2, p.770.
24 *The International Standard Bible Encyclopedia* (Peabody: Hendrikson, 1994), Vol. 2, p.1276.
25 *Zondervan Encyclopedia of the Bible*, Vol. 1, pp.865,867.
26 *International Standard Bible Encyclopedia*, Vol. 4, p.2993.
27 "The Threat of a New Islamic Alliance," *Charisma*, April, 1991, pp.54.
28 *Asian Report*. Quoted in *Kindreds*, Vol. 4, No. 4, 1993, p.4.
29 Cited in Bennett, *Saga*, p.230.
30 "Cooperation is the best defense," *Jerusalem Post*, Sept.15, 1992.
31 "Target Ready," *Jerusalem Post Magazine*, Oct. 8, 1993.
32 "'Barak' missile test successful," *Jerusalem Post*, Oct. 22, 1993.
33 "'Israel at cutting edge of technology due to Arrow.'" Ibid., June 16, 1994.
34 Adapted from "Successful First Flight of Arrow missile defense system," *Innovation*, Nov.1990. Cited in Bennett, *When Day and Night Cease*, pp.181,182.
35 "Spy satellite for Arab Emirates 'serious threat'. Defense officials claim US sale will narrow technological edge," *Jerusalem Post*, Nov. 19, 1992.
36 Ibid.
37 *Voice of Israel Radio*, April, 4, 1995.
38 Sura 2:97-98.
39 Rabin quoted on *Voice of Israel Radio*, April 18, 1995.
40 "More Scuduggery," *Jerusalem Post*, Aug. 19, 1992.
41 Ibid.
42 *Voice of Israel Radio*, Feb. 19, 1995.

BIBLIOGRAPHY

Archbold, Norma.
The Mountains of Israel: The Bible & The West Bank. Jerusalem: Phoebe's Song Publication, 1993.

Avneri, Arieh.
The Claim of Dispossession: Jewish Land Settlement and the Arabs, 1878–1948. New York: Herzl Press, 1982.

Bard, Mitchell G., and Himelfarb, Joel.
Myths and Facts: A concise record of the Arab-Israeli Conflict. Washington: Near East Report, 1992.

Bar-Illan, David.
Eye on the Media. Jerusalem: *The Jerusalem Post,* 1993.

Becker, Jill.
The PLO: The Rise and Fall of the Palestine Liberation Organization. New York: St. Martin's, 1984.

Netanyahu, Benjamin.
A Place Among The Nations: Israel and the World. New York: Bantam, 1993.

Bennett, Ramon.
When Day and Night Cease (2nd ed.). Jerusalem: Arm of Salvation, 1993.

Bennett, Ramon.
Saga: Israel and the Demise of Nations. Jerusalem: Arm of Salvation, 1993.

Berger, David. (Ed.)
History and Hate: The Dimensions of Anti-Semitism. New York: Jewish Publication Society, 1986.

Brown, Michael L.
Our Hands Are Stained With Blood: The tragic story of the "Church" and the Jewish people. Shippensburg: Destiny Image, 1992.

Comay, Michael.
Zionism, Israel, and the Palestinian Arabs. Questions and Answers. Jerusalem: Keter, 1983.

Dashti, Ali.
23Years: A Study of the Prophetic Career of Mohammad. London: George Allen & Unwin, 1985.

Dawood, N.J.
The Koran. London: Penguin 1993.

De Haas, Jacob.
History of Palestine, the Last Two Thousand Years. New York, 1934.

Dodd, Peter., and Barakat, Halim.
River Without Bridges: A Study of the Exodus of the 1967 Arab Palestinian Refugees. Beirut: Institute for Palestine Studies, 1969.
Dolan, David.
Holy War for the Promised Land. Nashville: Thomas Nelson, 1991.
Evans, Mike.
Israel—America's Key to Survival. Plainfield: Logos International, 1981.
Freud, Sigmund.
Beyond the Pleasure Principle. London: Hogarth Press, 1922.
Gonen, Amiram. (Editor-In-Chief)
The Encyclopedia of the peoples of the world. New York: Henry Holt, 1993.
Grace, Peter.
The Rape of Lebanon. Beirut: Evangelical Press, 1983.
Grant, George.
The Blood of the Moon. Brentwood: Wolgemuth & Hyatt, 1991.
Green, D.F.
Arab Theologians on Jews and Israel. Genève: Editions de l'Avenir, 1974.
Gulston, Charles.
Jerusalem: The Tragedy and the Triumph. Grand Rapids: Zondervan, 1979.
Hogg, Ian V.
Israeli War Machine: The Men; The Machines; TheTactics. London: Hamlyn, 1983.
Hull, William L.
The Fall and Rise of Israel: The Story of the Jewish People During the time of their Dispersal and Regathering. Grand Rapids: Zondervan, 1954.
King Hussein.
My War with Israel. New York: Morrow, 1969.
Kah, Gary H.
En Route to Global Occupation. Lafayette, LA: Huntington House, 1992.
Katz, Samuel M.
Battleground: Facts and Fantasy in Palestine. New York: Bantam, 1973.
Katz, Samuel M.
Israel Versus Jibril: The Thirty-Year War Against a Master Terrorist. New York: Paragon House, 1993.
Keretzky, Frank.
The Media's Propaganda War Against Israel. New York: Weidenfeld & Nicolson, 1984.
Kierman, Thomas.
Yasir Arafat. London: Sphere Books, 1976.

Bibliography

Krantz, Les.
Facts that matter: Everything you need to know about everything. Los Angeles: Price Stern Sloan, 1993.

Laffin, John.
Fedayeen: The Arab-Israeli Dilemma. London: Cassell, 1973.

Laffin, John.
The Arab Mind. London: Cassell, 1975.

Laffin, John.
The PLO Connections. London: Transworld, 1982.

Lederman, Jim.
Battle Lines: The American Media and the Intifada. New York: Henry Holt, 1992.

Lewis, Bernard.
The Political Language of Islam. Chicago: University of Chicago, 1988.

Lewis, Bernard.
The Arabs in History, 4th rev. ed. New York: Harper-Colophon Books, 1966.

Liebler, Isi.
The Case For Israel. Australia: The Globe Press, 1972.

Livingstone, Neil., and Halevy, David.
Inside the PLO: Cover Units, Secret Funds, and the War Against Israel and the United States. New York: William Morrow, 1990.

Morey, Robert.
The Islamic Invasion: Confronting the World's Fastest Growing Religion. Eugene: Harvest House, 1992.

Moskowitz, Irving.
Should America Guarantee Israel's Safety?. New York: Americans For A Safe Israel, 1993.

Patai, Raphael.
The Arab Mind. New York: Macmillan, 1983.

Peters, Joan.
From Time Immemorial: The Origins of The Arab-Jewish Conflict Over Palestine. London: Michael Joseph, 1984.

Pritz, Ray A.
Nazarene Jewish Christianity. Jerusalem: Magnus, 1988.

Rolef, Susan Hattis. (Ed.)
Political Dictionary of the State of Israel. Jerusalem: Jerusalem Publishing House, 1993.

Sachar, Howard M.
A History of Israel: From the Rise of Zionism to Our Time. New York: Alfred A. Knoff, 1991.

Shimoni, Yaacov.
   Biographical Dictionary of the Middle East. New York: Facts On File, 1991.

Slater, Robert.
   Rabin of Israel. London: Robson, 1993.

Shorrosh, Anis A.
   Islam Revealed: A Christian Arab's View of Islam. Nashville: Thomas Nelson, 1988.

Twain, Mark.
   The Innocents Abroad. New York: Literary Classics of the United States, 1984.

Twain, Mark.
   The Complete Essays of Mark Twain, Charles Neider, (Ed.) New York: Doubleday, 1963.

Waller, Valerie Luke.
   A Stranger in the Land. Houston: Daughters of Truth, 1984.

Weizman, Ezer.
   On Eagles' Wings. Jerusalem: Steimatzky's, 1976.

Complete Works of Josephus Flavius. Grand Rapids: Kregel, 1980.
Encylopædia Judaica. Jerusalem: Keter, 1971.
The World Almanac and Book of Facts. New York: Pharos, 1993.

Notes

Notes

Notes